DEDICATION

❖

This book is dedicated to the memory of Bala Mohammed, M.K.O. Abiola, Kudirat Abiola, Ken Saro-Wiwa, Chima Ubani and all the unsung foot soldiers of our struggle for democracy and nationhood!

About the Author

Chido Onumah is a Nigerian journalist. He has worked in Nigeria, Ghana, Canada, USA, India and the Caribbean. He has been involved for more than a decade in media training for professional journalists as well as promoting media and information literacy in Africa.

He is currently coordinator of the African Centre for Media & Information Literacy (AFRICMIL), Abuja, Nigeria. AFRICMIL is a pan-African centre dedicated to a new vision of media and information literacy as a key component in the education of young people in Africa. From 2002 to 2004, Onumah worked as director of Africa programmes, Panos Institute, Washington, DC, U.S.A., helping journalists in West Africa as well as in the Caribbean, report in detail on issues that are frequently underreported or misreported issues such as HIV/AIDS, environmental degradation, and ethnic and religious conflicts.

Onumah was educated at the University of Calabar, Cross River State, Nigeria, and the Western University, London, Ontario, Canada, where he earned an MA in journalism. He was associate editor of The Insight newspaper, and assistant editor of African Agenda magazine both in Accra, Ghana. He served as coordinator, West African Human Rights Committee, Accra, Ghana, and correspondent for African Observer magazine, New York, and AfricaNews Service, Nairobi, Kenya.

In 2003, Onumah spent some time in Haiti and Dominican Republic where he worked with, and reported on, people living with HIV/AIDS, as well as on cross-cultural dialogue between African and Caribbean journalists. Between December 2001 and January 2002, Onumah was in New Delhi, India, on fellowship with the Indian Express newspaper, reporting on international issues.

CHIDO ONUMAH

"There are two basic questions that must be answered by all of us Nigerians. One, do we want to remain as one country? Two, if the answer is yes, under what conditions?"
- Chief Bola Ige

NIGERIA IS NEGOTIABLE

Essays on Nigeria's Tortuous Road to Democracy and Nationhood

Foreword by Hafsat Abiola-Costello

Nigeria is Negotiable!
Essays on Nigeria's Tortuous Road to Democracy and Nationhood

First published July 2013

Copyright© Chido Onumah

Published by
African Centre for Media & Information Literacy
27, Asheik Jarma Street, off Mike Akhigbe Way, Jabi, Abuja. P. O. Box 6856 Wuse, Abuja, Nigeria
+234 (0) 7040448533; Email: info@africmil.org

The right of Chido Onumah to be identified as the author of this work has been asserted by him in accordance with copyright laws.

A catalogue record for this book is available from the National Library of Nigeria.

ISBN: 978-978-932-476-7

All rights reserved. No part of this publication may be reproduced, transmitted, or stored in a retrieval system, in any form, or by any means, without the permission in writing from the copyright holder.

Between 2006 and 2007, he served as pioneer coordinator of the crime prevention unit (Fix Nigeria Initiative) of the Economic and Financial Crimes Commission (EFCC) in Nigeria, working on a civil society anti-corruption agenda for the country, and in partnership with the Wole Soyinka Centre for Investigative Journalism (WSCIJ) developed programmes on ethics and investigative reporting for Nigerian journalists.

Between 2001 and 2002, Onumah volunteered for the London Cross Cultural Learner Centre, London, Ontario, Canada, working on integration and provision of information for refugees and new immigrants to Canada. Since 2005, he has been a volunteer for the World Computer Exchange (WCE), Hull, Massachusetts, USA, seeking donations of used computers from corporations, universities, and non-profit organizations, and assisting in recruiting community organizations, universities and secondary schools in Africa that benefit from the services of the WCE.

In June 2012, Onumah was part of twelve senior news editors and producers from around the world selected for the International Reporting Project's (IRP) 2012 "Gatekeeper Editors" trip to Kenya. The trip to Kenya was part of a special IRP bloggers' trip focusing on family health, reproductive issues and the impact of population growth.

The group visited urban and rural residents, talking to youth leaders, doctors, health officials and leaders of NGOs while studying the environmental, health and social impact of population growth. It also visited maternity clinics and sanitation projects in Kibera (reputed as Africa's largest slum settlement). It travelled to Lake Victoria to the towns of Kisumu and Kogelo where it examined the impact of overpopulation on local health issues, looked at cultural and religious aspects of population growth and the efforts of local women (in- cluding Sarah Obama, President Obama's step grandmother) working with village groups. The group travelled to the pristine region of Laikipia, where it examined the effect of human population growth and migration on wildlife and water resources.

Onumah has earned a number of awards, including the Clement Mwale Prize for courage in journalism, AfricaNews Service (Kenya) 1997; Kudirat Initiative for Democracy (KIND) Award for excellence and courage in journalism (Nigeria), 1999; Alfred W. Hamilton Scholarship (Canadian Association of Black Journalists), 2001; William C. Heine Fellowship for International Media Studies (Canada), 2001; and the Jerry Rogers Writing Award (Western University, London, Ontario, Canada), 2002.

Onumah is the author of *Time to Reclaim Nigeria (Essays 2001-2011)* 2011. He has edited books on various subjects, including *Making Your Voice Heard: A Media Toolkit for Children and Youth* (2004); *Anti-Corruption Advocacy Handbook* (with Comfort Idika-Ogunye) 2006; *Guide to International Anti-corruption Laws* (2007); *Youth Media: A Guide to Literacy and Social Change* (with Lewis Asubiojo) 2008; *Understanding Nigeria and the New Imperialism* (with Biodun Jeyifo, Bene Madunagu, and Kayode Komolafe) 2006; and *Sentenced in God's Name: The Untold Story of Nigeria's "Witch Children"* (with Lewis Asubiojo) 2011.

Onumah is married to Sola and they have four children: Femi, Mobolaji, Dotun and Moyosore.

Contents

Dedication	iii
About the Author	iv
Contents	vii
Foreword	xii
Preface	xv
Prologue	xvii
Introduction	xix
Author's Note	xxi
Acknowledgements	xxvi
List of Selected Abbreviations	xxx

Section One: June 12 and the Democratic Alternative — 1

A JUNE AGO: In the middle of the Barricade
By Chiedu Ezeanah — 2

1	Thoughts on the "political class"	4
2	The triumph of illusion	6
3	A transition and an illusion	8
4	Cry the bedeviled country	10
5	Demo-crazy	12
6	Welcome "Nigerjevo"	14
7	The triumph of treachery	17
8	Democracy and American hypocrisy	20
9	June 12 and the democratic alternative	24
10	Why Abiola lost out	31
11	Transition and illusions	36
12	New beginning or dead end?	40
13	Democracy without democrats	43
14	Democracy as diversion	47

15	"Power shift" and its opponent	50
16	A misplaced outrage	56
17	When democracy insults	58

Section Two: Of Heroes and Villains — 63

A JUNE AGO: Requiem for the Fallen Horseman:
For Moshood Kashimawo Olawale Abiola
By Chiedu Ezeanah — 64

1	A minister's burden	66
2	Compelling reason for pessimism	68
3	In memory of the Ogoni thirteen	70
4	Ikoku's African revolution	72
5	For citizen Ubani, et al	76
6	Abacha's second coming	78
7	Abacha's image problem	82
8	The problem with Nigeria	86
9	As evil descends	90
10	Remembering Saro-Wiwa	93
11	Countdown to autocracy	96
12	The making of a deity	99
13	Before they select our next President	102
14	Abacha's blitzkrieg	107
15	Abacha's tragic end	110
16	Kofi Annan's diplomatic gaffe	113
17	The general in a labyrinth	117
18	The wrong man	121
19	Saro-Wiwa: three years after	126
20	Between 1979 and 1999	131
21	Gospel according to Gidado	135
22	Obasanjo and the end of the Nigerian state	138
23	Babangida's heritage	146
24	Of heroes and conspirators	149
25	When an apology falls short	153
26	Babangida's death wish	156
27	When Patience is not a virtue	159

28	In sympathy with Ribadu	162
29	Jonathan, Abati and the Ribadu report	166
30	A governor, three ministers and their burden	170
31	Our not-so-distinguished senators	174
32	Memo to Doyin Okupe: what is President Jonathan hiding? (1)	178
33	Memo to Doyin Okupe: what is President Jonathan hiding? (2)	182
34	David Mark and his anti-gay crusaders	186
35	No country for petty thieves	190
36	The "risen" First Lady	194
37	Orji Kalu's "fake degree"	198
38	IBB's two-party solution	201
39	Please, pardon President Jonathan	205
40	What does Obasanjo want?	209
41	The Achebe I knew	213

Section Three: Matters Miscellaneous — 218

A JUNE AGO: A Busted Dance:
For Kudirat Olayinka Abiola
By Chiedu Ezeanah — 219

1	Appropriateness of pricing	221
2	Towards a new beginning	223
3	A cycle of rubbish	225
4	The state and the people	226
5	Far from world order	229
6	The task before the youth	231
7	The way we live	233
8	Leftists and transition politics	235
9	Market "foxes" and the rest of us	237
10	Lesson of world revolutions	240
11	Beijing and superpower antics	242
12	Solving the housing question	245
13	Global tackle for poverty	248
14	The paradox of law and order	250

15	A nation on trial	253
16	Season of bulldozers	255
17	ASUU and our national dilemma	258
18	The paradox of power	261
19	In the grip of history	264
20	Requiem for the state	267
21	Nigeria: open sore of a continent	270
22	A tale of two countries	272
23	Time to snub dictators	275
24	Exporting terrorism	278
25	Where is Russia going?	280
26	Any respite for minorities?	282
27	Who will stop America?	285
28	The shame of a nation	289
29	Humanitarian intervention or US terror?	291
30	This barbarity must stop	296
31	The new killing field	298
32	Time to end subsidy on inefficiency	302
33	In praise of corruption	305
34	Of presidential media chat and asset declaration	309
35	President Jonathan's one child policy	312
36	Murder incorporated	316
37	The N5,000 note déjà vu	320
38	The fuel subsidy conundrum (1)	321
39	The fuel subsidy conundrum (2)	324
40	The Nigeria Police Force as a metaphor	329
41	The assault on public education	333
42	The "fake universities" syndrome	337
43	President Jonathan as "Big Brother"	341

Section Four: Nigeria is Negotiable — 346

	A Poem for my Country By Chiedu Ezeanah	347
1	Postponing the evil day	349
2	The masses and the draft constitution	351
3	National question and stability	353

4	Before we democratise	356
5	The Nigerian tragedy	358
6	Nigeria: divided we stand?	360
7	Charter of demands for a new Nigeria	366
8	Was there a country?	370
9	Before Nigeria implodes!	373
10	The moral imperative of a Sovereign National Conference	377
11	Nigeria is negotiable	380
12	How not to build a nation: reflections on Nigeria @ 52 (1)	383
13	How not to build a nation: reflections on Nigeria @ 52 (2)	386
14	How not to build a nation: reflections on Nigeria @ 52 (3)	389
15	How not to build a nation: reflections on Nigeria @ 52 (4)	392
16	Piracy as democracy	396
17	Nigeria won't break up	399

Section Five: 2015 and all that Jazz — 404

1	2015 and all that jazz	405
2	In defence of President Jonathan?	408
3	2015: Let the race begin	412
4	Can APC cure Nigeria's headache? (1)	416
5	Can APC cure Nigeria's headache? (2)	420
6	Let's negotiate Nigeria	423

Appendix 1	428
Appendix 2	436
Index	444

FOREWORD

BY HAFSAT ABIOLA-COSTELLO*

In May 2013, on the eve of the 14th anniversary of the return to democratic rule, an article in Nigeria's most popular newspaper, Punch, reported that the IMF observed that in spite of 12 years of growth, poverty in Nigeria was rising. The IMF, the article reported, was mystified by this apparent paradox. I was also mystified until I read Chido's book. I would, therefore, recommend this book – *Nigeria is Negotiable* – to that important international organization.

A leadership course I attended, also in May 2013, taught me about the golden rule in communication; that is, an explanation needs to cover the WHAT, HOW and WHY. What: in the period under review by the IMF, i.e, from 2000-2012, Nigeria experienced significant growth but also an increase in the proportion of people living in poverty. How: even though the growth was diversified, with only a third coming from the oil sector, the government had been unable to put in place a sufficiently robust framework that would ensure that the poor would get an equitable share in the benefits of said growth.

Chido's book then covers the question why, by highlighting why the democratic government of Nigeria failed to do this most democratic of things – ensure the economic empowerment of the majority of people. I had agreed to write the foreword to Chido's book six months before I finally sat down to read it. I accepted because I respect his work. Indeed, my organization, the Kudirat Initiative for Democracy (KIND) recognized his brilliant reporting during the height of the brutal Abacha regime with a KIND Award for Excellence and Courage in Journalism in 1999. We had stayed in touch over the years and I wanted to support him. But when faced with the actual task of reading his book, I started stalling.

Reading about the June 12 period, for obvious reasons, is difficult for me, even now, 20 years after. It is difficult to think about all that we lost and all that we stood to gain; to bear witness to how the main beneficiaries of so much sacrifice by so many were largely those who betrayed the cause; and to acknowledge the limits to the commitment espoused for democracy by its most vocal champions in the western world.

Yet, the reasons for my reluctance also made the exercise of reading the book that much more critical. Perhaps, revisiting the past might well aid us in understanding the present and defining the future. Knowing the consistency that Chido had brought to the cause assured me that travelling on such a journey with him as the guide would be a worthwhile undertaking.

And on a transatlantic flight from New York to Brussels in May, after six months of stalling, I finally read the over 400-page collection of essays. It was interesting to see what Chido's work might teach me about how one translates an abiding love for one's country into visions and strategies for reclaiming Nigeria.

Chido's book takes us on this journey. Writing as he did throughout the June 12 effort and the 1999 transition to the current political dispensation, we experience again the many concerns of the progressives during the IBB, Abacha and later Abdulsalami transitions: their hopes for a successful transition and later disappointment and anger when the election was annulled under IBB, hijacked under Abacha and finally completed under Abdulsalami; and the complexity and diversity of their responses.

Peppered with thought-provoking quotations, such as that attributed to Frederick Douglass that, "Those who profess to favour freedom, and yet deprecate agitation, are men who want crops without plowing up the ground; they want rain without thunder and lightning; they want the ocean without the awful roar of its many waters", and effective literary devices such as his fictional rendition of what occurred during M.K.O.'s last meeting with the US State Department officials, Chido's essays reflect the workings of a mind that is able to cut through the abundance of subterfuge inherent in a bankrupt political system intent on resisting change.

The result is incisive analysis and the deployment of logic in the service of strategy, so simply rendered, that the reader might easily fail to appreciate its value. But the truth is that most intellectuals in Nigeria are incapable of such disinterested analysis. Their personal concerns so obfuscate the road that they can no longer point people in any direction outside of that which advances their personal agenda.

In conclusion, I would like to say that I am glad that this is Chido's book as opposed to that of a visitor to Nigeria, no matter how distinguished his scholarship. For to reclaim Nigeria, we must reclaim our stories as we reclaim our memory from forgetfulness while staking our continued existence on a new bid for justice, for true federal- ism and for power vested in the Nigerian people.

So, do read this worthy tome, then let us strategize again in another bid for Nigeria, knowing that as imperfect as the progressive politicians may be, we cannot afford to leave the fate of 170 million people to the forces of regression that have governed our affairs so far.

Aluta continua. Victoria ascerta.

- *Hafsat Abiola-Costello is the founder of China-Africa Bridge and China Africa Forum, which promotes mutually beneficial cross-cultural collaboration between China and Africa, with a specific eye on women's contributions to the economy. In 2000, Abiola-Costello was honored as a Global Leader of Tomorrow at the World Economic Forum in Davos, Switzerland. In 2003, she was elected as a Fellow of the Ashoka: Innovators for the Public in recognition of her international status as a social entrepreneur. In 2006 she was nominated to be a founding councilor at the World Future Council.*

    Abiola-Costello is the founder of the Kudirat Initiative for Democracy (KIND), which seeks to strengthen civil society and promote democracy in Nigeria. She is currently the Special Adviser to the Ogun State governor on Millennium Development Goals (MDGs).

Preface

❖

BY DR. CHIDI ANSELM ODINKALU*

Nation building is not a project for the faint-hearted or for those with a short memory. It needs statesmen and women, thinkers and active citizens. And it takes very little for granted. In this book, essayist, activist, and organizer, Chido Onumah, explains all this using as his raw material Nigeria's contemporary political economy and history.

In law as in politics, countries are defined by a population within bounded territories under a common sovereign. Boundaries, howsoever defined, are, however, not facts of nature; they are artificial. They can be formed, re-formed, un-formed, negotiated and re-negotiated.

Within one generation, for instance, the Soviet Empire collapsed into middling, hardly remarkable, entities; Yugoslavia disintegrated into a collection of warring states and statelets; Germany evolved into one country from two; Ethiopia went the other way, becoming two countries instead of one, (indeed, Menelik II had sold Djibouti to the French about 116 years ago to finance the modernisation of Addis Ababa); Sudan has similarly become two countries (in which further splintering cannot be ruled out) and the United Kingdom itself could be reduced to England and Wales in 2014 depending on the outcome of the proposed referendum on Scottish Independence.

A little further back in time but still not too long ago, Tagore's India, the subject of the composition "Mind Without Fear" in his Nobel Literature Prize winning collection, *Gitanjali*, went from one territory to three countries (India, Pakistan and Bangladesh) in just under a quarter of a century.

In this collection, Chido Onumah makes a case for not taking Nigeria or its citizens for granted. It is at once a passionate cry for a better country; a compelling argument for rational debate about the future of the country; and an articulate appeal for committed citizenship.

This book contains a compilation of essays composed over a twenty-year period going back to 1993. Some were written in Nigeria; others were composed during exile. During this period, the standards of our educational system and its capacities for preserving and communicating accurately our contemporary history have degraded sharply. The capacity for transcending narrowness in explaining or understanding Nigeria has also similarly suffered.

In this book, Chido Onumah shows what is possible when national issues are tackled with rigour and intellectual honesty.

Somewhat more than the arguments that it seeks to put forward, therefore, this book is also a record of Nigeria's contemporary history in the last quarter century, from the perspective of a Nigerian whose growing up happened during the period. Fittingly, it is published on the cusp of the Nigerian centenary.

This book does not set out to win a popularity contest. Its passion is relentless; its prose is committed and its logic takes few prisoners. Most who read it will find something in it to disagree with and also much in it to agree with. But such is the enterprise of nation building. If this book reminds us of the unfinished tasks of nation building at the exclamation point of Nigeria's Centenary, then the author has served a brilliant purpose.

- *Chidi Anselm Odinkalu, Ph.D., is the current chair of the Governing Council, National Human Rights Commission (NHRC) in Nigeria. He was a senior legal officer for the Africa Program of the Open Society Justice Initiative. Odinkalu is a lawyer and rights advocate. He received his Ph.D. in law from the London School of Economics and Political Science.*

  Prior to joining the Open Society Justice Initiative, Odinkalu was senior legal officer responsible for Africa and Middle East at the International Centre for the Legal Protection of Human Rights in London, Human Rights Advisor to the United Nations Observer Mission in Sierra Leone, and Brandeis International Fellow at the Centre for Ethics, Justice and Public Life of the Brandeis University, Waltham, Massachusetts. Odinkalu is widely published on diverse subjects of international law, international economic and human rights law, public policy, and political economy affecting African countries.

Prologue

BY DR. ANTHONY AKINOLA*

The ghost of the annulled presidential election of June 12, 1993, has remained with us for 20 years. It will continue to haunt the perpetrators of that unpatriotic act for the rest of their lives.

The election of 1993 was not intended to lead to democracy; it was the culmination of political deceit by Gen. Ibrahim Babangida, author of the annulment, who had postponed his transitional programme on two previous occasions, 1990 and 1992. The annulment, as it was, was Babangida's desperation to hang onto power for as long as he possibly could.

General Babangida could not, on his own, have held our nation's fortunes to ransom as he did with the annulment of a free and fair election; he had the support of top military officers who were basking in the atmosphere of corruption and self-enrichment at the expense of the rest of us. They were generals who could not rise above ethnic bigotry.

Of particular note was Gen. Sani Abacha who eventually became military ruler between November 1993 and June 1998, having pushed aside an interim government hastily cobbled together in the aftermath of Babangida's forced exit on August 27, 1993. There had been "gossip" of a presumed "pact" between Babangida and Abacha that the latter would also take his turn in becoming Head of State and Commander-in-Chief of the Armed Forces.

The Abacha regime was characterised by unprecedented terror and assassination of political opponents and activists, not least because of the determination of the latter to actualize the mandate Nigerians gave Chief Moshood Abiola, the winner of the 1993 presidential election.

The dishonesty of members of the so-called political class was quite evident in the sustenance of the Abacha regime, as was also that of foreign interests whose pre-occupation was mainly with oil.

Gen. Abacha, just like his military predecessor, Gen. Ibrahim Babangida, embarked on a make-believe constitution-making and a transition programme that was intended to crown him as an "elected" Head of State.

There were to be only five political parties supporting a "consensus" candidate that would have been himself. However, fate did not allow Abacha's joke of a transition to further infuriate our sensibilities; he died in mysterious circumstances on June 8, 1998.

Sadly, Chief Abiola could not claim his mandate, as he also died in suspicious circumstances a month after the death of his tormentor, Gen. Abacha. Have we learnt any lessons from the events of 20 years ago when our democratic aspirations were badly dashed by a tiny minority of corrupt and unpatriotic generals?

This is the question that will continue to agitate honest minds as we must negotiate to achieve peace, stability and progress in a nation severely divided by the cleavages of ethnicity, religion, language and culture. Of course, Nigeria is Negotiable!

Nigeria is Negotiable, a collection of informed journalistic essays and commentaries, reminds readers of the political injustices and cruelties of an era. It calls for discussions on the way forward.

With persistent corruption, religious extremism, armed robbery, a new culture of kidnapping, co-existing with political intolerance and endemic chaotic elections, it would be dishonest to assume that all is well with our nation.

Our overbearing rulers, when outlining guidelines to their proposed constitutions, had tended to preclude certain issues from discussion – even when such issues were central to the stability of state and society.

Issues, suppressed or swept under the carpet of political opportunism, have a way of resurfacing with a vengeance.

- *Anthony Akinola, Ph.D., is a Nigerian political writer. A graduate of Political Science and Law from Howard and Oxford Universities respectively, he is the author of The Search for a Nigerian Political System (1986); Rotational Presidency (1996) and Democracy in Nigeria-Thoughts and Selected Commentaries (2013).*

INTRODUCTION

BY PROF. YAKUBU ABOKI OCHEFU*

Chido Onumah's collection of essays provocatively titled *Nigeria is Negotiable* is an effort at putting to the fore, the fundamental question of nation building in Nigeria since independence. Beginning from the Berlin West Africa Conference of 1884-85, the "nego- tiated" existence of what eventually became Nigeria in 1914 has al-ways been a part of its historical experience.

Under British colonial rule, the economic and administrative structures of the country were continuously rejigged until independence in 1960. Indeed, the process of decolonization of Nigeria has been identified by a number of historians as the building block of what Chido appropriately refers to as the "tortuous road to democracy and nationhood".

Between the official versions of the decolonization history that give a prominent role to our nationalist heroes for winning independence from the British and others who believe in the "conspiracy theory" of decolonization, the process of how the region with the least democratic credentials ended up as the driver of a new democratic enterprise epitomizes aspects of the negotiated experience.

As a country on its "third missionary" journey to a truly democratic nation, the fundamental questions of nation building that began over 100 years ago have not been fully and or properly answered. The corporate existence of the country has been formally broken once and pronounced broken once. It took a horrible civil war to restore the entity when it was broken and an equally brutal attempted coup when it was pronounced.

Beyond this, the crisis that engulfed the Niger Delta and the current insurgency in some parts of northern Nigeria have fuelled the speculation that the prediction by the National Intelligence Council of the United States that Nigeria may be a failed state from 2015, may come to pass. However, as the NIC itself notes: "The predictions are dire in some instances, but not irreversible, not all doom-and-gloom. Let's take in the good, the bad and the ugly, and make more excellent the good, beautify the bad, and reject the ugly".

Chido's essays for me draw our attention to the need to do a very simple thing: Learn from our past and the past of others who have democratised and modernised their countries. With essays going back 20 years, the book reminds us of aspects of our recent democratic experiences and, more important, our failures. It helps us to sharpen our thinking and focus on some lapses like investments in education and basic infrastructure. It questions our collective attitude towards corruption in general and penchant for impunity in particular.

For Nigerians like myself who are incurable optimists in the Nigeria project, the book is at once a reminder of how easy it is for a giant to fall. The current attack on our polity that is being driven ferociously in a religious and ethnic vehicle has produced outcomes that Chido himself could not have imagined twenty years ago.

When the erudite Nigerian historian, Obaro Ikime, wrote a book titled *The Fall of Nigeria* which details how the various polities in Nigeria lost their independence to the British, one sarcastic review asked whether Nigeria fell or she was pushed.

As we approach 2014 that marks 100 years of our negotiated existence, a "humpty dumpty" scenario can easily be envisaged. If this happens, the colonial map that was drawn in 1960 will certainly change.

We must collectively negotiate to ensure that we retain the map but change the way we exist under that map.

- *Yakubu Aboki Ochefu, Ph.D, attended the University of Birmingham, UK, where he earned an M.A. in Political Economy and Economic History in 1985. He earned a Ph.D in economic history from the University of Calabar, Cross River State, Nigeria. He started his academic career at the University of Calabar where he taught history from 1985 to 1992. In 1993, he was one of the pioneer staff of Benue State University where he helped establish the History Department. He held various positions in the University such as Head, History Department, Dean, Students Affairs, Deputy Vice-Chancellor and Professor of Economic History and Development Studies.*

  He is currently a Professor of History and Vice-Chancellor, Kwararafa University, Wukari, Taraba State, Nigeria.

Author's Note

HOW CAN WE FORGET?

Many Americans like to boast that they remember where they were and what they were doing when the young and charismatic president, John Fitzgerald Kennedy, was shot on Novembe 22, 1963, in Dallas, Texas. I am sure many Nigerians of my generation and older would remember where they were and what they were doing that balmy day, June 12, 1993.

The election that took place that day was the culmination of the political transition orchestrated by self-styled evil genius, Gen. Ibrahim Badamosi Babangida (IBB). Eleven days after, on June 23, after efforts to manipulate the results failed, IBB, through his goons, announced the annulment of the election won by Chief Moshood Abiola, who would later die in detention.

On August 27, 1993, exactly eight years after he seized power, IBB "stepped aside", leaving the quivering head of the Interim National Government (ING), the not-so-earnest Ernest Shonekan, in charge. Shonekan's makeshift government lasted until November 17, 1993, when he was supplanted by IBB's evil alter ego, Gen Sani Abacha. The rest, as they say, is history.

June 12 this year marks the 20th anniversary of Babangida's failed diabolical political experiment. The country has come full circle. Today, the remnants of that perfidious era, including David Mark who now holds court as the Senate President of the Federal Republic, call the shots in our so-called democratic order.

I remember June 12, 1993, vividly. The last time there was an election in Nigeria before that auspicious day in 1993 was ten years earlier in 1983. I had just left secondary school and seething with rage at the way politicians of the Second Republic had desecrated the nation. I was 17 years old and could not vote. There was a military coup that year – the fifth in the country's tortuous political history.

By the late 80s, as a student at the University of Calabar, I found myself, like many students of that era, on the frontline of the quest to return the country to democratic rule. For me, and many of my generation, June 12, 1993, was the first opportunity to vote and perhaps have a say in the governance of the country. It wasn't an easy decision. After a decade of military rule Nigerians had become bruised and battered, wary of a military government that couldn't justify its messianic pretentions. I grew up under military rule. I had experienced enough of the military to distrust their role in government.

However, nobody wanted to give IBB any justification for remaining in office a day longer than expected. Nigerians put behind them the myth about ethnic and religious divide. One of the two parties that IBB created, the Social Democratic Party – SDP (the other being the National Republican Convention – NRC) had two Muslim candidates, Moshood Abiola (from Ogun State in the South-west) and his running mate, Babagana Kingibe (from Borno State in the North-east). It didn't matter. Abiola defeated Bashir Tofa, the presidential candidate of the NRC, (a Muslim from Kano in the North-west) in his home constituency.

That was how sophisticated the electorate was twenty years ago. June 12, 1993 mattered because for the first time in the post-independence electoral history of Nigeria, there was no focus on religion or ethnicity. For the first and only time Nigerians were going to have a president they actually voted for. There were hardly any reports of electoral violence. Even the elements (no rainfall throughout the election in the rainy month of June) conspired to deny IBB a reason to stop the election.

It was a golden opportunity to set the country on the path of genuine democratic reconstruction, but IBB squandered it. Expectedly, our politicians moved on. They were co-opted into Abacha's transition and for them June 12 became history. Abacha's Minister of Information, Prof. Jerry Gana was one of the earliest people to sing the dirge of June 12.

In May 1994, as Nigerians prepared to mark the first anniversary of the June 12, 1993 election, Gana reminded us that "The (Abacha) military administration did not actualize the June 12 election in spite of its opposition to the annulment for fear that certain sections of the country could rise against it. If they actualized June 12 when they came in, another section would rise".

Gana admitted that the annulment was a terrible error, but that Nigeria's corporate existence could not be sacrificed for it. According to him, "The annulment is a painful one, but we cannot because of it allow the people of Nigeria to be destroyed. Somebody has made a mistake like somebody made in 1966, like somebody made in 1984, like somebody made a mistake by stopping Jerry Gana in becoming a president by annulling my own primaries".

Of course, it was a costly mistake that cost lives and threatened the very existence of the country. On 11 June 1994, president-elect Moshood Kashimawo Olawale Abiola, declared himself president. The Abacha administration hunted Abiola down, arrested him and imprisoned him. Abiola would die in prison on July 7, 1998, a month after Abacha expired.

While I was working on this book, I had a phone conversation with Odia Ofeimun, the famed poet and former president of the Association of Nigerian Authors (ANA), who informed me that he was working on a book on June 12. He said it was important that Nigerians did not forget; that for too long progressives had yielded the political stage to recidivist politicians to the detriment of the country. I couldn't agree more.

How can we forget that there was an election on June 12, 1993; that the election was annulled; that some of those who oversaw the annulment and their collaborators still call the shots in the country? How can we forget the ignoble roles of the likes of Arthur Nzeribe and Abimbola Davies of the infamous Association for Better Nigeria (ABN) who put themselves and their organization at the service of the military junta?

Any nation that lacks memory is doomed. How can we forget Kudirat Abiola, wife and mother, who was gunned down in broad daylight in a Lagos street because she dared to question the rationale for her husband's detention; Pa Alfred Rewane who was brutally murdered in his bedroom for supporting pro-democracy activists as well as many unsung heroes and heroines of the June 12 struggle?

Six years after he "stepped aside", IBB was on hand to help install Olusegun Obasanjo, Abiola's kinsman, as president of the 4th Republic, perhaps as part of efforts to "compensate" the South-west for the loss of Abiola. In retrospect, twenty years after he caused the June 12 debacle, this is how IBB explained his treachery:

> *"The emergence of Obasanjo came about as a result of what happened in the country; the country was in a very serious crisis and we had to find the solution to these problems and therefore we needed a leader known in the country. We did not believe in foisting somebody who is not known; so, we looked for a man who has been involved in the affairs of this country, who held positions either in the military or in the cabinet and who has certain beliefs about Nigeria.*
>
> *"Now, all of us that were trained as armed forces, there is one belief that you cannot take away from us; we believe in this country because this is part of our training. We fought for this country, so when you have a situation like that, you need a leader that has all these attributes and quite frankly, he quickly came to mind".*

IBB actually used the word "foisting". We all remember how Obasanjo – the pseudo-democrat who told us that Abiola, the winner of the June 12, 1993 election was not the "messiah" – foisted an ailing Umaru Musa Yar'Adua on the nation in 2007 after eight years of misrule.

The "Abiola is not the messiah" mantra was Obasanjo's simple way of dismissing Abiola's victory on June 12, 1993, and upholding the subsequent annulment of the election. Obasanjo may have believed that Alhaji Shehu Shagari was the real messiah. That was why he handed power to him in 1979 even though it was clear he (Shagari) did not win the presidential election of that year.

Thanks to the likes of IBB, Obasanjo and their "politics of settlement", today we are saddled with President Goodluck Jonathan, one of the greatest beneficiaries of our "negotiated existence". Unfortunately, Nigeria was first negotiated on the terms of a marauding band of merchants and empire builders; and subsequently by a military cabal and its civilian collaborators. Now is the time to negotiate it on the terms of the mass of our people who bear the brunt of its lop- sided and unjust features. This is essentially what this book is about.

As part of the process of reconciliation, President Jonathan can honour Abiola as the second democratically elected president of Nigeria. If he can pardon convicted serial treasury looters and grant amnesty to militants and terrorists, he certainly can honour Abiola. That should kick-start the much needed national dialogue on the future of Nigeria.

There are 124 essays in all, divided into five parts, covering events in Nigeria and beyond in the last quarter century. Section One covers the period around the June 12, 1993 election. Section Two focuses on some personalities, past and present, and the roles they played and are still playing either in advancing our democracy or undermining it. Section Three consists of essays on miscellaneous topics. Section Four comprises essays that proffer solutions and "the way forward" for Nigeria. Section Five looks at the upcoming general election in 2015, the intrigues surrounding President Jonathan's re-election bid and the antics of those who want to stop him. Each essay is separate and can be read on its own. Those with any kind of link have been put in chronological sequence for easy reference.

All the essays in this book have been published in more or less the same form as they appear here, sometimes under different titles, in newspapers, magazines, and online journals around the world, including *The Punch, Sunday Punch, The Guardian, Thisday, Leadership, Tempo, Daily Trust, Sunday Trust AM News, The News, PM News, The Insight, Nigerian Compass, People's Daily, PH Telegraph, National Interest, Socialist Standard, African Agenda, London Free Press, Africa World Review, AfricaNews Service, African Observer, African Suntimes, Saharareporters, Premium Times, Africa Undisguised, Nigeriavillagesquare, Nigeriaworld, 234next, Elombareports, Osun Defender, Huhuonline, Gamji.com, Newsdiaryonline, NigerianMuse, ChatAfrik, El Pais* and *chidoonumah.com*.

Acknowledgements

The materials that make up this book date back to almost a quarter of a century. In that period, I encountered many people who impacted me one way or another. I thank my parents – my dad, Elder E.E. Onumaegbu and late mum, Comfort Onumaegbu – who allowed me to be who I wanted to be, and my siblings, Polite, Newman, Franca, Faith and Fidelia, for tolerating me. I am grateful to Dr. Lambert Onumaegbu and his wife, aunty Celine, Chief Ibem Onumaegbulam, Chief Sunny Onumaegbu, Emmanuel Onumaegbu, uncle Ikem Iwuoha and his wife, aunty Angela, for their guidance and support over the years.

I am greatly indebted to Edwin Madunagu whose writings and views shaped and continue to shape much of my ideological and political beliefs. Much credit goes to the "the master poet of his generation", Chiedu Ezeanah, iconoclast, Godwin Onyecholem, Danlami Nmodu, Richard Mammah, Austin Uche-Ejeke, Tayo Odunlami, Peter Anyasi, Uche Akpulu, Igwilo Nwachukwu, Moyosore Jolaolu, Chika Oduah and master designer, Femi Jolaolu, who accommodates my many requests with an equanimity that is beyond belief. Without their prodding and magnanimity in reviewing the manuscript, this book would not have materialised.

No words are enough to thank Dr. J. 'Kayode Fayemi, Governor of Ekiti State and Ogbeni Rauf Aregbesola, Governor of the State of Osun for finding time to read the manuscript. Prof. Anthony Ochefu, Hafsat Abiola-Costello, Dr. Chidi Anselm Odinkalu and Dr. Anthony Akinola made this book possible with their contributions. Godspower Onumaegbu, Tunji Wusu, Idris Oba, Sam Aderenle and Olufemi Anjorin deserve praise for retrieving much of the material that went into this book.

Special thanks to Prof. Wole Soyinka, Asiwaju Bola Tinubu, former

Governor of Lagos State, Babatunde Fashola (SAN), Governor of Lagos State, Owelle Rochas Okorocha, Governor of Imo State, Prince Eze Madumere, Deputy Governor of Imo State, Senator Ibikunle Amosun, Governor of Ogun State, Comrade Adams Oshiomole, Governor of Edo State, Alhaji Tanko Al-Makura, Governor of Nasarawa State, Senator Babafemi Ojudu, Senator Oluremi Tinubu, Alhaji Lai Mohammed, National Publicity Secretary, Action Congress of Nigeria (ACN) and Engr. Buba Galadima, National Secretary of the Congress for Progressive Change (CPC).

I appreciate the support of Mallam Nuhu Ribadu and his wife, Zara, Mallam Idris Othman, Ibrahim Lamorde, Executive Chairman, Economic and Financial Crimes Commission (EFCC), Prof. Ben Nwabueze (SAN), Dr. Tunji Braithwaite, Makin Soyinka, Ladi Olorunyomi, Prof. A.Y. Ribadu, Bukar Abba, Dr. Ezinne Nwadinobi, Prof. Biodun Jeyifo, Prof. Manjunath Pendakur, Prof. Biko Agozino, Laolu Adegbite, Hon. Idowu Obasa, Femi Falana (SAN), Usman Iya'a Abbas, Ayo Olowoniyi, Joshua Daramola, Odia Ofeimun, Ngozi Moses-Saromi, Abiodun Odude, Jay Oelbaum, Farouk Adamu Aliyu, Uba Sani, Ibrahim Modibbo, Uche Onyeagucha, Kunle Ajibade, Bayo Onanuga, Comrade Charles Ezugha, Hon. Abike Dabiri-Erewa, Prof. M.A. Mainoma, Dr. Mohammed Bawa, Ayo Obe, Dr. Abdulmumin Jibril, Dascha and Alex Paylor, Gretchen Maynes, Charlene and Clayton Root, Chantal Philips, Pastor Ingrid Shultz, Fred and Elfrieda Klassen, Olumide and Deola Folarin, Dr. Yao Graham, Dr. Sam Amadi, Chairman, Nigerian Electricity Regulatory Commission (NERC), Farida and Isa Dogonyaro, Abdulrasheed Maina, Chief Ganiyat Fawehinmi, Mohammed Fawehinmi, Prof. Pat Utomi, Mohammed T. Ibrahim, Olisa Agbakoba (SAN), Eugenia Abu, Prof. Tunde Samuel, Dr. Benson Akintola, Pastor Tunde Bakare, Yinka Odumakin, Dr. Osagie Obayuwana, Asishana Bayo Okauru, Ifueko Omoigui-Okauru, Mohammed Mohammed and Pastor Wole Oladiyun.

I am grateful to the following for their encouragement: Prof. Bene Madunagu, Dapo Olorunyomi, Prof Chinweizu, Col. Abubakar Umar (retd.), Nike Ransome-Kuti, Olajide Bello, Sunday Edem, Dr. Oshita Oshita, Dr. John Iyang, Jamilah Tangaza, Dr. Usman Bugaje, Dr. Sola Olorunyomi, Prof. Princewill Alozie, Alton Grizzle, Mike Akwa, Austin (Canoways) Emaduku, Dr. Jose Manuel Perez Tornero, Dr. Samy Taiye, Jordi Torrent, Carolyn Wilson, Oluseyi Soremekun, Prof. Audrey Gadzekpo, Prof. Kwame Karikari, Dr. Laura Cervi, Federico Olivieri, Alozie Orji, Prof. Wale Adebanwi, Rev. Fr. Paul Irikefe, Prof. Ebenezer Obadare, Prof. Ishola Ajiferuke, Prof. Omolade Adunbi, Prof. Ogaga Ifowodo, Prof. Mitu Sengupta, Chile Okoroma, Dr. Isaac Osuoka, Dr. Ike Okonta, Dr. Garuba Abari, Kayode Komolafe, Mike Membu, Simon Kolawole, Dr. Keziah Awosika, Prof. Bolaji Aluko, Seun Kuti, Henry Oriabure, Ohi Alegbe, Sunday Dare, Folake Bello, Ibrahim Magu, Gertrude Ngozi Okeke, Pastor and Mrs. Emmanuel Olaoluwa, Dr. Rosaline Okosun, Dele Alake, Ben Ogazi, Wale Okuniyi, Che Oyintumba, Prof. Okey Ndibe, Prof. E. C. Osondu, Prof. Akin Adesokan, Joe Igbokwe, Prof. Farooq Kperogi, Ibrahim Nawagui, Elvis Obieroma, Semiu Okanlawon, Omoyele Sowore, Rudolph Okonkwo, Franklen Oparaocha, Edmond Enaibe, Nonye Macebuh, Michael Yese, Vera and Emeka Amadi, Jenkins Alumona, Osita Nwajah, Dr. Chris Nwokobia, Dr. Bunmi Aborisade, Henry Ugbolue, Yemi Odetola, Daniel Alabrah, Musikilu Mojeed, Dr. Chijioke Uwasomba, Dr. Okey Ekeocha, Pastor Dan Effiom, Uchenna Akweke, Kehinde Adewole, Elor Nkeruwem, Victor and Joy Femi-Walsh, Seun Adenuga, Pastor Sylvester Egogo, Dr. Joseph Uwazota, Kennedy Etoroma, Sufi Alli, Gibson Tano Akwevagbe, Austin Paul, Godwin Ogbona, Yomi Kuku, Chris Beatty, Riva Levinson, Lekan Akinosho, Chris Otaigbe, Constance Ikoku, Sanya Ojikutu, Okey Nwanguma, Ben Ihenacho, Osita Okechukwu, Abimbola Jaiyesimi, Dachung Bagos, Apollo Goma, Wale Bakare, Vera Opara, Patricia Ekpo, Pastor Sunday Ogidigbo, Tobi Oluwatola, Ohimai Godwin Amaize, Terry Bagia, Mike Nnaekpe, Jola Ajibade-Kusimo, Dr. Adegboyega Dada, Bukola Oreofe, Pauline Vander-Pallen, Nana Kweiba, George Koomson, Fortune Alimi, Philip Muskwe, Akwetey Ofori, Frank Opara, Mike Ekome, and Oliver Enyinnah.

I am thankful to my colleagues at the African Centre for Media & Information Literacy (AFRICMIL), particularly Lewis Asubiojo, whose tireless effort ensures the Centre is kept alive when I am AWOL, Taiwo (Jante) Adebowale, Kingsley Paul, Wale Abimbola, Stanley Metibogun and Nonso Alozie.

My professional colleagues and friends in civil society, Innocent

Chukwuma, Hon. Yusuf Ayo Tajudeen, Wale Adeoye, Emma Ezeazu, Kayode Oladele, Clement Nwankwo, Nwagwu Ezenwa Samson, Richard Akinnola, Salihu M. Lukman, Steve Aborisade, Dr. Kole Shettima, Dr. Hussaini Abdu, Mahmud Abdul, Fola Odidi, Oma Djebah, Bamidele Aturu, Lekan Otufodunrin, Max Amuchie, Maxwell Kadiri, Toyin Akinniyi, Motunrayo Alaka, Yakubu Afuye, Peter Ocheikwu, Ola Doifie, Ify Okoli, Nnimmo Bassey, Chioma Chuka, Attah Joseph, Raxy Ekwebelam, Victor Oruche, Steve Onwuka, Prof. Pius Adesanmi, Eze Joseph, Dr. Nduka Otiono, Festus Ogbeide, Emeka Aneke, Robo Oduwole, Denja Yakub, Jaye Gaskia, Betty Abah, Akinbode Oluwafemi, Adeola Fayehun, Akeem Lasisi, Abbas Jimoh, Dr Jibrin Ibrahim, Louis Odion, Kadaria Ahmed, Sina Oke, Wilson Uwujaren, Chris Oluka, Nwanyinma Okeanu, Felicia Bot, Princewill Egbe, Layo Olutimehin, Angel Israel, Omena Abenabe, Abdul Alaya, Folashade Awunah, Sumner Shagari Sambo, Ikeogu Oke, Paul Onomerike, Jiti Ogunye, Charles Musa, Comfort Idika-Ogunye, Lateef Raji, Majek Adega, Dr. Kezia Awosika, Hawa Baba-Ahmed, James Peters, Kehinde Bamigbetan, Kingsley Obom-Egbulem, Juliet Offiong, Eric Isagba, Toye Adegboye, Ikechi Onyekpere, Azuka Onwuka, Tolu Ogunlesi, Greg Odogwu, Tunji Ajibade, Kola Ogunbiyi, Naja'tu Mohammed, Ibiba Don-Pedro, Cyril Oriabure, Stephnora Okere, Nosa Igiebor, Nwaogu Donatus, Massiv Rex, Maurice Archibong, Rv. Fr. Walter Onumaegbu, Bayo Olupohunda, Festus Owete, Francis Abayomi, Harry Iwuala, Rv. Fr. Emmanuel Ojeifo, Beruk Abraha, Blessing Jona, Fanta Sidibeh, Marjorie Kyomuhendo, Abdou Jatta, Adama Lee Bah, Kingsley Uluocha, Eze Onyekpere, Chude Jideonwo, Ejike Asiegbu, Niran Adedokun, Lekan Sote, Jide Ojo, Uche Igwe, Mannie Ochugboju, Osaro Odemwigwe, Tolu Jinadu, Toni Kan, Tony Akiotu, Ubong Ekong, Amina Salihu, Sunday Ejoku, Theo Ayoma, Tive Denedo, Jacob Emaguna, Lucky Okumogwe, Bolanle Asimolowo, Abubakar Ibrahim, Steve Madojemu, Gbile Oshadipe, Gbolahan Olalemi, Alex Uriri, Niyi Ibietan, Anwal Musa Rafsanjani, Nasir Kura, Adagbo Onoja, Fr. John Patrick Ngoyi, Deshola Komolafe, Dr. Amanze Akpuda, Yusuf Alli, Shettima Yerima, Idris Akinbajo, Gbemiga Ogunleye, Ozo Esono Omosigo, Wole Oni, Willie Obase-Ota, Orlando Oaikhena, Lanre Suraj, Lanre Arogundade, Sunny Moniedafe Abubakar Usman, Dotun Eyinade, Sani Tukur, Maremi Olofinjana, Stellamaris

Oparaugo, Rex Iyobosa, Richard Akinwunmi, John Odah, Femi Ipaye, Felix Ofou, Ade Atobatele, Tony Iyare, Omor Bazuaye, Deji Bademosi, Emmanuel Ogala, Dele Ajaja, Gbenga Bamgbose, Diego Okenyodo, Dolapo Abimbola, Bashiru Adigun, Egghead Odewale, Kayode Ogundamisi, Horatius Egua, Daniel Elombah, Olarewaju Thomas, Uzor Maxim Uzoatu, Gbenga Olorunpomi, Yomi Gidado, Tunde Aremu, Ifeanyi Ugorji, Attah Ikharo, Sheddy Ozone, Wahab Gbadamosi, Benedict Okoro, Eze Eluchie, Dayo Aiyetan, Lara Owoeye-Wise, Ken Henshaw, Gbenga Aruleba, Kunle Adewale, Aminu Ardo, Jahman Anikulapo, Joel Nwokeoma, Issa Bayero, Kenneth Ozegbe, Dr. Anthony Kola-Olusanya, Dr. Emma Shehu, Emeka Madunagu, Helen Chukwunwike, Adebayo Bodunrin, Martins Oloja, David Akoji, Basil Ugochukwu, Theophilus Ilevbare, Dr Omano Edigheji, Mohammed B. Attah, Ahaoma Kanu, Fred Adetiba and Martins Obono, deserve special mention.

Without the painstaking effort, many years ago, of Ophelia Owusu-Danquah who volunteered to put in soft copy many of the essays in this book, there would not have been the desire to undertake this project. My managing editor at the Insight newspaper in Accra, Ghana, Kwesi Pratt, Jnr., his wife, Mariam and their children, Maame Ama, Payin and Kakra, provided not only refuge, but a platform to continue writing when I was out of Nigeria during the Abacha dictatorship.

Of course, my greatest gratitude is reserved for my family. My spouse, Sola, has been supportive in ways words can't describe. My darling children, Femi, Mobolaji (who assisted in retyping some of the essays), Dotun and my little princess, Moyosore, who kept prodding, "Daddy, finish your work", provided the impetus to work.

I take complete responsibility for any shortcomings associated with this book.

Chido Onumah
Abuja, Nigeria
June 12, 2013

LIST OF SELECTED ABBREVIATIONS

ABN - Association for Better Nigeria
ACE - Alliance for Credible Election
ACN - Action Congress of Nigeria
AFRC - Armed Forces Revolutionary/Ruling Council
AFRICMIL - African Centre for Media and Information Literacy
AIT - Africa Independent Television
ANC - African National Congress
ANPP - All Nigeria Peoples Party
APC - All Progressives Congress
BBC - British Broadcasting Corporation
CAN - Christian Association of Nigeria
CBN - Central Bank of Nigeria
CBOs - Community Based Organizations
CD - Campaign for Democracy
CDHR - Committee for the Defence of Human Rights
CEN - Conference of Ethnic Nationalities
CCB - Code of Conduct Bureau
CIA - Central Intelligence Agency
CJN - Chief Justice of Nigeria
CLO - Civil Liberties Organization
CMA - Conscientizing Male Adolescents
CNON - Coalition of National Organizations of Nigeria
CONAKAT - Confederation des Association du Katanga
CPC - Congress for Progressive Change
ECOMOG - Economic Community of West African States Monitoring Group
EFCC - Economic and Financial Crimes Commission
ERC - Electoral Reform Committee
FDCA - Federal Capital Development Authority
FCT - Federal Capital Territory
FEC - Federal Executive Council
FoIA - Freedom of Information Act

FNI - Fix Nigeria Initiative
GEJ - Goodluck Ebele Jonathan
GNPP - Great Nigeria People's Party
GPEI - Global Polio Eradication Initiative
ICPC - Independent Corrupt Practices and Other Related Offences Commission
IGP - Inspector General of Police
IMF - International Monetary Fund
INEC - Independent National Electoral Commission
ING - Interim National Government
KIND - Kudirat Initiative for Democracy
MAI - Multilateral Agreement on Investment
MAMSER - Mass Mobilization for Self Reliance, Social Justice, and Economic Recovery
MIP - Mass Interest Project
MPN - Movement for Progressive Nigeria
MUSON - Music Society of Nigeria
NADECO - National Democratic Coalition
NAFDAC - National Agency for Food and Drug Administration and Control
NAN - News Agency of Nigeria
NANS - National Association of Nigerian Students
NBA - Nigerian Bar Association
NCDC - Nigeria Centre for Disease Control
NDP - National Democratic Party
NDPVF - Niger Delta People's Volunteer Force
NEC - National Executive Council
NEITI - Nigeria Extractive Industries Transparency Initiative
NESG - Nigerian Economic Summit Group
NGOs - Non Governmental Organizations
NIPSS - National Institute for Policy and Strategic Studies
NITEL - Nigerian Telecommunication Limited
NLC - Nigeria Labour Congress
NMA - Nigerian Medical Association
NNPC - Nigerian National Petroleum Corporation
NPA - Nigeria Ports Authority

NPN - National Party of Nigeria
NPP - Nigerian Peoples Party
NRC - National Republican Convention
NUC - National Universities Commission
NUJ - Nigeria Union of Journalists
NUNS - National Union of Nigerian Students
NUT - Nigeria Union of Teachers
OPEC - Organization of Petroleum Exporting Countries
PDP - People's Democratic Party
PHCN - Power Holding Company of Nigeria
PPPRA - Petroleum Products Pricing Regulatory Agency
PSSGTG - Private Sector Supporters for Good and Transparent Governance
SAP - Structural Adjustment Programme
SDP - Social Democratic Party
SNC - Sovereign National Conference
SNG - Save Nigeria Group
TNCs - Transnational Corporations
TI - Transparency International
TTA - Third Term Agenda
TUC - Trade Union Congress
UN - United Nations
UNICEF - United Nations Children's Fund
UPN - Unity Party of Nigeria
WAI - War Against Indiscipline
WASPs - White Anglo-Saxon Protestants
WTO - World Trade Organization
YAO - Youth Alliance for Obasanjo
YEAA - Youth Earnestly Ask for Abacha

SECTION ONE

JUNE 12 AND THE
DEMOCRATIC ALTERNATIVE

A June Ago

In the Middle of the Barricade

BY CHIEDU EZEANAH

Today a name unites divided tongues, today
bayonets engulf the name.
Today is all wings and no flight.

It was June 12th invented by the Trickster-General.
It was June 12th in all the tabloids hawking images
of the eagle combating the horse in the rainwind.

It was the month and the day
of the triumphant horseman
chosen by the crossroads suspended by iron.

Who could feel June and forget?
We look at the stable, but no messages,
no horseman, no horse...

We sing the June that's outgrown guns.
We sing the pit of curfews that surround us.
But where's the horseman, where the horse?

We look at the stable and we say-
what if the furies of the present outgun the furies of the past?

We look at the stable and we say-
stout General splitting the chariot
of June, break this June gently.
Can you remember the shrieks of hope yelling all day long
in the middle of the barricade?

Can you remember the skulls busted
and the unknowing road that gushed blood
in the middle of the barricade?

Can you remember the heavy phrases-
"Political logjam", "Political impasse"
in the middle of the barricade?

Can you remember
silence had always been there
full of armed felons in the middle of the barricade?

Can you remember
the vague dunes in the palms they read
in the middle of the barricade?

Can you remember
the Generals vindicating the ruin
in the middle of the barricade?

Can you remember
we were laden with a land absconding
in the middle of the barricade?

Can you remember, or, do you think
the port-bellied Generals are set
for Saint Rawlings Day?

We come with footnotes from walking into massacres.
We come with chants of the wronged but overthrown.

Who could feel June 12th and forget?

1. Thoughts on the "Political Class"
September 1993

The cancellation of the June 12 elections has revealed the seedy side of the amorphous conglomeration called the "political class".

It has also revealed those who until now never stopped talking about democracy, the rule of law and social justice, but would vitiate them at every little opportunity; those doubled-faced high priests of peace who are stealthily fanning the embers of war.

I have never seen a group of people so "incurably debased by selfishness; so passionately consumed by self-pity". Simply put, the "political class in Nigeria has no desire to avail itself of any real programme". In the past two months, we have watched how cowardly opportunism has become an art; we have seen people staunchly defending the indefensible.

For some time now, the byword in the country has been peace! peace! and more peace! The "political class" has been convulsed by the frenzy of peace and unity. But the position of the "political class" as champions of peace is suspect. The "political class" wants peace at all cost even if it stands in the way of justice!

Our politicians are quick to remind us that democracy abhors violence. However, they are oblivious of the fact that democracy is not a friend of chicanery, disrespect for the rule of law and the unmitigated fettering of the wishes of the people. And that peace won at the expense of justice is not only perilous and illusory, but a harbinger of violence and war.

It is not strange that the "political class" so-called is obsessed with peace and unity; that its every statement and proclamation starts and ends with the thesis: "The unity of the country is nonnegotiable". It is also not strange that our politicians are not talking about people's right and justice.

But, is it not certain that peace and national unity can only become reality by the destruction of those structures which are antithetical to peace and unity? Is it not primarily because we have compromised justice in the past; because we have tried to get peace at the expense of justice, that our people have been forlorn? And nobody is guiltier in this show of shame than our vacillating political elite.

To say that the "political class" in Nigeria has been the greatest obstacle to lasting peace and enduring democracy would be repeating the obvious. It is instructive to note that our "political class" lacks political will; that the only thing in its political arsenal is rabid opportunism and consummate greed. Therefore, it quavers and totters any time its interests appear to be threatened. This may sound scathing, but it is the true position of things.

Bamidele Aturu, "The real political class", The Punch (7/2/93), gave a graphic description of the phenomenal wavering of this class when he noted,

> *"Right from the time it submitted itself to the humiliation of joining government-created parties, ascribing to state formulated manifestoes and constitutions, the political class has conclusively demonstrated itself as a class which does not even know its interest".*

As if that was not enough, it went through all imaginable torture and humiliation of being banned, unbanned and banned again at will without a response. All in an attempt to grab power!

This has been the modus operandi of our "political class". It has not been able to reconcile its self-interest with that of the populace. That is why it succumbed to the blackmail of an Interim National Government (ING); that is why it fails to appreciate the fact that when Nigerians from all walks of life march in protest against the cancellation of the June 12 election, they need nobody to propel them; that they are expressing their inalienable right.

However, our vacillating "political class" sees it differently. Our politicians, unabashedly, see these agitations as nothing but attempts by "disgruntled elements" – as if the current morass is not enough to make people disgruntled – to cause disaffection and undermine the unity of the country. The truth, on the contrary, is that the "political class", playing the marionette and allowing itself to be manipulated, is doing so not because it is genuinely interested in peace.

Typically, our "political class" has failed to diagnose the reasons why this much-vaunted peace has eluded us. It fails to realize the fact that peace does not come by chance; that people make effort to achieve it. Peace is a means to an end not an end in itself. The ultimate end is justice.

Therefore, our "political class" must realize that, in its sinister quest for peace, it must fight for justice and the restoration of rights. To think otherwise is to make it politically obsolete; it is to achieve "peace" while the "war" rages on.

2. THE TRIUMPH OF ILLUSION
APRIL 1995

In this season of infamy, "when the rule of law is a charade and justice is mocked; when our rulers do not obey the most elementary law of decency and common sense in their desire to cling to power; when the country moves from one uncertainty to another and the citizens sentenced to perpetual suffering", it is bewildering how our rulers manage to play the ostrich.

It is bemusing that our rulers still invoke such clichéd expressions as "Nigeria is the freest country in the world". Only recently, our head of state told the world that, "There is no human rights abuse in Nigeria. On the contrary, people in Nigeria have been free in expressing themselves even sometimes over-expressing themselves". Of course, he did not fail to tell the world that it was a court that halted the announcement of the results of the June 12, 1993 election.

Our military overlords have no redeeming feature. As Mao Tsetung noted, "Imperialists will never become Buddhas until their doom". When on November 17, 1993, Nigerians woke up to the fearful prospect of a supposed change in government, they did not need a soothsayer to tell them the event was only meant to tighten the cord that had held the country and its increasingly traumatized citizens together for almost a decade of fascism.

Of course, Gen. Abacha's position as the de facto leader in the

Interim National Government was not in doubt. So the November 17, 1993, event was a fait accompli. Therefore, I do not think any twisted logic can justify this grand deception. However, the "triumph" of this illusion cannot go unnoticed and uncelebrated. The perpetrators of this ignominy are rolling out drums and cymbals are clanging with deafening echoes in celebration of our march to democracy.

High-sounding speeches chronicling the achievements of the regime are some of the highpoints of this deception; and the witness: a population that has to contend with ever soaring prices, unemployment, poverty, diseases, and even death. Those who have nurtured this illusion to maturity can only feel a sense of fulfillment and raise glasses in defiance of the thunderous opposition.

We can only shudder at the unmitigated decline of the social, political and economic life of Nigerians in the past one year. And the hypocritical homilies of those who try to paint a colourful image of the Nigerian situation are only a sad reflection of their disposition to fascism.

Of course, what the military is celebrating is the veneration of the state, represented by a cabal, over the wellbeing of Nigerians and the drastic limitation of their political, social and personal freedoms. It is celebrating the collapse of social values and national ethos which has placed the masses at the mercy of the regime; people kowtowing each day to pay homage to the regime at great cost.

The regime is celebrating the unquestionable authority it enjoys and the bashing of the fundamental rights of the citizens. It has proven attractive to the regime as the only way it can move the country forward. Any opposition amounts to high treason. While basking in the illusion that it is advancing the unity of the country, the past one year has witnessed unabated persecution of minorities.

The regime's ruthlessness is only aimed at shoring up undivided loyalty. Of course, Nigerians are enmeshed in ethnic solidarity because those who claim to be the bastion of the country's unity have consistently failed to inspire in them any nationalistic feeling.

The curtailment of rights which is constantly made worse by the non-observance of the basic tenets of human rights should inspire in the regime a sense of celebration. Finally, the regime should not forget to celebrate the transition programme it has foisted on the nation. Of course, the parody that is the constitutional conference is expected to chart a new beginning as the country searches desperately for new values and new ideals.

It is evident, however, that Nigerians cannot get a reprieve from a regime that sees political and press freedom as a threat to national security; a regime that upholds the travesty of justice. As the illusion prevails, Nigerians cannot but feel nostalgic about what life was before this rude awakening; and for the perpetrators, nothing but a feeling of triumph.

3. A Transition and an Illusion
March 1996

Nigerians, the rulers and the ruled, seem to be engaged in a battle of wits. The latter, consumed by the problem of survival, has literally given up the struggle and resigned itself to fate. It has responded mechanically to the crisis confronting the society by serenading itself with various religious antidotes.

The political class, for various reasons, has joined the "Any Government in Power" bandwagon, securing whatever perquisite it can for itself. Like mercenaries, this group has been a veritable tool in the hand of the military in its uncanny attempt at "moving the country forward".

Amongst the civil populace, however, we have those who are impervious to the machinations of the military; those who prefer to pose critical questions at this crucial junction of our national development. They form the opposition; those who cannot comprehend how the country can start a journey to democracy with a patently undemocratic step.

But, just as the anomie persists and palpable contradictions envelope the country, the government does not look perturbed in prosecuting its transition programme. And with the election of local government chairmen in the zero-party polls, Nigeria is expected to have begun the march to "enduring democracy".

We must be grateful to the present military regime for not burdening us with the debate of a hidden agenda. We all know how diversionary and time-consuming such a debate was under Babangida's transition. From the outset, the present government has not hidden its intention about the kind of transition it planned to run.

To prove this point, the government organized a constitutional conference election immediately it came to power. While very few Nigerians participated in the election, the government was not bothered. And as more Nigerians opposed it and called for its termination, the regime, beating its chest in triumph, put a seal of approval on the conference.

Another election, or better still selection, is around the corner and we can be sure that no matter how it goes, the country must "move forward". It does not matter much that Nigerians who have had over half a century experience in party politics are subjected to a novel idea which reduces them to a people incapable of "playing politics".

Like its predecessor, the present transition being foisted on the populace is two pronged: economic and political. On the economic front, we are faced with a continuum. Exactly a decade ago, the preceding military regime prodded by the International Monetary Fund, introduced the Structural Adjustment Programme (SAP). SAP, with its twin policies of privatization and commercialization, has not only impoverished the entire country, it has depoliticized a great majority, since one must eat before "playing politics".

The present regime does not appear enthusiastic about changing the *status quo ante*. On the contrary, there is renewed resolve to pursue SAP to its logical end. Politically, the situation is not different. The government has put in place a programme which will see the military quit by 1998.

The question is, what new hope does the transition programme offer considering the helplessness pervading the polity? An examination of the transition might not be difficult to prove that this programme which appears to deny and ignore the wishes of the people is illusory. In an attempt to create a separate image and character for itself, the present government has tried to cultivate the grounds for popular democracy by putting in place certain transition structures. And without much trouble, it has buried the June 12 issue on whose back it rode to power.

For a military regime embarking on a transition to civil rule, nothing could be more enduring than the dismantling of military structures to smoothen the way for would-be successors. The increasing militarization of the polity does not point to this fact. Pro-democracy and human rights activists are being hounded just as the press is receiving the greatest knocks in its tortuous history. There is nothing like a mass-oriented political structure, devoid of government's influence, that is a part of the transition programme.

Except it wants to maintain its stranglehold on power, the government ought to allow the people run the transition. In the end, they will set the criteria that will determine the success or otherwise of the programme. The need for the transition programme to be handled by a transitional government becomes imperative.

Considering the antecedents of the military, however, it may be asking for too much to entrust it with the duty of laying the foundation for a genuine democratic dispensation that will not only minimize the ethnic and class contradictions in the country, but rescue her from the grip of a moral crisis.

What this means is that patriotic forces may have to intervene politically to stem the slide.

4. Cry the Bedeviled Country
March 1997

Last week, Gen. Sani Abacha talked about his desire to lead Nigeria as a civilian president in the tradition of Jerry Rawlings and Yahya Jammeh. It was a great relief of sorts.

At least, nobody, except perhaps an incurable optimist, would be in doubt that the languid general is set to become the next "democratically elected" president in Nigeria's Fourth Republic. Of course, Abacha is deluding himself. In the midst of massive opposition and resolve by Nigerians against the horrors visited on them by the junta, he is flying the kite of self-perpetuation.

During his infamous confession to the Financial Times, Abacha said he was willing to succeed himself if his constituency (whatever that means) so desired. Abacha does not have any constituency, not even in the army. The so-called constituency is nothing but a handful of mercenary soldiers who earn a living pandering to the general. We can be sure that this imaginary constituency will prod him on, to his destruction, as long as the general pays his dues. His other constituency, perhaps, is the "political class" who cannot resist the temptation of a few more naira to quench their insatiable lust for filthy lucre.

For a man who is set to self-destruct, it is difficult for him to see clearly the writing on the wall. It is a pointer to his intelligence that he cannot comprehend danger even when it stares him in the face. As the Nigerian state sinks deeper into tyranny, and further away from democracy, Abacha will test his transition with the local government election next month. Notwithstanding the result, Abacha and his gang of pseudo-democrats will have something to say to the world.

Not surprisingly, Abacha has mentioned that the December 1996 local government election was postponed because of bomb threats to polling centres. Certainly, he must, in his characteristic vindictiveness, crush those who are purportedly trying to derail his transition.

Abacha's excuse is untenable. He is the sole beneficiary of the crisis in Nigeria. As long as there is crisis, Abacha will remain in the business of unleashing terror and making sure that all forms of opposition are crushed for his ignoble quest to rule Nigeria like a fiefdom.

The picture I see of Nigeria is ugly and horrific and we can no longer pretend or deny the fact the only option left is an open confrontation with the despotic regime of Sani Abacha which breeds the crisis on which its very existence rests and is set to return our beloved country 100 years backward.

---

5. DEMO-CRAZY
APRIL 1997

"Tension in Nigeria", "Opposition leader survives murder bid" and "Grave dangers ahead".

These are some recent headlines on the lingering political crisis in Nigeria. For a distant observer, the goings-on in Africa's most populous nation may sound incredible, but the situation aptly captured by these headlines is real and a clear manifestation that Nigeria is at present mired in an uncontrollable out-break of violence.

This orgy of violence, which for the most part is state induced, has left Nigerians bewildered and portends a serious threat to the survival of the country. It is, therefore, not without reasons that continued and heightened interest in the macabre political events in Nigeria is on the increase.

In a few months, it will be 30 years since a bitter civil war to "safeguard Nigeria" broke out. Twenty-seven years after that internecine war with eight governments and various attempts at moving the country forward – a phrase that has become fashionable for successive military regimes – Nigeria still hangs on the precipice, torn asunder by military buffoonery and plundered by an equally rapacious and quivering political class.

This crisis, engendered by the military high command, is made to look superficial while the perpetrators themselves are absolved of all guilt in the growing human rights abuses and violation of fundamental freedom. Those who believe that theirs is the only option to move Nigeria forward have obdurately held the country in a vice-like grip since independence and specifically since June 12, 1993, when that damnable general who styled himself the "evil genius" and likened himself to the erratic footballer, Diego Maradona, contrived to upturn the popular will.

That sadistic display of military arrogance was preceded by mind-boggling financial impropriety. The Babangida transition cost Nigerian taxpayers over 50 billion naira during a period of eight years. The remnants of that mindless waste are scattered all over Nigeria. Yet, Gen. Sani Abacha, in a most unintelligent mimicry, claims he is pursuing a transition to democracy.

Of course, there is nothing new about what is going on in Nigeria. What we have is history repeating itself. And as Karl Marx observed in *The Eighteenth Brumaire of Louis Bonaparte*, when history re- peats itself what is usually seen is a farcical replication of a tragedy. If Babangida was a tragedy, Abacha certainly is a farce.

Had the military regime of which Abacha was the de facto deputy allowed the June 1993 elections to prevail, by October this year Nigerians would have been at the threshold of another election. However, the junta does not think the way peace-loving Nigerians think. The military must chart its own course for Nigeria and define her democratic future, even if in a chaotic manner.

Sometimes, I wonder why a country inflicts so much pain on itself. But, does it really matter as long as gun-toting men have a territory to control? We all know that Abacha's democracy is manufactured through decrees, not by the will of Nigerians; a democracy of bullets, certainly not of the ballot box.

One can hardly distinguish the deeds of the so-called political parties from the words of the military junta. In the end, supposed democrats would be groveling before the military (Abacha most likely) to lead them. It cannot be otherwise since the general doles out state money to parties and runs them as an extension of his kitchen cabinet.

Undoubtedly, Gen. Abacha stands at the head of the long list of problems with Nigeria. His denial of basic democratic rights will certainly ruin Nigeria. I have yet to see any country in history where a person was jailed simply because he won an election.

Welcome to Abacha's Nigeria where elected leaders are thrown into prisons and people are handpicked to stand elections. Let the whole world appreciate Abacha's democracy where a president elect is in prison and people (including Abacha) are jostling to become "elected president" in his stead.

Surprisingly, those who claim they are the bastion of democracy, freedom and human rights are tongue-tied and looking helpless, tacitly giving approval to the Abacha regime as it rides roughshod over Nigeria.

Democracy and its irony!

---

6. WELCOME "NIGERJEVO"
JANUARY 1998

Last December, the expected happened. Another phantom coup purportedly designed to derail Gen. Sani Abacha's tortuous and self-serving transition was uncovered. It demonstrated, once again, the extent to which the regime, like pigs, would go in devouring its kind.

The ethnic dimension of the arrests, the spurious reasons which the regime gave (moving the capital back to Lagos, etc.) as the motive of the "coupists", the fact that the "coupists" were trailed for three months, the invitation of duplicitous traditional rulers to watch video and audio tapes of the plot (when did coup plots become home videos for "bloody civilians"?) and the nature the trial would take, confirmed not just the theatre of absurdities which Nigeria has become, but the degenerate extent our puny Samson would go to succeed himself.

Gen. Abacha's pettiness defies logic. Like other bankrupt dictatorships, as the opposition intensifies, the more maniacal it becomes. It is certainly not strange that irrationality has taken over as the desperate junta plots another democratic charade. This coup must, therefore, be derided, not so much for the empathy for the Oladipo Diyas and Abdulkareem Adisas who have played various damaging roles and helped in propping up Gen. Abacha, but for the fact that it is meant to befuddle Nigerians and strengthen the hands of the regime while prolonging its hold on power.

Expectedly, the division has caught on, if only temporarily, as it did three years ago when the regime also hatched another coup to consolidate its own coup of November 17, 1993. Pro-Abacha crowds have hit the streets again condemning the coup and calling for the effete General to continue as president after October 1998. It is not surprising that some newspapers, for want of what to write, have also joined the rented crowd of pro-Abacha protesters in condemning the coup.

The issue, of course, is not whether there was a coup or not. Indeed, one would be hard pressed to believe, considering the notoriety of this regime and the untold hardship it is inflicting on Nigerians, that there are no persons seriously plotting to overthrow it. We have to look beyond Gen. Abacha, and his ridiculous coup theory, to the morbid interest he represents.

Gen. Abacha should, therefore, not assume that anybody would take him seriously. Gen. Oladipo Diya and his supposedly co-conspirators are nothing, but the latest pawns in the chess game of self-perpetuation. Many more, including some of those who are shouting themselves hoarse and inventing spurious theories to justify the coup, would have to be sacrificed as long as this scam of a transition is allowed to hold sway.

Clearly, Nigerians cannot allow themselves to be distracted by this bogus claim. Gen. Abacha's transition is simply a sham. The talk of a civilian vice-president (most likely from the East or West) to replace Gen. Diya is only to trump up a suitable reason why Gen. Abacha should not hand over. With a civilian vice-president and civilian state administrators in April, Gen. Abacha's roller-coaster ride to the presidency is as certain as the fact that night would replace day.

The only antidote to this political brigandry is for people to stop imagining what Gen. Abacha would do or not do. He and his cronies are creatures of the past. Nigerians should just write off this regime. We have to realize that we cannot, not withstanding its democratic posturing, place our hopes on a military regime which is nothing but the armed wing of an oligarchy for whom political power is the ultimate aphrodisiac. Strangely enough, those who have the capacity to act appear too unconcerned. Indeed, never in the history of post-civil war Nigeria has the country come so close to Sarajevo.

Nigeria has never had it so bad. The country today appears to be a fusion of Hitler's Germany and Stalin's Russia. People are not only denouncing their friends and families, it has become almost impossible to eke out a living without pandering to the maximum ruler. Nothing can work until you chant "Hail Abacha" or are adorned in Gen. Abacha insignia. Whether one lives or not depends on the whims of this latter-day Fuhrer. Life in Nigeria has become "nasty, brutish and short". We are reliving some of the tales from the Idi Amins, Bokassas and Kamuzus Bandas which we only read about years ago.

Clearly, Nigeria is in crisis. And if talking or even praying could avert the looming disaster then Nigeria would have been saved a long time ago because our people have talked and prayed enough. Now is the time for the decision whether we want to move forward as a nation or perish together. Foday Sankoh, the grand old man of Sierra Leonean politics, who is currently getting a whiff of Gen. Abacha's despotism once remarked that, "When a society demands a change, there is no need attempting to change it on old principles". In situations like this, history provides us with a good guide: Sarajevo, Kigali, etc.

What this means is that we can ill afford to leave the future of Nigeria in the hands of military adventurers. This historical tragedy and aberration called the Nigeria Army cannot be tolerated any further in the national interest. Under the pretext of being the bastion of stability and national unity, this Army has sustained the internal colonialism going on in Nigeria. Each day witnesses new, and always dangerous, plots, ruses and lies which serve just one purpose: the preservation of an oligarchy.

In the last decade and half, we have moved from democracy to military rule; from diarchy to an annulled election; from imprisoning an elected president to a farcical transition programme and an orchestrated plot at self-succession. We can only hope that the next stop is not "Nigerjevo"!

7. THE TRIUMPH OF TREACHERY
January 1998

Very often, subtly or otherwise, we are confronted by those who proclaim that Gen. Sani Abacha should be given a chance. You hear these comments from recidivist politicians and government officials who wouldn't mind one more political appointment with all the perquisites attached as well as from journalists who, in the name of "objectivity" or "responsible journalism" allow themselves the fantasy of indulging the Abachas of this world. I often wonder if any journalist worth his salt would have asked the world to give Hitler a chance. How do you give evil a chance? The logical implication of that argument is simple: permission to exterminate all non-Aryans. This is what treachery is all about.

Treachery is not limited to our "responsible journalists" so-called or even to those a friend aptly described as "stomach-direction politicians". Even diplomats and statesmen are bound by it. Why has treachery become a pervasive phenomenon? Is it due to what has been spuriously called human nature or because its logic is more appealing to our fantasies, given that the gains are more often than not immediate?

It was not surprising that Commonwealth leaders who met in Edinburgh, Scotland, recently, firmly resolved not to impose sanctions on the Abacha regime. They were certain in their estimation that he is pursuing a credible transition programme and should be given a chance. Asked after the meeting if the Commonwealth conference in 1999 would welcome "President Abacha", British Prime Minster, Tony Blair, answered: "That is a hypothetical question". Chief Emeka Anyaoku, Commonwealth Secretary General, put the icing on the cake when he added that the organisation would accept any leader elected by the Nigerian people.

These two answers sum up the attitude of the international community to the political crisis in Nigeria, which to all intents and purposes, does not favour the Nigerian people Anyaoku talks about so blithely. It is easy to understand the sentiments of Tony Blair and others like him. It is business as usual; so it does not matter much if more Nigerians are thrown into jail or executed to keep Gen. Abacha in power; it matters even less if Gen. Abacha denies Nigerians electoral freedom so that he can conveniently emerge as the next "democratically-elected" president of Nigeria.

The important thing is to have, preferably, a dictator who will maintain Britain's age-long plundering of Nigeria's vast resources and keep it as the hunting-ground of rapacious industrial and financial monopolies (Shell, UAC, etc.).

However, it is difficult to place Anyaoku who is a Nigerian. Such cynicism as expressed in the statement "any leader elected by the Nigerian people", in the present dispensation, smacks of opportunism and a veiled attempt to legitimize Gen. Abacha's incongruous transition. Is he saying that he is unaware of the numerous limitations placed on Nigerians by Gen. Abacha's transition?

The consequence of this statement is that Gen. Abacha can gather a handful of people, purport to have held an election and declare himself winner and president of Nigeria. Interestingly, Anyaoku says nothing or pretends to be oblivious of the fact that Nigerians chose a president four years ago in the person of Chief M. K. O. Abiola and they deserve the right to know what has become of him and his mandate.

That is the sorry case of what happens to people who detach themselves from reality and are ready to be seduced by official lies. If only the Anyaokus of this world are aware of the looming catastrophe and grief they are causing Nigerians. Certainly, there are enough reasons why this charade cannot and should not be allowed to complete its cycle. If Gen. Abacha succeeds, with the help of Anyaoku and others, in making himself president, we will be saddled with this monstrosity for another decade or more.

Suddenly, the history of Nigeria is being rewritten; falsified or destroyed where it cannot be twisted. Nothing is right except that which serves to glorify Gen. Abacha. The rented crowd that parades our streets everyday and the attempts by Gen. Abacha's political parties to draft him into the elections are clear indications of the level of bankruptcy of the Abacha regime. In the coming months, he will arrest more journalists as well as human rights and pro-democracy activists if only to satiate his lust for power.

Gen. Abacha, like all despots can go on deluding himself into believing that he is conducting a credible transition. He contends that the rules for democracy in Africa are different from those in the West. Let us grant him the right to philosophise even though it is known that intellectual exercise is not one of his many fancies. There is no definition of democracy which allows a president to be imprisoned after winning an election and the majority disenfranchised, arrested and imprisoned because a military ruler wants to succeed himself.

The attempt at the perpetuation of "Abachadom" will tell Nigerians in plain language that the annulment of the June 12, 1993 presidential election was all about the preservation of the rule of an oligarchy of which Gen. Abacha's military is the armed wing. This oligarchy, it appears, is tired of ruling through arms, now it must continue its ignoble rule in a "democracy".

However, if we allow the indignities heaped on us by this regime in the name of democracy and transition, we may soon realize to our regret that we are singing the dirge of our beloved country. The whole attempt at democracy is nothing but an effort to sustain the myth surrounding the oligarchy referred to and cushion the devastating effect of dictatorship which is gradually being ingrained in our consciousness. Clearly, there is nothing to be said in favour of Gen. Abacha and his transition.

Undoubtedly, it is the history of brutality under Gen. Abacha that makes it compelling for us to oppose this regime; that makes it impossible to have a greater preoccupation than finding an antidote to this regime. We cannot leave the future of Nigeria to some mercenary statesmen and diplomats who have found pleasure in Gen. Abacha's own treachery.

Nigeria's tortuous history, the painful experiences of the last decade and the rise of fascism in the last four years make it inevitable that progressive forces in Nigeria must continuously follow the path of liberation. Africa definitely cannot afford another travesty of democracy in Nigeria.

After four years of brutal dictatorship and conscious effort to erase the past and befuddle Nigerians, it is time to break the cycle of horror and shame. The international community cannot pretend to be unaware of Gen. Abacha's scheming. However, if it decides to act in that manner, it is the historical task of progressive elements in Nigeria to bring to an ignominious end this regime led by Gen. Abacha who, it is clear, has no vision for a democratic Nigeria.

8. Democracy and American Hypocrisy
April 1998

"Washington has been too willing to downplay democracy and human rights for the sake of natural resources or diplomatic alliances". - New York Times: March 20, 1998.

One of the high points of President Clinton's six-nation African tour was the endorsement of the higgledy-piggledy transition of the military cabal in Nigeria. At a press conference in South Africa, Mr. Clinton remarked, in reference to Abacha's plot of self succession: "If he stands for election, we hope he will stand as a civilian". He added, "There are many military leaders who have taken over chaotic situations in Africa that have moved towards democracy. And that can happen in Nigeria". That endorsement was expected. Indeed, it was long overdue because pro-democracy and human rights forces in Nigeria had become weary of Washington's game of hide and seek with the inglorious regime of Sani Abacha.

Mr. Clinton did not surprise anybody, except those confused activists who had hoped, particularly after the annulment of the June 12, 1993 election won by Moshood Abiola, that Washington would send a strike force to pull down the Babangida regime and restore the winner of the election. Somehow, it was not a misplaced hope, considering Washington's much-touted defence of democracy and its newfound role as the policeman of the world.

The fact that Mr. Clinton gave his support to the vicious military dictatorship in Nigeria and was optimistic that the regime could guarantee a democratic future for Nigerians once again confirmed Washington's double standards in dealing with the African continent and the underlying interest in America's foreign policy.

"Washington has been too willing to downplay democracy and human rights for the sake of natural resources or diplomatic alliances", the New York Times noted in its editorial of March 20, 1998. Clearly, nobody is better placed to serve this purpose of giving access to Africa's natural resources and providing a base in support of US diplomatic alliances than the various mad men who have sprung up (often with the help of Washington) within Africa and much of the developing world.

The US supported Mobutu Sese Seko after killing Patrice Lumumba, the first prime minister of the Republic of the Congo (now Democratic Republic of the Congo), and scuttling Congo's burgeoning democracy; and Mobutu, in return, provided a springboard for Washington against its bogeyman, communism. Today, the US has found it convenient to recant and is calling for democracy in the Democratic Republic of the Congo.

On February 4, 1966, Osagyefo Kwame Nkrumah, the first prime minister of Ghana, was overthrown in a CIA sponsored coup. The result was the abortion of Ghana's fledgling democracy. More than three decades after, the country is still grappling with the rudiments of democracy under a military dictator that is making a travesty of democracy; yet Washington is contented and applauding that "democracy is spreading".

Just name it! Where has Washington stepped into that she has not messed up? The US supported Ferdinand Marcos and his murderous gang in the Philippines; provided a slaughter slab for the butcher of Uganda, Idi Amin; aborted democracy in Chile and installed the hydra-headed monster, Pinochet; wrecked Haiti, courtesy of the Duvalier clan. In all these places, the US was looking for a mad man who would preside over the wholesale transfer of natural resources to America's multinationals and do her dirty job in its so-called war with communism.

Nothing mattered beyond the immediate economic and political gains of Washington. Not even the sight of mutilated bodies of defenceless and innocent kids who were the victims of the dastardly actions of such scum as Jonas Savimbi and his cohorts who were armed and financed by the US could move her to change her position.

Those who are familiar with America's foreign policy and the unwholesome interest underlying it will observe that nothing binds the society together and nothing pushes it to act other than the quest for trade and profit. That is why she is threatening fire and brimstone in the Gulf; it is for the same reason that she has actively supported Africa's "khaki presidents".

The so-called abolition of slavery in America was facilitated by the industrial revolution which had made indentured workers irrelevant just as technological advancement has rendered millions jobless today; not out of any patent desire to uphold the dignity of man or equality of races. Of course, the whole concept of electoral democracy in America is a sham.

Evidently, Washington supported the Boers in South Africa because the former is a society built on apartheid laws and America glorifies that history. The ANC was labelled a terrorist organisation (the usual refrain) while America's Military Industrial Complex (MIC) got gold mining concessions and supplied the weapon for the reign of terror of the white racist regime.

It is therefore easy to see why Washington has left the Nigerian people to the mercy of a ruthless dictator who despises and destroys what he cannot understand – and there are very few things he understands. Propelled by the theory of market forces and free trade, which also formed part of Mr. Clinton's African itinerary, siding with dictators against the people is the only way America can maintain her stranglehold on the local market.

The American society is a predatory society and it can survive only by aggressively expanding and conquering new markets from which to extract profit. What Washington aims at creating in West Africa, as in other areas that are under its sphere of influence, is a club of IMF/World Bank puppets. The reason is simple. "West African despots – as always, quislings of America and her Western accomplices – who mutate into civilian presidents, make all the difference between the acceptance or rejection of the West's obnoxious economic policies and by extension, the survival or collapse of their businesses".

The examples of Ghana, Burkina Faso and The Gambia are indicative of this trend. The IMF/World Bank and their host governments cannot be too sure what the "new man" would do (a case of the devil you know); so why not support a Jerry Rawlings, Blaise Campaore or Yahya Jammeh even where their transition to civil rule succeeds only in furthering neopatrimonialism.

As one of the puppets of international monopoly capital, Washington is sure Abacha will execute structural adjustment, devaluation, privatisation and such other infernal policies the IMF/World Bank may deem necessary to recommend for Nigeria's underdevelopment. This support, and manipulation of Abacha, is necessary to prevent the toiling masses from uniting in a revolution that would threaten international monopoly capital.

The largest, most powerful companies in Nigeria are Shell-BP (British/Dutch); Unilever, (British/Dutch) and Chevron, (American). Their global turnover vastly exceeds the combined budgets of all African states. Abacha and his likes all over African are nothing but gatekeepers of international capital, allowing profits to pass freely out of their countries into the pockets of multinationals; and Nigeria is nothing more than a hunting ground for these rapacious multinational companies whose interest Abacha has vowed to preserve. As long as he does so, these companies and their military backers will keep him in power (as military or civilian president), to rule on their behalf and maim and kill in their interest as witnessed in the Shell-BP backed ethnic cleansing in Ogoniland.

The fallout of Mr. Clinton's visit to Africa is that the world would move into the new century with all the prejudices, including the onslaught of imperialism (courtesy of America) which have made the 20th century a nightmare. It is difficult to imagine what could be a greater threat to world peace in the new millennium than the American state. Martinique psychiatrist, philosopher and revolutionary, Frantz Fanon wrote that, "Each generation must, out of relative obscurity, discover its mission, fulfill it, or betray it".

Africa's emergent activists, from Cape Coast to Cairo, must enter the new millennium boldly determined to confront the monster of imperialism. Those who are ready to liberate Africa from the clutches of poverty, illiteracy and general underdevelopment and expand the frontiers of democracy cannot look up to the West, America particularly. They must be ready to struggle for these rights. The US has committed too many grave crimes against the African continent that apologies would only serve to obfuscate these crimes.

Imperialism, it has been said, is like common cold. "You either fight it or go to bed with it". There can't be half measures or a middle course. This is a new era in which people, particularly the exploited and marginalized, cannot afford to look for salvation from outside.

Certainly, the US will fail in Nigeria as she failed in Vietnam, Cuba, and everywhere else she has sought to extend her bloody fang.

---

9. June 12 and the Democratic Alternative
February 1998

The realities of the June 12, 1993 presidential election and its subsequent annulment place an historical task before all true patriots, if only to clear, once and for all time, the ambiguities of the trajectory of Nigeria's political future. Danbala Danju writing in the December 1997 issue of Nigeria Now, published by the London-based New Nigeria Forum, summed up his solution to the seemingly intractable political crisis in Nigeria in the following words: "The alternative is neither Abacha nor Abiola". The gist of his argument is that there is an alternative beyond the present monstrosity and an Abiola presidency.

Danju's position raises several fundamental questions which must be discussed not just openly but frankly. He begins by acknowledging that, "Modern Nigeria is basically a colonial creation" and that British imperial interest was the underlying factor in this fusion. He argues further that the nationalists who took over at independence were not interested in the fundamental restructuring of the exploitative social relations (and hegemonic ethnic relations – my words) prevalent in Nigeria which led to the consolidation of a tiny unproductive ruling class. The policies which this predatory ruling class (both military and civilian) has pursued, including intense suffering and impoverishment, "pose a serious challenge to the corporate existence of the country".

According to Danju, "The economic hardships being experienced by the majority, coupled with the liquidation of formal political parties have made ethnicity, regionalism and religious bigotry important avenues for the articulation of the frustrations and deprivations of the masses…and it was against this background of worsening economic crisis and widespread rejection of SAP that Gen. Ibrahim Babangida's political transition programme was unveiled".

Danju contends that, "Although the democratic forces rejected the entire transition programme as portending greater danger to, than a harbinger of democracy, no concrete steps were taken to forestall Babangida's hidden agenda". "As the charade continued", argues Danju, "Only those that the regime's handpicked electoral committee approved were allowed to participate".

He advances his thesis by saying that, "IBB's transition programme that culminated in the June 12, 1993 presidential election was fundamentally skewed against workers, peasants and their intellectual allies… and that the political parties: the Social Democratic Party (SDP) of Abiola and the National Republican Convention (NRC) were dominated by the unprincipled moneybags-politicians whose conception of politics was that of an investment from which to make the maximum profit rather than service to Nigerians". Danju finds it hard to believe that, "Along with the electoral frauds and irregularities that characterized the entire transition programme some sections of the democratic movement call the elections free and fair".

Thus for him, "It is inconceivable that the struggle for the liberation of Nigeria would be headed by characters such as Abiola and Tofa who openly were beneficiaries and conscious collaborators in the systemic exploitation of Nigeria". He contends that, "Workers must fight for an end to military dictatorship and reject Abacha's so-called transition to democracy and this must not be hijacked to mean demanding another bourgeoisie such as Abiola as president." The idea that the Nigerian bourgeoisie under Abiola will usher in a democratic era and development", he argues, "is fundamentally mistaken".

Danju welcomes the emergence of a "Democratic Alternative" (DA) as "a broad movement of workers, students, youth and revolutionary intellectuals across the country with the explicit objective of capturing power for socialist transformation" and concludes that, "The task must be for the DA to intensify the organizational efforts to not only accelerate the demise of military rule, but capture state power and inaugurate a programme of socialist democracy".

Reading this, and the somewhat jaded conclusion on the current crisis, it is difficult to accuse Danju of lack of commitment or sincerity; perhaps it is his perception or understanding of the problem that is suspect. It is therefore necessary to explore some of the myths of our political evolution. In addressing the issue of democracy and the future of Nigeria, two markedly different questions have to be raised: the class and ethnic or national questions.

How do class and ethnic questions affect politics in Nigeria today? It is easy or rather conducive for some "radical" elements in their analysis to see the class question as the basic contradiction in Nigeria, which unfortunately is an underdeveloped capitalist society. Regrettably, this viewpoint only serves to compound the problem. Clearly, in addressing the class and national question, the colonial experience is instructive.

Undoubtedly, the question of North/South dichotomy in Nigeria, as in much of neo-colonial Africa, will remain a vexed issue for a long time probably up until the period when Africa's toiling masses assume control of the continent's political, social and economic climate. This North/South divide which was created by colonialism has been compounded by capitalism which aggravates uneven development.

It is, therefore, not difficult to see why ethnic consciousness is salient in Nigerian politics. Whether we assume that it is being manipulated by the ruling class on both sides of the divide is not the issue. As Richard Sanbrook notes in *The Politics of Africa's Economic Stagnation,* "Ethnic consciousness…is neither irrational nor ephemeral. From the perspective of ordinary people, ethnicity appears no less sensible a basis for political mobilization than class. Ethnic mobilization is, after all just a means to end, a way of forging a coalition to pursue scarce material benefits…ethnicity is, moreover, a surprising flexible basis for political solidarity".

During the struggle for independence in Nigeria, as in many parts of Africa, ethnic nationalism was substituted for "Nigeria nationalism". The reason is simple. A majority, if not all the contending ethnic nationalities, saw the colonialists as a common enemy. But the fact that these pan-Nigeria groups simply collapsed to their different ethnic domains immediately after independence shows that the ethnic pull was not just a flash in the pan.

In the Nigerian experience, it was particularly so because there emerged, with the help of the quivering colonialists, a palpable dominant class, which, apart from controlling the peasants and workers within its territory, sought in a most belligerent manner to control its counterparts, the ruling classes, in other parts of the country. The situation was made worse by the fact that before the coming of the colonialists and the attendant amalgamation, some of these ruling classes had waged bitter wars of annihilation or survival as the case may be. These wars are still on today.

What is going on in Nigeria currently has much to do with the question of poverty, as Danju would want us to believe. But, it has much more to do with an orchestrated plot in favour of ethnic domination or even annihilation. Perhaps, this would help in addressing the more serious question of why the June 12, 1993 election was annulled and why, strangely enough, those who clamour for the restoration of the mandate are made to look like ethnic chauvinists while those who plotted the annulment are assumed to have acted to satisfy their whims and could not have been led by ethnic considerations. This is a question Danju consciously or unconsciously failed to raise. Conversely, he raises the rather innocuous question of the election not being free and fair.

The June 12 election was adjudged free and fair for the simple reason that following the rules laid down by the Babangida regime, nothing appeared to have gone wrong. Danju was right when he asserted that the transition was skewed against workers and peasants.

But, where and when have bourgeoisie democracy and elections been in favour of workers and peasants? Even in the so-called advanced democracies – the US, Britain and France – the result has been pitiably the same. The 1979 election in Nigeria was, of course, skewed against workers and peasants. There were irregularities and controversies. But, it could not have been annulled.

If Tofa had won the June 12, 1993 election, we would not be arguing today whether the election was skewed against workers and peasants. The situation would not have created the opportunity to pose such a question. He may well have been re-elected to his second term of office. For Abiola, it was, as the cliché goes, a completely different ball game.

The dominant power bloc in the North, whose handmaiden Babangida was, could simply not tolerate what it perceived as a "power shift". Clearly, this, more than anything else, including Danju's hysteria about economic hardships, intense suffering and impoverishment, poses the greatest challenge to the corporate existence of Nigeria.

Apart from the present, the most tortuous period of Nigeria's history was the decade between 1960 and 1970 when the country was relatively buoyant and prosperous and political parties flourished. This era witnessed the census crisis, the crisis in the Western Region, the January 15, 1966 coup, the counter coup seven months later and, of course, the civil war almost immediately. What this tells us is that the problem is deeper than we are ready to accept.

Today, there are internal colonies in Nigeria in which people have to contend first for their rights and dignity as Nigerians before they pose the question of hunger. Of course, there is hunger in the East, West, North and South. There is also political and social alienation which has nothing to do with the fact that one is a peasant or worker but so much to do with the fact that one is from a section of the ethnic divide. June 12 broke this North/South dichotomy at the level of the masses. If the election had not been annulled, it would have been much easier to mobilize the same masses on a national basis for the ultimate task of entrenching a new order.

Surprisingly, we have not learnt our lesson as a nation and the annulment of the June 12 election would remain a sad reminder of how far removed from nationhood we are. If we accept that the election was skewed against workers and peasants, but according to the regime's rules it was free and fair, why then was it annulled? Was it because Babangida was sympathetic to workers?

It certainly was not a case of Babaginda not wanting to leave power – he did leave eventually. If Babangida so desired, he would not have allowed the election to hold. He and his cohorts were malevolent enough to carry out such plot. Sadly, it was the same judiciary that had been humiliated and rendered prostrate throughout Babangida's rule and barred from adjudicating on the transition that he latched onto as a reason for the annulment.

It is a measure of how the ruling class in the North perceives political power and its interest in the *status quo* that it would not lend its voice to the clamour for an end to Abacha's ignominious rule. Of course, it does not strike some of our radical critics that there is something significant in the fact that a section of the bourgeoisie is vehemently opposed to the present regime while a section is supportive or unconcerned.

It is not enough for such critics to dismiss the former as past collaborators. Understandably, the ruling class in the North cannot raise its voice in opposition to this regime. For this class, political has become a pastime. Babangida abdicated power but not before creating an interim government with Abiola's kinsman (Ernest "Buthelezi" Shonekan) as head. I am not sure the colonialists went this far in their heinous game of divide and rule.

Then came the *coup de grace*. Before Babangida finally "stepped aside", he signed a decree which stated that in the event of the resignation or death of the spineless head of the interim government, the highest ranking minister would take over. There is the contention that this decree was promulgated several weeks after the interim government was set up only to be attributed to Babangida when the need arose.

Whatever explanation is accepted, the issue is, how are ministers graded to know who is the highest ranking? Is it the ministry they control or the number of years they have served a particular regime? This clarification is necessary if only to explain the emergence of Abacha and the fact that he is an "arrangee" successor.

Of course, it is the desire for political power by the Northern ruling elite that makes it blurt out every now and then that "the unity of Nigeria is nonnegotiable". This unity claptrap is not borne out of any desire for national cohesion or quest for a united and prosperous nation but an opportunity to maintain a stranglehold over what it perceives as its geo-political conquest.

What the foregoing means is that "radical" critics across the country must be circumspect in their analysis of the on-going crisis. The ethnic or national question in Nigeria must not be treated lightly because it is still at the pristine level, which Samir Amin describes in his book *Class and Nation, Historically and in the Current Crisis*, as a situation (in Europe) where nationalities were oppressed by absolute feudal regimes.

Under the present dispensation, it does not suffice for our "radical" critics to be interested only in the economic empowerment of workers. They can only deny the existence and urgency of the national question at their own peril. Those amongst them who are genuinely interested in resolving the crisis must of necessity, in the words of Amin, "explicitly put in its programme, the immediate and real struggle against all forms of discrimination, inequality, and oppression based on ethnicity, language, religion, or custom". This is necessary because it is possible that, "The vanguard (read Democratic Alternative) could fail to get the exploited workers to accept a struggle for economic emancipation within the framework of a large, unwieldy and disunited nation".

It is pertinent to end this essay by restating the obvious: there is a hegemonic power bloc in Nigeria; a power bloc whose roots predate our colonial history. And as long as this class is allowed to hold sway, we cannot create a nation much less a just social system. Our "radical" critics cannot hide from this historical reality; for as Amin remarks: "The struggle for socialism in the periphery of the imperialist system cannot be separated from, and even less opposed to, the struggle for national (ethnic) liberation. The fact of imperialism obliges us to envisage the transition to socialism as resulting from the historical fusion of the goals of social and national (ethnic) liberation".

How the June 12 mandate would be restored would be determined by so many factors which I cannot possibly enumerate here.

---

10. WHY ABIOLA LOST OUT
JULY 1998

Events in Nigeria in the last one month have all the noticeable qualities of a tragicomedy. Former dictator, Sani Abacha, dies suddenly of "heart attack". A new military strongman, Gen. Abdulsalami Abubakar, takes over. He promises to release all political detainees, including Chief M.K.O. Abiola whose incarceration made it possible for Abubakar to occupy that all-powerful position of head of state and commander-in-chief. The international community – the EU, UN and Commonwealth – is impressed. It sends representatives to parley with Abubakar who reassures them that Abiola would be released. He also pleads with them to persuade Abiola to renounce his mandate. They oblige him. He sets a date for Abiola's release.

Before his release, the Americans come in to seal the deal. Abiola holds a meeting with the American delegation. Midway into the meeting, he demands a cup of tea, starts coughing and feeling uneasy. It takes some time before the doctors arrive. He is rushed to a clinic. About an hour later, he is pronounced dead. The American who was with him – I understand he is a diplomat, not a pathologist – when he "took ill" swears in the name of freedom and liberty that he did not suspect foul play.

Meanwhile, Abubakar, in a nation-wide broadcast tells a bewildered nation: "It is with a very heavy heart that I address you for the second time since destiny (arms and treachery, better still) bestowed upon me the mantle of leadership of our beloved nation. Exactly one month ago, we were shocked by the sudden passing away of our late head of state, Gen. Sani Abacha. As we conclude the official 30 days mourning of this great loss, we are now challenged by another national tragedy; the passing away yesterday of Chief Moshood Abiola was as sudden as it was tragic, particularly as he died on the brink of his release from detention...Government has already ordered full and transparent autopsy to establish the actual cause of his death. The autopsy is being undertaken in co-operation with the family and the participation of expert pathologists from the United States, United Kingdom and Canada as requested by his family".

Right now, the experts are working on the remains of Chief Abiola to determine the actual cause of his death. Chances are that they will not find much. Indeed, it is Nigeria that should be undergoing a post-mortem to find out why a nation with so great human and material resources should be lying prostrate. Maybe because successive rulers in Nigeria have allowed "destiny" rather than the will of the citizens to prevail.

Of course, there are enough reasons to conclude that the man who would have been president in 1993 based on the popular will of Nigerians was killed. Yes, killed! It was not necessary to poison Abiola. The betrayal was enough to kill him. The renewed international conspiracy against him, headed by America, must have been too much for the late Chief to bear. The man was made to look like a villain; ostracised, vilified and dumped.

One could picture what transpired between Abiola and American Under Secretary, Thomas Pickering, in that infamous meeting:

Pickering: Good day Chief. I am sure you recognize me. I am Under Secretary, Thomas Pickering. It's nice meeting you again after so many years.

Abiola: Of course, I do recognize you even though I have lost touch with the outside world.

Pickering: How is your health, Chief?

Abiola: I am not in the best of health. As I told members of my family when they visited in, sorry what year is this?

Pickering: 1998.

Abiola: I think that was in 1995. I told them that the condition here was like digging a grave for a living person. It has not changed. I have asked repeatedly to see a doctor and I have repeatedly been denied that request. They killed my wife. They want to kill me too.

Pickering: I am sorry about that Chief, but it is understandable. You know, these military boys are savages. Actually, why I came to see you is to seek your release and see what role you could play in the credible transition to civilian rule being put in place by the new regime.

Abiola: So what happens to the mandate given to me by Nigerians? Are you and your government saying you want me to renounce the mandate given to me by Nigerians? You know that is impossible.

Pickering: Why can't you be a realist, Chief? It's been five years since that election. As Mr. Annan, the UN Secretary-General told you, nobody is interested in that mandate anymore. In fact, people are saying if you were made president in 1993, your tenure would have elapsed a year ago. Even the pro-democracy forces you hope will support you are disorganized. They think June 12 is now history.

Abiola: You say you are Mr...

Pickering: Pickering.

Abiola: And your status?

Pickering: Under Secretary in the State Department in Washington.

Abiola: Does this mean this is the official White House position?

Pickering: I am afraid it is, Chief.

Abiola: I used to think that America abhorred military rule; that she valued the rule of law and respected democratic rights.

Pickering: Well we do, Chief. But we are also realists. You must be aware of the dictum that in politics there is no permanent enemy only permanent interest. You have to give up this mandate which has elapsed and go back to your family and business. I guess by now your businesses are in ruins if they have not collapsed completely. I am sure you know how many millions of dollars your detention has caused your personal fortune. But we are ready to cover that cost.

You just name your price. We could get you on the board of Mobil, Chevron or Cargill and in just one year, you are back. We, I mean the American government supports your unconditional release. But you must understand that we are not in a position to influence every action that the Nigerian government is contemplating.

Abiola: Why do you have so much faith in these military boys? They are incorrigible. The only credible election this country has witnessed was cancelled by these boys. Abacha was part of that regime. The same for Abubakar. They were all part of the diabolical plot to subvert the popular will of Nigerians.

Pickering: Well, Chief, you know how difficult it is to persuade the military to give up power. However, Abubakar is a professional soldier. I think we can trust him. More important, I think we can do business with him. You know, Chief, that the stakes for the US here are considerable. Need I remind you that your country is the fifth largest supplier of oil to the US and that US firms account for about half of Nigeria's petroleum and natural gas output? You know that scum of a general, I mean Abacha, really wasted Nigeria's oil resources. Over 10 billion dollars in oil export every year and there is nothing to show for it. Much of it diverted to personal account overseas. Oil concession was injudiciously given to cronies. We know that Nigerians want democracy and we will do everything to bring democracy to Nigeria. Who, but a professional soldier, can ensure this American dream of democracy in Nigeria while guaranteeing the cordial relations between both countries along that line I talked about earlier.

Abiola: Why are you doing this to me? I mean, why is the United States engineering this conspiracy against Nigerians and me. Is it a crime to win an election? I have been held hostage for four years. As if that is not enough, you come here to humiliate me by this untoward request. Why do you think Nigerians deserve anything less than democracy and the government of their choice? What do you think Nigerians would say if I walked out of this door and said thank you for supporting me for four years, I have had enough?

Pickering: I am deeply sorry, Chief, but that is the way things stand. You either accept our offer or you lose both ways. I know you are too smart to attempt losing both ways.

Abiola: What did you say? Lose both ways? What are you Americans planning? Why are you do...?

Abiola is overwhelmed by the treachery and the thought that he could be ruined financially and perhaps even killed. He begins to cough and feel uneasy. The scenario above may appear hypothetical, but it fits into the scheme of the rulers in Washington.

Abiola had so much faith in the United States. That was why – to the chagrin of pro-democracy forces – he went there in 1993, shortly after the annulment of the June 12, 1993 presidential election which he won. Although he was disappointed with the response he got, he did not lose hope. Unfortunately, the treachery had to run its full course.

Even though Abiola represented all that America would cherish, her spirit of free enterprise and liberty so-called, the American establishment simply could not trust him. He was far too enmeshed in "dangerous politics" and was seen to have support from the "radical" opposition in Nigeria that does not condone the misdeeds of the new slave masters. Abiola paid a price; a price all those who adore or have faith in the American system will pay eventually.

Guatemala is a handy example. It was in Guatemala in 1954 that the CIA, acting on behalf of the United Fruit Company (now Chiquita Brands), organized the overthrow of the newly elected democratic government of President Jacobo Arbenz. That damnable act which dimmed the democratic aspirations of Guatemalans later spread to Chile and other South and Central American countries.

The point being made here is, as far as America is concerned, expediency is the name of the game. Just as the United Fruits Company was interested in who governed Guatemala in 1954, the new imperialists – Chevron, Mobil, Texaco, Cargill and their sisters, Shell, Elf and Agip – are interested in who rules Nigeria. A few pertinent questions would buttress this position.

Why did Bill Clinton not persuade, first Babangida, and later Abacha, to release the results of the June 12, 1993 election? Was it because America did not believe the election was free and fair? Why would Mr. Clinton prefer Abacha running for president in a travesty of democracy rather than calling for the winner of a democratic election to be installed president? Multinational corporations, in two words. The bogey of communism is gone, supposedly, with the collapse of Soviet Union. The greatest threat to international capital now is the indigenous people.

One can hazard a guess about the kind of democracy America is envisaging for Nigeria – the IMF/World Bank democracy she has endorsed for the West African sub-region and the Asian continent – a democracy that will make Nigeria the outpost of international monopoly capital. It is for this reason that during a press briefing in Washington on July 8, State Department official, James Rubin, said amongst other things that when the new transition programme in Nigeria occurs there should be an election that is "free and fair".

Free and fair indeed. What happened to the free and fair election held on June 12, 1993? America would do well to wash her hands off the democratic experiment in Nigeria. When she had the chance to do something she blew it. But the new imperialists are too foolhardy to learn.

Of course, their forebears did not learn in Vietnam and Cuba.

---

11. Transition and Illusions
August 1998

If the pronouncements of this regime are not taken seriously, it is simply because of what they are: a ruse; and if the heading of this piece sounds like the title of a theatrical play, it could as well be because governance in Nigeria has been reduced to a farce. Interestingly, Karl Marx observed a long time ago that when history repeats itself what takes place is a farcical replication of a tragedy. This assertion is very true of the present dispensation, and this tragi-farcical experience will play itself out very soon.

If memory fails you, let me reiterate that the present illusion is not without precedent. In August 1985, a certain Maj. Gen. Ibrahim Babangida took power amidst smiles and a feeling of conviviality. He promised to exorcise the political horrors of the past and restore democratic rule. Before the euphoria died down, Nigeria was in the throes of death. It was a tragedy of infinite magnitude; a tragedy whose necessary outcome was the emergence of a psychopath who could not draw a line between personal ambition and national interest.

Today, 13 years later, another general is in the saddle, amidst smiles and talk of transition to democracy; and all you can see is a farcical reminder of the tragedy that convulsed the nation not too long ago. It is amusing how these military bigots become so easily predictable. Every step, every action, and indeed every statement, by the present regime smacks of the same line of perdition that Abacha, and Babangida before him, pursued in their transition, where all the rules served to disfranchise the people and reinforce totalitarianism. If Babangida was a tragedy, Abubakar certainly is a farce.

The tenet of the Babangida tragedy was to break with the past. It did not matter if such innovation brought the nation to its knees. He introduced option A4, allowed only two parties, one "a little to the left" and the other "a little to the right" – strange ideas that had little to do with the reality of the Nigerian situation. This will be the hallmark of the farce Abubakar is taking the country through.

Abubakar would want to be different. Well, he has already started by naming the bastion of his fraud the Independent National Electoral Commission (INEC). Of course, in consonance with this farce, Abubakar is expected to bring fresh ideas. These ideas, which to all intents and purposes, are not meant to improve the deplorable political landscape, will obviously mark him out as the handmaid of feudalism.

A scenario analysis would look like this: a president and five vice-presidents in line with Abacha's geo-political demarcation of Nigeria. Abubakar could also take the country almost four decades back and introduce a president and a prime minister in which case the North, considering its hypothetically larger population, will produce the prime minister.

He may, while creating new avenues of executive power, introduce a president whose powers are drastically whittled down. Finally, he may do any other whimsical thing that he deems necessary for self-preservation. In all this, however, the views of ordinary Nigerians count for nothing because these gendarmes of feudalism have only one mission and one vision: to maintain the *status quo*, at all costs.

Like Babangida, Abubakar and his disciples who now serve as the overseers of this neo-colony called Nigeria, are not perturbed by the economic crisis convulsing the nation. Their attempt at democracy is nothing but a design to placate imperialism and maintain the neo-colonial state structure. While it took some years for Babangida to initiate the transfer of the national economy to foreign control; the present monstrosity, a grotesque mediocre by all standards, has vowed to undertake the complete transfer of the Nigerian economy to his foreign backers before he leaves office in May.

Of course, there are those who have indulged in trying to understand this farce. They are worried that party registration was dogged by irregularities, that voters' card were not made available in certain areas; on and on the complaints keep coming. They are less concerned, as one writer put it, with the institutional deformity which throws up Nigeria's military tyrants. Therefore, while the collective amnesia persists, the military overlord charts his own course for Nigeria and defines her democratic future, even if in a chaotic manner. Regrettably, the military has accomplices too willing to do its bidding.

Just a little over a decade ago, Babangida waged a virtual war against our politicians. As usual, he began by throwing the bait of democracy. The politicians jumped on the gravy train. Since his war was also psychological, he knew that no amount of humiliation was too much for them to bear. He banned them many times over without as much as a comment from them. He imprisoned some, yet they did not learn any lesson. Of course, Babangida's transition ended in a fiasco, and the politicians as always relapsed into their usual state of forgetfulness.

The exit of one psychopath saw the emergence of another; and yet another transition gravy train. From the outset, Abacha did not hide his disdain for our politicians. However, that did not deter them. They soon forgot the horrors they went through under Babangida and jumped onto Abacha's transition train. What the politicians lacked in fortitude and integrity, they made up with clownery and servitude. Abacha's transition was not lacking in rogues, thugs and villains. We were never in short supply of the things that gave politics the epithet: dirty game.

Apparently, there is no end to the trauma that politicians will subject Nigerians in the name of politics. We have hardly overcome the grand deception of the Babangida-Abacha era and the party has begun again. The self-flagellation that is going on among our politicians who are lining up behind Abubakar's transition leaves one with the bitter feeling that nothing has been learnt from the distortion the military has subjected politics in Nigeria. Suddenly, our politicians have cleared the mist from their eyes and you can be sure that they will, once again, place themselves at the mercy of the military.

If politics, as designed by the military in Nigeria, has gone beyond what is acceptable to being downright farcical, you wonder why the hysteria that still grips the political class. It shows that politics is not only an avenue for self-indulgence, but a rear opportunity to settle the question of bread and butter. And if self-abnegation is lacking among our politicians, it is simply that "politics in Nigeria – the pastime of scoundrels and opportunists – offers few rules that are edifying". Abubakar's farcical transition can only reinforce this proposition.

Every illusion, however, like a house built on sand will sooner or later implode. Of course, Abubakar's transition will soon prove demonstrably false because the illusion will implode under the weight of its contradictions. We can only hope that this implosion does not consume the nation. As this illusion wears out, democratic and progressive forces have very limited options.

They can settle in their armchairs and watch as the comedy unfolds or come to the inevitable conclusion that the only credible alternative is to wrest power, by any means necessary, from those who have held the country hostage for decades.

12. New Beginning or Dead End?
August 1998

> *"The present crisis will not burn itself out. On the contrary, when it appears to have subsided, it will be found only to have coiled us into force for change that would either sweep out the military with ignominy or exploit its innate contradiction, its competitive lust for power and its sectional injustices".* – Wole Soyinka.

Once again, another General has announced his desire to give Nigerians "genuine democracy". Expectedly, the announcement was received with trepidation; trepidation not just for the lack of substance, but also for the tragedy whose imminence is being elongated. Of course, Abubakar's speech, suffused with cant and platitudes, did not come as a surprise to many Nigerians who have since given up on the painfully ludicrous theatrics of the military.

Confusion about the priorities of the beleaguered Nigerian nation seems to be deepening. Never in the history of Nigeria – except, perhaps, during the civil war – have Nigerians faced so complex a problem; yet never before has the country witnessed this deliberate and total incapacity on the part of its rulers to address its problem. This idle and arbitrary resolve to prosecute this illusion to its logical end will, of course, prove futile and disastrous.

Not surprisingly, the international community, led by the United States and Britain, who are clearly detached from the Nigerian debacle and whose commitment is matched only by the amount of oil available for sale, have become the cheerleaders of this theatre of the absurd that Abubakar is directing; an absurdity that has the potential of consuming the unstable theatre. There cannot be any meaningful electoral process in Nigeria no matter the support of these vultures hovering over it. Western leaders pressing for the lifting of sanctions or applauding Abubakar's transition must appreciate this feeling.

Of course, we know the West is not interested in any genuine electoral process. In 1996 when Sierra Leoneans questioned the rationale for holding elections without first resolving the grievances and multiple disagreements which had plagued the nation, Britain and the US, obsessed with elections, dismissed their complaints, arguing that they were crying wolf. They hurriedly put together and supervised a flawed electoral process which crumbled fourteen months later. Today, they are glad spending millions of dollars in clearing the mess. That is the same path they are advocating for Nigeria.

Having waited for so long for someone to repair the "bad boy" image Abacha had created for its business fortunes in Nigeria, the West seems contented now that things are gradually returning to the *status quo ante* when it was business as usual. They are praising Abubakar as a career soldier par excellence. We all know that that term has long lost is meaning as far as soldiering in this part of the world is concerned. He is being proclaimed as the long awaited messiah. You wonder again, which vermin has the neo-colonial military institution in Africa thrown up that the United States and Britain have not found favour with?

Clearly, Abubakar is torn between an insatiable quest for glory and an indescribable desire to self-destruct. The man must either be genuinely naive to think that what he is offering Nigeria is democracy and, therefore, it counts better than the quest for a Sovereign National Conference organized by a government of national unity, which he sees as undemocratic; or he thinks, in his foolhardiness, he can ride on the crest of international recognition so-called to bamboozle Nigerians. There is reason, however, for him to stop, not to carry this charade any further; for in the end, Nigerians are the ones to decide the way out of this impasse.

Abubakar has done everything to show that he is, in his words, "fully committed to the socio-political transition programme of late Gen. Sani Abacha's administration and will do everything to ensure its full and successful implementation". What he has not done, and would probably not to do, is to take a firm decision on the political future of the country he and his cronies have cruelly saddled themselves with the task of running. Perhaps Abubakar's greatest asset is the claim that he is a career soldier who has no political ambition – a rather spurious reason why he was given an edge over his senior colleagues.

The man is simply incapable of taking decisions, either good or bad. One moment he is embracing the programmes of his predecessor; the next moment he is attempting to wash his hands off a regime he helped nurture. Abacha lacked intellectual capacity; he was cruel and vindictive, a monster if you like. But, the man knew what he wanted. Except, of course, Abubakar wants to engage in "mercy killing" by tantalizing Nigerians with the prospect of an election before unleashing his own blitzkrieg. The prospects are there.

Expectedly, the ever-present and willing recidivist politicians are preparing for another "transition" joyride. The question is: how long does it take to build political ambition? What does it take to turn the massive security apparatuses of the state against the people? Abubakar's address has shown that the military is not only incapable of "moving Nigeria forward", but also indifferent to the problems confronting Nigeria and Nigerians; problems which largely are the creation of the military. The new military strongman purportedly consulted with every interest group before arriving at his panacea for the Nigerian crisis; but there are no indications that the consultations meant anything to him.

There are those who argue that the issue is for the next president of Nigeria to come from the south, a rather simplistic and opportunistic argument that tends to diminish the enormity of the crisis. Firstly, the presidency of Nigeria is not a souvenir or gift that is to be handed down by the military, working in concert with a medieval ossified force, at its whims. Secondly, what is the guarantee that the military will not abort any dubious transition that it manages to put in place? None at all!

The root of the problem in Nigeria is the "super race" psychology and slave owner mentality of a tiny bunch of individuals who think they are divinely mandated to chart a unilateral course for Nigeria. Handing out the presidency to the south like a Christmas hamper cannot solve that. The only way out is to obliterate the basis for this infernal theory by destroying that which gives it legitimacy, including the military. Nigerians must come together to discuss how this "monolithic edifice" called Nigeria must be rebuilt. It is not for the military or indeed any other group to do it single-handed.

Rescuing Nigeria from its present state of captivity is, of course, one stage of the struggle which must necessarily include the liberation of the impoverished and exploited majority. However, what Nigeria needs now is a multilateral vision to avert the looming tragedy.

The present regime lacks the initiative to do that. And from the way it is going, there is no way out of the *cul-de-sac* the military has plunged Nigeria.

---

13. Democracy without Democrats
September 1998

There is a disquieting political mood in Nigeria. Since June 8 when the damnable dictator, Sani Abacha, expired thanks to the antics of professional prostitutes, the Nigerian political crisis has worsened.

The new prefect, Abdulsalami Abubakar, basking in the support of international conspirators, has launched another bogus transition programme which he purports will return Nigeria to democracy after almost two decades of military rule. Under the guise of democracy, all the vultures who found no space in the previous gravy train due to Abacha's megalomania are now hovering over, waiting to gather the carcass of the political fiction called Nigeria.

While progressive and democratic forces have rightly condemned the ruse, the military government is bent on prosecuting its fraudulent and bogus transition to the end. In this renewed efforts at denying Nigerians their democratic rights and subverting their sovereign will, three distinct, yet markedly connected groups, are discernible, each pursuing its own iniquitous agenda. Largely, the driving force in this trinity of evil is imperialism with America as the arrowhead. The Nigerian military and the contemptible political class, a class that must be vanquished if Nigeria is to move forward, follow in that order.

America has played her part, succumbing to the diabolical machination that Abiola was the major obstacle to efforts at creating, under the cover of democracy, an enabling environment for multinational corporations to flourish. The next stage in this orchestrated attempt at short-changing Nigerians is for Abubakar to visit the White House where Clinton will put a seal on his transition programme, thereby qualifying it to bear the "democratic" tag. For certain inexplicable reasons, South Africa has been caught in this web of intrigues.

Remember, that was where, last March, Clinton made his infamous speech endorsing Abacha and his transition. Only recently, Abubakar appeared before the South African parliament and the feeling is that the venerable Mandela did conclude that, "This is my son, whom I love, with him I am well pleased". Clearly, the US is not interested in Nigeria's quest for democracy; and it is evident that while contending with the military and the political class, progressive and democratic forces in Nigeria must condition themselves for the *coup de grace* from this virulent interventionist.

The role of the military in the current political debacle is simple: to act as a stabilizing force in the power equation. The military in Nigeria is nothing but the armed wing of a feudal oligarchy that has no strain of democratic inclination and, therefore, cannot, seriously speaking, be a harbinger of democracy.

Expectedly, this army of occupation has treated Nigerians as prisoners of war and her resources as war booty. Abubakar, the new point man of this oligarchy and a loyal servant of Abacha, has resumed the democracy singsong. Of course, there is nothing new about the clamour for democracy. Talking about democracy is the pastime of all the generals who have misruled Nigeria, Abubakar will not be an exception.

Clearly, there is no difference between Abacha and Abubakar; the only possible difference being that between six and half a dozen. What we are witnessing is another grand design to befuddle Nigerians and provide a veneer for the internal colonialism that is going on in the country. Abacha may have been a devil, but his aspirations are being fulfilled by his successor.

Abubakar, just like his cousin, Ibrahim Babangida, the self-confessed evil genius, has adopted populism; but students of politics can confirm that populism is an intrinsic part of fascism. Presently,

Abubakar is on a mission of pacification; with the murderous state machine at his disposal, it would not take anything to railroad people into jail and visit mayhem on the country when it becomes necessary.

Another accomplice in the new democracy fiasco is the ubiquitous political class. Like every institution that colonialism bequeathed to Nigeria, this class is riddled with its own contradictions. Totally bereft of idea and grovelling at every turn, these power-besotted politicians and their counterparts, the "stomach-direction" politicians have once again embarked on another political merry-go-round.

It is not difficult to see why the political class in Nigeria cannot fight based on principles; why it must, at every turn, bend like a twig to accommodate the insults, humiliation and treachery of the military. That the political class in Nigeria is the most unprincipled on the continent is only repeating the obvious. Of course, politicians everywhere are prone to the iniquities which the dominant free market ideology has visited on mankind. Because the political class in Nigeria enjoys short-term gains, it has allowed the military to ride roughshod over it and cannot expect to be supported by external forces.

Take the Congo crisis as an example. Soon after the opposition began its struggle in the Democratic Republic of the Congo, South Africa called Joseph Kabila to negotiate with him, just as the US did when Kabila rattled the late Mobutu at the height of the Congo crisis last year. Today, parties in the Congo crisis are settling for a national conference to follow a cease-fire. It would be asking for too much to expect those who claim they abhor military rule in Nigeria to set their own terms for a new democratic order.

The humiliation which began in the heyday of the Babangida regime when certain elements within the political class were banned and others jailed, finds expression in the ludicrous party registration exercise conducted by Abubakar's so-called independent national electoral commission. Yet the politicians are scrambling to be part of the infamy.

Nigeria's professional politicians cannot learn. Of course, with this kind of political class everybody is at risk, and the prospect of democracy couldn't be farther away. If Abiola refused the terms of the military, why is it that a lot of those who supported him have found succour in Abubakar's transition? Could it be treachery or the ingrained division within the political class in western Nigeria where the support for Abiola was most visible? Whatever it is, certainly, it won't be out of order to place Abiola's death at their doorsteps. What they have proved is that they supported the theory that Abiola was the obstacle that had to be removed for them to come on board.

Interestingly, Nigeria does not have a constitution so the political class in the south as a whole which is clamouring for power shift does not even know on what terms it is seeking political power. Is the country going to have an executive president? Will it be the French system or another contraption that will maintain the *status quo*? What will be the power relations among the various groups that make up Nigeria? These are questions that should be agitating the minds of our politicians.

Nigeria will not collapse if these recidivist politicians will for once stand up and be counted on the side of integrity. Nigerians cannot place their hope on this regime which is grossly incapable of grappling with their problems. The single most important question in Nigeria today is the nationality question.

There is no way democracy, or for that matter unity, will return to Nigeria; not now, not in the future, until ethnic privileges and the issue of ethnic oppression are tackled. The solution has gone beyond power shift which the political class in the south is comfortable with. Power shift to the south will only provide the dominant class in the south another opportunity to replicate the contradictions in present-day Nigeria.

When people say they are different, that they have distinct languages, religions and cultural lives and therefore want national rights, no genuine democrat can afford to deny them these rights which are basic democratic rights. Nigeria is a land of oppressed nationalities and the only way to end national oppression is to guarantee the right to self-determination for the oppressed nationalities, not through power shift.

Democracy is meaningless if groups, particularly oppressed nationalities, do not have the right to self-determination. Nobody should be under the illusion that those parading themselves as democrats and their accomplices who are overseeing the current transition programme can acquiesce to this fundamental principle of democracy and the demand for a sovereign national conference.

14. Democracy as Diversion
September 1998

That the Nigerian military has become an embarrassment is not in doubt. This group of gun wielding men never fail at every turn to show the world how hopelessly irrelevant it has become. The duo of Buhari and Idiagbon who seized power in 1983 launched the "War Against Indiscipline and Corruption" (WAI-C) which was supposed to instill discipline in the ordinary Nigerian, who in their own estimation had become highly wayward and lawless.

The war also included a battle against drug and currency trafficking. Before the war could run its course, 54 suitcases belonging to a traditional ruler who was closely linked to the regime had slipped past the hard-nosed security men at the Murtala Muhammed International Airport. It was rumoured that the suitcases were filled with foreign currencies. The suitcase imbroglio is now part of our inglorious history of military misrule.

Babangida who toppled the Buhari/Idiagbon regime went a step further. He inaugurated a political bureau to start a transition to democratic rule; rejected the report of the bureau; set up and funded two political parties to contest elections and finally annulled the result of the presidential election. He did eventually "step aside" when pro-democracy forces made Nigeria ungovernable for him, but that was long after he had adorned the title of president. Today, the ball is in Abacha's court.

Notwithstanding the generally accepted concept of democracy, Abacha appears set to give it a new meaning; nothing the world has witnessed or will ever witness. Nigeria's transition to democracy has come a long way since 1986 when Babangida set about the process of returning the country to civil rule in 1990. Undoubtedly, this transition is the longest, most tortuous (we have lost count of the number of people who have been killed much less those imprisoned to keep the transition on course) and perhaps the most expensive transition to democracy in recorded history.

However, it is not the fact that the transition to democracy in Nigeria entails the conversion of a brutal military dictator to a civilian president that makes it novel; after all, Jerry Rawlings, Yahya Jammeh and others in the sub-region have craftily taken that perfidious route. Recently, a group that goes by the dubious name of traditional rulers tried to lend their voice to the infamy by calling on Abacha to continue in office.

He reportedly told them he was relying on God (for a man who has repeatedly said he will hand over to a democratically elected president by October 1, 1998) on the presidential issue and his final decision would be in the interest of the nation. The intriguing thing about Abacha's transition is that centuries after the demise of the divine rights of kings, our stone age dictator hopes to install himself president through the most idiotic claim – divine intervention.

In 1993, Abacha took over power and promised to hand over to a democratically elected government after a short stay. Five years later, the question is not that of democracy but theocracy of the crudest and most bizarre form. Clearly, Abacha must be a rare species of cretin to imagine that Nigerians cannot see through his antics and the circumstance of his emergence.

In February 1997, Abacha told a not too surprised nation that he could be the next civilian president if his constituency (the military) so desired. The feeling that the armed forces have become a de facto political constituency that is altruistic and the bastion of nationalism must be exposed for its arrant falsity.

That Abacha cannot keep his words is a reflection of the psyche of the army of which he is commander-in-chief: a spineless, pepper soup-drinking army; "an army of anything goes; an army that openly prefers political appointments over and above regimental appointments no matter the relevance of such appointment to their carrier progress". It is tragic that this is the calibre of men who have run Nigeria for decades.

Abacha's antics only confirm the theory that people and groups who wield unlimited and uncontrolled power often regard themselves as infallible; that anything they do is predestined, and they do not have to justify them to anyone. This is the unfortunate reality of the Nigerian situation.

There is a prevalent illusion among a section of Nigerians that it does not make any difference if Abacha transforms to a civilian president considering the chicanery of our politicians. There is something cynically interesting about this attitude. It is the feeling that the problem in Nigeria is basically the question of democracy. If the issue were simply that of democracy or installing a civilian president, Abacha certainly knows what to do.

Clearly, there cannot be a ballot-box solution to the present crisis. In 1993, there was an election in which a president was elected. The election, of course, was annulled and the winner imprisoned. The perpetrators of those criminal acts still roam the streets not perturbed by their villainy. The ongoing battle, therefore, is not just that against a despotic military regime that is trying, albeit unintelligently, to enthrone "lasting democracy", but against the remnants of an antiquated feudal system that is set to take the country 200 years backward.

In contention is the issue of how Nigerians perceive one another, the irreconcilable contradiction emanating from the quest for hegemony and domination. It is this hegemonic mindset which has given the likes of Abacha carte blanche to unilaterally define the future of Nigeria.

Regrettably, this feeling of omnipotence is now being pushed to a nauseatingly dangerous end. Since there is nobody (except the hunted pro-democracy activists) to question Abacha, only those to justify his malleable actions, the potential czar of the new theocratic kingdom of Nigeria thinks he can ride roughshod over Nigerians. Abacha and his cohorts, however, are not under any obligation to call this charade democracy. The reason is simple: democracy can never happen in a country where people express a murderous inability to tolerate one another or live together.

Abacha is presiding over the most brutal and primitive regime Nigeria has ever had. The objective of Abacha's transition to democracy is nothing other than to reinforce the psychology of hegemony and further make nonsense of the fiction called Nigeria. It is not for nothing that the regime wasted six million dollars and co-opted state apparatuses in organizing a pro-Abacha rally.

It is a pointer to the kind of power he wants to wield in the new dispensation; a power akin to that exercised by the biblical beast in which nobody could buy or sell except he or she had the mark of the beast; in this case Abacha's insignia.

The power bloc which Abacha represents has seen the irrelevance of its military wing (which it has relied on for so long), partly due to the global disdain for military rule, but more importantly because of the potential threat it poses to the unity of Nigeria which in its narcissistic thinking is "nonnegotiable". It must now strengthen itself in a completely new fashion.

It is a risk which the political oligarchy, in whose hand Abacha is but a tool, must embark upon in its latest and most vile attempt at clinging on to power. The alternative is to provoke a civil war which it hopes to prosecute and emerge as the victor.

Abacha and his cohorts must realize however that at no time has this seemingly futile attempt at despotism become more irrelevant. If Nigeria witnesses another disaster in the form of an Abacha presidency, we may well sing its dirge.

I have very little doubt that these vermin who are parading as political leaders can last longer than progressive forces want them to.

---

15. "Power Shift" and its Opponents
November 1998

"Sick intellectualism" is a popular term in Iran. Unfortunately, that term has taken root in Nigeria. "Sick intellectualism", according to its proponents, is "arrogant, impudent, and opportunistic". But it is not just that. It is equally cowardly and "not prepared to face danger".

Nowhere has "sick intellectualism" been so manifestly expressed as on the question of "power shift" in Nigeria. For the records, I do not subscribe to the notion of "power shift". The reasons are that first, it simply does not make sense; and second, it has a way of just scratching the surface of the monumental problems confronting Nigeria.

A "power shift", considering the present structures in the country, rather than solving Nigeria's myriad problems, will replicate the contradictions that are visible in every aspect of our national life. As a democrat, I am also opposed to the issue of "power shift" which tends to reduce the basic question in Nigeria today to a Southerner becoming president, rather than addressing the issue of ethnic domination and subjugation, not just at the political level but also at the social, religious, cultural, and educational levels.

I believe, and all true democrats will agree with me, that when people say they are different, that they have distinct languages, religions and cultural lives and, therefore, want national rights, they ought to be granted these rights. But there are those who oppose the notion of "power shift", not because they think the alternative they proffer will offer hope, but because they see it as a way of maintaining the *status quo.*

They resort to "sick intellectualism" to obfuscate and compound the problem. Felix D. V. Audu, (Power Shift to the South, The Guardian, September 27, 1998) falls into this category. Audu starts his piece on a very clumsy note. According to him, "There are also some prominent politicians who are not happy with the idea of 'shift' as if no southerner can win at the polls without the mechanical power shift. They are quick to point to the inconclusive 1993 presidential poll that M. K. O. Abiola almost won via a 'free and fair' process".

What is this if not "sick intellectualism"? If intellectuals like Audu can still come out boldly to say that the 1993 presidential election was inconclusive, surely, the Nigerian project is doomed. Many months after the self-acclaimed evil genius came out publicly to apologize and ask for forgiveness for annulling the election, the Audus of this world are still masking their contempt for Nigerians by making statements such as "inconclusive presidential poll that M. K. O. Abiola almost won".

Audu tries to play God and a surrogate of British colonialists when he writes that, "Fate more than anything else decided for Nigeria its political arrangement, called federation...by 1914, there was the historic amalgamation of the Northern and Southern provinces. The politics of amalgamation when analyzed on sentimental grounds seem to be saying that the action was to sustain the northern administration. In real terms, however, we know that amalgamation was to the good of all the people living in the area called Nigeria".

Maybe the amalgamation was not to sustain the northern administration as Audu wants us to believe. But, can he convince himself that peoples of the different groups – some had fought bitter wars of annihilation and survival as the case may be – that were put together were consulted before the amalgamation? Or that without colonialism these groups would have come together since according to him amalgamation was to the good of all the people living in the area called Nigeria?

When Audu writes that, "We are so interdependent that even a group that contemplates secession does so at its own peril" what you see is the arrogance of a slave owner. He writes as if all the nations that were joined to create Nigeria did not exist before colonial plunder and brigandage; that they had no culture, no form of government or system of governance, and no economic life. If these groups were indeed nations on their own before Britain coupled them in 1914 for its own administrative convenience, why should separating them become a matter of life and death?

Audu's proclamation is also a tacit warning that those who are contemplating secession will be crushed. Contrary to Audu's thinking, the continuous tinkering with the structure of Nigeria since independence when the country was made up of regions has not been done with the aim of making the federation function. Even though it was necessary for the Mid-west to be a region of its own in the spirit of federalism, that gesture would not have been extended to them if it did not serve to reduce the size and power of the old Western region. The same principle was applied to the creation of 12 states in 1967 to "weather the national storm", in the words of Audu.

According to Audu,

> *"Within the 38 years of Nigeria's independence, almost all the major regions in the country had in one way or the other produced a president. When the 1966 coup swept the government of the First Republic, J.T.U. Aguiyi-Ironsi, an Igbo, stepped in as leader from the Eastern region. When another counter coup was staged in 1966, Yakubu Gowon emerged as the Nigerian leader...it did not take long before the army got tired of Buhari's 'Iron discipline' and replaced him with Gen. Ibrahim Babangida who proclaimed himself president.*
>
> *"Babangida's presidency peaked with the annulment of the 1993 presidential election and when the crisis attained dangerous dimension Gen. Babangida had to 'step aside' from power and install Ernest Shonekan as head of the Interim National Government. Shonekan is a Yoruba. The failure of the Yoruba to accept Shonekan as head of a legitimate government gave blank cheque to the military and this led to the emergence of Gen. Sani Abacha from the North".*

Fine argument in the spirit of "sick intellectualism". Perhaps, it is only Audu who is not aware that the Interim Government was not designed to succeed; that its legality, which the courts also disproved, was in doubt from the outset; that it was a contraption put in place by Babangida and those he represented to assuage the feeling of the Yoruba. Has Audu forgotten the debate that centred on whether Shonekan was commander-in-chief of the armed forces or not?

The conclusion one draws from Audu's piece is that he does not believe that Nigeria has a problem. He talks glibly about the issue of "power shift" coming up now that Gen. Abudulsalami Abubakar has shown "a firm commitment to return the country to civil rule by

29th May next year" as if this is the first time Nigerians are hearing the words "firm commitment".

Abacha was firmly committed to democracy and return to civil rule. Babangida showed even firmer commitment – at least he organized elections – to return the country to civil rule. Of course, Gowon showed the same commitment. When people say the ruling class in the North has overbearing political power in what is supposed to be a federation, they are not fantasizing. That power was visible during the civil war. It was manifest in the annulment of the June 12, 1993 presidential election, in the politics of extermination that took place in Ogoniland and the dogged refusal to grant the request for a Sovereign National Conference.

Strangely, while not admitting that there is a structural problem with the Nigerian federation, Audu unknowingly admits that the North wields political power when he argues that, "Will it not be a very sound political understanding to say that if political power shifts from one region to the other, economic power also shifts to the one that had relinquished political power? It will be suicidal for the country to vest both political and economic powers in one geographical region".

What Audu is saying in essence, even though he may not admit it, is that Nigerians are edgy because of the touchy issue of imbalance in the country. Of course, when people express such murderous inability – note Audu's term "suicidal" – to live together, you do not solve the problem by "shifting power", either political or economic.

It is high time we accepted the reality that the history of this nation is flawed. And if the military - the bastion of this lopsided structure – is not stopped, this flawed past will ruin us all. It is this flawed history that made it possible that the freest and fairest election in Nigeria's tortuous history was annulled in June 1993; it is the same flawed past that has made Abubakar the new imperial lord who is ready to barter Nigeria for recognition and support. Of course, as James Baldwin admonished: "To accept one's past – one's history – is not the same thing as drowning in it; it is learning how to use it. An invented past can never be used; it cracks and crumbles under the pressures of life like clay in a season of drought".

Audu concludes that, "Perhaps the challenge for the future of Nigeria lies squarely in the hands of INEC (Independent National Electoral Commission) that has the responsibility of refereeing the political games". How can we place our hope in an electoral commission that is independent only in name? A commission whose existence and structure follow certain established patterns; a commission that cannot appoint its own state officers.

Audu is right when he says that, "The idea of power shift is undemocratic". However, his submission that, "In the spirit of the true federal democracy, let Nigerians produce effective and qualitative leaders through competitions via free and fair elections", is suspect. There was a free and fair election in June 1993. What happened to that election and the leader that emerged? Audu knows that with the present structure and the feeling of mistrust and suspicion which people like him are championing with their theory of economic power shift as a compensation for losing political power, democracy will be a nightmare in Nigeria.

The future of Nigeria lies in restructuring the geo-polity so that the country can – either as a unit or confederation of independent states – begin again on a purposeful note. Now is the time to do what the British could not do because of their selfish economic interest: organize a national conference where all the groups that were lumped together to create Nigeria will have to affirm their commitment or otherwise to their forced coexistence.

Nobody can deny Nigerians this opportunity except those who are ready to spill blood to protect this unstable polity. Yes, Nigeria needs federalism and democracy, but not the type being forced on it by the military or advocates of political and economic power shift.

British foreign secretary, Robin Cook, said recently in his eulogy to the Abubakar regime that Britain has "played a major role in Nigeria's history, and it has not always been an easy one". Interestingly, he failed to tell the world that British parochialism which led to the "mistake of 1914", and has created new slogans such as "political and economic power shift", is the major cause of this difficulty. We are indeed living through a period of "sick intellectualism", and if it is allowed to triumph, Nigeria may yet prove the costliest mistake of British colonialism.

16. A MISPLACED OUTRAGE
FEBRUARY 1999

I had thought (considering Gen. Abdulsalami Abubakar's outburst of enthusiasm about the outcome and the verdict of election observers, both local and international) that the December 5 Local Government Council elections in Nigeria would go down in history as the most successful, if for nothing else, for its acceptance by the political class, that ubiquitous confederacy of scoundrels. I was wrong, terribly wrong. My assessment or conclusion, of course, was not the product of naiveté. I only surmised based on the alacrity with which our politicians plunged headlong into Abubakar's transition, in defiance of reason, good judgement and obvious inadequacies.

From the politicians' point of view, the impression was that the transition programme was on course. Very much like them, they did not have the courtesy of allowing the so-called independent body in charge of the elections to announce the final results before they went to town with all manner of complaints. Everybody is complaining. There have been reports of missing ballot boxes, the presence of ghost-voters, murder of voters and the influence of money. Some of the politicians have described the election as a sham and are calling for fresh election, by extension, casting serious doubts on the future of the transition programme.

Judging from the all too familiar nature of the military and transition politics in Nigeria, the outrage of the politicians is misplaced. Indeed, listening to the protestations leaves one with the feeling that our politicians have just arrived from Mars. One wonders what they were expecting when they joined this incongruous transition.

Did they think the word "Independent" was enough to confer on the electoral commission true independence? It was barely a month after the death of Abacha, and with it his self-succession plots, that Abubakar launched his supposedly new transition programme. Of course, like dogs, our politicians began to salivate immediately Abubakar dropped the political bone. Nothing could deter them; not even the fact that the new regime was an extension of the preceding one or the knowledge that the transition was not designed to succeed.

If the foregoing could not deter our politicians, certainly it was expecting too much to assume that they would listen to the clarion call to reorganize Lugard's house before embarking on another phony transition. It made no meaning to them that if Nigerians had suffered so much under Abacha in particular, and the military in general, it was necessary to sit down and reflect on the way forward. One after another, they all got on the gravy train.

Those who claimed they were principled democrats lost sight of the fact that this is a carefully orchestrated transition to meet certain ends; that even though Abacha is dead, his long shadow casts menacingly over the present transition. Never mind that those who unabashedly formed themselves into Abacha People's Party are also at the receiving end of the transition. How else can Abubakar show that he is in control of the transition programme? Surely, the man knows those who will not succeed him.

The hue and cry did not start with the elections. From the outset, there were complaints about the process of both party and voter registrations. Analysts are of the opinion that this is just the tip of the iceberg of the monumental complaints that will trail the transition programme when the real thing begins. What all this points to is that Nigerians must look to something else, a third force perhaps, for their salvation.

After the humiliation our politicians suffered under Babangida and Abacha, one would have thought that they had learnt some lesson and would conclude that "never again". It does appear, however, that the military has a way of taking the wind out of the sails of our politicians. Or is it a case of sheer greed for power and the perks of office? Whatever it is, our politicians have not shown the kind of fortitude Nigeria needs to get her out of the present crisis.

It is not for nothing that all the political parties, conveniently recycled at the behest of the military, do not have programmes and policies that seek to address Nigeria's endemic crisis. They do not appreciate the enormity of the crisis; that is, if they even believe that there is a crisis. All they think of is one man (no woman, please) controlling Nigeria and its vast human and material resources. Nigeria does not need a hero. The problem in the country today goes beyond looking for a national figure who is acceptable to Nigerians in every nook and cranny of this beleaguered country. After all, we had one a few years ago and he died in detention – or so they claim.

It is in light of this that we must look at Nigeria's former military head of state, Gen. Olusegun Obasanjo's jostling for the presidency. Obasanjo does not wish Nigeria well to say the least. If twenty years after he left power, things have not worked to his satisfaction that he now wants to come back, then he should realize that there is more to it than meets the eyes. It is for this reason also that those who profess to be surprised and outraged at the outcome of the December 5 election shouldn't expect anything better but rather look beyond the present transition if they want to remain relevant.

Of course, the baseless complaints by a section of the political class that appears not to be favoured by Abubakar's transition demonstrate not only the impotence of the political class as a whole but also the bankruptcy of its current position. Clearly, they would rather self-destruct than allow a life of gross self-indulgence slip out of their hands.

In the end, as the Nigerian crisis goes from bad to worse, if the political class does not shift from its position of tardiness, confusion and utter helplessness, it will join the military and that section of the international community that has given Abubakar's lopsided transition the thumbs up, as the three-headed monster that the Nigerians would have to confront in the days ahead.

17. WHEN DEMOCRACY INSULTS
MAY 1999

The final acts of despotic governments often defy logic. They are predictable only in that they signal the coming apocalypse to their reign of terror". So wrote DeWayne Wickham in his book, Fire at Will. How remarkably true this is of Nigeria. The transition programme in Nigeria, and specifically, the emergence of Gen. Obasanjo as the president-elect defies logic and it signals the reinvention of the military's reign of terror and its total disregard for the rights of Nigerians.

As repulsive as this rape of democracy is, it has, regrettably, received the overt approval of a section of the international community. Of course, this tragedy is not totally unexpected. It must be viewed from the background of an imperialist world order that has always glorified dictatorships, military or civilian, and raised the issue of democracy when it suited its purpose. Not surprisingly, part of the outcome of the New World Order as initiated by America was the emergence of a new democratic culture for Africa. Suddenly, the West which had, ironically, supported all manner of ignoble dictators started applauding democratic transitions.

However, the democracy that the West introduced was one in which the citizens who ought to be the bastion of democracy were required to play an increasingly diminutive role. Of course, at every juncture, the West has supported the state in Africa for specific reasons. It used to be a vehicle for colonial exploitation; later a buffer against communism. Much later, it became the instrument for the propagation of various infernal economic policies.

Undoubtedly, this renewed interest in the so-called democratic states in Africa is a passing phase in the general struggle to relegate the mass of the people to positions of "hewers of woods and drawers of waters". Once the state fulfills its historical role as "an organized force serving the interest of international capital", as it has done conscientiously and ferociously, since the Structural Adjustment Programme swept through the continent, the issue of genuine democratic representation in the way the state is run matters even less.

The West has gleefully supported this system whose only credential is election. Once elections – more often than not, not free and fair – are held, the country is touted as a democratic nation. The current transition programme in Nigeria is symptomatic of this renewed attempt to deny citizens their democratic right as a way of ultimately curtailing their economic freedom. This transition is not premised on any democratic foundation. We are told by defenders of the current order that the issue at stake is to ensure that the military relinquishes power. We are led to believe that, after all, democracy is not perfect and therefore we should accept whatever we are given with the belief that we can improve on it.

"Democracy is a process...election is just an important event in that process", argues Gen. Obasanjo. Is it not strange how unconvincing our rulers often sound? Even the most entrenched political nit-wit knows that democracy is imperfect to the extent that we want it to be. Elections themselves must be subject to the dictates of democratic norms. Do the people want elections? Who designs the electoral rule?

Should it be at the behest of a single individual, or a minority that believes that with money and the right connection they can become the dubious representatives of the people? These are questions every true democrat ought to be asking. To view elections as the first step in any democratic dispensation amounts to placing the cart before the horse. Indeed, that politicians could actually contest elections without a constitution explains not only their character but also their dubious intentions.

Of course, the shenanigans of our politicians are only an alibi; a façade to belittle the enormous potentials that democracy offers because it suits those who want to use the so-called democratic order as a means to an end. They ignore the fact that democracy entails the greatest public participation and plurality of opinions. As Pik Smeet noted, "The most damaging thing to the cause of true democracy is the repeated assurances that what we have nowadays is democracy, and so all the sleaze...all the secret negotiations and dirty deals get lumped together to suggest in people's minds that democracy is not all that great".

The military regime in Nigeria has taken this sleaze further to an asinine level by conducting a supposedly democratic transition without a constitution. One wonders whose interest the constitution is meant to serve. Certainly, not the interest of those who were not consulted while the process lasted.

For some people, however, the democratic transition is on course.

This anti-democratic posture presupposes that, to paraphrase Smeet, we are one country, one people, working together for a common interest. This lie allows the military and their political accomplices to present us as if we have one common goal. It allows them to limit democratic choice because there is only one national interest and therefore one general programme, one set of policies to be followed. It means that since Gen. Abubakar has, for example, conducted elections, he is obliged to oversee the wholesale privatization of the Nigerian economy.

Is it not part of democracy that the citizens should know and acquiesce to the sale of their collective wealth, more so if that damnable act is being undertaken by a rogue military class whose only claim to legitimacy is the gun? Democracy is about building the structures of society so that citizens can develop faith in the system; it is about the right to self-determination, an issue the West is defending with murderous ferocity in Yugoslavia. People must agree to live together under certain conditions before embarking on the luxury of elections. Elections are just a seal of that commitment to live according to the will of the majority.

It is too dangerous for us as a nation to place our hope on the electoral victory of one man, whether for the purposes of dialogue or expanding the frontiers of democratic freedom. There are those who claim that Gen. Obasanjo has learnt his lessons. I disagree. The only lesson Obasanjo has learnt is that power can be bought or gotten by groveling and pandering to those who have it in excess.

Obasanjo believes that, "Under my leadership, we shall continue the process of deepening the democratic process through dialogue". By ignoring the fact that democracy should proceed from the known to the unknown, as his Excellency is wont to do, we are only taking one step forward and two steps backward. Dialogue of the type that is expected to build democracy cannot be between unequal partners.

Of course, the issue goes beyond Obasanjo and his proclivities. The conditions the military has created are such that chairs and all manner of missiles would be thrown in the various assemblies if they are ever constituted. This, of course, is nothing compared to the role of the military in the so-called democratic dispensation; the monumental ethnic minority question and various structural imbalances in the country; and finally how to sound the death-knell of those who have consistently raped the country and are opposed to the creation of a new nation and a new democratic culture.

It is really disheartening when the military class and their accomplices insult our intelligence in the name of democracy, and it is difficult to imagine what kind of peace one would wish for a nation that is totally lacking in justice.

Section Two

Of Heroes and Villains

A June Ago

Requiem for the Fallen Horseman
For Moshood Kashimawo Olawale Abiola

By Chiedu Ezeanah

I'm Muslim, but my religion is love - M.K.O.
Sunlight in the hut of night, sieving
aches for potions, aches for love...

Nothing, not the bewilderment
brewed before disturbed him

that calls and returns, to flock
for the first and repeated time

to mother and father,
to obliterate forever

the lamenting rings
of sons disappearing from a house of night.

Sieving the noon-trees,
he dared the crossroads-

What's the use of a birthplace, that
cannot be assailed for a ladle of milk?

The lone image that turns and returns-
 he's your locked cry uttering nothing.

He left fragrances of love in the air.
The air has never known its hinderer:
The crossroads no longer
has a memory of light.

One despot deposes the other,
renames the roads after his name.

Horseman alone, with
bone and blood wooed

into intimacies of iron,
stammering for love.

Nothing changed
at the crossroads

nothing changed
the pestilences...

Horseman alone, hero alone-
we ask - why did he love

the wild ways he beloved
the Trickster-Generals?

With his torch of love
and riffling proverbs,

to sack the Generals
he chummed with Generals.

Lone horseman in a blind Time...
Hero alone broken by iron...

One despot stole his torch,
another caged him.

One despot killed his wife,
yet another took his life.

Traversing twin-rivers echoing woes,
killings we did not sow, yield song...

How bounteous is our captivity
as harmony flows as iron growls...

Iron flourishes, love fails,
can iron endure the rust?

1. A Minister's Burden
May 1994

There is something infectious about being in government, especially in Nigeria, which is lost to lesser mortals like us. All too often, people are wont to change once bitten by the government bug. The academic becomes effete; the politician abandons politics for "politricks"; the professional soldier becomes a chevalier d'industrie. In short, otherwise sensible people lose their senses.

We know that "power corrupts", but there is no theory to the effect that being in government reduces one's ability to appreciate simple logic. In a few days, the country will celebrate the first anniversary of the June 12, 1993 presidential election. Though some people would like us to forget that date, it just refuses to go away.

One of such persons is the officious Minister of Information, Prof. Jerry Gana. The minister was on hand some days ago to sing the dirge of June 12.

> *"The military administration did not actualize the June 12 election in spite of its opposition to the annulment for fear that certain sections of the country could rise against it. If they actualized June 12 when they came in, another section would rise",* he affirmed.

Gana admitted that the annulment was a terrible error, but that Nigeria's corporate existence could not be sacrificed for it. In the words of the minister,

> *"The annulment is a painful one, but we cannot because of it allow the people of Nigeria to be destroyed. Somebody has made a mistake like somebody made in 1966, like somebody made in 1984, like somebody made a mistake by stopping Jerry Gana in becoming a president by annulling my own primaries".*

The minister sure has a duty in trying to advance this faux pas, but suffice it to say the annulment of the June 12 elections is one mistake too many. The only pertinent question that is worth raising here is: Who is opposed to the validation of the June 12 election? I am sure the Minister does not have in mind those who turned down religious and ethnic persuasions by voting massively across the country for the winner of that election.

Is it not appalling that an election was annulled not because it was not free and fair, but because some whimsical individuals felt it should be annulled? Yet, our information minister does not see any need to revisit the issue or tell the world the truth about it.

It is terrible when our ruling class and its courtiers substitute their consciousness, their inordinate desire, their whims, for the wishes of the masses whose life-long desire is to get bread and butter in an atmosphere of peace and tranquility.

The problem of the country is basically that of power relations. It is at the root of the annulment of the June 12 election and we cannot run away from it or gloss over it. It is true that some people see the June 12 victory as an attempt to balance power. Yet for many, it was a progressive attempt to advance unity and democracy.

We must state, at the risk of sounding repetitive, that if Gana is really interested in Nigeria, it should not take him time to realize from hindsight that no greater threat to the corporate existence of Nigeria assails us today than the annulment of the June 12 election. No matter from which angle we view it, the annulment is the greatest threat to peace and unity and has the capacity of tearing Nigeria apart.

The resort to escapism, blackmail and treachery will only succeed in postponing the evil day. June 12, we must concede, is not an end in itself, but a means to an end. If and when it is actualized, it can only be a step, a temporary relief, in our quest to reconstruct our polity into a humane, progressive, egalitarian and peaceful society. However, we have to start somewhere.

If the ruling class is desirous of saving what remains of this contraption called Nigeria, then it must put its house in order with regard to June 12. The best the ruling class in the country can get now is to revert to June 12 one way or the other, or face the possibility of a sudden and violent change. And we can be sure, notwithstanding the lies spewed by pied pipers, the risk of reverting is certainly much less.

Our information minister should not behave like the miserable schoolmaster who, in the words of Leon Trotsky, "for many years was repeating the description of spring to his pupils within the four walls of his stuffy schoolroom, and when at last, at the sunset of his days as a teacher, he came out into the fresh air, does not recognize spring and rises to prove that spring is not spring after all, but only a great disorder in nature because it is taking place against the laws of natural history".

For all practical purposes, the June 12 phenomenon, its verdict and implications will remain ever fresh in our memories. And unless we do something about this verdict, many of us may not live to write or read its history.

---

2. COMPELLING REASON FOR PESSIMISM
OCTOBER 1995

Karl Marx in *The Eighteenth Brumaire of Louis Bonaparte* while complementing G.W.F Hegel's assertion that every major event, phenomenon or personage in history usually appeared twice, stated that the first appearance was usually a tragedy and the second a farce.

That historical assertion appears to stand for all time. Edwin Madunagu strengthened this statement in his piece titled "Historical Parodies", The Guardian 23/6/94, when he wrote that, "History's second edition of a major event is always fake".

Today, history is repeating itself and, as expected, it cannot but be a debasement of its earlier occurrence. It is this time-tested analysis of political events that compels us to be pessimistic about Gen. Sani Abacha's transition programme which is being touted as the only event that can move Nigeria forward. Undoubtedly, Nigeria needs to move forward from its 35 years of tardiness. For a country with so much resource, it is not only compelling but also desirous that the citizens be wary of the endless military rule, which rather than moving it forward has continually taken it backward.

Babandiga's transition programme, though not the first in Nigeria's political history, could be described as a major political event or phenomenon. We are all witnesses to the novelty of that prodigious and mind-boggling transition. In his attempt to be distinct, Babangida introduced novel programmes, including the establishment of two political parties, even though Nigerians had prior to then over half a century experience in party politics.

Also, in his attempt to bring "enduring and lasting democracy", he went ahead to ban those whom he termed old breed politicians and humiliated them when the occasion warranted. In all these actions, Babangida had support. Recidivist politicians and fawning professors not only acquiesced to his antics, but they went the extra mile to find a philosophical foundation for them. Babangida was elevated to the position of messiah by the political class so-called even when it was clear that he was transitioning to nowhere.

Presently, we have in place what can be described as the second transition, which is clearly a mirror of the preceding one. Abacha and Babangida's transition have so much in common that we are reminded of the statement about historical personages and events repeating themselves and the consequences of such repetition.

Apart from the fact that the personages – Babangida and Abacha – share common backgrounds (they are military men, they jointly aborted the Second Republic and also jointly terminated the Buhari-Idiagbon regime) there are many historical parallels between the transition programme announced by Gen. Abacha and what we witnessed under the Babangida regime.

When this regime came on board, it promised that its tenure would be very brief. It is, however, not surprising that the regime had to wait for two years before it could announce its own transition programme. Expectedly, the programme did come with its own novelty. The regime has gone ahead to introduce what has been referred to as the modified French presidential system which may well be a euphemism for modified confusion. What's more, our esteemed court historians and effete professors are battle ready again to provide intellectual explanations for this new political hoax.

Since every regime succeeds itself – and the present will not be an exception – it is expected that it will come out with its own containment policy, either tacitly or in the open by registering only those parties it wants to register or making it impossible for others to join the race just as it happened under Babangida's dictatorship.

And like its predecessor whose programmes and policies the present regime is trying to modify, we can be sure that none of the very grave problems which are threatening the foundation of the entity called Nigeria will be addressed; issues such as restructuring the country in consonance with the principles of federation and creating a humanistic socio-economic climate.

As the country prepares for the Fourth Republic, a product of another extended transition, contradictions and shattered hopes are the only benefit the citizens can reap. It is not possible that a regime – like its predecessor – which has impoverished the people, paid no attention to their wishes and assaulted the national psyche can avail itself of any real programme.

Certainly, there are compelling reasons for pessimism because the transition programme which is regarded as the elixir for the country's socio-political woes is fake. And until we come to terms with this reality, the illusion will go full circle.

3. In Memory of the Ogoni Thirteen
December 1995

Very few Nigerians will forget November 10, 1995, in a hurry. Many people are yet to overcome the trauma that accompanied the wanton destruction of human lives on that fateful day. That inglorious day can rightly be described as one of the saddest days in the history of post civil war Nigeria. Events that led to that macabre dispensation of justice are no longer news, but suffice it to say that there is more than meets the eye in the death of thirteen Ogoni citizens and many others unmentioned in what has now become the Ogoni tragedy.

The Ogoni tragedy is succinctly captured in the statement that the 13 Ogoni sons were killed for the survival and enjoyment of non-Ogonis. Herein lies the philosophical foundation of the Ogoni massacre. Expectedly, the Nigerian state has drawn the ire of the international community even though its spokespersons are quick to say that it is not in its character to annihilate its citizens.

Of course, without the death of the four prominent Ogoni last year, the state would still have caught up with Saro-Wiwa and all others who stood in its way in its attempt at "moving Nigeria forward". The military zone which Ogoni, the once fertile and peaceful town, had become before the "Ogoni 4" were killed makes this plausible. Closed to the outside world by a well-orchestrated and intimidating military onslaught under the guise of maintaining peace, it was inevitable that the Ogoni saga had to take its present course.

Saro-Wiwa was a man of vast potentials. Very few men had stirred so much public discontent against the state. More than anybody else in recent times, he had taken on the behemoth called the Nigerian state single-handed and paid dearly with his life. Just as the Nigerian state claims in its undiplomatic gaffes that the world was looking for an avenue to knock Nigeria before the Ogoni hanging, it is evident that the state was looking for ways to cut Saro-Wiwa to size before the killings of May 21, 1994.

The "Ogoni Thirteen" and their forgotten compatriots died for the survival and benefit of the Nigerian state. Certainly, the state must now heave a sigh of relief and strengthen its resolve to maintain peace, even with the lives of her citizens. The military and the ruling class whose infamy has been sustained by the stupendous oil wealth from the restive Niger Delta community must of necessity raise their glasses to toast the demise of the man who threatened their survival.

They must make merry that "peace" has finally returned to Ogoni and that Shell, the fiend whose every finger drips of blood, can now return to recoup the millions of dollars it has "lost" in the past two years. Presently, Ogonis, and non-Ogonis, are being goaded to paint a blissful picture of the Ogoni tragedy and gloss over the agony of the Ogonis occasioned by the unmitigated onslaught of the state.

In the most uncanny ways, we are told why Ken Saro-Wiwa and eight others had to die; how he had magnified the problem of his people and brought untold hardship on them; how it is impossible for every Ogoni citizen to own a Mercedes Benz car, even with the vast oil wealth; how he was given a fair trial; and of course, how justice had been done! It is difficult to believe, however, that in its machinations, the state has allies, willing elements within the ravaged oil producing community who are ready to "sell their birthright for a mess of pottage".

Even more painful is the fact that these same elements are trying very hard to paint Saro-Wiwa as a villain and diminish what he stood for. However, those who are gloating over the death of the distinguished author must of necessity realize that the Nigerian state cannot give them justice. And that at each occasion, that overriding interest which seeks to devour, will always have its way. For patriotic Ogonis, the death of thirteen eminent sons in less than two years must be a terrible blow and a harrowing anticlimax to a purposeful and genuine struggle. But it was expected.

What remains to be done is for the living to prosecute that struggle, not minding the opposition; because no matter how people try to vilify Saro-Wiwa, the late president of MOSOP, the struggle he led was logical, historical, and inevitable. Anyone in doubt should go to Rwanda, Bosnia or the former Soviet Union.

---

4. Ikoku's African Revolution
April 1996

Olusegun Mayegun's piece, "Farrakhan's betrayal" which appeared in some national dailies must have stirred the hornet's nest, at least in government circles. Expectedly, one of the most scathing criticisms of that article came from Mazi S. G. Ikoku, a member of the Transition Implementation Committee.

Writing in AM News, 21/3/96, under the title "Apropos Farrakhan's African revolution", the ebullient politician tried laboriously, albeit unsuccessful, to defend military rule and by extension the present military regime. For those who know Ikoku's ideological antecedent, his tirade against Mayegun must have come as a surprise. However, the article in question proved a point and it was not difficult to understand Ikoku's mission.

Of course, if we dismiss his mission and concentrate on the logic of his presentation it would not be difficult to see how effortlessly he has tried to undermine his much-touted African revolution. Mazi Ikoku's analysis of the dialectics of substructure and superstructure phenomenon and its relevance to the present impasse was quite instructive and illuminating. Hear him:

> *"I submit that the fundamental contradiction in our situation today is neo-colonialism, that 'latter-day theory' (Nkrumah) that strives to reconcile national sovereignty with imperial hegemony".*

He argues that,

> *"Until we recognize the primacy of the struggle against economic and cultural colonialism, operating under the cover of pseudo independence or formal political sovereignty, as the foundation of our economic stagnation and backwardness, social malaise and political trauma, we run the risk of continually applying ineffective remedies and in the process making our political therapy rather irrelevant".*

Quite true! But, we must go beyond this simplicity in theory; for to think that the issue is as straightforward as it appears is illusory and not in consonance with reality. Of course, neo-colonialism does not operate in a vacuum. It is aided by structures within the neo-colony, which in the case of Africa, and most of the developing world, include the military.

Nigeria's military establishment is a neo-colonial institution. It was created by the colonialists and nurtured by them; and it has remained inefficient, except in the service of its former masters.

Though it sees itself as the bastion of nationalism, beyond the façade lies a ruthless collaboration with the enemy. The military has ruled the country for 36 years now without anything to show for it. Rather, the living conditions of Nigerians have continued to decline. However, it has not just been ruling; it has continuously served the interest of neo-colonialism.

Mazi Ikoku identifies neo-colonialism as a political-economic system assiduously foisted on developing countries since the historical UN Resolution of December 1960. This, we are told, is made possible through the IMF/World Bank. Of course, we all know that the Structural Adjustment Programme (SAP), the monstrous baby of the IMF/World Bank in the last decade, was introduced in Nigeria by a military regime. Since then, no regime has found it necessary to link SAP with the unmitigated suffering of the masses.

In trying to create the African revolution, therefore, we must raise two salient issues. First, contradictions exist between us and the external enemy (neo-colonialism) and contradictions also exist within our polity. Second, and more important, there is no eternal law on which one must be tackled first. It is a matter of expediency.

For us to develop and build the African revolution, we must get rid of the military because it has proved an anathema in almost every part of Africa. "The African revolution, while still concentrating its main efforts on the destruction of imperialism, colonialism and neo-colonialism is aiming at the same time to bring about a radical transformation of society" (Nkrumah, *Class Struggle in Africa*). This cannot be done until "military rule and all forms of tyranny are removed" (Mayegun).

In his *Class Struggle in Africa*, Nkrumah also went ahead to admonish that,

> *"In Africa, the internal enemy – the reactionary bourgeoisie – must be exposed as exploiters and parasites, and as collaborators with imperialists and neo-colonialists on whom they largely depend for the maintenance of their positions of power and privilege".*

Anyway we look at it, the military is no less a part of the reactionary bourgeoisie". It is true as Mazi Ikoku pointed out that "military rule could move a neo-colony forward and could also serve as the instrument for sustaining neo-colonialism". Of course, where the former situation prevails, the military joins the rank of nationalist forces to ward off neo-colonialism. However, where the latter phenomenon is dominant – and this is most often the case – what role should the people play?

Ikoku agrees that, "Every situation has to be studied in depth and on its own merits and demerits in order to expose its inner dynamics". The suffering masses of this country know who their enemies are - neo-colonialism and its collaborators, both military and civilian - and they do not need any charlatan to define the course of the struggle for them.

It is good enough that Farrakhan rails against the evil of the American society and for us to be wary of it, but there is nothing friendly in his recipe of accommodating the military; certainly not when it has not played any liberating role. Our country has never been so divided, yet we keep looking for imaginary enemies.

The unprecedented horror and miseries that confront our citizens are, for the most part, the product of despotic and self-serving military incursions. And since the African revolution is not only a struggle against "external enemies" but also against what Nkrumah calls the "internal enemy", our struggle therefore must start within. Of course, it cannot end within until the total liberation of African as envisaged by Nkrumah.

Ikoku's defence of military rule and his attempt at fanning the embers of pseudo nationalism will only defer the African revolution.

5. For Citizen Ubani *et al*
July 1996

Recently, human rights and pro-democracy groups met to ruminate on the first anniversary of the detention of Chima Ubani, Secretary-General of the Democratic Alternative (DA) and Head of Human Rights Education at the Civil Liberties Organisation (CLO). The occasion afforded the groups an opportunity not just to reflect on the fate of Chima Ubani and other detainees languishing in various detention camps across the country, but the question of democracy and a humanistic society.

The date was Thursday, July 18, 112996. Though an informal gathering, most guests were on edge as Mr. Abdul Oroh, Executive Director of CLO and Dr. Tunji Abayomi, lawyer to imprisoned Gen. Olusegun Obasanjo, who were in detention with Ubani recounted the agony the young man was going through.

What struck me was not so much the condition of the detainee, knowing that it could be worse. However, Ubani's continued detention reminded me that July 18, 1995, had joined the dark dates in the annals of Nigeria's tortuous political history. I was immediately reminded of June 23, 1993, when the June 12 election of the same year was annulled; July 8, 1993, when about 200 pro-democracy activities had to pay with their blood in protest against the annulment; June 23, 1994, when the winner of that election was imprisoned; August 19, 1994, when Frank Ovie Kokori and Wariebe Agamene, President and Secretary-General respectively of the National Union of Petroleum and Natural Gas Workers (NUPENG) were arrested and thrown into detention.

I also remembered January 17, 1995, the date Sylvester Odion-Akhaine, Secretary-General of the Campaign for Democracy (CD), began a detention process that almost cost him his life; July 17, 1995, when four journalists were sentenced to life imprisonment for their alleged complicity in a coup plot; October 6, 1995, when elder statesman, and pro-democracy supporter, Pa Alfred Rewane, was brutally murdered.

I did not forget January 30, 1996, when people's lawyer, Chief Gani Fawehinmi, began what has become a horrid detention experience; February 14, 1996, when Femi Falana, the steadfast advocate joined the band of those detained without charges or trial; and of course, June 4, 1996, which witnessed the gruesome murder of the indefatigable Kudirat Abiola. The dates, of course, are endless; and if I did not remember all, it was simply because one's brain was suffused with what the gale of arrests and detention holds for the future of Nigeria.

Expectedly, so much was said about Ubani that day; and so much has been written about him. What I would want to add is that Ubani represents the best in us, Nigerian youth. Intelligent, articulate and of firm resolve, Ubani portrays the quintessence of what our generation ought to be; and the more he stays in detention, the more our inadequacies as the bastion of an open and just society come to the fore. Therefore, as conscious elements within a decaying society, Ubani's one year in detention should help us in posing once again, the question: what is the role of the youth in the future of Nigeria?

"Politics" is back once again; and as always, our politicians, so-called, are jostling for positions. Not one of them has raised questions about the rationale for the wave of arrests without trial going on in the country. Certainly, it says a lot about the character of those whom the future of this country will eventually be handed to.

What this means is that Nigerian youth should once again rededicate themselves to, not just the termination of military rule, but also the quest for an open society with the full complement of basic rights and democratic freedoms, including the freedom of association, expression and social security. We have seen everything there is to see, and there cannot be any doubts in our minds where the country is headed.

We have seen an election annulled after wasting over 40 billion naira in a transition programme. We have witnessed the incarceration of the winner of that election, and the dastardly murder of his wife. We have observed our colleagues and friends go through mind-bending experiences in detention just because they dared to question the *status quo*. We have also seen that Nigeria presently seems to be a haven for, and beneficial to, only those who are armed, in whatever guise; either as soldiers who are in power, as policemen and "task forces" at checkpoints, as assassins who now have a regime of their own or as robbers who have taken over our streets.

There cannot be any further doubts that what is now under construction in Nigeria has nothing to do with democracy; it will not guarantee us freedom and our basic rights. Our task, therefore, is to keep the fire of the pro-democracy and fundamental human rights struggle aglow.

This admonition was inspired by the invocation of Sylvester Odion-Akhaine, a "fellow" of what is now referred to as the "Chartered Institute of Detainees", that, "The best you can do for a political detainee is for him to know that his associates have not abandoned the cause for which he was detained". Odion-Akhaine was emphatic at the gathering for Ubani that, not minding his temporary deprivation, the real tonic the latter needed was the assurance that his colleagues had not "sold out".

I know Ubani would not entertain any doubts that his constituency is alive to the struggle for which he was incarcerated. Anybody who can reach M.K.O Abiola, Gani Fawehinmi, Chima Ubani, Ovie Kokori, Femi Falana, Femi Aborishade, Nnimmo Bassey, et al, should ask them to take heart; that "the pot of agony is still boiling"; that the struggle is certainly on, notwithstanding all odds; and that victory is certain.

---

6. ABACHA'S SECOND COMING
JANUARY 1997

The release last month of human rights lawyers in Nigeria, in the wake of the visit of the Commonwealth Ministerial Action Group (CMAG), did not come as a surprise to many people. If anything, it goes to show the true character of Nigeria's maximum ruler, Gen. Sani Abacha, as a political schemer. I am sure he did not expect Nigeria to cheer.

That spurious gesture also confirms the statement that Nigeria has become a veritable nightmare, particularly in the past three years. The poor showing of the military junta in terms of human rights abuses and political contraction is underscored by the fact that those political detainees released recently were in detention for almost a year without trial or any formal charges.

The junta, squirming as always, had hoped to secure some diplomatic points with such half-witted political manoeuvre. However, no amount of face-saving measures or diplomatic window-dressing can obviate the fact that Nigeria and Nigerians have remained worse off under Abacha's rule.

Living in Nigeria today can best be described as living behind prison walls. Nigeria has become a large military barracks with Abacha and his henchmen as sentries. Pro-democracy and human rights activists are arrested and detained at will. Newspaper vendors are arrested for selling certain publications, while numerous publishing houses have come to accept security operatives as complement staff.

In a characteristic fascist manner, the Internal Security Task Force of the regime prowls the precinct of minority ethnic groups perceived to be restive, mowing down defenceless citizens in an orgy of violence and bloodletting. Decrees of every imaginable garb are rolled out daily by the supreme commanders to take care of such mundane things as students' protest or the proscription of such innocuous organizations as the Academic Staff Union of Universities (ASUU).

That is the prevailing condition under the rule of a brutal military junta. Specifically, the economic situation has been most distressing in the last few years with majority of Nigerians having to live without the bare necessities of life. On the other hand, citizens have been gradually, but systematically, incapacitated politically. The reason for the latter action is not difficult to decipher.

Gen. Abacha, like a snake, is set to shed his skin; in this case, his tight and fading military uniform. Nobody should doubt this presupposition because Abacha's notoriety for scheming is legendary. He was man Friday for two military regimes and like a sleuthhound guided himself patiently to his prey: the presidency.

On December 31, 1983, Abacha heralded the coming of the fifth military regime in Nigeria. Two years later on August 27, 1985, he announced the emergence of yet another military contraption. That action saw him rise to the position of army chief. By the time the former dictator, Gen. Ibrahim Babangida, stepped aside on August 27, 1993, Abacha had risen to the position of Defence Minister and de facto second-in-command of the regime. Then on November 17, 1993, his patience ran out. He not only announced the toppling of the weary Interim National Government (ING) led by the quivering Ernest Shonekan, he decided it was time for him to taste the pudding he had helped to prepare on previous occasions.

He promised a quick return to civil rule. However, that was not to be. Surprisingly, today the major issue at the centre of political discourse in Nigeria is not whether the errant military regime will bring democracy or not but the ignoble quest by Abacha to succeed himself. Initially, it began as a rumour (indeed, every major political event in Nigeria which has come to pass started as rumour), then his political marionettes started giving impetus to the call.

First, it was the former Chief Justice of Nigeria, Mohammed Bello, who opened the floodgate of the Abacha-for-president campaign. He told a bewildered nation that nothing in the constitution barred the infantry general from being the next civilian president of Nigeria. For the information of readers, Nigeria does not have a constitution. The military junta suspended the prevailing constitution when it took over power. Two years after it set up a conference of ragtag politicians to write a constitution to suit its ambition, Nigerians are still wondering what is going on.

Then came the outburst by the chair of the Transition Implementation Committee (TIC), Justice Mamman Nasir, who contended that "Gen Abacha is eligible to contest" the planned presidential election in 1998. It did not stop at that. The venerable, I mean renegade, Sam Gomsu Ikoku of the famous Nkrumah Ideological School, Winneba, Ghana, and Vice Chairman of the TIC, hit the nail on the head: "Abacha should contest to ensure continuity and checkmate the politicians who do not have much to offer".

Expectedly, Abacha has put in place structures that will ensure a smooth transition, not for the benefit of Nigerians but to satisfy his ego. Starting from the amorphous constitutional conference which he formed immediately he came to power, to the five political parties registered recently, everything the general has done, point to his disregard for political freedom and the rule of law.

Rather than allowing Nigerians to form political parties (the first political party formed by a Nigerian came into existence over 70 years ago, before the mendacious general was born), the situation is the other way round, not minding the fact that Babangida's failed example where he foisted two political parties on Nigerians is not too distant to learn from. The five parties, all little better than government parastatals, are already scrambling to conscript Abacha as their flag bearer.

One does not expect anything less from Gen. Sani Abacha. As chairman of the Economic Community of West African States (ECOWAS) and head of the club of soldiers who become civilian presidents, Abacha must fulfill his historical mission. We may ask: what moral justification does Abacha have to be a referee in his own game or a judge in his own case? It does appear, however, that morality does not count much when guns lead the way.

Abacha is not just making a mockery of democracy; he is struggling hard to create a miserable caricature, to rehash the bad dream which started a decade ago when Gen. Babangida inaugurated the first chapter of this unending transition programme. Babangida was less brusque in his approach when he announced two political parties and told a not too surprised nation that he knew those who would not succeed him.

Abacha is not talking of those who will not succeed him because it is he and his ambition that is at stake. Abacha seized power on November 17, 1993, amidst protest and opposition. For three years now, he has maintained a stranglehold on power, riding roughshod over Nigerians. Even though the campaign against his murderous regime is on the ascendancy, he still feels secure, and like the ostrich hides his head in the sand and pretends all is well.

This ploy cannot fool anybody. Abacha's foibles are innumerable. He is obstinate and incapable of keeping his words. When he cajoled a section of the human rights community and the political class to support him in 1993 so that he could reverse the atrocities of his predecessor, some people must have thought he was serious. Today, they definitely know better.

There are enough reasons, therefore, to be skeptical when Abacha talks about democracy. Abacha is your quintessential dictator. This is evident as much through his antics as through his misdeed. Seriously speaking, I see history repeating itself in the attempt by Gen. Abacha to succeed himself. I see Gen. Abacha going with measured grace through the part trodden by the likes of late Samuel Doe, the infamous dictator of Liberia. The second coming of Abacha will certainly be a farcical experience. If and when there is a real attempt at democracy, even the congenitally blind would see it.

For now, Nigerians can only muster the courage to confront the Janus-faced general when the time comes. It is inevitable because West African military leaders have to be cured of their paternalistic tendencies and Nigeria should lead the way. Their irascible mien is turning the sub-region into a political cauldron. In the case of Nigeria, it is certain that when people's power takes control, the blustering generals will scamper.

It happened three years ago.

7. Abacha's Image Problem
March 1997

It has become a common feature of the defenders of the tottering military regime in Nigeria to put up puerile arguments in defence of the junta headed by Gen. Sani Abacha.

For three years, Nigerians and others concerned about the contraption put in place by the military high command have been subjected to "Abacharite" history by those whose official duty seems to be to rationalize the existence of Abacha's regime and provide a basis for its continued manipulation of the people's will.

These jesters in Abacha's court do not spare any occasion to inform the world that the supreme commander is sincere about his handling of the political crisis in Nigeria. However, in this morbid act, they often go too far, sometimes sounding incoherent, unintelligent and even ridiculous. One of such attempts to shore up the plummeting image of Nigeria's infamous dictator was the advertorial "Nigeria: 36 Years of Nationhood" which appeared in Ghana's Daily Graphic newspaper of December 30, 1996.

Those behind the facile attempt to downplay the absolutism of the Abacha regime say he is committed to laying a foundation for democracy in Nigeria. Nigeria's Acting High Commissioner to Ghana, Kennedy Apoe, was quoted in the Graphic report as saying: "Gen. Abacha is sincere about the transition program…in fact, the success of the local government election on a nonparty basis as well as the large membership of the political parties (estimated to be about 25 million) are pointers to the confidence which the people have in the administration of Gen. Abacha". Nothing, of course, could be further from the truth.

What the High Commissioner failed to tell us is the use or essence of democracy when it is placed in a straitjacket? What about the monumental abuse of human rights going on in Nigeria under "Abacharite" democracy? Of course, the March 1996 election was a caricature that went on under the guise of democratic polls.

Eligibility was only open to those whom the junta "trusted". The election proper could not have been more farcical. Apoe's "large membership of political parties estimated to be about 25 million" is a figment of his imagination. It is an open secret that Abacha's five political parties recruited the dead as well as underage children to swell their membership in order to meet the electoral commission's arduous condition that parties had to have a specific number of members in different wards before they could be registered.

In an effort to cover up the murder of Ken Saro-Wiwa and eight others on November 10, 1995, the High Commissioner explained that Ken Saro-Wiwa and his compatriots were tried for the murder of four prominent Ogoni citizens by a competent judicial tribunal chaired by a highly respected high court judge and not a military tribunal.

Perhaps, the High Commissioner should have had the common courtesy of telling those who did not witness the judicial charade that the condemned men had no right to appeal. Witnesses were bribed by the government to testify falsely during the trial and the defence lawyers had to withdraw when the intimidation became unbearable. Weeks before the judgement, Abacha's special adviser on legal matters, Professor Auwalu Yadudu, had stated on more than one occasion that Ken Saro-Wiwa was "indeed guilty of murder".

However, the biggest test of credibility for the "save Abacha" campaigners is their inability to rewrite the history of Abacha's ascendancy as Nigeria's supreme ruler. In a piece in the West Africa magazine, Abacha's official megaphone, Dr. Walter Ofonagoro, Nigeria's minister of information, was at his quintessence. Those who are familiar with the effete former history teacher at the University of Lagos would not lose sleep about his interpretation of Nigeria's political history, at least from June 12, 1993. For the benefit of others, it is necessary to expose Ofonagoro's sense of history.

Just as Apoe did in the Graphic report, Dr. Ofonagoro in his interview ignored the reality of the June 12, 1993 presidential election. According to Ofonagoro, "The election held on June 12, 1993, was between two parties: NRC and SDP, but two days before that election, on June 10, there was an injunction at an Abuja High Court restraining the electoral commission from holding the elections on the grounds that there were irregularities in the primary elections and that the rules had not been complied with".

After the election, according to Ofonagoro,

> *"The chief judge of the Abuja High Court ruled that an election held in defiance of a court order is improper and invalid and therefore null and void. He directed the National Electoral Commission to stop processing the results. He gave this order on June 16, 1993 (when) only 14 states' results had been processed. Nigerian at that time had 30 states plus the Federal Capital Territory, so 16 states were yet to be processed. Under the rules governing the election, a candidate had to win a majority of the votes cast plus one-third of the votes cast in two-thirds of the states*

of the federation. Now two-thirds of 30 is 20, so the minimum number of states one needed to win to claim victory and an overall majority was 20".

This was how the minister tried, albeit unsuccessfully, to defend the folly of the military regime of which Abacha was the de facto deputy when it annulled the election.

We are told by the chroniclers of the Abacha regime that the election ran into trouble just two days before it was held. But this is just a red herring. Even though the court gave a ruling, it must be stated that it acted *ultra vires*. First, the petition on which the court based its ruling was brought by the Association for Better Nigeria (ABN), an insidious and unregistered association of worthless individuals who later recanted and exposed how the Babangida regime nurtured and paid them to frustrate the election. It is pertinent to add that this also took place when the regime had clamped down on all unregistered associations or groups to forestall any disruption of the election.

Second, that the electoral commission had to ignore the ruling of the court was not its own making. The decree setting up the commission exempted it from interference by any court of law in Nigeria. All these were part of efforts by Babangida to show the world he was serious about handing over power to a civilian government.

Let Ofonagoro know the following facts: the Abuja High Court did not order the annulment of the election. Even if Babangida inferred that from the court's ruling, he ought to have been charged for contempt when he failed to stop his electoral commission as the Abuja High Court so ruled before the election.

If Ofonagoro is so interested in the rule of law, and his venerable courts, he should ask his masters to dismantle all military tribunals in Nigeria. All detained human rights and pro-democracy activists currently in detention without trial should be charged to court. Above all, the winner of the presidential election held on June 12, 1993, M.K.O. Abiola, who has been in detention without trial for three years, should be released.

Evidently, Abacha's town criers will not tell the outside world that it was the manipulation and confusion engineered by Babangida and

Abacha in June 1993 that paved the way for Abacha to install himself as Nigeria's ruler after the ineffective head of the interim government, Ernest Shonekan, was toppled in a palace coup on November 17, 1993.

Since that date, Nigeria has lived under barefaced dictatorship. It is, therefore, bemusing that some paid courtiers think they can prop up a dictator by peddling lies and distorting history.

---

8. THE PROBLEM WITH NIGERIA
APRIL 1997

"When a society demands change there is no need attempting to change it on old principles". - Foday Sankoh

A new philosophy is sweeping through Nigeria. That philosophy is "Abachaism". Decadent and moribund as it were, "Abachaism" is making itself the dominant ideology in Nigeria through chicanery and coercion.

It is important, therefore, to reflect on the emergence of this phenomenon and what is portends for Nigeria's democratic aspirations. After he took over the reins of government in a most comical palace coup on November 17, 1993, Abacha who has been a key figure in Nigeria's political crisis since December 31, 1983, when he announced the end of Nigeria's Second Republic, set out to inaugurate his own political transition programme.

He promised a brief tenure and quickly arranged a phony national conference made up of handpicked political dilettantes to put together a "new constitution" on which a "genuine and everlasting democracy" would be built. Today, two years after that inauspicious body submitted the draft constitution and just a little over a year to the end of Abacha's transition programme, the draft constitution has yet to be made public.

The constitution is being implemented behind the scene to suit the whims of Abacha at each point of his transition programme. It certainly would be asking for too much to want these military bigots to subject the constitution to a referendum.

Abacha of course is keeping the constitution for obvious reasons. Holed up in Abuja, Abacha, who has failed to honour every important national assignments, including the November 17, 1996, burial of Nigeria's first president, Dr. Nnamdi Azikiwe, for fear of reprisals from the public, knows that the only way he can achieve his aim of self-perpetuation is through a dubious manipulation of the constitution.

This involves the use of decrees and or clandestine organisations to shore up support where necessary. It is no coincidence that "Abacha for president" campaigners are springing up each day. Some of these startlingly banal groups go by such name as, "Youth Earnestly Ask for Abacha '98", "Movement for Abacha for President" and the "General, Dr. Abacha for '98 presidency".

The last name is particularly striking. Abacha delights in gloating over his numerous "intellectual" achievements, his multiple honourary doctorate degrees, including his "recognition" by the World International Property Organisation (WIPO). It should be expected for as Wole Soyinka said when he lampooned the "all-too-common desire among semi-literate African dictators to obtain academic recognition while at the same time decimating the intelligentsia in their respective countries": "The more moronic the ruler, the greater his desire for intellectual recognition".

Notwithstanding their futility, these imbecilic campaigns go on with ample support from state structures. Of course, these campaigns are little different from those engineered by a diabolical group called Association for Better Nigeria (ABN) under the Babangida/Abacha regime.

While Abacha's special duties minister, the ubiquitous Wada Nas threatened to deal with persons campaigning for Abacha's presidency, Abacha's chief press secretary, David Attah, was reported to have called on Nigerians to exert "sufficient pressure on Abacha to convince him to continue with the good works that everybody says he has done, but in a purely civilian setting".

As this double-talk goes on, new strategies are being worked out for Abacha's grand design. Without any modicum of decency, federal civil servants are being forced to wear Abacha badges which come in two forms, one with Abacha in military uniform and the other in civilian clothes with the inscription, Dr. Sani Abacha.

Abacha, however, should know that he is a poor mimic. Nigerians have passed through this road before. This same dubious political regimentation happened barely three years ago. Nigeria's political elite must suffer a kind of collective amnesia to imagine that "Abachaism" can work. The realisation of his limited vision and the presence of an unyielding opposition have forced Abacha to strengthen his absolutism: a new decree which gives him absolute power to sack local government chairmen was recently promulgated.

The new decree empowers Abacha to overrule the choice of the people notwithstanding the fact that the choices were made at his instance. It also empowers him to annul elections and dissolve elected government in the same manner he and his commander-in-chief did four years ago. However, Abacha must be made to realize that he is playing a very dangerous game. At no time has this futile effort at totalitarianism become more irrelevant as the present. What he has set out to do is to destroy the fundamental principles of Nigeria's federalism.

Expectedly, Abacha's illusory political experiments are being opposed in all nooks and crannies of Nigeria and even outside, and this has left the general wondering why he should be the object of such vitriolic attack considering the fact that he is not Nigeria's first military ruler and probably won't be the last; his regime is not the first to detain people without trial or even engage in the morbid business of extra-judicial killings.

So why the fuss about "Abachaism"? "Abachaism" represents all that is antithetical to democracy. Abacha, in his self-delusion, believes he is the best thing that has happened to Nigeria. In his omnipotent parochialism, he must, through despotism, maintain a stranglehold on Nigeria and Nigerians.

Abacha cannot claim any messianic role. He and his cohorts remain the major obstacle to the realization of democracy and prosperity in Nigeria. When on December 31, 1983, Abacha announced the termination of Nigeria's Second Republic, he told a skeptical nation that he and his gang had to intervene because, among other things, "Our hospitals have become mere consulting clinics". If hospitals in Nigeria were consulting clinics more than a decade ago, today they are death chambers as they not only lack basic infrastructure, but cannot administer the basic drugs for very minor illnesses.

Nigerians, and indeed people around the world, must therefore brace up to kick out Abacha. Opportunistic and crooked politicians, military adventurers and ethnic chauvinists who see in Abacha the only way forward must realize that Abacha's new order is nothing but shameless opportunism and that Nigerians deserve a better deal.

It is pathetic that the United States and her apparatus of democracy are doffing their hats for Abacha. An election-monitoring group, the second from the US, which monitored the recently concluded sham local government elections in Nigeria reportedly declared them "peaceful and open". For this group, this is a strong indication of "Nigeria's determined march to democracy".

If what democracy means to these groups is just for people to queue at a polling station and cast their votes then we must be wary. The disqualification of candidates by the regime did not mean anything to these holidaymakers (after all, they were sponsored by the regime) disguised as election observers; the stringent registration exercise, fraud, irregularities and violence mattered even less.

It is only in Abacha's democracy that parties that do not meet certain representation during an election would be proscribed; that local council chairmen cannot attend party meetings except by special permission of military administrators; that an electoral commission has to succumb to the orders of a minister to toss a coin to determine the winner of an election. Yet our purveyors of democracy do not see the possibility of Nigeria becoming a one-party state under Abacha's anvil; and that the presence of so many parties is just a façade of political pluralism.

Consciously or unconsciously, the US and her democratic institutions so-called are creating another monster in the mould of Mobutu. In the case of Mobutu, it took them three decades (or so they want us to believe) to discover how despicable their monster was; in the case of Abacha, it won't be that long, but the consequences would certainly be grave.

Surprisingly, Abacha was reported last month to have welcomed a summit in Togo – another haven of dictatorship – on the crises in Zaire, describing the fighting as "disheartening and dangerous to Africa's peace and security". Those who know Abacha will agree that the difference between him and Mobutu is that between six and half a dozen. The illegal detention, torture, harassment, extra-judicial killings and the general climate of insecurity in Nigeria make Mobutu's murderous rule pale in comparison.

If the US, and others in league with her, cannot denounce Abacha, it would not be asking for too much to say that they should stop propping him up. What the present political impasse in Nigeria, which is principally the handiwork of military adventurers, requires is the immediate release of Abiola and all political prisoners, the setting up of a government of national unity to be headed by him and the convoking of a Sovereign National Conference (SNC) of representative of all interest groups in Nigeria: labour, academia, students, market women, religious group, ethnic minorities, etc.

Anything short of this would give Abacha the freedom to ride roughshod over Nigeria.

---

9. AS EVIL DESCENDS
May 1997

Once again the West seems appalled (at least that is the impression you get) by the political trickery and murderous game Abacha is playing with Nigeria and Nigerians. The spin-doctors at the State Department in Washington and Foreign Office in London appear to be concerned (I hope I am not too presumptuous) about the imminent crisis which the Abacha junta is set to unleash on Nigeria.

What is the reason for their righteous indignation? The fact that there would be no presidential election on August 1, 1998, despite over three years of political manoeuvres. Suddenly the West is acting as if the unexpected had happened. Unctuously, it is pretending as if it did not know there was never meant to be an election. It speaks as if it has just discovered Abacha's criminal inclinations.

Of course, the West has always been known to maintain double standards in these matters. However, knowing Abacha, one would have thought the West would have learnt its lessons. But, that did not happen. The West gave Abacha the legitimacy he sought and he is reveling in it.

We did hear such refrain as "give the transition programme a chance". Lyndon LaRouche and his Executive Intelligence crap often called those who questioned Abacha's monkey tricks "naysayers". London on its parts was busily trying to "constructively engage" the regime. What about the mother of all alibis provided by no other than President Bill Clinton, ruler of the purported bastion of democracy, America?

The sudden discovery by the West of Abacha's political deception is hypocritical. The West saw Abacha, tutored him and propped him up against pro-democracy and human rights activists and above all against the democratically-elected president who is spending his fourth year in prison. Now that Abacha has become a hydra-headed monster, the West seems incapable of dealing with him. Clearly, Abacha has embarrassed his Western backers who undoubtedly would be gravely disappointed at his tactlessness. He could still have added some finesse to this political travesty.

It is a measure of the level of dementia of the man who seized power under duplicitous circumstances in 1993. Abacha is literally incapable of grappling with the processes of governance. He is so dim-witted that he must try all dirty tricks imaginable to make himself the next "democratically selected" president of Nigeria. What Abacha wants to do with Nigeria has become manifest. So, when the likes of Dagogo Jack, Chairman of Abacha's electoral commission, speak of "enthroning lasting democracy", what they mean in effect is enthroning lasting dictatorship.

Under Abacha, who was not born when the first political party in Nigeria was formed, democracy has taken a completely new meaning. In which political process can five parties select a candidate for an election when the candidate does not belong to any of the parties and has signified his intention to contest the election?

It is even more ridiculous considering the fact that the electoral guidelines do not permit independent candidates. But this is Nigeria, a country where all you need to turn a man into a woman is a decree at the pleasure of the maximum ruler. Nothing operates according to law in Nigeria. Abacha makes laws and violates them with impunity.

It is also a measure of how insecure the man Abacha is. It certainly would not come as a surprise if the planned referendum is called off and Abacha continues in office under the so-called civilian dispensation. The next stage of this debacle, therefore, is for Abacha's band of sterile and unthinking sycophants to fly the kite of continuity.

Unfortunately, Abacha's misdeed is not limited to the field of politics. Anybody who bothers to find out how the economy of Nigeria has been run in the past five years will not only shudder but also come to the inevitable conclusion that Nigeria is witnessing brazen dictatorship and banditry. Nigeria produces oil, yet fuel shortages have become a feature of her national life; the common person cannot find, much less afford, kerosene a byproduct of petroleum for daily use.

Virtually all roads in Nigeria are decrepit when all it requires to put them in good condition is bitumen derived from petroleum. Currently, the country imports 10-14 cargoes of petrol and diesel per month at the cost of $40 million because the nation's refineries are incapable of producing enough petrol for local use. This, of course, is part of the general anarchy the Abacha junta has created in the economy through corruption and mismanagement.

Since Abacha is a man who is ever ready to destroy that which he cannot understand, it is not impossible that if he is left unchecked he would drag 100 million Nigerians with him on his journey to perdition. Nobody, even incurable optimists, is in doubt that evil has descended on Nigeria and Nigerians have to brace themselves up for a long-drawn-out battle.

With his latest political faux pas, Abacha has closed every peaceful option to the resolution of the political impasse in Nigeria. Clearly, he is not interested in dialogue. Last October, after much pressure from human rights and pro-democracy activists, he promised to release political detainees, to no avail. Only recently, after the visit of the Pope to Nigeria, Abacha again gave the impression that he could be taken seriously. Clearly, he is buying time.

Of course, Abacha can still redeem himself. His best option now is to abdicate his post and allow Nigerians to freely decide on the future of their country. However, will this man who is set to be the 20th century's last monster read the writing on the wall? I gravely have my doubts.

10. REMEMBERING SARO-WIWA
NOVEMBER 1997

In November 10, 1995, a horrifying event took place in Port-Harcourt, the oil city in South-south Nigeria. It was the murder of Ken Saro-Wiwa, internationally acclaimed author and environmental rights activists and eight of his compatriots. Two years after, echoes of that mindless and depraved application of state power still reverberate around the world.

The international community is justifiably appalled and concerned now as it was two years ago when the murders occurred. It is not the novelty or cruelty of the deaths (Saro-Wiwa was reported to have given in only after the fifth attempt of the hangman) or the fact that nine innocent souls were wasted; after all, military regimes in Nigeria have turned the country into a killing field and made a vocation of murdering Nigerians depending on their whims.

Those murders were a measure of how nauseatingly murderous and despicably arrogant the Abacha junta has become and the extent it would go in the pursuit of its imaginary enemies. They showed the degree to which the junta could imperil Nigerians and Nigeria, as it has done in keeping the winner of the June 12, 1993 presidential election, Chief M.K.O. Abiola, in prison since June 1994. They also confirm the regime's lack of commitment (except through hostage taking and assassination) to the resolution of the political problems in Nigeria; problems that were caused by the avarice and inordinate ambition of a discredited military cabal.

Saro-Wiwa and his compatriots stood for many things, not the least was the impetus they gave their Ogoni nationality in its struggle for self-determination and against environmental degradation; a struggle borne out of the need to extricate itself from the clutches of internal colonialism and the booby trap which Nigeria has become. Abacha showed no scruples in the Saro-Wiwa case and he is even less circumspect now; for him power is the ultimate aphrodisiac.

Clearly, his reign of terror is not limited to vanquishing minority rights activists. Between November 10, 1995, and now, many more unresolved politically induced assassinations, including that of Kudirat Abiola, wife of Chief Abiola, have taken place. So well has the Nigerian state honed its repressive apparatus that it is not content slaying innocent Nigerians at home, but has to go in search of its perceived enemies beyond the frontiers of Nigeria to the furthermost parts of the earth.

Sembene Ousmane was right when he noted that, "Power is a citadel, you must be granted admittance. If you force your way in, you'll have to use violence to remain". Notwithstanding the campaigns of various countries and international rights groups engaged in undiluted condemnation of the Abacha regime, it continues its recourse to violence and intimidation, its vicious campaign of arrest and detention without trial. Put in another term, the public must be reduced to apathy and subservience for these infernal violators of human rights to maintain their stranglehold on power.

Just like every other bankrupt dictatorship, the current dictatorship in Nigeria is making a benevolent gift of democracy to Nigerians. However, Abacha remains undecided, or so he claims, whether to be a judge in his own case by contesting the hoax of an election scheduled for October 1998. Listen to the head of Nigeria's ignoble military regime in an interview with Radio Nigeria some weeks ago:

> *"We have heard their request, it is a very difficult request, (in reference to some duplicitous traditional rulers calling on Abacha to run for president) it is something one has to think about... we pray that God will guide us so that whatever God decides will be in the best interest of all of us".*

Abacha who seized power in the chaos precipitated by the annulment of the June 12, 1993 election which he and his predecessor engineered cannot now claim to be under the direction of God. Abacha's greatest problem is how to reconcile his ambition and the fervent desires of Nigerians to be rid of the embers of an ossified dictatorship and usher in democracy and freedom.

The justifiable struggle by Nigerians against a desperate military dictatorship shows that when a people are denied justice and freedom for so long they are forced to struggle to regain same. It was in one of such struggles against these latter-day fascists that Saro-Wiwa and his compatriots met their deaths. As we remember them two years after, we cannot but wonder how many more Nigerians have to die before Abacha and his goons fulfill their ambitions.

We cannot talk about Saro-Wiwa and his compatriots without talking about the collapse of the Nigerian state. Their deaths remind us of not only our inadequacies as a nation and how our duplicity, complicity and oppressive tactics can only create more deaths, but the fact that there is nothing sacrosanct about the monstrosity called Nigeria.

Not minding Abacha's claims about democracy, it is clear through his dubious transition programme that in the months ahead his regime will trample on the rights of Nigerians to freely elect their leaders. It is, therefore, not surprising that two years after Saro-Wiwa, Ogoniland remains uninhabitable because of oil pollution and an overbearing military presence. Shell's monstrous instruments of death still dot every nook and cranny of the oil community.

Today, numerous Ogoni citizens, pro-democracy and human rights activists are languishing in Abacha's dungeons. In Abacha's perception of justice, no trial is needed, neither are victims entitled to know their offences. Not even the decadent Apartheid regime in South Africa could have been so cynically brutal.

Four years after Abacha seized power, it has become evident that military dictatorship in Nigeria is a spent force and has no relevance. But, it has to take the efforts of the likes of Saro-Wiwa and company to make this reality sink in. We remember the "Ogoni 9" as if it was yesterday when their pains and anguish at the hands of the gruesome hangmen of a regime of equal status brought tears to our eyes and created deep gulfs in our hearts.

Adieu Saro-Wiwa, Saturday Dobee, Nordu Eawo, Daniel Gbooko, Paul Levera, Felix Nuate, Baribor Bera, Barinem Kiobel, and John Kpuine as well as other unsung heroes and heroines of the struggle for democracy, freedom and justice in Nigeria, all for whom Abacha's regime meant one thing: horrid death. May your spirits not rest in peace but continue to haunt your bloodthirsty murderers.

11. Countdown to Autocracy
December 1997

It did not come as a surprise. Well, except perhaps to incurable optimists. The telltale signs that Abacha desires to be the next "democratically elected" president of Nigeria have always been palpable. It was just a matter of time before it became a *fait accompli*. And it took no less a person than Abacha's Minister of Special Duties, the honourable Wada Nas, a man gifted with an incredible talent for doublespeak to bring this fact home.

In a speech in Abuja, Nigeria's capital, on Tuesday, November 11, 1997, Wada Nas (Wada Noise is more like it considering his proclivity for doublespeak) was reported to have called on political parties to let Abacha stand unopposed in next year's presidential election.

Wada Nas, whose penchant for unguarded public utterances has become not only provocative but also nauseating, remarked that no candidates had put themselves forward for the election, meaning an

Abacha presidency was the only option. His words: "The political parties should on their own come together and draft him as their common candidate. The draft Constitution allows this".

Perhaps, Mr. Nas shares the notion that Nigerians suffer collective amnesia. Alternatively, his flight of fancy may derive from some delirium which leads to temporary loss of memory. Or how else can it be explained that it was Wada Nas who in April this year declared as illegal and unauthorized the various "Abacha-must-succeed-himself" campaigners and organizations? Indeed, no day passes in Nigeria without some political vermin squeaking for Abacha to succeed himself.

Mr. Nas, the all-knowing political fixer of Abacha's transition went on to denounce the groups as "phantom organizations" which have not only taken to a "futile flight of fancy" but constitute a serious threat to the political transition programme of the federal government as well as the sincerity of its avowed commitment to handing over to a democratically elected civilian administration in October 1998".

Wada Nas' volte-face, through a statement so puerile that a child could see through it, serves to complement the efforts of some duplicitous traditional rulers who in October called on Abacha to contest the 1998 election, and more importantly to prime Nigerians for the inevitable: the ascension of Abacha as a "democratically elected president". Talk about farce, political chicanery and mimicry and you may have just succeeded in diminishing the perfidy of Abacha and his bungling ministers. Abacha certainly is the most outrageously self-parodying ruler that Nigeria has ever had.

We do not need to look any further. The conspiracies that have been hatched in the past four years are ready to explode before our eyes. Those state functionaries who are campaigning for Abacha are no longer doing so under a shadowy political climate. They seem to have made it clear that the choice facing Nigerians is choosing Abacha as president or relinquishing their democratic aspirations, which essentially is no choice.

We should not doubt them for once. Abacha's transition is not only laughable; it has an in-built mechanism for chaos. With the winner of the June 12, 1993 presidential election, Chief Moshood Abiola, numerous pro-democracy and human rights activists and journalists in jail, and others in exile, Abacha has succeeded in neutralising a large section of the opposition. Since the credible opposition is not represented in Abacha's five political parties, all you have are political dandelions who dread even mentioning the word presidency much less declaring their interest in it.

Is it not surprising that less than a year to the presidential election, not one politician in a country of over a hundred million people with close to a century's experience in party politics, has come out to even declare his intention? For Wada Nas, this is not a blot on Abacha's bogus transition but a confirmation of Abacha's unsurpassed acceptance.

There is yet another game plan. With Abiola in prison, the country faces the intricacies of having two presidents. It does appear that it is only Abacha who can solve this riddle. And he has made this possible by making sure, according to Mr. Nas, that the draft constitution makes it possible that political parties could come together and draft Abacha as their common candidate.

It is instructive to note that three years after Abacha's puppets in the much pilloried constitutional conference presented the draft constitution to the largely ineffectual (except in doing Abacha's bidding) Provisional Ruling Council, the public has yet to know what it looks like or what it portends for them.

Yet in the midst of the treachery, the world gloats over Abacha's transition. At the just ended Commonwealth Heads of Government Meeting in Edinburgh, Scotland, Commonwealth heads of government could not convince themselves enough to declare Abacha and his regime a pariah, opting to give him one more year to complete his political hoax.

What justification is there for describing what is going on in Nigeria as a democratic transition? Certainly, nothing other than the fact that Abacha and his band of political masquerades have created a façade of democratic transition. Nigeria has not been able to hold credible elections in close to four decades of independence. We have not conducted an acceptable census – the simple act of counting human beings. Nothing has changed.

The situation cannot be any different now with the hiccups in Abacha's transition. It is even less plausible considering the fact that the only credible election in Nigeria – the June 12, 1993 presidential election – was annulled by a regime in which Abacha was the de facto second-in-command.

It is time to move Nigeria forward, away from the unmitigated incompetence of Abacha. We cannot afford to delay any further. The call to give Abacha time is nothing but a call to entrench autocracy. Just as the world stood up (except those whose hypocrisy could not be hidden by their economic interests) to repudiate Apartheid, the world must once again rise to the challenges of the bloodthirsty regime of Mr. Abacha. Just as Nigerians dispensed with the perfidious regime of Ibrahim Babangida, they must brace themselves up to confront the very last of the inglorious military regimes to rule Nigeria.

---

12. The Making of a Deity
December 1997

Gradually, but steadily, Nigeria's military ruler, Sani Abacha, is turning himself into a deity of sorts. The way he is going about it, Idi Amin, Bokassa, Mobutu and other bloodthirsty dictators in Africa will fade in comparison.

In the last one month, Nigerians have been treated to some of the most bizarre machinations of leadership. It started with Abacha's Minister of Special Duties, Wada Nas, calling on politicians to endorse Abacha as the next "democratically elected" president of Nigeria. His reasons: the constitution allows it; and nobody else appears interested in the presidency or is capable of ruling Nigeria.

Then came the introduction of "Abacha" brand television of a "businessman" who clearly was being propelled by the government. Since it is obvious that there is no better way our puny Samson can endear himself to Nigerians, it won't be difficult to appreciate the efforts of these imbecilic enthusiasts of Abacha succeeding himself.

However, Abacha's devoted pawns are not limited to business. Not long ago state governors were seen proudly parading Abacha badges. A few days before the dissolution of his cabinet, Abacha's morally delinquent ministers took out full-page advertisements in newspapers congratulating Abacha on his "good governance". Interestingly, to leave nobody in doubt about how indispensable he has become in the politics of Nigeria, Abacha used the occasion of the fourth anniversary (November 17) of his palace coup to launch the Sani Abacha Foundation for Peace and Justice.

What a name for an essentially propaganda outfit! Nobody is left in doubt that Nigeria is a land of chronic injustice; a country where peace is threatened because of the avarice and lust of power of one man: Sani Abacha. President-elect, Moshood Abiola, has been in prison since June 1994. Last month marked the second anniversary of the murder of minority rights activisit, Ken Saro-Wiwa, and eight of his compatriots. Numerous journalists, human rights and pro-democracy activists, including a former head of state are languishing in jails across Nigeria. What greater injustice or threat to peace can a people face?

Clearly, what Abacha is doing is to cloak his brutal dictatorship and his desire to succeed himself behind some democratic rhetoric and all the talk about transition and economic recovery. Of course, not many people take Abacha seriously. As one of Nigeria's authoritative news magazine, Tell, reported:

> *"In a political setting increasingly unfriendly to the tradition of free speech, the few politicians of clout still allowed to participate in the current transition have, in well-measured utterances, corroborated the open secret that Abacha is in the race for his present office".*

They have done so by simply abandoning the quest for the presidency even though Abacha has "assured" the world severally that he would hand over to a "democratically elected" president in October 1998. Sam Mbakwe, the ebullient former governor of Imo State, according to Tell magazine, "would have loved to run for the presidency were there a vacancy in Aso Rock", Abacha's official residence.

The tale of what is now referred to as the Etiebet Affair is worth retelling here. According to the magazine,

> *"Don Etiebet, a former oil minister under the Abacha administration and a friend of the general, had formed the National Centre Party of Nigeria (NCPN) on whose platform he had hoped to contest next year's presidential elections. His was the only party that did not endorse Abacha for president. The local government election was an opportunity to teach Etiebet a lesson or two".*
>
> *"His NCPN is said to have swept the polls in his constituency, the states of Cross River and Akwa Ibom. An announcement of the election results, in a move that was a replay of the June 12, 1993 presidential elections won by detained Moshood Abiola, was suspended. The next day, armed soldiers surrounded the local secretariat of the National Electoral Commission of Nigeria in Uyo, Akwa Ibom State, and hours later, the much-beloved United Nigeria Congress Party UNCP (which has endorsed Abacha) won the election.*
>
> *Etiebet was arrested and taken to Abuja where he was held hostage and his life threatened until he agreed to back out of his presidential ambition. To make the coup against him a complete success he was forced to renounce his membership of the NCPN, a party which he is said to have spent well over 100 million naira to establish and build nationally. He finally did the impossible: announce his membership of the UNCP!"*

Olusola Saraki, a senator in the Second Republic, says the magazine, valued his safety very much. Saraki once declared: "The issue (of contesting the presidential race) is in God's hands". Translation: only "God" (read Abacha) can determine who contests. Of course, the head of Nigeria's military junta is never tired of playing "God".

Abacha recently declared as "unfair and unacceptable the growing tendency by some members of the international community to target Africa and other parts of the developing world over alleged non compliance with their own perception of democracy and human rights".

It is bewildering and inexplicable that Abacha thinks it is proper to intervene militarily in Sierra Leone while at the same time denouncing those who merely make comments about his inhuman and murderous reign.

The only explanation, unfortunately, is that Abacha sees himself as a political deity.

---

13. BEFORE THEY SELECT OUR PRESIDENT
MARCH 1998

In this season of anomie, when the general feeling is to confine our ubiquitous generals to the barracks, there is a tendency to accept half measures, to look for the easy way out. What do I mean? It is simply that in our desire to end the cycle of military misrule we have unwittingly conceded too much ground to the military in deciding the shape of things to come; that is, the nature of post military democratic order. However, no combatant wins a war by conceding such grounds to the enemy.

This concession has, of course, created room for all manner of charlatans and political simpletons to aspire to rule Nigeria. I am not excited about the calibre of men who are positioning themselves to redeem the dilapidated Nigerian state. And I am sure many Nigerians share my lack of enthusiasm. Of course, at the end of the day, since we have left it to the military to decide, the next president will be that person the military high command trusts to defend its interest. Ask Babangida for clarification. However, before he does that, we can at least make that choice which nobody can deny us: expose the moral bankruptcy of some of those who aspire to rule us.

Virtually all politicians in the race for the presidency of this country carry with them an excess political baggage which when off-loaded shows that they care for this country, to paraphrase DeWayne Wickham, in much the same way that pimps care for their whores: just what they can get out of them. Are we going to have President Iwuanyanwu who thought Abacha was God's greatest gift to Nigeria? Or we should expect President Rimi, the renegade apostle of Talakawa (masses) politics who thinks that power shift is undemocratic – as if Nigeria as a country has any democratic basis – not because he genuinely believes it is, but because it will take the wind out of his feudal sails?

Will they give us President Falae, the unrepentant high priest of structural adjustment? Or President Saraki, another apostle of the Abacha-for-life campaign who has yet to explain his role as senate leader in the rot that was the Second Republic? It could be timorous President Etiebet who abandoned the party he established just not to be left out of Abacha's gravy train. Perhaps, they will settle for President Obasanjo whose anti-human rights record is nonpareil. Or President Ekwueme, former vice-president of the inglorious Second Republic, who thinks the idea of a Sovereign National Conference is meaningless?

Will we be saddled with President Akinjide whose only credential, apart from being the counsel of the National Party of Nigeria (NPN) in the infamous twelve two-third case twenty years ago, is that his romance with the North which dates back to the sixties has, in his own words, "blossomed over the years, culminating in my appointment as Justice Minister in the Second Republic"?

Of course, space will not allow a thorough analysis of the liabilities of these politicians; suffice it to say, however, that all the presidents-in-waiting have one thing in common: they do not think Nigeria has problems beyond their assumption of the presidency. There is, however, a voice of reason among this babel of presidential voices: that of the redoubtable Chief Bola Ige. After Chief Obafemi Awolowo, Chief Ige's political mentor, no politician has been so courageous and forthright in addressing the problems of Nigeria.

Reading Chief Ige's speech titled "Towards the Beckoning Glory of the 21st Century" rekindled hope that at least there are politicians who have solutions to Nigeria's myriad of problems. Chief Ige understands and is bold to admit that one of the greatest problems facing Nigeria today is the internal colonialism confronting its peoples; the murder of fellow Nigerians, particularly in the Niger Delta, by those who think they have a monopoly of violence. I crave the indulgence of readers to quote Chief Ige extensively:

> *"Let me now raise fundamental issues that must be addressed and tackled in the first twelve months of our Presidency and which undergirds everything I have hitherto spoken about. There are two basic questions that must be answered by all of us Nigerians. One, do we want to remain as one country? Two, if the answer is yes, under what conditions? These are the questions being asked by the angry Ijaw youth, the jobless Yoruba graduate, the disconsolate Kano businessman and the marginalized Igbo youth. I believe strongly that most Nigerians would want Nigeria to continue as one country. What is in contention is on what terms. I know that we have a duty to address the conditions under which we must live together...I believe strongly that we need to answer the question: on what terms do we to live together?*
>
> *"This is necessary for two main reasons. One, Nigeria was not conquered by the British as Nigeria, but as separate independent states. In pre-colonial Nigeria, to take an example, the Oba of Benin was the sovereign of the Benin Kingdom. He held the powers of the head of state and government, conducting treaties, waging wars and governing his people according to the tradition and constitution of the Bini people. Then Benin was conquered and when Nigeria became independent, the sovereign right of the Bini people was not restored. Only two weeks ago, the Military Administrator of Edo State, peopled mainly by the subjects of the Oba of Benin, suspended the Oba from*

the traditional council. I do not want to go into the merit of that case. But, this is only an indication that the Oba of Benin is no longer a sovereign and the power that suspended him was not elected by the Edo people. Second, we should not shy away from the reality that the Nigerian people had no say in the creation of Nigeria. That was entirely the outcome of British colonial conquest. But we must make the very best of our situation.

"By the time the military leaves next May, we should take steps to hold a Conference appropriately designated to examine the state of the union. Every nationality, no matter its size, big or small, must be represented. We need to have a new Act of the Union that would form the bedrock of the new Nigerian Commonwealth. Unless this is done, the future of Nigeria is bleak. I do not belong to the group of Nigerians deluding themselves that we can keep Nigeria forever as it is. I am not a subscriber to Operation Fool the Nation, OFN.

"I am a realistic optimist. That is why I feel sorry for my colleagues in the People's Democratic Party, PDP, who think nothing has changed. They do not know, or they refuse to know, that June 12 and the martyrdom of Abiola have changed the face of Nigeria forever. They don't know that the crisis of the Niger Delta is one of the outcomes of the June 12 crisis. I do not want to consider the alternative. The truth of the matter is that Nigeria has no future except the nationality question is answered. We have a duty to Nigeria to save her and rescue her from the hands of philistines".

I subscribe to Chief Ige's vision; that is why I have taken great pains to quote him elaborately. However, I do not share his illusion. What is this illusion? It is the belief that we can reconstruct Nigeria on the foundation laid by the military. There couldn't be a more dangerous misconception. According to Chief Ige,

> "We have learnt not to compromise principle for temporary gains and not play politics for expedient and short-term considerations. We are not only working to end military rule; we are on the threshold of a new decade, a new century and a new millennium. We are participating in politics, (read Abubakar's transition) not because we believe the military is right in setting rules for democratic practice, a job for which they are not qualified, but because we are duty bound to encourage the military to leave power and assume their traditional role of protecting the citizens of Nigeria, their employers, instead of ruling them".

Fine polemic. However, we cannot in a bid to "encourage" the military to leave power give them carte blanche the right to decide the outcome of the new order. To do that is to abdicate our responsibility; it is to concede our inalienable rights to the military; it is to lay the foundation for chaos and engender the quick return of the military. For in the end, whoever emerges as president is duty bound to defend the deleterious decrees and unseen constitution which the military, at its convenience, will foist on Nigerians.

If we desire a new order, we must be ready and willing to secure it through political action no matter the opposition from the military. Was it not Frederick Douglas who said, "Those who profess to favour freedom, and yet deprecate agitation, are men who want crops without plowing up the ground; they want rain without thunder and lightning; they want the ocean without the awful roar of its many waters". The present regime has already shown that it is up to no good by releasing a decree that limits the powers of state governors in the so-called new political dispensation.

Our politicians, and I mean those that can be taken seriously, must appreciate the need to consider other options beyond the convulsive measures that the military has decreed. In this regard, there are very limited choices. It is either the military at the behest of civil society agrees to initiate the process of a government of national unity and ultimately a Sovereign National Conference or civil society takes the initiative to secure the kind of society it wants.

There can be no half measures, no compromises.

14. ABACHA'S BLITZKRIEG
MAY 1998

The harrowing events of the last one month are generally expected. Specifically, I refer to the April 15 and May 1 massacre of pro-democracy activists in Ibadan, the subsequent arrest of dozens of activists and the death sentences and various terms of imprisonment handed down by the secret military tribunal headed by Gen. Victor Malu whose exploits in Liberia have become a nightmare for citizens of that country.

Undoubtedly, by the time you read this piece, those detained allegedly for leading the Ibadan protests would have appeared in court, charged with all manner of criminal offences. They would be lucky to escape the Saro-Wiwa experience; certainly not when some of them have already been tagged "prisoners of war". It wasn't a slip of the tongue by whoever uttered it. Abacha and his cohorts are waging a war against Nigerians.

It is not beyond the regime to try the detained activists for offences that attract life imprisonment or death as penalty. While that war is being fought on that front, the ritual – that is, the regular pilgrimage to Abuja to grease the ego of the "strong man" – would have started to ensure that Abacha does not supervise another round of bloodletting by ordering the execution of Gen. Diya and his alleged co-conspirators.

It is instructive that the fate of Diya and others now rests on the whims of one man, even when the Provisional Ruling Council, supposedly the highest decision making organ of the Abacha regime, has given its own verdict. About a decade ago, Russian author, Dmitri Volkogonov, made what can be described as a quintessential assessment of the psychological build-up of dictators. Prior to the publication of his book, *Stalin: The Triumph and the Tragedy*, which was a political profile of Joseph Stalin, he was asked to draw a parallel between the lives of dictatorial figures he came across during his research and the life of the subject of his book: Stalin.

This is his reply: "At some stage, people wielding unlimited and uncontrolled power come to regard themselves as infallible, to believe that no constraints apply to them and that anything they do is predestined. They need no advice, no one dares to question their actions, and they do not have to justify them to anyone. Any decision taken by such a ruler is glorified". This is the situation in Nigeria today under the country's maximum ruler.

Of course, it is not for nothing that the Abacha regime is becoming increasingly repressive. The reason is simple: no military regime has trod the road of perdition which this regime is treading in such a brazen manner. And Abacha knows that the only way he can prosecute his illusion is to silence as many people as possible through death, and imprison as many as his prisons can accommodate.

Those who still harbour the illusion that the days ahead will witness a subdued onslaught against pro-democracy and human rights activists only diminish the capacity of the Abacha regime for blood spilling. Like the Atlantic sharks during centuries of the Trans-Atlantic Slave Trade, this regime has "acquired more of a taste for blood" than any other military regime in Nigeria's chequered history.

Interestingly, the ubiquitous vermin, Daniel Kanu, of the infamous Youth Earnestly Ask for Abacha (YEAA) '98, and others like him, are already laying the foundation for the much-expected blood bath. Kanu and his duplicitous followers who represent the very worst of Nigerian youth have promised to make Nigeria ungovernable if Abacha does not succeed himself.

Also in this enterprise of presaging anarchy and bloodbath is the mealy-mouthed political contractor, Godwin Daboh, who thinks that only Abacha can bring "genuine and lasting democracy" to Nigeria. Recently, in an interview with the Voice of America, Daboh observed that there was nothing wrong if the blood of Nigerians flowed to nurture this dubious political transition.

These and other separate, though related events, provide the groundwork for what to expect in the next few months. Abacha's antecedent is a ready insight to the impending blitzkrieg. As the defence minister in the no less iniquitous regime of Gen. Ibrahim Babangida, Abacha, in July 1993, supervised the slaughter of more than 200 Nigerians who were protesting the annulment of the June 12, 1993 presidential election.

It was also on the bidding of the military high command that Abacha's protégés, Lt. Col. Dauda Komo and Major Paul Okutimo, supervised the "wasting operations" in Ogoniland which culminated in the hanging of environmentalist, Ken Saro-Wiwa and eight of his compatriots. Clearly, in line with his dictatorial proclivities, Abacha has turned the Nigerian Army and security apparatuses into mercenary forces and the guardsmen of iniquity whose only allegiance is to himself; and as long as he can, he would use these organs to glorify any decision he takes.

Those who care to think back would remember how Abacha's armed forces conducted unprovoked bombardment of Mabella and Magazine Wharf in the east end of Freetown on September 4, 1997, and the subsequent attacks on other areas of the city, killing, maiming and mutilating innocent civilians in their unsolicited and clearly hypocritical desire to restore democracy to Sierra Leone.

Why did Abacha's soldiers slaughter defenceless civilians in Sierra Leone? Why were pro-democracy activists massacred on two occasions in less than one month in Ibadan? The answer lies in the psychology of dictators. Abacha believes that no constraints apply to him and that everything he does is predestined. Perhaps, it is for this reason also that the nation will soon witness another presumably divine directive; that is, the confirmation of Abacha as the next civilian president of Nigeria.

As far as this regime is concerned, human life has no value. On the contrary, power means everything and the end justifies the means in this maniacal quest for power. This descent to barbarism engendered by despotism of the most archetypal form has often occasioned discussion about brutalities spawned by dictatorial figures in history. In the wake of the death of Pol Pot, one of the most brutal mass murderers this century has witnessed, someone was quick to liken

Nigeria's military ruler to the deceased former ruler of Cambodia.

Of course, the comparison matched in more ways than one; more than anything else, they share the same pedigree as bloody dictators. Pol Pot, like Abacha, also believed that whatever he did was predestined and in the interest of Cambodians. However, the reference is also a reminder of the reality of the words of G.W.F Hegel': "What experience and history teach is this – that people and government never have learned anything from history, or acted on principles deduced from it".

There are enough reasons to believe that Abacha is set to run Nigeria in the same manner in which his forbears – Hitler, Idi-Amin, Bokassa, and, of course, Pol Pot – tried but failed. And since he is incapable of learning from history, he surely will be another victim of history.

---

15. Abacha's Tragic End
June 1998

History casts very long shadows". At last, Africa's number one outlaw has gone the way of all tyrants: "They either die unsung or are chased out of office". It is inevitable. Very few people will mourn Gen. Abacha; fewer still will be shocked that he died; except, of course, the millions who would have wished to see him go on trial for his crimes against the Nigerian people.

Abacha sought power and relished it. Unfortunately, when he needed power most, it eluded him. About two weeks ago, he was expected in Nigeria's commercial capital, Lagos, a city he had not visited and could not visit for four years. A week to his visit, Lagos was paralyzed by his security apparatuses. It was an opportunity for Abacha to assert himself by defying the anticipated affront of Lagosians to his five years of misrule.

To the chagrin of the state military administrator, the effete general did not show up. The just-ended OAU Summit in Burkina Faso was another chance for Abacha to showcase himself after his triumphal entry into Sierra Leone, but as much as he would have loved to, he could not defy death.

Although he was in poor health, Abacha clung to power. He knew he was in the throes of death, but he did not want to go down alone. He wanted Nigeria and Nigerians to be part of his descent to the abyss. It is a measure of his depravity that even at the point of death, he never imagined a successor.

It was not for nothing that Abacha bore the tag "Africa's No 1 outlaw". When he seized power on November 17, 1993, he promised a quick return to democratic rule; but that was not to be. In the five years that he reigned, Nigeria witnessed an archetype of military despotism which marks the period as the cruelest and most shameful period of her national history.

This allusion to Abacha's brutal rule is not overdrawn; neither is the epithet that he was the most vicious and most corrupt ruler in the history of Nigeria. Abacha mindlessly engraved his name on the plaque of notorious dictators. Under Abacha, Nigeria became an absolute police state. He declared war on every aspect of the nation without batting an eyelid. The bestiality of his regime knew no frontiers. He unleashed wanton viciousness and terror. The press was shackled and citizens jailed and assassinated indiscriminately.

The squirming general had hoped to secure diplomatic points when he charged pro-democracy activists for treason last year. Such half-witted political manoeuvres like his incursion into Sierra Leone were meant as face-saving measures for his illegal regime. In a characteristic fascist manner, Abacha's internal security task force prowled the precincts of minority ethnic nationalities, mowing down defenceless citizens in an orgy of violence. Decrees of every imaginable garb were rolled out daily by the supreme commander to strengthen his insatiable quest for power.

Abacha was the quintessence of Nigerian generals who, in the words of Randall Robinson,

> *"Govern to steal and steal to govern. They talk of elections with no real commitment to hold them. They talk of de-*

mocracy with no notion of the freedoms implied. Their parameters for governance are set at the fore and aft opportunity points for self-enrichment: power achieved not to render public service, but only to steal as much as possible for as long as possible. The generals are so well beyond accountability as to make hypocrisy unnecessary".

While the Nigerian State reeled in tyranny and a state of total collapse and, of course, further away from democracy, Abacha launched his transition programme. For a man who was set to self-destruct, he flew the kite of self-perpetuation. Not given to serious mental efforts, Abacha constructed the most disingenuous transition the world has ever witnessed. The idea of democracy was simply beyond him; and neither logic nor common sense, no matter how common, was a tool of governance. It was not for him to be circumspect on national problems – which more often than not he did not understand. He was simply an embodiment of brute force.

In 1995 and late last year, his regime concocted coups. Those shameless ploys were made for two reasons: first, the regime had the opportunity of turning its opponents to felons and jailing them. It is difficult to understand why Abacha who gloated over bloodletting did not carry out the execution of the coup plotters. Second, the coup palaver had the effect of steering national discourse from pertinent issues.

For a long time, Nigerians engaged themselves in intellectual gymnastics as to the veracity or rationality of the claims. These diversions, chicanery and treachery were necessary to keep Abacha in power. Nigerians have nothing to show for Abacha's five years of maniacal reign other than impoverishment and the denial of their basic democratic and fundamental human rights.

Now that Abacha is no more, those who had ranted "no Abacha, no Nigeria" or had hoped that without Abacha succeeding himself Nigeria would grind to a halt must accept that they have become irrelevant. Of course, the scum that they are, it may not be long before they create another monster if only to eke out a living from the new power-besotted generals.

However, if Nigeria ceases to exist, it would not be because of the lack of fortitude on the part of the citizens, but because of the rapacious profligacy and wantonness of Abacha and the generals who have stepped into his ignoble shoes. But, the flame of democracy in Nigeria cannot be extinguished because of the irresponsible and repressive actions of a degenerate bunch of generals.

Nigeria has got to a stage where these generals should be confronted with a fait accompli. The legality of the present regime – that is, if it has any – must cease on October 1, the day the military junta under Abacha freely elected to hand over power to a democratic government. From then onwards, this regime becomes persona non grata as far as the governance of Nigeria is concerned.

It does not have to worry about securing time for election. There is an elected president who is spending his fourth year in detention. Nigeria can move on from there with the convocation of a Sovereign National Conference of the genuine representatives of the various nationalities in Nigeria to discuss the geopolitical future of the country.

It is often said that Africans do not speak ill of the dead, but nobody will doubt that Abacha's death was, to use a cliché, good riddance to bad rubbish; and no epitaph could be better than that written last year by the Association of Nigerians Abroad:

> *"We shall create a museum in memory of your dastardly reign. So that the world may never forget. So that our children may never forget".*

---

16. KOFI ANNAN'S DIPLOMATIC GAFFE
JULY 1998

Since the death of Gen. Sani Abacha and the assumption of supreme power by the new self-appointed ruler in Nigeria, the ranks of those who have taken interest in the Nigerian debacle have expanded to include all manner of political jobbers. We have seen the

Wada Nases and Ebenezer Babatopes, people who contributed in no small way to the heinous agenda Abacha attempted to foist on Nigeria, recanting and calling for new attitudes and ways to "move Nigeria forward".

Perhaps the most tragic aspect of this doublespeak is the attitude of the international community so-called. The suddenness with which the international community, represented by the European Union, the Commonwealth and the United Nations, is embracing the remnants of the mendacious generals who have misruled Nigeria for 28 years leaves much to be desired.

The sickening hypocrisy of the representatives of these organizations leaves one wondering how they think they can run the world on injustice and double standards. Well, they have managed to do just that. Liberia, Sierra Leone, Kosovo, and more recently Guinea-Bissau, are clear examples.

Some people say the gestures of the new military rulers in Nigeria may have spurred the current position of the Kofi Annans and Emeka Anyaokus. Of course, except they are victims of collective amnesia, it is not difficult to remember that former dictators, Ibrahim Babangida and the late Sani Abacha started by releasing political detainees. Indeed, the present regime whose existence, like that before it, has no basis in law, is doing nobody any favour by releasing political detainees. It is only wiping the slate clean to give it enough space for its own equally dubious script.

For five years, Abacha held Nigerians hostage and the best Nigerians got from Kofi Annan was undignified silence while Emeka Anyaoku became adept at inconsistent outbursts. Why did they not make efforts to stop Abacha? It was not in the interest of their masters in Washington and London to do so. Clearly, no matter how the West, particularly the United States and Britain, hated Abacha for his excesses, it is conscious of the fact that only the military can guarantee its iniquitous grip on Nigeria. So it wasn't necessary for a Kofi Annan or Emeka Anyaoku to persuade Abacha to change his mind. Now, they have to be on their guard to prevent the new military regime from losing grip.

It is not for nothing that Anyaoku is deeply involved in the fresh shenanigans to subvert the popular will of Nigerians. Of course, he once believed that Abacha was pursuing a credible transition programme and ought to have been given a chance. So, the less said about him the better. My grouse is with the new henchman (they both are really) of imperialism.

Kofi Annan's manifesto which calls on Abiola to renounce his mandate is an open cheque for the military to continue riding roughshod over Nigerians. It is also in line with the thinking of the American establishment as echoed by President Bill Clinton during his six-nation Africa tour in March. It is not surprising for a man who owes his position to the benevolence of the same establishment.

Echoing the feeling in Washington has become his forte. His prescriptions for Africa's economic recovery tell it all. As one writer put it:

> "Those who chanced upon UN Secretary General, Kofi Annan's recent report on Africa's ills, requested by the UN Security Council...could be forgiven for thinking it was written by President Bill Clinton on behalf of the US corporate elite".

Annan recommended deregulation and the privatization of state-controlled industries and denounced the role of military forces in African states. Yet he failed to remind us that virtually all military regimes in Africa have had support from Washington or were the creation of his masters in the White House. Understandably, after four years in solitary confinement with bare medical care and not too certain whether pro-democracy forces will back him to the hilt, Abiola may decide not to play Mandela and acquiesce to the overtures of the military over- lords backed by their international hatchet men.

In that case, he loses every moral right to seek a fresh mandate from Nigerians, as advocated by Tom Ikimi, the official spokesman of tyranny. One is not making excuses here, but these are very grave possibilities. If that happens, the new military chaperon should not claim any moral victory. And the reason is simple: as long as the June 12 issue is not resolved on the side of justice, Nigeria cannot start on the road to nation building.

Of course, the June 12, 1993 election would have defined the face of the new Nigeria: a nation unencumbered by the fettering vestiges of feudalism and colonialism. People simply fail to see the issues at stake or if they do, they tend to gloss over it. The reality is that on June 12, 1993, the masses made a very fundamental political statement which confounded our power-besotted rulers.

What is this fundamental political statement? It is simply that Nigeria's impoverished and forgotten masses were able to overcome the bogey of ethnicity and religious deceit by the ruling class and show that these are weapons in the hand of this inglorious class to maintain its stranglehold on the country. Whether Abiola holds on to that mandate or not is gradually becoming unimportant. Progressive forces opposed to these twin evils and many other cankers that have spawned destruction, destitution and death in Nigeria, will not renege on their struggle until the dawn of a new and positive era.

Those who diminish June 12 seem to have a permanent fixation about Abiola and what he does or does not represent and they are now given to the utterly absurd contention that Abiola is not the messiah or that the tenure of his mandate has elapsed. However, the conservative political class and the international community must understand that the military poses the greatest threat to Nigeria's corporate existence; that every day the military stays in power diminishes the prospect of rescuing what is left of Nigeria.

Undoubtedly, those who call for a transitional government of national unity to be headed by Abiola do so with the conviction that beyond its prospect of engendering national reconciliation, the highly ethnic and unprofessional military is incapable of being a midwife of democracy in Nigeria.

More important is the fact that the problem with Nigeria, a country where no census has been conducted "without sheep and goats raising eyebrows", is not all about election. It is also about the geopolitical imbalance that has created internal colonies within a neo-colony; about the rapacious misconduct of multinationals in league with the Nigerian state.

An interim government made up of genuine representatives of

interest groups in Nigeria to really discuss which way Nigerians want Nigeria to go remains the best concession these forces of reaction can get; for as Annan would agree, when armed bandits decide to rob you of your right, you have no choice but to retrieve that right by any means, including the use of arms.

17. The General in a Labyrinth
October 1998

There is a rising chorus by Western leaders which borders on the acceptance of Nigeria's purported march to democracy. The reasons, notwithstanding how devious they are, are understandable.

More than any ruler before him, the new maximum ruler in Nigeria, Abdulsalami Abubakar, has demonstrated that he is capable of securing oil concessions on behalf of the West and safeguarding "big business". All this, however, is in spite of the clamour by Nigerians for a Sovereign National Conference to oversee a restructuring of the "geographical expression" called Nigeria, and the conviction that the problem with Nigeria is not ballot-box democracy – at least, June 12 1993, proved this point.

Two phenomena explain the latest hopeless situation Nigerians have found themselves. One is the arms morality of international politics. This pernicious doctrine states that persuasion count for little in people's quest for liberty, justice, and freedom; that until you bear arms, nobody, including those who have turned talking about liberty, justice, and freedom into a favourite pastime will listen, much less come to your aid.

Abubakar's transition, therefore, is being hyped up far beyond its worth by the West not because they believe he can restore democracy to Nigeria – after all, they also believed Abacha really wanted to put Nigeria on the democratic path. The only reason the West has adopted Abubakar and is supporting him against Nigerians is that he controls the means of coercion. Of course, taking sides with dictators is the only way the West can maintain its stranglehold on the local market.

The second is that the shenanigans of the military in Nigeria – unnoticed by far too many who are blinded by their selfish interests and others who cling to the illusion that the military can restore democracy – have become enduring. Soldiers, particularly the type bred in Nigeria, are indeed a curious lot. Just three months ago, Abubakar was the chief of defence staff of one of the most iniquitous regimes in human history.

He and his colleagues participated in the mayhem perpetrated by the Abacha regime; they watched with glee as Abacha tore apart the fabric of the Nigerian society; as he destroyed real and imaginary opponents. They were ready and would have actually helped him in his self-succession bid. All that is now history, according to those who think it is their prerogative to dictate the rules of democracy in Nigeria. Today, Abubakar is the messiah. You are expected to take this political skullduggery as a fait accompli or be termed a trouble-maker and an enemy of democracy.

Abubakar's latest manoeuvres stem from the same age-old psychological warfare which the military has visited on Nigerians. After going through Abacha's murderous reign – which Abubakar contributed to significantly – who would not welcome a reprieve, even if it comes from the devil? This partly explains why, in the past, coups had a soporific effect on Nigerians. It was visible after Murtala Muhammed overthrew the profligate regime of Gowon in 1975; we saw it when Babangida and Abacha toppled the high-handed regime of Buhari/Idiagbon in 1985 only to unleash greater terror on Nigerians subsequently.

Of course, Abubakar would not have made an impression and everybody would have seen through his facade if on assumption of office he did not order the release of political prisoners, all of whom were held without charge or trial. How would he have set out implementing his agenda if he did not extend an olive branch to the opposition? How would he have taken full charge of the nation and its vast resources if he did not sound as the great conciliator? The important thing, however, is not meeting with what the military has often referred to as "various interest groups and shades of opinion". What is important is rejecting whatever advice or genuine suggestions these highly expendable groups may proffer.

Abubakar believed in Abacha. He said that much during his October 1 speech when he surmised that the military had always taken power in the interest of the nation. Such weasel words have become the refrain of the military whose main interest has always been to divide and rule by playing upon the psyche of Nigerians. Whose interest were Abacha and his cohorts representing when they looted the treasury and cannibalized Nigerians?

We really must have two nations in Nigeria – the nation of the military and that of civilians. It is not surprising that in his tough talk and so-called house cleaning, Abubakar has said nothing critical of Abacha or his regime. That certain individuals are being exposed for their alleged corruption should not stir our blood. Abacha would have done the same. After all, scoundrels like Umaru Dikko, Uba Ahmed, Adisa Akinloye, and Joseph Wayas who led the government that Abacha overthrew in 1983 were heroes of his transition programme.

Having, in partnership with Abacha, completed the destruction of everything Nigerians hold sacred, Abubakar has taken over and is singing a lullaby in the name of transition to democracy. He wants to send Nigerians to sleep, to forget the past and renounce their agitation for a genuine and worthwhile political transition. Regrettably, Abubakar is yet to explain his complicity in Abacha's murderous regime.

The country is still waiting for him to explain his role in Abiola's murder; to tell Nigerians who killed Pa Alfred Rewane, Kudirat Abiola, Shehu Yar'adua, and journalists: Bagauda Kaltho, Chinedu Ofoaro and Tunde Oladepo; who ordered the extermination programme code named "wasting operations" in Ogoniland; and of course, who orchestrated the many phantom coups that were meant to quarantine officers from a section of the country.

As part of the psychological warfare against Nigerians, Abubakar – knowing that the military has sufficiently primed Nigerians along ethnic lines – is sure that chaos will be the hallmark of the transition programme he is foisting on Nigerians. If what we hear and read that the political class in the South insists that the next president of Nigeria MUST come from the South – a development that undermines the essence of democracy – then Abubakar's future in Aso Rock, Nigeria's power base, is guaranteed.

Abubakar knows that the ultraconservative political class in the North, in whose service he is and for whom he is nothing but a tool, will not accede to the principle of rotating the presidency of Nigeria, which the political class in the South naively thinks is the panacea to Nigeria's political crisis. He knows that Nigerians will boycott his sham elections and that it will take nothing to overthrow any government put in place by the military notwithstanding his anti-coup rhetoric.

Alternatively, Abubakar may design a constitution – the trump card of the military – that whittles down the power of the president while creating new levers of power. Whatever he does, the aim remains the same: to ensure his continuity or that of any other person the military subclass will throw up.

If Abubakar is interested in addressing the Nigerian crisis, all he has to do is put in place structures that will guarantee a stable polity and by extension democracy. The mere fact that he has done everything to the contrary shows that Abubakar cannot be taken seriously. His tactics can be likened to the bikini syndrome: "what is revealed is interesting; what is concealed is more so". For a man who has barely seven months to leave office, Abubakar's public relations gimmicks leave much to be desired.

The fact that he is roaming the world begging for recognition goes to show that Abubakar has yet to unfold his agenda. What the so-called international community – which is grieving more than the bereaved as far as Abubakar's topsy-turvy transition programme is concerned – must realize is that Nigerians have come to the conclusion that the military, a patently corrupt and undemocratic institution, whether under the control of an Abacha or Abubakar, cannot restore democracy in Nigeria.

The world is indeed an unfair place to judge Abacha and Abubakar differently; and those who are consorting and parleying with

Abubakar, massaging his ego and making him feel he has a moral or even legal right to govern are nothing but accomplices in the tragedy that is inevitable because the prefect-general will not emerge from this labyrinth.

---

18. THE WRONG MAN
NOVEMBER 1998

I am not very comfortable with religiosity; and the reason is simple. As one writer put it,

> *"Religion has a way of validating many of the crimes against humanity. All too often, many a deluded crank inflicts heart-wrenching tragedies on society in defence or propagation of one religion or another".*

Equally, more often than not, people mask their folly under some religious apparel, purporting to be under divine control when embarking on personal misadventure. The renewed presidential ambition of Gen. Olusegun Obasanjo (retd.), Nigeria's former head of state, started on this religious note.

Shortly after his release from Abacha's dungeon, the self-styled born-again general told a bewildered nation that if it was the will of God he would contest the supposed presidential election in Nigeria next February. Initially, many thought such a nugatory idea was mere wishful thinking or part of the general's well-known witticism. Then, in a final act of self-absorption, the retired general announced, a few days ago, his ambition to rule Nigeria again, 20 years after he vacated the same post.

Of course, Nigerians are quite familiar with these spiritual interventions. It was the will of some god somewhere that the June 12, 1993 presidential election should be annulled. This same god willed that Abacha should seize power and unleash mayhem on Nigerians; that the new overlord, Gen Abdulsalami Abubakar, should assume control after Abacha expired. Obasanjo himself was thrown into jail because this god willed it. Now, this same god has sanctioned Obasanjo for the position of president in Abubakar's so-called transition to democracy. I seriously doubt if such a god exists anywhere. However, that is neither here nor there. What matters is that the general is determined to rule again.

Obviously, considering the hue and cry that has trailed the Obasanjo-for-president declaration, a lot of people find fault with his ambition; and expectedly, many have vowed to put up resistance against it, even to the point of death. Their grievances against Obasanjo are legion.

Personally, I think every right thinking person should be concerned about the Obasanjo-for-president hullabaloo; for nothing is more appalling than to watch someone self-destruct. So what is it that people have against Obasanjo that makes him unsuitable for the presidency of Nigeria at this crucial juncture?

Pro-democracy groups insist Obasanjo has an unabashed dislike for democratic processes. They say he is not a democrat; that he has never been. They point to the twelve two-third debacle in which Obasanjo surreptitiously handed power over to a civilian government that did not win the 1979 presidential election going by the electoral provision that to be declared winner, a candidate must win in 13 states. Under Obasanjo, Nigerian legal luminaries created history when they proved that twelve two-third and 13 are the same thing.

These pro-democracy groups and their allies are quick to point to the infamous "Abiola is not the messiah" testimony which was Obasanjo's own way of dismissing Abiola's victory on June 12, 1993, and upholding the subsequent annulment of the election. Obasanjo may have believed that Alhaji Shehu Shagari was the real messiah that was why he handed power over to him in 1979 even though it was clear he (Shagari) did not win the presidential election of that year. For pro-democracy activists, if Abiola was not the messiah, certainly Obasanjo is the wrong man. For them, there is no difference between an Obasanjo presidency and the tragedy of Abacha's abortive self-succession plan.

Human rights activists speak of the many violations of human rights under the regime of Gen Obasanjo. Of particular interest to them is the first penal colony in the history of Nigeria, the notorious Ita Oko outpost, created by Obasanjo. Academics also have reasons to be opposed to the Obasanjo-for-president bandwagon. It was during his reign that they suffered the first serious attack on academic freedom – the era of "teachers not teaching what they were paid to teach" which led to the dislocation of many academics. Out of frustration, many sought greener pastures overseas, while others simply gave up academic life.

Students, of course, are not left out in the anti Obasanjo-for-president hysteria. Those in tertiary institutions, the most vocal group yet, have gone to town with a litany of complaints. Most of them remember that their first contact with gun-toting soldiers was during Obasanjo's regime when soldiers were drafted to maintain discipline in secondary schools. However, that is not their greatest worry.

They have not lost sight of the fact that the worst student demonstration – in terms of opposition from the government and casualties – in the history of Nigeria took place under Obasanjo whose regime launched a fierce attack on students that saw the proscription of the umbrella organisation of students, the National Union of Nigerian Students (NUNS).

Those concerned about financial impropriety say it was during Obasanjo's regime that Nigeria witnessed her first major financial scandal: the 2.8 billion naira proceeds from oil sale allegedly flown out in a presidential jet. Labour and workers have their own grudge, while journalists are vexed by Obasanjo's attitude towards them, exemplified in alleged cases of assault and the menacing signpost at his Ota Farm haven – the only visible legacy of Obasanjo's disastrous "Operation Feed the Nation" programme – which expressly bars journalists.

"Puritans" proclaim Obasanjo is not a stable family man, whatever that means. They argue that he is not reliable and cannot keep his words. They point to his "I won't join any political party" vow made about two decades ago and the more recent "I have been to the highest as a head of state and to the lowest as a prisoner, there is nothing left to aspire to" declaration.

On a humorous, but no less serious note, Obasanjo (thanks to pepper soup and Gulder Lager beer) has been described as the first publicly confirmed case of a Nigerian army officer to have developed a potbelly. The potbelly so irritated Afrobeat maestro, Fela Anikulapo-Kuti, that, in one of his many songs, he decried it as a menace to good governance.

These humorists remind us that just a few years ago, in a mordant critique of his predecessor in office, another born-again general, who had incredibly planned a comeback, Obasanjo was quick to warn against the futility of such an exercise with his sarcastic question: "What did he forget in the state house?" Is it possible that Obasanjo forgot his hoe? They also remind us that as a mark of his seriousness, Obasanjo, at the height of the anti-apartheid struggle, when the *gendarmes* of apartheid went berserk, advocated juju as a means of liberating black South Africans.

There are those who contend that they are not surprised that the evil genius of Nigerian politics, Ibrahim Badamosi Babangida, (IBB) is supporting, and even funding, the Obasanjo-for-president campaign. Birds of a feather, they say, flock together. Some extend their distaste for this unholy alliance a bit further by positing that, knowing the records of IBB, it is not impossible that the campaign in support of Obasanjo is a ploy to derail the already hamstrung transition. It is the view of this group that the power-besotted rulers in the North have come to the conclusion that if they must relinquish power, then it must go to one of their kind, in this case Obasanjo; if for nothing, at least to compensate for his effort in making Shagari president.

External watchers argue that like all military dictators, Obasanjo is unrepentantly anti-democracy, and that he won't be different from the many military rulers on the west coast of Africa who transmute into civilian presidents and whose brand of democracy is no more than glorified military dictatorship; that Obasanjo will – he showed these signs as far back as 1978 – implement structural adjustment, devaluation, privatization and other anti-people policies that have made these village tyrants in West Africa parading as statesmen the darling boys of the IMF/World Bank and the West .

Even the clerics are worried. For them the voice Obasanjo heard that echoed "run, Obasanjo, run" which he has interpreted to mean he has been sanctified for the presidency could also mean "Obasanjo run away" from the presidency. Not surprisingly, Biafran nationalists say they won't forgive Obasanjo for his mopping-up operations in the eastern part of the country at the end of the civil war, a war that was fought ostensibly to seek control of Nigeria's vast oil fields. Ethnic jingoists say they can't trust Obasanjo, who in what seemed to be a grand design to maintain the dubious record as the only Egba and Yoruba man to rule Nigeria, showed no sympathy when the presidential election won by his kinsman, the late Chief M. K. O. Abiola, was annulled.

Agitators for ethnic self-determination are of the view that the Nigeria Obasanjo will inherit, assuming his ambition comes to fruition, is one totally polarized and suffused with irreconcilable contradictions; and that since Obasanjo, avowedly anti-democracy, does not believe in the basic democratic principle which guarantees groups the right to self-determination, he will definitely crack down on this group of Nigerians. Obasanjo's land use decree fiasco which deprived many nationalities of their land and its resources by handing them over to an omnipotent but insensitive federal government is another sore point.

Finally, there are those who are of the opinion that Obasanjo has neither the inclination nor ability to be president. Why do they say this? They point to his book titled *Not my Will* in which he stated that it was not his will to be head of state in 1976. Twenty-two years after, they argue, he still cannot make up his mind; he has to seek spiritual intervention or wait for the nudging hands of power brokers in the North before he makes up his mind to vie for president.

It appears every aspect of the Nigerian society has a bone to pick with Gen. Obasanjo over his ambition. However, when ambition becomes a disease, how do you cure it? Someone has argued that if in just three years in office (1976-1979) the retired general has a record which makes Abacha's misrule look like a birthday party, then, Obasanjo must reconsider his ambition, or better still the diabolic intentions of those who are prodding him to contest for president.

It is not impossible that Obasanjo, in the tradition of his alter ego, IBB, will publicly apologize for his actions. That is left for him and the gods to decide. The only lesson I can draw from this Obasanjo-for-president campaign is this: those, as the saying goes, the gods want to destroy they first make mad.

❖

19. Saro-Wiwa: Three Years After
November 1998

"When I decided to take the words to the streets, to mobilize the Ogoni people and empower them to protest the devastation of their environment by SHELL, and their denigration and dehumanization by Nigerian military dictatorship, I had no doubt where it could end... death! This knowledge, however, has given me strength, courage and cheer and psychological advantage over my tormentors. Whether I live or die is immaterial...we must keep on striving to make the world a better place for all". – Ken Saro-Wiwa

This is a season of remembrances, unfortunately, for very tragic reasons. In November 1993, the Nigerian state – in a manner characteristic of all dysfunctional neo-colonial state – spewed up a demented general, the most delirious ruler this continent has witnessed. Exactly two years after, this general and his cohorts, amidst many other crimes against Nigerians, murdered the internationally acclaimed author and environmentalist, Ken Saro-Wiwa and eight of his kinsmen. The grisly execution stunned people all over the world, including, surprisingly, those who had shored up the regime and given it international recognition.

That singular act of barbarism did not come as a surprise to many who understand and appreciate the character of the Nigerian state. It had to happen if only to prove the point that the internal colonialism going on in Nigeria is not a fluke. Of course, Saro-Wiwa, considering his prescient knowledge of military dictatorship, knew that Abacha, at the height of his bestiality, could do anything.

However, as a man of ideas who believed in non-violent struggle he might have thought that reason would prevail in the resolution of the age-long minorities question in Nigeria. He took lightly the reality that in matters of national oppression or subjugation, reason, for the oppressor, counts for nothing. Ask the ethnic Albanians in Kosovo, the East Timorese under Indonesia, and the people of Chechnya in Russia.

Regrettably, those who supervised the murders are the ones running Nigeria today. Expectedly, they have made concessions – just as the British colonialists did when agitation from the subjects became unbearable – but when it is convenient for them, they will kill and kill again.

As we mark the third anniversary of the murder of Saro-Wiwa and his compatriots, we cannot – this is the only service we can offer their restless souls, which undoubtedly, will continue to haunt their bloodthirsty murders – but reflect on the convoluted history of a country that throws up the likes of Babangida, Abacha, and Abubakar and makes it possible that the only way they can respond to the democratic aspirations of their people is through murder.

A look, even a cursory one, at the Nigerian political landscape gives the indication of a country on the brink of disintegration. However, Nigeria started to disintegrate from the outset; when Britain contrived to create a lopsided federation and empowered a bigoted political class as part of her divide and rule doctrine. Of course, if those who inhabit this political fiction today feel alienated and have grown impatient with the tantrums of those who have run it for so long, it should be expected as the logical consequence of British colonialism, the precursor of this sham.

Nigeria was created by force and is being held together through force. The British unashamedly intended it to be so. Unfortunately, there are those who still insist that we cannot talk about the future of Nigeria. They say the unity of Nigeria is nonnegotiable; or better still, there is no need to undo what has been divinely instituted. Remember, not too long ago, in what smacked of Apartheid tactics, a military regime banned any discussions, gathering, and even thoughts about the future of Nigeria; it became a treasonable offence to discuss the future of Nigeria. Others diminish the severity of the crisis by talking of power shift to the South.

Yours sincerely received one of such responses recently. Though it was not based on the absurd politico-religious bigotry or the issue of power shift, the author nevertheless showed himself as one of those who do not appreciate the enormity of the current crisis and, therefore, the approaching storm. Whoever he is (he did not give his name), this patriotic Nigerian, considering the tone of his piece, had this to say about an earlier piece titled, "The General in a Labyrinth": "Rather than criticize this man, Gen. Abubakar to death, why not for once offer constructive, proactive mechanism to achieve lasting peace and technological upheaval in Nigeria. I am of the opinion that you would rather have him wash your feet and call you sir than see that he is moving the country away from the tyranny of Abacha and into something acceptable by a majority of people. Can you tell us what you would have done, constructively and proactively, if you were in his shoes? I hope your approach will steer clear of any history of colonial Nigeria or reference to British Parliament".

The tirade continued ad nauseam, but the paragraph above is a fair representation of what is not included. Nigeria's colonial history is an interesting issue which must concern everyone, including those who brought the various nations together in 1914. What Abubakar needs to do immediately, considering the tragedy that was the Abacha regime of which he played an active part, and the impotent set-ups that transition programmes in Nigeria have become, is to allow Nigerians to convoke a Sovereign National Conference of their genuine representatives to decide how the country should be administered.

Is it possible, considering the long history of ethnic discontent in Nigeria, to discuss the future of Nigeria without reference to the history of colonial Nigeria or to the British Parliament? The answer, of course, is no. The amalgamation of Nigeria, simply put, had no democratic basis, and therefore cannot sustain democratic governance or withstand a transition to democracy, even within the most elastic definition of the term.

Nigeria was created on the terms of a marauding band of slave merchants and their progenies, now is the time to negotiate it on the terms of those who inhabit it and bear the brunt of its lopsided features. I do not think those who make this humble demand are asking for too much. While people may desire to shape the present, they cannot do so effectively without understanding the past. In a sentence, the only way we can appreciate the misfortune of the present is to understand the past.

If we are worried that 28 years after an internecine civil war, the division among Nigerians is more pronounced now than it was at independence; if we are concerned that many years after two multi-billion-dollar steel complexes were built, Nigeria is still a fourth-rate nation technologically; if we are worried that in its 38 years of flag independence, Nigeria has offered its citizens just ten years of civil rule; if we are worried that Nigeria is the poorest oil producing country in the world; if we are worried about the threats and prospects of secession, the ifs can go on indefinitely; if we are worried about these things, then there is nothing wrong in looking back, if only to see where we went wrong. But more important, there is nothing wrong in seeking to address the mistakes of the past, even if those mistakes were made by the British Parliament.

Am I too cynical about the Nigerian project? Maybe I am. Maybe also my cynicism is the result of not just failed dreams and wasted opportunities, but the idiocy of those who control power in Nigeria and have blocked every viable opportunity of looking for solution to the country's problems. It matters little to these people that this project was doomed from birth.

As long as they can pick the crumbs from the tables of their masters they are contented, ever ready to hold brief for them, to kill and maim at their behest. They talk of a grand plan to destabilise Nigeria. Intermittently, you see them handing out labels such as "agents of destabilization", "unpatriotic and disgruntled elements who are out to cause disaffection"; infernal labels that border on political narcissism.

It is the same line of thinking that conditioned the regime's response to the carnage at Djerhe (Jesse), Delta State, last month. Conspiracy theorists, including the head of the military regime, were quick to label the local inhabitants of the disaster prone oil community saboteurs; and as a punishment for their crime, they won't be compensated. It was the height of insensitivity to the plight of a people whose lives have been atrophied by years of oil exploration.

However, it tells a lot too about the psyche of the military oligarchy whose role as soldiers of fortune in the service of multinational interests is not in doubt. Abubakar and his Shell entourage couldn't careless about the social alienation caused by the activities of oil companies which has removed the people of Djerhe (Jesse) from their means of subsistence. They are not concerned about the structural dislocation which has occasioned fuel scarcity in a country that is one of the largest producers of oil in the world, so much so that oil spill is celebrated with fanfare.

Of course, the injustices in Nigeria cannot be redressed by labelling people. The so-called National Assembly as advocated by the military cannot resolve the problem. The injustices cannot be redressed by the outmoded song that, "We have agreed – nobody has been able to say where this agreement was reached – to remain one united Nigeria, so shall it be". The option that the proposed National Assembly will tackle the issue of restructuring is particularly flawed. The military reserves the right, since it has the right of life and death over Nigerians, to outlaw such a debate by ensuring that it is not included in the constitution.

If Nigerians condone this constitutional ruse, anybody that raises the issue of restructuring after the constitution takes effect will most likely be charged for treason. The military could also design a constitution where laws are passed through simple majority. In such a situation, the North, which will, as usual, have a majority in the Assembly can veto such debate without worrying about the consequence. Alternatively, the military could leave it open so that the chaos that will be generated by such a debate will necessarily lead to another military intervention.

Evidently, the Nigerian state is run on sectarian privileges; and if the country faces extinction today, it is simply because of what happened in the past: the history of the amalgamation and the treachery and intrigues surrounding it. Nigeria was not always there. God did not ordain it. We know when and how it all started. The lunacy of those who insist that the unity of this country – where people live in semi-colonies as conquered people and ethnic crisis are resolved with the same arbitrariness with which the British resolved the colonial question – is nonnegotiable will only spell doom.

As we remember Saro-Wiwa and all those fallen heroes and heroines of democracy, justice, and liberty, we cannot but ask: How many more will be murdered before people are granted their inalienable right to self-determination? How many more will be roasted alive before we realize our foolhardiness in maintaining the *status quo*?

Pertinent questions without any immediate answers. However, one thing is certain: time is running out on those who have undertaken the unenviable task of overseeing this neo-colony.

20. BETWEEN 1979 AND 1999
FEBRUARY 1999

Few people would remember that it was not long ago, 1979 to be precise, that Nigeria was saddled with a monstrosity. Two decades later, the nation has come full circle and history is about to repeat itself. The reason for this amnesia, which is not the thrust of this article, includes in part, the dreary reality that politics of transition programmes, thanks to Babangida and Abacha, has become the only meaningful occupation for survival in Nigeria. We cannot forget how Babangida and Abacha, just for a few naira, cajoled erstwhile respectable intellectuals, academics, professionals, musicians, artistes, and even footballers, to "underwrite" their infamy.

Indeed 1979 and 1999 bear more than a fleeting resemblance with 1999 poised to outshine 1979 in every area of political trickery and chicanery. As the sham continues; and as the new military rulers persist in making a mockery of themselves and democracy, you cannot but feel the terrifying similarity between 1979 and 1999. In 1979, Gen. Obasanjo's regime transferred political power to Alhaji Shehu Shagari.

Prior to the exit of the military in 1979, there were promises to return the country to democratic governance that failed to materialise. When Obasanjo grabbed power in 1976 after the death of Gen. Murtala Muhammed, he was saddled with a monumental problem which clearly he could not cope with. The result was a badly mangled transition in which he was forced to hand over power even though there was no clear winner at the end of the presidential election.

However, it was not only a dubious democratic experiment that Obasanjo bequeathed to the 2nd Republic. The lawlessness, tyranny and impunity that were the hallmarks of his regime were carried lock, stock, and barrel into the Shagari regime. Many Nigerians have yet to overcome the horrors of Inspector General of Police, Sunday Adewusi's "Gestapo", aka "Kill and Go", that supervised the mayhem that was the 2nd Republic. In the two decades since the 1979 debacle, the nation has been run in fits and starts. Today, the story is no different; it is, in fact, worse.

Last June, Gen. Abdulsalami Abubakar emerged as the new maximum ruler after the death of Abacha. The first signs of the schizophrenic nature of the regime and its total incapacity to comprehend the current crisis emerged few days after Abubakar took over when he promised to complete the transition programme of his predecessor. No sooner was the statement made than it was withdrawn. The regime also promised to hand over last October. It reneged on that promise. Of course, there are still no clear indications that the regime will quit in May as it has consistently promised.

The present regime, like that of Gen. Obasanjo, came into being with the pressing need to act out the scripts written by its predecessor. The catch here is that there is a compelling need to "hearken to the master's voice", while trying to be different, and at the same time making futile efforts to placate every facet of society. It is not for nothing that Abubakar's transition programme has shown visible signs of the "landslide victory" that brought Shagari to power in 1979.

However, it is in the area of state terror that this regime should be judged for what it is. With the number of political killings that have gone on so far, particularly in the Niger Delta, in the next five months, Abacha's butchery will pale into insignificance. Some people contend that not even the Boers would have gone to the extremes the Abubakar regime has in the Niger Delta – declaring a state of emergency and mowing down defenceless youth who are demanding their inalienable right to chart their destiny – considering the failed attempts of its predecessor in the same area. However, they fail to realize that we are dealing with an establishment more sinister than the Boers.

The vision of this regime explains the constellation of retired generals, military officers, and all the military apologists who are buying their way into positions of authority in the supposed civilian regime. Clearly, if this regime must relinquish power, it must hand over to those who possess the wherewithal to prosecute the campaign of terror which the military erroneously thinks is needed at this moment to maintain the Nigerian federation. It is also their own little, even if disastrous, way of showing that the military cannot be disgraced out of office, never mind they are being pummelled by a ragtag army in Sierra Leone.

Nigeria has a knack for creating history; it will not be different under Abubakar's transition. That gubernatorial elections, the last but one stage of his transition, took place last week without the benefit of a constitution caused little surprise. We now understand when the military high command chants the morbid phrase: "home-grown democracy". Unfortunately, it is either the military does not appreciate the importance of a constitution for a people clamouring for true federalism and a permanent end to military dictatorship or it is out to cause mischief. I am inclined to believe the latter.

Of course, it suits the regime to precipitate enough chaos as it can muster. The military regime is under no obligation to tag the current charade democracy whether home grown or foreign. Forget that the likes of Emeka Anyaoku, Commonwealth scribe and an adept at doublespeak – he honestly believed Abacha was pursuing a credible and genuine transition – described the election as an important step in the transition to democracy.

By the time this transition is revealed for the sham that it is, we would have recorded another landslide or, perhaps, hurricane victory. One man who is set to ride into Aso Rock aided by the ferocity of the hurricane is ex-head-of-state, ex-UN Secretary General aspirant, avowed enemy of press freedom, retired but certainly not tired general and pardoned coup convict, Gen Olusegun Obasanjo, who unfortunately was at the centre of the maelstrom of 1979. But we only have to look back – we can't afford any form of amnesia here – two decades ago to come to the inevitable conclusion that never has this nation had more reason to be wary of a presidential aspirant.

Going by his sordid records, what, for example, would be Gen. Obasanjo's answer to the crisis in the Niger Delta? Nothing, but greater violence. Not that any of the other candidates jostling for Aso Rock merits our attention; far from it. The truth, however, is that Gen. Obasanjo has exhibited an uncanny predilection for ruthlessness. He showed it during the civil war; it was manifested between 1976 and 1979 when, against his will, he ruled Nigeria. The man is just one plague this country cannot afford at this crucial juncture.

It does appear, however, that as far as this transition is concerned, Nigerians have very little say concerning the bizarre machinations of the military. But it must be made clear that the democratic meal Abubakar is serving Nigerians, the attempts to foist the military on the populace under the guise of democracy, is nothing but the "democratization of violence", and it offers no hope for the future.

A transition programme that has no resonance with the feelings and aspirations of Nigerians; a transition that simply ignores the objective reality of Nigeria's flawed federation is only a recipe for chaos. As we approach the last lap of this crisis prone transition, Nigerians have a duty to ensure that we do not return to the tragedy of 1979 by saying no to those who supervised that ignominy.

21. Gospel according to Gidado
March 1999

With two months to the end of Abubakar's transition, and hopefully 15 inglorious years of military dictatorship, the post-Abubakar democratic order is looking increasingly hollow. This hollowness manifests itself in the characters who are supposed to succeed Abubakar, but more important in the structures that the present regime will bequeath to the civilian regime.

Of course, those who know the antecedent of this regime and the fact that its transition programme, like the ones before it, is sowing the seeds of its own destruction, are not disappointed at the insincerity that has dogged it and they won't be proved wrong when it, inevitably, comes to a sticky end. Clearly, the illusion that the transition programme will usher in a sustainable democratic order is just what it is, an illusion. Not surprisingly, the regime and its backers have managed so far to carry it through.

In a few days, election observers of all shades will converge on Nigeria. Their concern, primarily, will be to watch Nigerians cast their votes for a president the military high command has presented to them as a fait accompli. However, the overwhelming interest the international community has taken in Nigeria's so-called democratic process is suspect. Of course, there are those who genuinely wish and would like to see Nigeria return to democracy, but their limited understanding of the Nigerian crisis will ensure that they are hoodwinked into believing that democracy is on the horizon.

There are others, however, who understand the labyrinth of the Nigerian crisis but who, in order to keep Nigeria in check, will acquiesce to the agenda of a power-crazed elite. Elections might as well be conducted without a constitution for all they care. It becomes completely irrelevant, in the light of this reality, who emerges as the next president under the transition programme. And by extension, the election itself is a grave distraction from the main issue: power relation among the various nationalities that constitute the Nigerian state.

Intermittently, this issue comes to the fore. And more often than not, the recipe, quite clearly an untenable one, has always been that greater force is the way out of the political impasse in Nigeria. It is this conviction that explains the murderous proclivities of successive military regimes in the country.

In their quest to maintain power, any voice outside the political *cul-de-sac* they have plunged the country is regarded as a treasonable offence. Of course, the military is not alone in this supercilious attitude. It is simply for this reason that the so-called democratic order, or better still, the processes leading up to it, must interest those who wish Nigeria well.

There is a new, well not really new, tune that is being sung by power bigots in Nigeria. It is what Professor Wole Soyinka, sardonically, referred to as the "gospel according to Gidado". In the February 1999 edition of Africa Today, Soyinka quoted from a lecture reportedly given by Alhaji Idris Gidado, secretary to the military government in Nigeria, at the Gamji Forum public lectures series on November 10, 1998. According to Alhaji Gidado,

> *"Mankind needs government, but in areas and situations where anarchy has prevailed, or is being incited by ethnic chauvinists and demagogues, the people will first submit only to despotism and authoritarianism. Those who genuinely care about democracy, therefore seek first to preserve a functioning government, even if despotic, and only when government has become habitual, can we hope to make it democratic".*

What a contradiction! Of course, it would not have stirred much interest if Alhaji Gidado's gospel remained a theoretical contradiction. However, it is not. It is a gospel that touches the very existence of the Nigerian state and best explains why successive military regimes, the present inclusive, have raped, murdered, and subjected Nigerians to all manner of indignity without any retribution for their crimes.

Wole Soyinka whose piece has renewed the interest in the issue of power relations in Nigeria, at least for those of us who did not have the privilege of listening to Alhaji Gidado at the Gamji Forum, meant it as, in his own words, "food for thought for everyone, young and old, soldier and civilian, to chew over into 1999".

I do not know how many people have read this gospel. It is even more difficult to know how many people are able to reflect, as the professor of literature had hoped, on its implications. But one thing is certain: Alhaji Gidado did not intend his remarks as a comic relief for those who are weary of military dictatorship. This gospel, therefore, is one that ought to be condemned in its entirety.

Alhaji Gidado's gospel is not without precedent. This is not the first time someone will attempt an interpretation of the lingering political crisis in Nigeria using antiquated and morbid solutions. If memory fails you, not too long ago, in a slavish and moronic attempt to play God and possibly rationalize the political contraption put in place by colonialism, Alhaji Maitama Sule made one of most astonishing comments since Nigeria was created in 1914.

A former Nigerian Ambassador to the United Nations and scion of the remnant of feudalism in northern Nigeria, Alhaji Sule was reported to have said God had wisely shared different talents among Nigerians. In his words,

> *"The easterners, the Igbos, for instance, are the business entrepreneurs. The west, the Yorubas make excellent administrators, civil servants and teachers. The north, the Hausas are blessed with the gift of leadership and must be accepted as such".*

Undoubtedly, this is one of the most cynical and infernal statement on political narcissism since Hitler developed his infamous theory of Aryan supremacy. Alhaji Sule did not say what will happen to those who, for whatever justification, found it necessary to upturn God's plan for Nigeria.

The answer, of course, can be found in Alhaji Gidado's gospel. What Alhaji Gidado really wants is unclear, but his solution to the political instability in Nigeria raises a lot of questions. For example, at whose behest will despotism and authoritarianism be unleashed on humankind (read Nigerians)? Whose interest, any genuine democrat is bound to ask, will the despot or tyrant be serving in the pursuit of repression?

Of course, anarchy, which Alhaji Gidado gives as justification for tyranny, is the product of despotism and totalitarianism. We can go on ad infinitum raising pertinent questions about Alhaji Gidado's anachronistic response to contemporary reality. Suffice it to say, however, that his exultation of tyranny can only suit a gathering of savages. Nigerians are not savages.

Perhaps, if it is so difficult to learn from history, the likes of Alhaji Gidado may do well to learn from the present. We know from painful and very costly experience, past and present, that despotism and totalitarianism, in whatever guise – to defend religion, ideology or hegemony – are not only out of vogue, they are simply unworkable solutions. Examples abound. Certainly, those who are supervising the current transition to democracy in Nigeria are not thinking of participatory democracy.

Their idea of governance is not to involve the people but to lord it over them. No amount of desire for democracy can justify tyranny; nobody who genuinely cares about democracy can condone despotism and totalitarianism. To all the election observers who have taken interest in Abubakar's transition and will be in Nigeria to cover the end-phase of this charade, particularly those from countries, purportedly the bastions of democracy, I therefore recommend the gospel according to Gidado.

After a thorough examination, they should ask themselves a simple question: is this jamboree worth all the trouble?

---

22. Obasanjo and the End of the Nigerian State
April 1999

It is true that when history repeats itself, and it happens quite often in places where people do not learn from history, what takes place is a farcical reply of a tragedy. Nowhere is this tragicomic reality better exemplified than in Nigeria and the emergence of Gen. Olusegun Obasanjo as the country's next ruler, twenty years after his infamous rule between 1976 and 1979.

For various reasons, not excluding the national trauma we all face under an Obasanjo presidency, those who contrived to bring about this political absurdity have done a great disservice to themselves and to Nigeria. Of course, the only way we can understand this farce and its implications for Nigeria is to look at the trajectory of the present crisis which dates back to the Babangida era.

It is unfortunate, and indeed quite bemusing, that a section of the political class is expressing misgivings about the charade the world witnessed recently. Last December, in an article titled "A Misplaced Outrage", which was an answer to many Nigerian politicians who were outraged at the level of electoral fraud that accompanied the December 5, 1998, local government election in Nigeria, I expressed consternation at the complaints, describing them as misplaced.

The thrust of that article was that "our politicians would rather self-destruct than allow a life of gross self-indulgence and an opportunity to compensate for their idleness slip out of their hands"; that the complaints were just the tip of the iceberg of the monumental complaints that would trail the transition programme when the real thing began.

Clearly, these politicians, including the purportedly principled ones, ought to be blamed for the ruin that has befallen them. They lost sight of the fact that the transition had clearly been carefully orchestrated; that even though Abacha was dead, his long shadow cast menacingly over the present transition.

Our politicians jumped headlong into Abubakar's transition claiming they wanted to end military rule at all costs. They did not check the traps and pitfalls and the likelihood of the military returning in another garb as it plans to do in the person of Obasanjo. They could have resisted Abubakar and insisted on a Sovereign National Conference, which has become inevitable; except, of course, the warmongers in our midst have their way. This war option is one that ought to be taken seriously. Those who want to precipitate another civil war in Nigeria have taken it for granted that they control the balance of military power and that, assuredly, another military conquest will permanently seal their hegemony.

Backing out of this transition certainly was too much a sacrifice for our politicians to make. However, while pursuing their selfish end, they unwittingly provided Abubakar's programme the shred of support it badly needed. Now they know better. They have suddenly come to the belated realization that what we are faced with is no better than Abacha's self-succession efforts. To think that they sincerely believed that Abubakar's transition was capable of producing a free and fair election!

But let us forget the politicians and their foibles since many of those ranting about, to use what has become a national catchphrase – "service to the nation" – will definitely find space in Obasanjo's gravy train. I hear Mr. Shonekan, erstwhile head of the imperial conglomerate, United African Company, (UAC), erstwhile head of the Interim National Government (ING) and Chairman of Abacha's Vision 2020 programme, has earnestly declared his intention to serve the nation if called upon to do so.

With the outcome of the presidential election, the myth of Abubakar's transition which held the international community, particularly America and Britain, in total stupefaction has been broken. Interestingly, by that singular act of deception, the military in Nigeria has revealed its true face; by employing all the trickery known and unknown in politics to foist Obasanjo on Nigeria, its wheel of treachery and power bigotry has rolled full circle and come to a halt. Where to go from here is what they cannot determine.

It should not be taken for granted that America and Britain were indeed stupefied by Abubakar's so-called reforms and by extension his transition programme. Long before Abubakar came on the scene, the US, for example, made it clear that it welcomed a new transition programme which excluded the winner of the June 12, 1993 election. For reasons that border on the often-trumpeted American national interest, the US dumped Abiola and welcomed Abacha's transition and even his self-succession plot if only there could be a semblance of electoral contest.

As I indicated earlier, to understand the emergence of Obasanjo we have to go back to June 12, 1993. When Babangida and the power-crazed establishment he represented agreed to leave power, after many aborted attempts, they allowed Moshood Abiola and Bashir Tofa to contest the 1993 presidential election. With the help of hindsight, and of course, Babangida's infamous confessions, it is now clear that they never, in their wildest imagination, assumed that Abiola would emerge triumphant.

If they knew, they would have either prevented the election or manipulated the election results to suit Abiola's opponent. Of course, they did try some element of destabilization by allowing a high court in Abuja to rule, a night before the election, that it could not be held even though there was a decree that prevented the courts from interfering with the electoral process.

From the annulment of the June 12, 1993 election, through Abacha's murderous rule, to the imprisonment of Oladipo Diya and company, to the death of Abiola in prison and the emergence of Obasanjo, the military wing of the dominant power bloc in Nigeria which never ceases to pose as the Nigerian military has been scheming to maintain the *status quo*. Clearly, Abacha's rise to power was the logical outcome of the annulment of the June 12 election and the limited powers of the Interim National Government.

With pressure from both human rights and pro-democracy groups in Nigeria and the efforts of a tiny but progressive section of the international community, Abacha was compelled to initiate a transition programme. Then again the question of who will control power in the post Abacha era became paramount. Meanwhile, the greatest threat to the oligarchy's continued grip on power, Abiola, was still alive and hopeful, even though in detention.

To stop Abiola, and prevent the emergence of a president from the South of the country which had become the battle cry, if only to assuage the South-west for the annulment, Abacha had to act. He had two options: one, to decimate the top echelon of the military from the South-west who looked set to control power – Gen. Diya and others – in the event that Abacha succumbed to his many terminal illnesses. Two, to embark on a self-succession drive, with the full back-ing of the military while bribing and coercing civilian accomplices. Of course, beyond his own damnable proclivities for murder, there was no way Abacha could achieve all this without slaughtering Nigerians. He did exactly that.

After imprisoning Abiola, Abacha had to reach for the jugular of others whom he saw as a veritable threat to his ambition. That was how Obasanjo, the man the West looked up to as a potential civilian president, came into the fray. Abacha checkmated Obasanjo by linking him to a phantom coup and jailing him. By demanding the release of Obasanjo alongside genuine opponents of the Abacha junta who were in jail, the human rights and pro-democracy movement built him into a hero of sorts. The morality of that action may be subject to debate, but what is not in doubt is that Obasanjo was the ultimate beneficiary.

Outside Nigeria, Obasanjo was touted as a democrat. It was assumed, erroneously, that he was jailed for his opposition to the Abacha junta and his demand for human rights and democracy. But it is common knowledge that Obasanjo relishes the abuse of human rights and that he is not a lover of democracy; except, of course, where he stands to benefit. For example, when the June 12, 1993 presidential election, Nigeria's freest and fairest, even in the eyes of international election observers, was annulled Obasanjo was one of those who campaigned vigorously against Abiola, the winner.

Of course, Abacha's megalomania proved too dangerous for himself, the establishment he represented adequately, and lastly, Nigeria as a whole. Abacha could still have been tolerated if there was not a popular alternative – Abiola in this case – to his misrule. The puzzle to resolve was: how do you get rid of Abiola without stretching the already frayed nerves of a section of the country? To resolve this riddle, Abacha who had already come to his wits' end became dispensable. With Abacha out of the way, it was only logical for Abiola to follow.

However, before that *coup de grace*, Abubakar emerged as the messiah. He ordered the release of some detained politicians and human rights activists. It is, however, interesting to note that immediately Abubakar took over he promised to continue the policies and programmes of his predecessor. Undoubtedly, if he had to hand over in October 1998 as he initially planned, that meant that elections would have to be held and possibly all those detained illegally, including Abiola, whom they feared might contest and win another election, would have to be released.

What happened next is now history. Immediately Abiola was out of the picture, Abubakar announced a new transition programme. At this stage, the oligarchy feared that to transfer power to itself in a civilian dispensation was like placing Nigeria on a keg of gunpowder considering the fact that even the otherwise docile and bribable politicians from the South were also calling for power shift.

It was left with two options: either to continue to hold on to power and risk the disintegration of the country or look for a puppet, preferably from the South-west, it could pull by the string if only to atone for June 12. Opting for puppets to provide a facade while it entrenches its dominance is a game the oligarchy is adept at. Enter Gen. Olusegun Aremu Obasanjo! After all, what does the presidency matter since anybody who controls the armed forces controls everything in Nigeria?

For a man who had publicly expressed his disinterest in the presidency of Nigeria, a man who claimed he had become bankrupt, thanks to SAP, one who could not even win his constituency, Obasanjo's rise from prison to power leaves a lot of questions unanswered. Interestingly, immediately he was released from prison, the Abubakar regime spared no pain whitewashing him. A presidential jet was placed at his disposal and he was granted pardon when others accused with him of plotting to overthrow the Abacha regime were languishing in jail. To make the pardon not appear as a plot, Gen. Shehu Yar'Adua, who died almost a year earlier, was pardoned posthumously.

The Abubakar regime did not stop at this overflow of magnanimity. To show that the regime was pursuing a genuine transition and that it was indeed concerned about the "political loss" incurred by the Yoruba nation, it ensured the emergence of a "moderate" Yoruba politician to challenge Obasanjo. With all these arrangements, the regime still did not take chances as Babangida naively did.

It kept the constitution to itself, as a backup plan, in the event that if its candidate lost out, it could still have rolled out another plan; say for example, the introduction of a parliamentary system which would create the position of a prime minister, most probably, from the north considering the dominance of the national assembly by the People's Democratic Party (PDP). This option is not ruled out completely until the constitution is made public.

Of course, between now and May 29 when Abubakar claims he will hand over is a very long time and anything can happen considering that Nigeria is a country of the impossible. In this regard, the outpouring of consternation and grief by the losers in Abubakar's transition can achieve two ends. It could prod the military into finding an alibi to continue in office. Alternatively, the military could ignore the politicians and install Obasanjo. Either way, we have a crisis. Clearly, there is no way the military would continue in office without exacerbating the present tension in the country. Handing over to Obasanjo, to ensure a temporary reprieve, has its own disturbing consequences.

Obasanjo, like Shonekan before him, is just a pawn, a neutered tiger in the power game that is convulsing Nigeria. He may delude himself that he is nobody's stooge, but the reality is that Obasanjo is going to run a hostage presidency. First, there are those within the military who are wary that Obasanjo might go for their pound of flesh for the humiliation he suffered as a prisoner. And he certainly would, judging from his antecedents. Second, there is the threat of the hawks within the military establishment who see themselves as the final arbiter on the future of Nigeria. Added to this is the fact that his people do not support him.

I do not know anybody who has managed to rule Nigeria without the support of his ethnic nationality. Other nationalities see him as a crude imposition on Nigeria. Even disinterested observers point to the electoral malpractice that preceded his victory as a sign that the man has little moral authority to rule.

Perhaps, Obasanjo's greatest albatross is the whole of the Niger Delta, though for a start the Ijaw nation. I can't imagine what his answer will be if the restive youth of the atrophied heart of Nigeria's oil wealth were to issue an ultimatum, say, on May 30. I am inclined to believe the man will act out the script of his predecessor.

After that showdown, it won't be long before America and Britain come to the realization, that is, if they have not, that election is the last thing Nigeria needs at this time. As Chief Gani Fawehinmi said recently in an interview with The Source magazine, "Placating an ethnic nationality or group is not the issue. In fact it is misdirected".

Paradoxically, America and Britain, two infamous bedfellows, are leading a legion of forces to Kosovo to defend the fundamental and inalienable rights of a little over one million Kosovo Albanians under the jackboots of Slobodan Milosevic and his Serb forces while the call for justice for ethnic nationalities in Nigeria, some twenty times the size of the troubled Serbian province, is treated with contempt.

Could it be that American national interest is not threatened yet or the crisis in Nigeria does not have the potential of threatening international stability? To quote the London Times' lead editorial of February 3, on the Kosovo crisis,

> "The people of this country (Britain) understand well that a trading nation with global interests must be prepared to deploy its forces where international stability is threatened".

As we close in on this end game, we cannot but concede that Obasanjo's Pyrrhic victory is welcome in that it heightens the prevailing contradictions in Nigeria. It is absurd to think that the military will grant a Sovereign National Conference; it is equally illusory to think that a civilian regime like the type that will emerge on May 29, will address Nigeria's myriad problems.

Obasanjo's presidency is at best a disaster; and at worse, the end of the Nigerian state.

23. Babangida's Heritage
May 1999

"The psychosis of Africa's 'Big Men' does indeed run deep". President Henri Konan Bedie of Ivory Coast pays the equivalent of 3.5 million CFA francs to acquire an honorary degree from a French university. Paul Biya of Cameroon mortgages his country to earn a doctorate degree from a foreign university. The list is endless. When they are not paying to earn a miserable degree and don the tag Dr. President this and that, they are probably building a monument that would be the only legacy of their infamy.

We saw it in Nigeria when that murderous cretin, Sani Abacha, contributed about 500,000 pounds to institute a Sani Abacha chair in a university abroad, at a time Nigerian universities were in a coma due to underfunding. Perhaps he was only following the tradition of his predecessor, that other exemplar of perfidy and self-styled evil genius of Nigerian politics, Ibrahim Badamosi Babangida.

Babangida, in his heyday, when the issue in Nigeria was not so much the surfeit of money as how to spend it, built a school of postgraduate studies in Liberia which he named after himself. If only Nigeria had a coherent foreign policy, that mindless wastage of public funds could have strengthened it. The country has nothing like a foreign policy, much less a coherent one.

What it all means is that each serving despot dips his bloody fangs into the national treasury to grab enough money for self-glorification. Even when Abacha was at his wits' end and the Nigerian nation on the brink of disintegration, thanks to his inglorious dictatorship, he still busied himself building a Sani Abacha Foundation for Peace and Development. It is best to imagine what form of peace and development the country would witness when the rulers were barefaced bandits who unabashedly flaunted their banditry.

The latest fad in this primeval display of egotism is here. They call it Heritage University; Babangida's Heritage University, to be precise. Reports have it that Nigeria's former military dictator has embarked on mass acquisition of land and property in Kaduna, northern Nigeria, where he intends to build his university. There are strong indications that all the effete intellectuals who perpetually trade their calling for a mess of portage, including those who provided the intellectual basis for Babangida's misrule, are ready to lend their service. But that is another issue.

Ordinarily, one would have welcomed this private initiative that seeks to address the crisis of tertiary education in Nigeria, not withstanding one's aversion to the commercialization and privatization of education. The questions that easily come to mind are: What is the source of funds for Babangida's multi-million-naira project? What job or business is Babangida involved in?

However, if these questions do not make sense since it is in our character to glorify wealth no matter its source, we must cast our minds back to the late '80s and early '90s when Babangida ran Nigeria, including her educational establishments aground. That was the era when professors in Nigerian universities could not afford to buy a car even if they decided to starve for a whole year and save the pittance that was handed out to them as salaries; when students were detained without charge or trial; when indiscriminate closure of universities and dismissal of lecturers were the rule; when lecturers could not teach because they lacked chalk; when lecture rooms reminded one of a market scene; when, for example, "lecturers teaching fluid mechanics had to use their lecture notes to demonstrate the motion and forces acting on fluid flowing in a pipe to their third year engineering students because the equipment for such a simple experiment – the smokescreen – was not available".

Yes, it was that bad. Therefore, Babangida cannot justifiably say he has any moral authority building a university when he destroyed the decent university system he inherited. Clearly, this project is not for the benefit of Nigerians, but to enhance Babangida's self-interest. Babangida's heritage is nothing but wanton profligacy and deceit. He seized power on August 27, 1985, for no reason, except of course, to advance his personal interest.

Eight years later, in June 1993, he annulled the presidential election that was to signal the end of his ignoble rule, again for no justifiable reason other than to satiate his maniacal love for power. In between these treasonable acts, he destroyed everything Nigerians held sacred. He corrupted the judiciary, perverted traditional institutions, literally bought the military and destroyed professionalism and esprit de corps, destroyed the economy through a combination of graft and ineptitude, and reduced academics to quivering sidekicks of dictatorship.

Many people would remember how that infamy ended. The reluctance, the ubiquitous wet handkerchiefs, the red eyes that fought hard to hold back loosened tear ducts. In all this, Babangida did have the common courtesy of saying he was leaving. He called his exit "stepping aside".

Looking back, that decision to "step aside" was not just a rehash of military jargon. It was a measure of the complicity and duplicity of a man who had something up his sleeve. Undoubtedly, Babangida plans to come back to the seat he vacated six years ago. If Obasanjo could do it, why not Babangida? After all, this is Nigeria where amnesia is part of the national psyche.

Lately, as part of his policy of reintegration, Babaginda has been making numerous public appearances, and most disturbingly calling for the reintroduction of the Structural Adjustment Programme (SAP). In one of such public display of tomfoolery, he was quoted as saying, in response to the anticipated backlash his pro-SAP views would elicit that, "It would be naive not to expect much opposition from parties whose interests would be or may appear to be adversely affected by the programme. But the nation cannot afford to sacrifice its future to satisfy a few unpatriotic elements".

Talk about patriotism or the lack of it. If there is a tag "most unpatriotic Nigerian", that badge of dishonour must go to Babangida. For eight years, he had the chance, goodwill and all, to transform Nigeria, but what did he do? He had the opportunity to implement his most cherished economic blueprint, SAP, but where did the policy leave Nigeria? Nigerians became poverty-stricken, the quality of life diminished drastically, and state institutions collapsed completely.

Life is indeed full of bizarre contradictions. It says so much about the character of Nigerians and the Nigerian nation that the likes of Babangida, who ought to face the law for their crimes, are not only walking the streets, shamelessly displaying their loot, but are the ones that will direct state policy in the next century.

Of course, one way Babangida plans to do this is through his so-called Heritage University. Apparently, there is no end to the chicaneries of Nigeria's ruling elite. I think the time has come for Nigerians to face the contradictions and challenges which the Babangida phenomenon represents because his heritage belongs nowhere else but the trash can of history.

24. OF HEROES AND CONSPIRATORS
JUNE 1999

Recent events in Nigeria bear remarkable similarity to those in Yugoslavia where Mr. Bill "the bomber" Clinton and his mechanical sidekick, Tony Blair, have waged a senseless and vainglorious war; a war that will not bring justice to Serbs or Kosovars because imperialism does not go to war to promote justice in the first place. And if reports of renewed trouble in Nigeria's Niger Delta, 24 hours after power was transferred to Mr. Olusegun Obasanjo, is anything to go by, then a long-drawn-out crisis looms. Latest reports put the death toll of the clashes between Ijaw and Itsekiri nationalities at well over 200.

The war in Yugoslavia is over borders, borders drawn by imperialist powers when they claimed victory at the end of World War I and saw nations as the spoils of war. The latest crisis in Nigeria is about borders, borders created by internal colonialists and their henchmen during years of sustained brigandage.

The war in Yugoslavia is also about heroism, albeit a very sinister one.

> "This has been called the American century because in it we were the dominant force for good in the world. Now we are on the verge of a new century and what country's name will it bear? I say it will be another American century".

That was George Bush in 1988 while accepting his presidential nomination.

> *"The NATO of the 21st century is being tested now before the new century begins. And we are determined to pass that test; using aircrafts and facilities from more than a dozen countries we are striking hard"*. – Madeleine Albright in 1999, during a speech in Washington on the New NATO.

Whether to open the new century as an American century or to test the capabilities of the New NATO, America, the most belligerent nation in the world and its leader, Bill "the bomber" Clinton, smarting from his sex imbroglio, are striking hard because they see themselves as heroes of sorts: the defenders of democracy and global peace.

It is not very clear the nature this heroism will take in Nigeria, but the present regime, basking in the illusion that it was democratically elected – and therefore whatever actions it takes are in the interest of the democracy-loving people of Nigeria who voted to put it in power – will soon, as the saying goes, show its true colors. Expectedly, troops have been deployed to the Niger Delta.

The regime may delay for a while before baring its fangs, knowing that whatever false steps it takes now would count against it. However, let us not waste time on speculations. There are a couple of actions that say loudly that the present regime in Nigeria is just a throwback to the oligarchy which has been the hallmark of modern Nigeria. Take the appointment last week of Gen. Victor Malu as Army Chief, an army riddled with crisis of confidence.

Gen. Malu, a product of the dog eat dog military system in Nigeria, led the joint West African forces (ECOMOG) in Liberia. He was later chairman of Abacha's military tribunal that tried the alleged coup plotters of December 1997, which included Abacha's second-in-command, Gen. Oladipo Diya, and some journalists. This development has left tongues wagging. Could his appointment be the outcome of a deal between this regime and the one preceding it? Could it be part of the much-touted reconciliation process which is nothing but an attempt to seek reprieve for the scoundrels in uniform who have tyrannised and desecrated Nigeria?

Perhaps, we could forget the past if only those who yesterday, in an undisguised and unmitigated display of self-abuse, were too glad to be counted among the hired thugs of the fiendish regime of Sani Abacha; those who shunned democracy or even the pretence of it; those who rather than speak out against evil, were too willing to dine with the devil himself; perhaps, we could forget if these people, thanks to the skewed transition to democracy, are not the ones who have taken control of the political landscape.

Even more intriguing is the question: Would Obasanjo have made Gen. Malu Army Chief if he (Malu) had been the one that jailed him during the 1995 fake coup trial? It is not unlikely then that a self-confessed murderer like Maj. Al-Mustapha, Abacha's Chief Security Officer, and a member of his murderous triumvirate that comprised Ismaila Gwarzo, National Security Adviser and Frank Omenka of the notorious Directorate of Military Intelligence, will find space in the new dispensation. After all, the police seem not to have a case against him and are calling on the public to provide evidence to enable them prosecute him.

Those posing as heroes today were, just a little while ago, conspirators in the grand design to enslave Nigerians perpetually. Let us go back twenty years when, in the words of Ike Okonta, Head of Strategy and Tactics of Environmental Rights Action,

> *"Obasanjo on the eve of his departure as Head of State bowed to pressure from the unitarist hawks and their oil company paymasters to enact the Land Use Decree in 1978". "He",* according to Okonta *"at one fell swoop, took away the sole livelihood of millions of poor peasants in the Niger Delta, turned them into tenants on their own property, and gave Shell and the other oil companies the ammunition they needed to rape and pollute the land without challenge".*

Professor Omo Omoruyi, a former director of the Centre for Democratic Studies, has indicated that the way the military, particularly the leadership, is constituted is at the root of the Nigerian problem. He has also revealed how,

> "Gen. Obasanjo frustrated an attempt to address the armed forces question at the Constituent Assembly in 1978 and deleted the landmark amendment on the creation of a new military as well as the amendment which was to create a new political class from the draft constitution submitted by the Constituent Assembly".

These two events, the crisis in the Niger Delta and the structure of the military, may yet be his (Obasanjo's) Achilles' heel. This regime, therefore, ought to be opposed because in many ways it is a continuation of the greedy rule of an oligarchy that has sought, in the last four decades, to decimate Nigeria and live on the spoils and is part of the plot to prevent Nigerians from determining their future. The mass hysteria that gripped a section of the international community would no doubt give way sooner than later as it becomes evident that the so-called democracy gift in Nigeria is nothing but a Trojan horse.

Genuine pro-democracy forces have no option but to expose this illusion of stability. The way out, of course, is to hold tenaciously to the demand for a Sovereign National Conference of genuine representatives of Nigerians which will ultimately put in place a new constitution and a truly federal system because it is hard to see how this deeply scarred nation can build a democratic society with a patently undemocratic process. However, there is a problem here. It is not impossible that the so-called elected representatives will demonize pro-democracy activists with such words as "anarchists", "troublemakers" and other high-sounding verbiage.

Like the hypocritical bunch of warmongers who have besieged Yugoslavia, what they cannot do, however, is to deny the fact that, as in Yugoslavia, the crisis in Nigeria has persisted because the social and political structures have served to undermine peace and progress.

Of course, those who are not only responsible for the problem but are principal beneficiaries cannot correct that.

25. When an Apology Falls Short
June 1999

American journalist and author, DeWayne Wickham, once wrote, "There are times when an apology just isn't enough to right an ugly wrong". This sentiment best addresses the ugly spectacle Nigeria has been confronted with in the last few days.

When the news broke two weeks ago that the Speaker of Nigeria's House of Representatives had lied about his age and educational qualification in order to get the lucrative job, very many people were confounded. The ex-(dis)honourable Speaker, Salisu Ibrahim Buhari, did not help matters when he stuck to his pernicious lies and threatened to sue the magazine (The News) that dared to expose his infamy. Like most politicians adept at double-speak and chicanery, Buhari had hoped that his bravado, and may be his pedigree, would overshadow his crime.

Last week Buhari bowed to public pressure, if not commonsense, and belatedly tendered his letter of resignation. He tried to fool a nation of over a 100 million people when he, while sobbing like a kid that was denied his lollipop, said his distasteful action was motivated by his zeal to serve his nation.

It is difficult to know if Buhari's tears were the product of a contrite heart. What is not in doubt is that it was a sorry sight; nauseating by the realization that Buhari received a thunderous applause from his fellow honourable colleagues who, I am reliably informed, also agreed to pardon him, just as there were protests in some places by, presumably, party supporters, against Buhari's ignominious exit. How many more honourable members secured their places through such high-sounding but no less dubious and contemptible credentials? We may never know.

Not too long ago, I had the rare privilege, courtesy of a friend who was on a visit, of knowing not only some of the people who, purportedly, were elected to represent him and millions of other helpless Nigerians, but also how they were elected. As my friend regaled me with tales of political trickery, violence and corruption that were the hallmark of the transition programme – evidently, in some cases, confirmed outlaws had actually found their way into the National Assembly as lawmakers – the only thought I could muster was that those who orchestrated this grand deception would not be disappointed.

Understandably, not a few people have called for Buhari's prosecution, if only to show that the current regime in Nigeria has a moral right to govern and dispel the belief that there is a gulf between intentions and actions. This call is welcome even though there is little that gives one hope that the law would be allowed to take its due course. The Nigeria Police would more likely arrest you for wandering in your neighbourhood than prosecute an executive miscreant.

However, there is another dimension to the Buhari saga. It is this aspect that should be of concern to those who are interested in the future of democracy in Nigeria. It was not Buhari's desire to serve his fatherland that led him to such villainous heights. It was his greed, his inordinate ambition and lust for power that took control of him. Of course, that greed, that repulsive ambition, that putrid lust for power was oiled by a system that itself reeks of decadence.

Buhari, of course, is as much a victim as a villain. He is a villain to the extent that his disgraceful act has taken the shine out of the little lustre that seemed to have enveloped the Nigerian nation after almost two decades of sadistic military repression, banditry and profligacy. But, his case is an equally pitiful one. As a victim, Buhari was responding to a system whose harbinger cannot pass the simplest test of propriety.

We are all witnesses to the fraud that was the transition that threw up Buhari and people like him; and they abound in every facet of Nigeria's so-called new democratic order: those who had laws bent in their favour; those who bought their way to exalted positions simply because there was no alternative. It was a system that from the outset disfranchised Nigerians and placed them at the mercy of political thugs and scoundrels who counted more on money rather than morality to attain their positions. It was a system that sought to diminish the true meaning of democracy and belittle the immense prospects inherent in a genuine and unfettered democratic order.

Of course, it is not presumptuous to say we have heard the last of the Buhari saga. After all, incurable optimists would ask, what would it add to or remove from Nigeria's determined march to lasting democracy? Whether the Buhari crisis and how it is resolved would add to or vitiate Nigeria's new democratic order is left to be seen.

There are, however, a few lessons to be learnt from the Buhari debacle. These lessons are simply that democracy and elections are two different things; that "free and fair elections", whatever that jaded phrase means, cannot be a true test of a genuine democratic order.

Since Buhari is the quintessence of the present order, we must begin to question the wisdom of our Euro-American taskmasters who deify elections and have solemnly sworn to force them down our throats when it suits their purpose. More often than not, they are not interested in the processes leading up to elections and really care very little what the vast majority of the people stand to gain at the end of every electoral victory. It is better to imagine the horror Nigerians would have gone through in the next four years in the guise of lawmaking if Buhari had not been exposed.

Let us pause for a moment and consider this: why was it possible that members of his party who ought to know him well could not detect that Buhari was far younger than he claimed to be and that he did not possess a degree from any of the universities he claimed to have attended?

What can we make of the political party that produced Buhari and ensured that he emerged as the Speaker of the House of Representatives? Is it possible that his party (the People's Democratic Party) knew about his lies but was overwhelmed by his financial generosity? There is little doubt that Buhari's electoral victory and the ovation he received as he bowed out disgracefully last week were signs of solidarity with a kindred spirit.

Now that the Abacha/Abubakar tragicomedy has claimed its first victim, the question is: How long will it take before this circus, inevitably, comes to an end? In these times, an apology is, certainly, not enough. Not even the prosecution of Buhari will suffice. Any system that produces the Buharis of this world calls for nothing less than a thorough overhaul.

26. Babangida's Death Wish
June 1999

Recently, as I sat pondering over the most cynical and provocative statement ever made by anybody since the political crisis in Nigeria took a morbid turn in June 1993, I received an e-mail from a friend in South Africa. It is important to state here that this friend is not a Nigerian. However, his comments showed that he had taken more than a passing interest in the Nigerian crisis, and that he understood it, contrary to the many patchy analyses of most foreign analysts. I would like to share his mail with readers.

> *"My brother, we must demand for a Truth Commission to find out the disappearances, human rights violations, murder – Giwa, prison conditions, the plane that killed several officers under IBB (including my roommate Major Bawah and other friends from Uganda), etc., as part of any genuine transition? IBB must face the music! So he thinks his life is more important than the thousands who have died (through economic policies, etc.) or by naked murder by the police and military? West Africans must learn to fight the military; this nonsense can no longer take place in Uganda. Collect a book on Uganda by Major Ondonga from Kabral or Nasser and read. Thanks for the piece. We need the right slogans across the country".*

The "nonsense" he referred to was the absolutism of the military in Nigeria; its excesses and highhanded actions which had been the subject of an earlier discussion between us. We had discussed the fact that the military enjoyed the best that the Nigerian state could offer. They lived in the choicest houses, owned property beyond imagination, drove the best cars, and did not pay for public utilities, including bus fares. The conclusion, of course, was that the military had not only become a liability but a veritable fetter to progress in Nigeria. My friend felt, and still feels concerned, about the Nigerian crisis and had gone ahead to offer very meaningful and practical solutions.

What had really caused me so much distress was, coincidentally, the same issue my friend had raised: Babangida. The former dictator was quoted in an interview with the New York Times that his annulment of the June 12, 1993 presidential election was wrong and that he regretted his action. Babangida said many odious things, including his admission that he betrayed his "very genuine friend for 25 years", Chief M.K.O. Abiola. "From the day we met", in reference to Abiola, "there was rapport. I had my friend there waiting to take over. Truly, it would have been a great destiny", Babangida was reported to have said.

Babangida was not alone during his confession. His son, Mohammed, who was present during the interview, was quoted as saying,

> "There were other generals, including the late Sani Abacha, who said that if power was ceded to a southerner like Chief Abiola, the North will have nothing left. They then put my father in a corner, they threatened him".

Interesting words! We would like to know, however, who these generals are. Are they still in service?

Under normal circumstances, one would have dismissed Babangida's statement as the ranting of a demented General, one who ought to be on trial for his crimes against Nigerians. However, these are not the best of times, and when generals rule anything can happen. Babangida's latest interview followed on the heels of another he had with the London Guardian, the summary of which was that he had no regrets for annulling the June 12, 1993 election. Echoing his cousin who now heads the contraption called government in Nigeria, he said there was no need for a national unity government to convene a Sovereign National Conference because that would be undemocratic.

I tried to make sense out of his recent outbursts, but the harder I tried, the more nonsensical they appeared. I told myself, here was a man who had the excellent opportunity of making history, of being a great statesman, but chose to play the buffoon and act as a spoilsport. The conclusion was that it is either Babangida does not appreciate the extent of his crime, or he thinks Nigerians are gullible and, therefore, would always fall for his claptrap.

For a man who visited unmitigated suffering on Nigerians and caused so much death, destruction and pain, one would have thought Babangida was a genuine penitent, but it appears the maniacal dictator is not through with Nigeria. Signs of what to expect emerged shortly before the inglorious death of Abacha when the self-styled "evil genius", in his denunciation of Abacha, said military rule was essentially authoritarian and had lost its appeal.

It is not impossible that Babangida, supported by foreign security apparatuses, masterminded the sinister events in the country in the last two months to plan for his re-emergence. Undoubtedly, Abacha pursued a perilous agenda which was not in the interest of the political monstrosity which Babangida represents. Abiola on the other hand was the greatest threat to these iniquitous power maniacs. Expectedly, the next line in this macabre drama would be the announcement that Babangida has become a born again democrat and would attempt to contest as a civilian president.

Apart from dubious western analysts, there are those who genuinely think Nigeria is on the threshold of a transition to democracy.

This optimism is borne out of the inherently faulty reasoning that the military in Nigeria is capable of self-correction. Babangida, of course, may be able to bamboozle these incurable optimists. For Nigerians, this is too much an idle postulation to merit any comment. Whilst seeing through this facade, we must return once again to the Babangida era. What Nigerians endured under Babangida has no historical precedent.

Fortunately, the former dictator, consciously or unconsciously, is openly calling for a trial which must out of necessity take place if Nigerians are to heave a sigh of relief and say never again will violations of their rights go unpunished.

Babangida should be ready to pay for his iniquities. He has called the trial upon himself. No amount of penitence would suffice.

27. When Patience is not a Virtue
October 2012

If you want to appreciate the integrity deficit of the Jonathan administration, look no further than the events surrounding the disappearance and appearance of the First Lady, Patience Jonathan.

For someone who never misses an opportunity to steal the spotlight, it was inevitable that the First Lady's absence would draw some attention. And it did. Regrettably, what started as speculation about her whereabouts soon turned into a comic relief and a national embarrassment. When it became apparent that the "resting in Germany" alibi was as lame as it was perfidious, we were told that President Goodluck Jonathan, accompanied by the chaplain of Aso Villa Chapel, Ven. Obioma Onwuzurumba, paid a visit to the First Lady in Germany.

The result of the secret visit, according to reports, "was a short news item aired on the Nigerian Television Authority (NTA) at 9pm and accompanied by a short video clip (shot and sent to NTA by the Presidency) showing the President and a gorgeously dressed First Lady who was heard saying, 'Let me take picture with my husband'".

Reuben Abati, the Special Adviser to the President on Media and Publicity, put a spin on that senseless but audacious attempt to hoodwink Nigerians. According to Abati,

> *"The video clip aired by NTA was a confirmation that the President's wife was hale and hearty contrary to what some people wanted Nigerians to believe. The video has put paid to all the lies that people who play politics with almost everything have been spreading. It was clear from that video that the scene was not a hospital scene".*

I am sure Abati hardly ever listens to his inner voice. If he does, he would know that he and his boss were the ones playing politics with the life of the First Lady. Abati noted that, "Government had been quiet since because it could not afford to be 'jumping into the fray' with everybody". Welcome to the world of fairy tales. We are supposed to believe this and just move on with our lives. Of course, if you believe Abati's tales by moonlight, you might as well believe that tooth fairies exist.

His position shows how unhinged the whole apparatus of governance in Nigeria has become. What were we expected to make of the fact that our ubiquitous First Lady, the Marie Antoinette of our time, went AWOL for two months? However, let me reassure Abati and his paymasters that even though they have joined the "wrecking crew" of our commonwealth, it is hard to find any Nigerian, including the inveterate enemies of the president, who wishes the First Lady ill health.

The grand secrecy and deception that surrounded the First Lady's sudden disappearance for two months was unnecessary and impish. One would think that after what the country went through in the hands of erstwhile First Lady, Turai Yar'Adua and her cabal, our so-called leaders would have learnt a lesson or two. How mistaken we were! It seems the more things change in Nigeria, the more they remain the same. Governance has become a huge joke. Nigerian rulers take Nigerians for granted because they are convinced they are not accountable to the citizens.

As if Abati's taunts were not enough insult, when the First Lady finally made it back to the country last week after a well-deserved rest in Germany, she cursed, bragged, and like a true Christian, thanked God Almighty for bringing her back safely to Nigeria and giving her a second chance. It is a bit mystifying that someone who claimed she was not sick or admitted in any hospital came back and thanked God for giving her a second chance! Nigerians are reputed to be the happiest people on earth, but I am not sure we are a country of 160 million dunderheads.

Typical of the First Lady, her return was marked by fanfare and welcome celebrations reserved for royals. Since Mrs. Jonathan went to rest and idle Nigerians kept busy speculating on cyberspace that she was in Germany for cosmetic surgery or getting treatment for a life-threatening ailment, the carnival-like welcome ceremony was only proper to confirm she is hale and hearty.

The First Lady denied ever staying in a hospital during her trip abroad and in a rambling tone, explained her sojourn in Germany:

> "Wherever there are good people, there are also bad ones. There are a few Nigerians that are saying whatever they like, not what God planned because God has a plan for all of us. And God has said it all that when two or three are gathered in His name, that He will be with them. And Nigerians gathered and prayed for me and God listened and heard their prayers. So, I thank God for that. God is wonderful and His mercy is forever. At the same time, I read in the media where they said I was in the hospital".
>
> "God Almighty knows I have never been to that hospital. I don't even know the hospital they mentioned. I have to explain what God has done for me. I do not have terminal illness, or any cosmetic surgery much less tummy tuck",

the first lady reassured Nigerians.

She may well be correct. She may not have visited a hospital. Perhaps, the Presidency bought an estate in Germany and got the doctors to treat her at home. There is a world of difference and rumour mongers can jump into the lagoon for all they care.

Not done with her tirade, the First Lady added,

> "My husband loves me as I am and I am pleased with how God created me. I cannot add. But, at the same time, I will use this opportunity to thank my beloved husband and my children and my staff in general and all Nigerians for standing by me during my trial time. God has given me a second chance to come and work with women of Nigeria, children and the less privileged. I have come to save Nigeria. I have come to work with Nigerians. I am there for them. Once more, I am pleased to be back. I love Nigerians. They are my family".

If the attitude of the First Lady is borne out of a feeling of guilt, that unlike her, thousands of women die every year from poor pre and post natal care and millions more do not have access to basic health care because of the poor health infrastructure her husband oversees, she shouldn't worry. We are used to our rulers getting treatment and possibly dying overseas, particularly in Germany.

If there is a group that should bear any guilt, it is the media. Where was the Nigerian media in this debacle? The same question was asked during the Yar'Adua crisis. If our journalists could not go to Germany and were happy to join the speculation game, they owed Nigerians a duty to raise pertinent questions when the First Lady returned.

The Patience Jonathan story is an insight into the secrecy that has dogged this administration. But, it is not just that. It is also a reflection of the reckless impunity and utter contempt Mr. Jonathan has, not just for the laws of the land, but the people he purports to lead.

If Nigerians appear impatient with the current administration, it is for very good reasons. There are very few options open to us as a nation beyond the current administration.

In the First Lady, this country finally has a saviour. Let's hope the second chance she asked for, which Almighty God has graciously granted her, is not to continue the plunder and deepen the culture of impunity and bad governance.

---

28. IN SYMPATHY WITH RIBADU
NOVEMBER 2012

I sympathise with Mallam Nuhu Ribadu, ex-Chairman of the Economic and Financial Crimes Commission (EFCC) and more recently Chairman of the Petroleum Revenue Special Task Force (PRSTF). It is often said that once bitten twice shy. That best describes the situation Ribadu found himself a week ago during the submission of his committee's report to the president.

Nine months ago when the public awoke to the surprise appointment of Nuhu Ribadu to head the PRSTF, it set tongues wagging. Many Nigerians had questioned the wisdom in accepting the job.

The objection ranged from the fact that the committee was set up by the Minister of Petroleum Resources (who is deeply enmeshed in the crisis in the oil sector) and not the president, to the fact that for an administration with a predilection for committees, this may just be another committee. The cynics had argued that it was an attempt to shore up the government's integrity deficit and boost its anti-corruption credentials.

I was one of those who had some reservations about Ribadu's appointment, but I did not make my feeling public. Even though I had worked with him closely at the EFCC and much later during his presidential campaign, I did not attempt to discuss his new job with him. I assumed that as a man of strong convictions, he had his reason for accepting the job.

I met Ribadu in late August. Prior to that meeting, we had not seen for eight months since the public presentation of my book, *Time to Reclaim Nigeria,* in Abuja, on December 15, 2011, which meant there was a lot of catching up to do. Part of our discussion centred on his committee's work. He expressed his frustration and explained some of the problems his committee encountered. He hinted about the pecuniary influence from oil "stakeholders" and the possibility of divided allegiance of some members of the committee.

Listening to him, I got a feeling that his was a committee primed to fail. I saw a man tormented by betrayal, yet upbeat. What was of interest to him was what to do to curb the monumental fraud his committee had discovered in the oil industry. He sounded to me like someone who knew the inevitable outcome of the report, but wanted to give the administration the benefit of the doubt.

Looking back, I am not sure he knew or felt at the time of our meeting that the government was contemptuous enough to undermine the report of a committee it set up. I left him and looked forward to the submission of his committee's report. The submission of the report turned into a fiasco, predictably so. So much has been written about the events surrounding the presentation of the PRSTF report to President Jonathan on November 2. What is missing in the narrative is the complicity of the Presidency, the Minister of Petroleum Resources and major oil multi-nationals in the effort to scuttle the work of the PRSTF.

For a man who promised to do things differently, President Jonathan is awfully predictable. Last week, as the nation waited patiently for the submission of the PRSTF report, I had noted that we would be treated to the same rhetoric that has become the hallmark of the Jonathan administration. It was exactly what happened; except that this time, the president conspired to embarrass himself and the entire nation.

When Reuters first put the PRSTF report in the public domain a little over two weeks ago, the Presidency promised that there was no attempt to "cover up" the findings of the committee. Diezani Alison-Madueke, Minister of Petroleum Resources, said a committee had been given ten days to look at the report and make some "input". The minister had received the report more than a month earlier, but decided to sit on it.

So what happened? Here is my take: I think the government was caught in a bind, it panicked and the result was the embarrassing situation that played itself out on November 2. The Presidency, it seemed, had been wondering what to do with the PRSTF report since August when it was submitted to the Minister of Petroleum Resources. A minority report by members who were not "comfortable" with the main report may have been an option. But, once the report became public, it changed everything. Enter Steve Oronsaye and Bernard Otti.

It is instructive that the report the Minister of Petroleum Resources promised would be ready in ten days was not presented to the president as expected. Instead, Oronsaye and Otti made themselves available or were recruited to wreck the final report submitted to the president. Their only reason: "the process adopted by the committee in arriving at its report was flawed".

Oronsaye's verbal diarrhoea at the submission of the PRSTF report could only have come from a man who had the backing of the Presidency. "What I am saying is that the President has said come and submit the report, so what, if we are not ready, we are not ready," Oronsaye asserted confidently and condescendingly. "When I say so what, the President has spoken, we should be man enough to tell the

President that we are not ready. That is the reason why you are handing over a report that is not process driven".

Two things are at play here. One, only a man that is incredibly reckless would speak the way Oronsaye spoke before the president. I do not think Oronsaye is a reckless man considering he is a career civil servant who rose to become the Head of the Civil Service of the Federation. The only other thing is that his comments were carefully scripted and contrived. This was evident when he offered the coup-de-grace in these words: "I don't know what the report contains. Therefore, in my view, I do not think the report should be accepted at this time, I challenge any member of this committee to take me on".

Expectedly, Ribadu, the chairman of the committee, took him on. As it turned out, Oronsaye and Otti, barely participated in the committee's work. According to Ribadu, "He (Oronsaye) was not at the inauguration and he never participated in the deliberations of the committee. The only time he came was when we wanted to start deliberations on recovery and he came on behalf of one company, Addax Petroleum, which owes $1.5 billion. That was the only time he came. In fact, he scuttled the payment of the $1.5 billion".

Whether it was for financial gains or compensation for their appointments while serving as members of the PRSTF – Oronsaye became a member of the board of the NNPC and Otti became a director in NNPC – both Oronsaye and Otti have written their names in infamy. So long as their sense of propriety did not detect a conflict of interest and instruct resignation from the committee, they will remain on the wrong side of history. They sold their conscience and mortgaged the future of their children for lucre.

President Jonathan, in his characteristic tepid response to official sleaze, "urged Nigerians not to be distracted by the small disagreement, but to focus on the subject matter of the committee which is the sanitization of the petroleum sector for the benefit of Nigeria and Nigerians". The president said he was "not surprised there are disagreements between the members of the committee on the Petroleum Revenue Task Force. It is about money. There are some lapses and probably not everyone agreed". He advised any member of the

PRSTF "who had a contrary opinion from those expressed in the report to submit his opinion to him through his chief of staff or the Minister of Petroleum Resources".

Clearly, we have heard the last of the PRSTF report, going by the president's dismissive response. Like Ribadu, I weep for Nigeria!

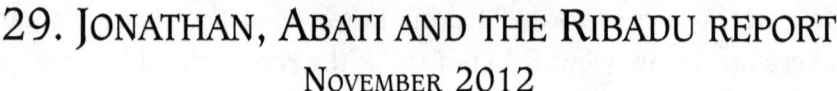

29. Jonathan, Abati and the Ribadu Report
November 2012

Reuben Abati and Doyin Okupe are amongst the best in their business. And by this, I mean the business of dissembling. That was exactly what Abati did in his latest treatise, "Jonathan and the Ribadu Report". I do not begrudge both Abati and Okupe. Their job is to be evasive and to try as much as possible to mislead while continuously throwing lies at us in the hope that some will stick; our responsibility is to cut through their BS. Indeed, it was a lot of BS that Abati attempted to heap on us in his last outing.

Abati began his latest assault on our collective sensibilities with an overdose of insult when he wrote,

> "It is so unfortunate that there has been so much ignorant carping and malicious tittle-tattling about the report of the Petroleum Revenue Task Force chaired by Mallam Nuhu Ribadu, both failings arising from a deliberate attempt to individualize what was actually a group work, a mischievous attempt to politicize one report out of three, and to smuggle into an emergent grand web of conspiracy, elements of blackmail, mischief and outright opportunism".

As the master of BS himself, Abati knows too well that the "putrefacious stench of the fart that seems to have overtaken the subject" comes from no other place than the Presidency. Here is a chronology of the Presidency and Abati's metamorphosis on the Petroleum Revenue Special Task Force (PRSTF) report.

A few days after the report was made public by Reuters, Abati claimed it was meant to embarrass the government. According to him, "excerpts from the report could not be taken as an official document because the committee had not formally submitted its report to the appropriate authority. As far as the Federal Government was concerned, the report in the public domain was suspicious". This was the first clear attempt to undermine the PRSTF report.

Abati then went on to qualify the task of the committee and foreclose the prospect of anyone being held to account:

> *"For the avoidance of doubt and for the benefit of the naysayers, the committees were set up as fact-finding and advisory bodies to generate ideas and recommendations about how best to strengthen the oil and gas sector and to further pursue the objectives of institutional integrity, transparency and accountability".*

Abati did not see anything wrong in Steve Oronsaye and Bernard Otti being appointed into different positions in the NNPC while serving on the PRSTF. "It is important to note that this committee and other committees had government officials and ex-staff as members", he intoned.

We all know the role Oronsaye and Otti played in their attempt to scuttle the report during its submission to the president on November 2. Their infamous intervention was done at great insult and inconvenience to the president. But, who cares? Of course, insult and inconvenience count for nothing when billions of dollars and the president's anointed are involved.

A week after the PRSTF submitted its report, as it became evident that the controversy instigated by the Presidency will simply not go away, Abati's second-in-command and Senior Special Assistant to the President on Public Affairs, the voluble Doyin Okupe, alerted us to paragraph four of the covering letter of the PRSTF report signed by Ribadu and the secretary of the committee, Olasupo Shasore, SAN.

The offending paragraph four which Okupe alludes to, states,

> *"The data used in this report was presented by various*

> stakeholders who made submissions to the Task Force at various dates, which have been disclosed in relevant sections of the report. Due to the time frame of the assignment, SOME (emphasis mine) of the data used could not be independently verified and the task force recommends that the government should conduct such necessary verifications and reconciliations".

The implication of this "overriding" paragraph four in Okupe's omniscient reasoning was that, "The committee had issued a disclaimer to its own report which will now make it impossible under our laws to indict or punish anybody except and until the federal government fully verifies and reconciles the facts as recommended by the committee in its submission to the government".

Can anything be more contradictory? Can Okupe be more ridiculous and fraudulent? The committee admitted that the reason it could not verify SOME of the data used was the "time frame" of the assignment. How does this constitute a "disclaimer" or absolve those responsible for the rot in the oil sector as indicated in the report?

In his desperate effort to stand reality on its head, Okupe shoots himself in the foot when he says the "disclaimer" will "make it impossible to indict or punish anybody except and until the federal government fully verifies and reconciles the facts as recommended by the committee in its submission to the government".

In one instance, he calls the committee's statement a "disclaimer"; in another, he praises the report by implying that the government will do what the committee recommends it does: "Conduct such necessary verifications and reconciliations". How addlebrained can one be in the defence of falsehood? Okupe's assurance that a White Paper will be issued and the recommendations would be fully implemented after the Presidency completes the uncompleted work of the PRSTF is as reassuring as asking Okupe to head the Economic and Financial Crimes Commission (EFCC).

Back to Abati and his disdain for truth and commonsensical argument. Abati accused Zakari Mohammed, Chairman, House Committee on Media and Public Affairs, of "talking absent-mindedly about 'lack of political will' to fight corruption" in his (Mohammed's) criticism of the president's handling of the PRSTF report. There is nothing new about Mohammed's postulation. Every right-thinking Nigerian holds that view.

This government has no redeeming feature. It was clear from the outset that the Presidency was looking for ways to undermine the PRSTF report to let itself and its cronies off. The Presidency was not interested in the committee's report. If it was, it would not have created so much ruckus around the report. It simply would have given the committee extra time to finish its work if it felt the report was incomplete.

With the PRSTF report, President Jonathan has met his Waterloo. Thankfully, the report has received the support of the Nigeria Extractive Industries Transparency Initiative, (NEITI). NEITI says the PRSTF report reechoes the findings detailed in its own report on the monumental corruption and waste in the oil and gas sector that have yet to be implemented.

Aso Rock under President Jonathan has become a graveyard of committee reports. We have lost count of the number of committees President Jonathan has set up since May 6, 2010, when he first became president. There is a common thread to all the committee reports: their non-implementation.

To say the government lacks the "political will" to fight corruption is to be charitable to the president. This government has made corruption the directive principle of state policy. This was evident the very moment President Jonathan failed the political-will-to-fight-corruption litmus test when he refused to publicly declare his asset at the inception of his government on May 29, 2011, and went ahead during a nation-wide TV interview in June to heap scorn on Nigerians by saying he did not "give a damn" about public declaration of asset.

At that very moment, President "IDGAD" Jonathan declared war, not on corruption, but against Nigerians.

30. A Governor, Three Ministers and Their Burden
December 2012

The Governor of the Central Bank of Nigeria (CBN), Mallam Sanusi Lamido Sanusi, created a media firestorm last week when he proposed that the civil service be cut by half. Sanusi, of course, is not new to controversy. In the last three and half years of being at the helm at CBN, Sanusi has been variously assailed and praised for such policies as Islamic Banking, the N150,000 ($1000) maximum daily withdrawal, the cashless policy initiative and the introduction of a single N5000 ($33) note, in a country where majority of citizens live on about $2 a day.

So, it was expected that his latest comments at the Second Annual Capital Market Committee Retreat in Warri, Delta State, would attract public attention. According to Sanusi,

"At the moment, 70 per cent of Federal Government's revenue goes for payment of salaries and entitlement of civil servants, leaving 30 per cent for development of 167 million Nigerians. That means that for every naira government earns, 70 kobo is consumed by civil servants. You have to fire half of the civil service because the revenue of the government is supposed to be for 167 million Nigerians. Any society where government spends 70 per cent of its revenue on its civil service has a problem. It is unsustainable".

He added that the country did not need 109 senators and 360 representatives to make laws. He called for an end to the "wastage" of funds on the maintenance of 774 Local Government Area chairmen, their aides, councillors and other appendages of the third-tier of government and the scrapping of states that are not viable.

Lending support to what appears to be the position of the Jonathan administration, the Minister of Finance, Ngozi Okonjo-Iweala (she and Sanusi are members of President Jonathan's Economic Management Team), who spoke a few days later at the National Economic Summit, had this to say in praise of Sanusi's position,

> *"Let me tell you, the targets of this fiscal tightening are human beings; they are the ones that must be eliminated to prune down the costs. The cost of personnel in the budget is 32 per cent and that is huge".*

Not surprisingly, the responses to Sanusi's comments were fast and furious. Some of the responses were genuine; others downright opportunistic. Take for instance the response from the National Assembly via the Deputy Chairman of the House Committee on Media and Public Affairs, Victor Ogene, who accused Sanusi, of heating up the polity with his "frequent controversial utterances".

According to Ogene, the National Assembly had a total budget of N150bn ($1bn) in 2012 to cater for 360 House members, 109 Senators, thousands of civil servants and political aides while the CBN had over N300b ($2bn). On Sanusi's suggestion to cut the civil service by half, Ogene was amazed that "a manager of the economy would come up with such a proposal in the face of the socio-economic challenges of today".

Coming from a member of a do-nothing House that wears scandal as a badge of honour, Ogene must have some cojones to lecture us about "socio-economic challenges". At the last check, Ogene and his colleagues cart home so-called quarterly constituency allowance (read security vote, because you hardly can find any constituent that benefits from that allowance) to the tune of N43m ($286,000).

Clearly, some of the positions that Sanusi canvassed are constitutional matters. Nothing can be done about those issues unless Sanusi himself supports the call for a genuine constitution of "we the people" or better still the restructuring of Nigeria. But on the call for the pruning of the civil service, you have to agree with Sanusi if you have encountered our civil servants or had the misfortune of visiting, for example, the Federal Secretariat in Abuja.

A typical day at the secretariat reminds you of a visit to a shopping mall with staff milling around aimlessly while those in the offices are busy channel flipping. With "ghost workers" everywhere, it is difficult, if not impossible, to get anyone to attend to your enquiries. Late last year, the Head of Service of the Federation, Isa Bello Sali, informed us that the government had uncovered 71,135 ghost workers on its payroll which cost the country N28bn ($186m) annually.

Undoubtedly, the civil service is bloated and needs to be trimmed for efficiency. But beyond this revelation, there is nothing spectacular about Sanusi's call. The rot and inefficiency in the civil service is part of the rot and inefficiency in the larger society. It is emblematic of a culture of entitlement, cronyism and waste of which Sanusi is an integral part.

In 2011, there was an allegation of impropriety in a land buyback scam in which the names of President Goodluck Jonathan, the Attorney General of the Federation, Mohammed Adoke, and Lamido Sanusi featured prominently. It was a bizarre story the mainstream media refused to touch. The sordid details are chronicled in my book, *Time to Reclaim Nigeria*.

We have the intrepid online publication, Saharareporters, to thank for that amazing investigative report. Days after Saharareporters published the story, the CBN, in a contemptibly inadequate response, acknowledged that it paid almost N20 bn ($133m) for a piece of land, originally owned by a government agency, NITEL, to build "a world class conference centre".

It seems our rulers know a thing or two about world class event centres because while Sanusi was busy dreaming of a lean, efficient and effective civil service, news came that the government was planning to build another banquet hall for Mr. President at the cost of N2.2bn ($15m).

"We noticed that it (the current hall) is inconveniencing; it is not in tandem with what is outside the country. Even smaller countries have better Banquet Halls near their Presidential residences", the minister of the Federal Capital Territory (FCT), Bala Mohammed, said in defence of the scandalous approval for the unbudgeted project by the Federal Executive Council (FEC) at its last meeting.

Again, this hollow argument about what obtains in other countries. Unfortunately, our rulers are too blind to see the good network of roads, constant electricity and reliable infrastructure in other countries. That our youth, the future of this country, migrate in droves to smaller countries like Ghana for university education is certainly not of concern to Mr. Mohammed.

Mr. Mohammed who appears beholden to President Jonathan is on familiar territory (no pun intended). He recently expressed outrage, during a ministerial inspection tour, that the construction of new homes for the four presiding officers of the National Assembly in one of the choicest parts of the capital city, Maitama Extension (which the minister had renamed Goodluck Jonathan District), was not going as planned. The presiding officers are the Senate President, David Mark and his deputy, Ike Ikweremadu, Speaker of the House of Representatives, Aminu Waziri Tambuwal and his deputy, Emeka Ihedioha.

At a budget defence last year, the minister told lawmakers why their leaders needed new residences outside their current Apo Legislative Quarters residences. "We were there on inspection and so we cannot guarantee the safety and security of principal officers of the National Assembly who take decisions on very serious and sometimes critical issues that may impinge on the sensibilities, perception and feelings of others. We must as a government protect the principal officers of the National Assembly", the minister said.

These new, secure and luxury homes will cost about N1bn ($7m) each for the Senate President and the Speaker. Add another N1bn ($7m) for the homes of their deputies and do the math. The minister did not disappoint during his 2013 budget defence. His ministry, he confirmed, will spend N2bn ($13m) in 2013 as part of the N7.1bn ($47m) approved for a "befitting" residence for the Vice President, Namadi Sambo. The week in review ended with an affront from our oil goddess, Diezani Alison-Madueke, who clarified why the Ministry of Petroleum Resources would spend N6.2bn ($41m) on the Petroleum Industry Bill awareness campaign. The less said about this the better.

The preceding examples, a drop in the ocean of brazen pillage currently going on in the name of governance in the country, represent the face of the decadent culture in Nigeria that we need to do away with quickly. There is something sinister about our democracy. It is that our so-called elected representatives see their position as an opportunity to get their share of the proverbial national cake. It is, therefore, not surprising that the highest decision-making body in the country, the FEC, as well as MDAs have become veritable money laundering platforms in the guise of contract awards.

While Nigerians die in their dozens every day from preventable diseases, poverty, terror and associated ills, it is this brazen plunder that should concern the likes of Sanusi and Okonjo-Iweala who still have the scruples to talk about reducing the cost of governance.

---

31. OUR NOT-SO-DISTINGUISHED SENATORS
DECEMBER 2012

Distinguished Senator David Alechenu Bonaventure Mark is a very lucky man. Indeed, he is one of the luckiest Nigerians dead or alive. In the last three decades, he has featured prominently on the national stage as minister of communications, Governor of Niger State, four-term senator and two-term Senate President.

Other things being equal, Senator Mark may yet end his long and illustrious career by emerging as President of the Federal Republic, an ambition I am sure he does not take lightly, the constant denials by aides notwithstanding. Senator Mark has had occasion to take shots at the Jonathan government on the problem of insecurity, poor infrastructure and the government's fiscal policies. It is the mark of a military strategist. In all, though, he is a loyal party man; and a patient one at that.

Every now and again, aides of the Senate President alert us of mischief makers "bent on causing disaffection between President Goodluck Jonathan and the President of the Senate". The reference is to the cacophony of voices championing the 2015 presidential ambition of Senator Mark. The Special Adviser, Media and Publicity, to Senator Mark, Kola Ologbondiyan, had this to say recently in response to one of the ubiquitous "Mark for President 2015" groups:

> *"It is imperative to state and emphatically too, that Senator Mark and President Jonathan are on the same page in*

the onerous task of providing democratic dividends for Nigerians. It is therefore irresponsible, mischievous and misplaced for any set of Nigerians to embark on overheating the polity at this time of our national history. The Senate President is faced with providing qualitative legislative leadership for our nation and (has) urged mischief makers not to distract him".

I had the fortune of encountering Senator Mark in all his power and splendour earlier in the year. It was during a casual visit to a friend, a former legislator, at the Apo Legislative Quarters in Abuja. After my visit, my friend decided to drive me home. A few metres down the road, as we drove out of my friend's house, we were halted by a detachment of policemen.

While I wondered impatiently what was going on, my friend who obviously was used to the drama just rested both hands on the steering wheel and waited as a convoy of more than ten vehicles, including three black limousines, a bomb disposal van, an ambulance, numerous police escort jeeps with heavily armed policemen, crawled into an imposing edifice a few metres ahead of us.

After about five minutes, we were given permission to continue our journey. My friend commented off-handedly, "That is the Senate President". My immediate reaction was amazement and then revulsion when I realize d that the Senate President was coming from his office a few kilometres away. My mind wondered furiously about what democracy was costing the mass of our people; the cost of maintaining the Senate President's fleet of vehicles and aides; of the imposing house we just drove past and the fact that the Minister of the Federal Capital Territory, Senator Bala Mohammed, was building a new official residence for the Senate President and the three other presiding officers of the National Assembly, the Deputy Senate President as well as the Speaker and his deputy, for more than N1bn each.

So, it was a bit of a surprise when Senator Mark spoke recently during his condolence visit to the family of the late Senate Leader in the Second Republic, Dr. Olusola Saraki, in Ilorin, Kwara State. While praising Saraki, the Senate President noted,

> "Baba is not dead. He lives on because a man who lived as he did does not die. In everything, he was always himself. He did not pretend. He was a natural man doing what he loved best. He did all he did from the bottom of his heart. Unfortunately, there are many actors and pretenders on the political scene in Nigeria today. Politics should be played with honesty, with honour and a lot of integrity".

It seems Senator Mark never misses an opportunity to say the right things. But, doing the right things is a different kettle of fish. Someone once asked,

> "What manner of 'god' is the office of Nigeria's Senate President that the occupant should earn six times more than what President Barack Obama of the United States takes home and three times more than what the British Prime Minister earns, in a country where over 65 per cent of the citizens wallow below the $1 benchmark?"

That is the tragedy of the Nigerian situation. This piece is as much about David Mark as it is about the "hallowed chamber" he leads. It was prompted by an event earlier in the month involving the chairman, Federal Civil Service Commission (FCSC), Deaconess Joan Ayo.

During its 2012 budget performance before the Senate Committee on Establishment and Public Service Matters, Deaconess Ayo was confronted by the vice chairman of the committee, Senator Babafemi Ojudu, who alleged that there was rumour making the rounds that "some staff of the commission were compelling young job seekers to part with N500,000 ($3,000) to get jobs".

Senator Ojudu noted, "Such a rumour is not good for the image of this committee, it is not good for the image of your commission and the image of the country." The FCSC chairman responded by saying the commission had zero tolerance for corruption and corrupt practices and that she was hearing the rumour for the first time from Senator Ojudu. She challenged the senator to show proof of the alleged money-for-job scandal.

Of course, Deaconess Ayo was being economical with the truth. I do not know if Senator Ojudu was able to provide proof as requested by Deaconess Ayo, but the exchange threw up an issue that is equally troubling. Talking about rumours, we have heard allegations that senators collect bribe before approving budgets. But this pales in comparison to the fact that many government agencies now insist that job seekers must get letters from senators before they are considered for employment.

And this is no rumour because I have been involved with two federal agencies where this issue came up. It seems the only reason our senators enjoy this privilege is that they have control over the budget of these agencies. It is understandable if senators use their influence to help their "constituents", but it is criminal for them to legalize it.

Dr. Sam Amadi, Chairman/CEO of the Nigerian Electricity Regulatory Commission (NERC), put this phenomenon in perspective during the 7th Ralph Opara Memorial Lecture organized by the National Association of Seadogs (NAS), on Friday, November 2, 2012. In a speech titled, "Terrorism, Insecurity and Irredentist Movements: the Challenges for Nation-Building in Nigeria", Dr. Amadi noted,

"Today, Nigerian leaders have added to their sin of the exclusion of Nigerian citizens from the wealth of the nation, the sin of excluding them from employment opportunities. Every employment in private and public sector in Nigeria today is based on a letter of sponsorship from one Senator or Governor or Minister.

> *"Poor Nigerian working family that spent life savings to educate their children have little hope of them getting a good job because the people in power distort the recruitment process from merit to privilege. This is the new aristocracy in a republic. Recruiters in the public service will not ask for aptitude. They ask for a letter from a Senator, Governor or Minister. What will the much deprived graduate without such reference letter do if he is never considered for employment many years after leaving school than to seriously consider resort to violence and criminal enterprise?"*

This is what the average job seeker in Nigeria has to contend with. Senators Mark and Ojudu cannot say they are not aware of this phenomenon. And, if they are not aware, I am using this medium to bring it to their attention. They should denounce the agencies that are bringing the Senate into disrepute.

For the amount of money the country spends maintaining the Senate, the last thing we need is for our so-called lawmakers to become a menace to society by shamelessly acting out the despicable role of thoughtless enablers and overseers of an extremely dysfunctional polity.

32. Memo to Doyin Okupe: What is President Jonathan hiding? (1)
December 2012

I refer to your press conference of Thursday, December 6, 2012, in which you tried, albeit unsuccessfully, to do a cleanup of President Jonathan's anti-corruption credentials. You would agree that your presentation was all fury and little substance. I know as the Senior Special Assistant to the President on Public Affairs, your responsibility is to make the president look good in public. In your press conference, you listed a number of things that the government has done (and is doing) to show that President Jonathan is serious about fighting corruption.

To save space, I shall focus only on one. In a sense, the issue I have chosen for discussion appears to be the most important. Not only because it was the first in the list of accomplishments you enumerated in your speech, but because it is pivotal and at the heart of whether the president has the "political will" to fight corruption and whether we should believe him or not when he claims he is fighting corruption. I am talking here about the Freedom of Information Act (FoIA).

This is what you said about the FoIA:

> "The signing of the Freedom of Information Act into law by President Jonathan in May 2011 represents a watershed in the anti-corruption crusade in Nigeria. This piece of legislation, which had been virtually stalled by successive administrations since 1999, was signed into law by Mr. President to usher Nigeria into the league of countries where TRANSPARENCY (emphasis mine) in governance is entrenched and citizens are GRANTED UNFETTERED ACCESS TO INFORMATION (emphasis mine) about government activities.
>
> "This is the fulcrum upon which good governance rests in all known democracies and it is noteworthy that the present administration took the bull by the horns to lay this very important foundation for the war against corruption in Nigeria in the early months of its inception and 24 hours after the bill was presented to him by the National Assembly. You will agree with me that without a legal framework for whistle-blowing, the fight against corruption would be meaningless".

Well said. I couldn't agree with you more on the importance of the FoIA. Yes, it is to the credit of the government that the very first law the president signed was the FoIA. The problem, however, is that the law has been observed more in breach. And we can thank the president for his shining example. Perhaps, as a latecomer to the jamboree that is the Jonathan administration, you are not privy to certain things. Or is it a case of selective amnesia? The blustering presidential aide that you are, perhaps your impulsiveness got the better of you.

Whatever the problem, it is important that we set the record straight for posterity. Warily, to test the FoIA and the president's sincerity, on July 28, 2011, almost two months to the day the president signed the FoI bill into law, the African Centre for Media & Information Literacy (AFRICMIL) sent a Freedom of Information request to the Code of Conduct Bureau (CCB) asking "to be allowed to inspect and obtain copies of the 2007 asset declaration of President

Goodluck Ebele Jonathan; the asset declaration of President Goodluck Ebele Jonathan after the end of his tenure on May 28, 2011; and the current asset declaration of President Goodluck Ebele Jonathan when he assumed office on May 29, 2011".

AFRICMIL made the request in good faith and in accordance with Paragraph 3, Part I of the Third Schedule to the 1999 Constitution of the Federal Republic of Nigeria, as amended, which provides that "the Code of Conduct Bureau shall have power to: (a) receive declarations by public officers made under Paragraph 12 of Part I of the Fifth Schedule to this Constitution; (b) examine the declarations in accordance with the requirements of the Code of Conduct or any law; (c) RETAIN CUSTODY OF SUCH DECLARATIONS AND MAKE THEM AVAILABLE FOR INSPECTION BY ANY CITIZEN OF NIGERIA ON SUCH TERMS AND CONDITIONS AS THE NATIONAL ASSEMBLY MAY PRESCRIBE (emphasis added)".

Paragraph 11 of Part I of the Fifth Schedule to the Constitution provides that: "(1) Subject to the provisions of this Constitution, every public officer shall within three months after the coming into force of this Code of Conduct or immediately after taking office and thereafter - (a) at the end of every four years; and (b) at the end of his term of office, submit to the Code of Conduct Bureau a written declaration of all his properties, assets, and liabilities and those of his unmarried children under the age of eighteen years".

Pursuant to the aforementioned constitutional provisions and Section 2 of the Freedom of Information Act 2011, which states that "Notwithstanding anything contained in any other Act, Law or Regulation, the right of any person to access or request information, whether or not contained in any written form, which is in the custody or possession of any public official, agency or institution howsoever described, is hereby established", AFRICMIL made the request to the CCB to be allowed to inspect and obtain copies of President Goodluck Jonathan's asset declaration.

Regrettably, the CCB did not dignify the request with a response. After waiting patiently for almost three months and in line with the provisions of the FoIA, AFRICMIL filed a case at the Federal High

Court, Abuja. In the suit (No FHC/ABJ/CS/877/2011) filed on October 21, 2011, on behalf of AFRICMIL by Ashimole Felix of Che Oyintumba & Associates, AFRICMIL sought an order of mandamus compelling the CCB to comply with its (AFRICMIL's) request of making available to the public the asset declaration of President Goodluck Jonathan.

Mr. Lewis Asubiojo, who represented AFRICMIL in the suit, said,

> *"The organisation was concerned that even with the memo from the presidency that government agencies should subject themselves to the Freedom of Information Act, the CCB refused to act on its request". According to Asubiojo, "For a government that has proclaimed a transformation agenda and wants to fight corruption, it is important that President Jonathan leads by example, and one way he can do that is to make public his asset declaration".*

Since AFRICMIL's request over a year ago, we have gone from the ominous silence of the CCB, to Reuben Abati, the president's Special Adviser on Media, coldly confirming that "the president will not declare his assets on the pages of newspapers", to the president himself conceitedly stating publicly that he did not "give a damn" about making his asset declaration public. The assumption, of course, is that the declaration is with the CCB and was made as and when due.

In a June 2012 interview with SaharaTV's Rudolf Okonkwo, to mark Democracy Day, Abati had referred Nigerians interested in the president's asset declaration "to check with the Code of Conduct Bureau office". Regrettably, it is the same CCB that has "gone rogue" on the president's asset declaration. It is instructive to note that Sam Saba, chairman of the CCB, recently declared that the FoIA conflicts with the Constitution on the issue of making available to the public the president's asset declaration. He called for "judicial intervention to know what the law says".

President Jonathan says he is a transformative leader. Unless he just wants to transform himself, I see no reason why he should allow his asset declaration create so much uproar and overheat the polity unnecessarily.

33. Memo to Doyin Okupe: What is President Jonathan hiding (2)
December 2012

After the first part of this piece appeared last week, I received a couple of emails accusing me of several wrongdoings, from "disgracefully cherry-picking your press statement" to "being an agent of the opposition". One responder noted, "It is morally wrong to ignore all Okupe pointed out as regards progress in the fight against corruption. It is disgraceful to say the least. You don't have to kick the president at every twist and turn, just because you hate him".

Another intervener said matter-of-factly, "The President has complied with the law by declaring his assets, making it public is another thing entirely. There are many reasons it may not be desirable to make same public. One of the reasons is family pressure and the need to protect (his) investments". I do not know if the two responders above were speaking on your behalf, but one thing is clear: the issue of publicly declaring his asset is something President Jonathan cannot wish away as long as he lays claim to fighting corruption.

It is true that you said many things during your press conference of Thursday, December 6, 2012. For example, you averred,

> *"Since the present administration under President Goodluck Jonathan took charge of the affairs of this country, it has worked assiduously not only to transform the lives of Nigerians but also enhance the image and prestige of the country abroad.*

> *"A lot has been achieved in the intervening period with the transformation agenda of the administration. Despite these achievements, there is unbridled cynicism on the part of some individuals who have taken it upon themselves to mislead Nigerians by making unfounded and baseless allegations against this administration. The purpose of this campaign of misinformation and disinformation is to blind*

Nigerians to the sure and steady progress President Jonathan's administration has made in the eighteen months that it has been in power, to improve the quality of governance and deliver on the promises it made to the people.

"We seem to be living in a socio-political atmosphere of cynicism where theatrical actions, showmanship and other grandstanding are misinterpreted to mean political will in addressing a situation. This government does not believe in just arresting people for the sake of drama or playing to the gallery nor does it harbour the idea of deploying the anti-corruption agencies as tools to witch hunt political opponents, which were undisputable familiar practices in the past".

That was you waxing eloquent about President Jonathan's anti-corruption effort. Now that I have captured the essence of your message, I can go ahead to critique it. I decided to dwell on the Freedom of Information Act (FoIA) as referenced in your speech because, in my estimation, it provides a practical demonstration of the current government's fight against corruption or the lack of it. And the reason is simple: it touches President Jonathan directly.

You noted, and rightly too, that,

"All over the world, governments seriously desirous of tackling the menace of corruption usually adopt a holistic strategy which encompasses some or all of the under-listed benchmark: Enacting enabling laws, which clearly define what corruption is and spell out punitive measures; creating by law, the enabling environment for whistle blowing (FOI)".

It is on the strength of this that the Code of Conduct Bureau (CCB) should comply with the request by the African Centre for Media and Information Literacy and other organizations asking it to make available the asset declaration of the president. It is convenient for you to talk glibly about creating the enabling environment for whistle blowing, but nothing is more convincing than walking the talk. I am not being frivolous when I insist that the public needs to know what our transformative president is worth.

I have written about this before, but it is worth repeating. In 2007, President Jonathan, as vice president, declared his asset after much pressure from his boss, the late Umaru Musa Yar'Adua. In the intervening period (2007-2011), he did not do any other job (constitutionally, he is not allowed to) apart from being vice president, acting president, and president. So what could the president have acquired in four years that he does not want Nigerians to know about? In a sentence, what is President Jonathan hiding? If the president does not care enough about Nigerians to make his assets public, why would he care about steady power supply or good roads?

Of course, there is no law that says President Jonathan should declare his asset publicly. However, for someone who preaches transparency and accountability, he has a moral obligation to do so. Beyond this, however, it is important to emphasize that there is a law that says those who want access to public information (including asset declarations of public officers) can request such information. It is called the FoIA.

The president himself assented to it a year and half ago. On this issue, the CCB which is the custodian of asset declarations is under obligation to make available the president's asset declaration and those of other public officials on request. That is what the law says. There can't be any excuses or exemption. Nigeria is what it is today because we think the law is only applicable to certain people.

As the president's adviser, beyond laundering his image, it is also important that you give him genuine feedback and tell him the truth. The truth is that Nigerians (the much-touted happiest people on earth) are not happy. When I say Nigerians are not happy, I know am speaking the mind of millions of ordinary people, not those who are queuing to take the president's job or those you refer to as "cynics, 'latter-day saints' and emergency activists".

I am talking about the millions of Nigerians who are paying the price for the grand corruption and wanton pillage that have become the hallmark of the Jonathan administration; Nigerians that do not have the luxury of going to die in India or Germany because of the comatose state of healthcare in Nigeria.

If it is unpardonable for President Jonathan to say he does not "give a damn" about publicly declaring his asset, it is disingenuous for the CCB to say it is not in a position to act. It is equally contemptible for Labaran Maku, Minister of Information, to ask Nigerians, as he did recently during a workshop organized by the Federal Ministry of Information on the FoIA, "to examine the efficacy of the Freedom of Information Act in the fight against corruption by demanding for information on governance from public institutions".

Nothing typifies the impunity in Nigeria than the CCB's obfuscation on President Jonathan's asset declaration. Sam Saba, chairman of the CCB, claims protection under the 1999 Constitution for his organization's refusal to accede to public request for the asset declaration of President Jonathan. He argues that the FoIA conflicts with the Constitution and has requested "the National Assembly to enact an Act prescribing the terms and conditions under which the CCB could make assets declared by public officers available for inspection by Nigerians" as provided for in Section 3(c) of the Third Schedule of the 1999 Constitution which empowers the CCB to "retain custody of such declarations and MAKE THEM AVAILABLE FOR INSPECTION BY ANY CITIZEN OF NIGERIA ON SUCH TERMS AND CONDITIONS AS THE NATIONAL ASSEMBLY MAY PRESCRIBE" (emphasis added).

I thought that was exactly what the National Assembly did when it passed the FoIA. What else does Mr. Saba want the legislature to do? Make another law specifically for the asset declaration of President Jonathan? To think that it is the same CCB that wants the public to act as whistle blowers. I have spoken to some legal scholars on this issue and the consensus is that the aim of Mr. Saba and the CCB is precisely to subvert the objective of asset declaration.

Since the CCB that is legally bound to act won't do so, it is important that we look to the president to lead by example. I know the president is a good man at heart and that he aspires to be the most liked president, as opposed to his current status as the most abused, when he leaves office. His likeability will, however, depend on how he deals with the cancer of corruption which has made any form of progress impossible. And that begins with him publicly declaring his asset.

Nothing you say or do will convince us to the contrary.

❖

34. DAVID MARK AND HIS ANTI-GAY CRUSADERS
JANUARY 2013

I understand distinguished Senator David Mark, the President of the Senate of the Federal Republic, is a very pious man. I do not know Mr. Mark personally, but those who know him say the retired general is one person who pursues his cause with the zeal of a soldier. It was this zeal that he brought to bear as minister of communications in the regime of the "Evil Genius", Gen. Ibrahim Babangida, by making sure that the "ordinary people" did not have access to telephone and upbraiding university students for protesting fuel price increase when many of them did not have cars.

When Mark wanted to run for president a few years ago, he granted an interview in which he declared: "If I have my way, I will say whoever does not have a military background should not be made president", noting that "civilians don't have the requisite training".

According to Mark, even journalists should undergo military training because, "It gives you the confidence that you need and makes you to be everything". He went on: "I can tell you that a staff sergeant in the army is better than a university graduate in this country. That is the truth. If you give me a graduate and a staff sergeant, I will pick the sergeant because I can train the sergeant". The point Mark was trying to make was that nobody should deny him the opportunity to rule Nigeria simply because he was once a soldier.

Mark has since made his mark (no pun intended) on our democratic landscape. He has been a senator since the return to democracy in 1999. He is in his second term as senate president, the first and only senator to achieve this feat in the 4th Republic. He was one of the senators who supported the bill that sought to give President Obasanjo a third term in office. He was one of the few officers alleged to have played a prominent role in the annulment of the June 12, 1993 presidential election. And the way he is going, Mark may yet fulfill his ambition of being the president and commander-in-chief.

Mark's latest pet project is his crusade against gays and lesbians, that extraterrestrial, subhuman group that has descended on our great country, seeking to pervert our collective morality. Some people have argued that if Mark and his colleagues could expend a quarter of the time and energy they are expending hounding gays and lesbians, on pressing national problems, the country might be a safer and more prosperous place for her citizens. But, that is beside the point. We all know the Upper Chamber of the National Assembly is nothing more than a retirement home for public officers who have lost their immunity.

As a devout and morally upright Christian who aspires to be a Knight of the Catholic Church someday, I can understand Mark's antipathy toward gays and lesbians. However, to allow that to becloud his legislative judgment in a supposedly secular nation like ours, is to say the least, troubling. Unfortunately, that is exactly what he is doing by championing the anti-gay movement in the senate.

During his latest outing at a civic reception in honour of John Cardinal Olorunfemi Onaiyekan in Abuja, Mark said, "The need to nurture and preserve sanity, morality and humanity in our nation informed the decision of the Nigerian Senate to legislate against same-sex marriage and homosexuality".

It is important to read Mark's statement clearly. The issue is not just opposition to same-sex marriage, but to homosexuality as well. This clarification is important because, among other things, the criminalization of same-sex marriage which attracts 14 years imprisonment will equally be applicable to anybody that engages in homosexual acts if Mark's fantasy becomes law.

"We will not compromise on this. I want to invite you all to join the crusade of decency in our society. There are many good values we can copy from other societies but certainly not this one (same-sex marriage)", Mark implored his audience.

> "We have to prove to the rest of the world, who are advocates of this unnatural way, that we Nigerians promote and respect sanity, morality and humanity".

It was perhaps in keeping with Mark's injunction to prove to the rest of the world that Nigerians "promote and respect sanity, morality and humanity" that a few weeks ago, as reported by Steve Aborisade of Nigeriahivinfo.com, anti-gay crusaders apprehended three men in Ekwe, Njaba Local Government Area of Imo State, South-east, Nigeria. Their offence? Engaging in homosexual acts! The men were paraded naked, bound like farm animals. We can only imagine the fate of these men; citizens have been lynched or burnt to death for lesser crimes.

That is the face of the new Nigeria of moral warriors that Mark envisages. But, what haven't we compromised as a nation? We have compromised on corruption. We have compromised on probity and accountability. We have compromised on freedom, human rights, and the rule of law. Indeed, we have compromised on all the ethical standards that make a modern nation function. However, those things do not concern us. We only need to weed our society of these sexual deviants who are polluting us with their foreign way of life.

There are a few issues arising from the gay bashing that has become not only fashionable, but a comfortable distraction and a uniting topic between the ruling class and a section of the people they oppress. One is that homosexuality is foreign to our culture and that it was brought to us and is being promoted by Europeans and Americans. The other is that it is against religious doctrines. Of course, homosexuality is not a white man's "disease". Homosexuals are found in every society in the world, including ours.

One of the most insightful articles I have read on this debate is that by Wole Soyinka. In the piece, The Sexual Minority and Legislative Zealotry, the Nobel Laureate takes our legislative zealots and religious bigots to task on their fear mongering and distaste for science. It is a piece worth reading for anyone interested in understanding the anti-gay hysteria in Nigeria.

On the issue of "foreign interference", Soyinka noted,

> "The noisome emissions that surged from a handful of foreign governments last year should not be permitted to obscure the fundamental issue of the right to private choices of the free, adult citizen in any land – Asian, African, European, etc. Those external responses were of such a nature – hysterical, hypocritical and disproportionate - that, speaking for myself at least, I could only wonder if they had not been generated by a desperate need for distraction away from the economic crisis that confronted, at that very time, those parts of the world".

Now that we have laid the incubus of "foreign interference" to rest, perhaps we can address the other issues that rile our anti-gay crusaders. Some of those who attack gays and lesbians say homosexuality is "abnormal" and "unnatural". Others have gone a step further to query why the West that opposes polygamy supports homosexuality. This, of course, is a faulty analogy. We can have the debate about same-sex marriage, just like polygamy, but to criminalize homosexuality is the height of "legislative zealotry".

The debate on polygamy and same-sex marriage would also fall within the realm of the debate on whether a 50-year old senator can marry a thirteen-year old child. Of all the issues above, same-sex marriage, in my view, is the least upsetting. I have yet to see how same-sex marriage affects the rights of citizens or is a threat to society as do polygamy and paedophilia.

We all know where science stands on the issue of homosexuality. It does appear, therefore, that beyond the religious argument, there has not been any "persuasive" argument put forward by homophobes. But, we can't give in to the religious argument for obvious reasons. Nigeria is a secular state. The other reason is that it is a very slippery slope. If we hound homosexuals on the basis of religion, then we create room for other religious bigots who have made our country a living hell in their purported attempt to propitiate heaven.

Caution is the word, Mr. Mark. All the balderdash that homosexuality is not in our culture, is simply that: balderdash. The bottom line is that we are dealing with a relationship between two consenting adults. What crime has been committed? The crime of falling in love?

The lesbian, gay, bisexual, and transgender (LGBT) community does not pose a national security threat. Rather, those we need to wage a war against are bigots, whether they are religious, ethnic or sexual.

If we allow Mark and his colleagues to legislate on what adults do in their bedrooms, they may one day begin to think of legislating on what a woman, for example, does to her body.

35. No Country for Petty Thieves
February 2013

Nigerians are outraged, justifiably so, at the shenanigans of the country's judiciary which led to the ridiculously light sentence and eventual freedom last month of a man who pled guilty of robbing the country's police pension scheme of billions of naira.

The facts of the case speak for themselves. John Yakubu Yusuf, a former assistant director in the federal civil service, and six others are implicated in the theft of N32.8bn ($218ml) of police pension fund. They go on trial on a 20-count charge. Under a plea bargain agreement with prosecutors, Mr. Yusuf pleads guilty to three charges, including the 19th and 20th offences relating specifically to him (betraying trust and fraudulently converting N2bn ($13ml) of police pension funds to private use).

The maximum penalty for each offence is two years. Justice Abubakar Talba of the Federal High Court, Abuja, finds Yusuf guilty on three counts and orders that the sentences should run concurrently. He gives Yusuf an option of N250,000 ($1,700) fine on each of the three counts. In addition to the fine, Mr. Yusuf is ordered to forfeit to the State, 32 property, in Abuja and Gombe, and the sum of

N325 million ($2.1million) in restitution.

In his plea for leniency, Yusuf's lawyer, Theodore Bala Maiyakim, claimed his client had a serious heart condition. "He has saved the time of my Lord and being a first offender, with no previous record of conviction, I urge the court to temper justice with mercy and sentence him with least possible terms", Maiyakim said. Another version of this tale noted that Maiyakim had "urged the court to be lenient on his client as he has ailing aged parents and responsibility to pay the school fees of his children".

There are conflicting reports about what transpired and the exact amount involved in this criminal enterprise. According to the International Centre for Investigative Reporting,

> *"The prosecution and defence lawyers actually had an agreement on specific outcomes of the case which included a custodial sentence which was breached by the judge. Although no formal agreement was written or signed by any of the parties, the two sides agreed with the judge that first, the accused person would declare and forfeit all assets he acquired with proceeds of the funds he stole. Secondly, the parties agreed that he would be given custodial sentence with no option of fine".*

It is really difficult to know how much Yusuf and his daredevil gang stole. We may never know how high up this fraud goes; the very senior government officials, ministers, maybe, senators and reps, bank managers and sundry other perfidious criminals involved in what clearly is a well-coordinated plot. What is not hard to see is the effect of their barefaced thievery.

We can see it in the "untimely death" of many police pensioners; the families that have been ruined and impoverished; the thousands, perhaps millions of children who could not go to school because the person responsible for paying their school fees is dead or has been denied his paltry income.

However, all this is now academic. In a way, the Yusuf saga has become a byword for all that is wrong with our laws, criminal justice system, notion of crime and punishment and national psyche. Our mind-set is that when you steal public fund, you are stealing from nobody in particular; you are merely getting your share of the proverbial national cake. After all, those before you did the same and nothing happened.

We have a warped sense of nationhood and hardly realize, or couldn't care less, if our actions bring the country to her knees. The refrain is that everyone has a price. So, when you steal, you have to steal enough to bribe or pacify everyone, including judges, prosecutors and journalists.

Since the Yusuf judgement, the media (mainstream and social) have been awash with examples of how the country's broken legal system has succeeded in shortchanging the masses. We have been reminded of the six-month imprisonment of Tafa Balogun, a former Inspector General of Police, for corruption and money laundering; the two-year imprisonment of ex-governor Diepreye Alamieyeseigha of Bayelsa State for corruption and money laundering; James Ibori, former governor of Delta State, who appeared before Justice Marcel Awokulehin on 147 charges, was set free, only for the governor to be found guilty and sentenced to 13 years in prison in Britain; the six-month imprisonment (or golden handshake) given to rogue banker, Cecelia Ibru, for defrauding her bank to the tune of $1bn; the six-month imprisonment with an option of N3.5ml ($23,000) fine for ex-governor of Edo State, Lucky Igbinedion, for corruption; and the 30-month imprisonment of Bode George, former Chairman of the Nigerian Ports Authority, and national vice-chairman, southwest zone, of the People's Democratic Party for contract fraud. The examples are endless.

The Tafa Balogun case is, indeed, instructive considering it involves the head of a law enforcement agency. How is it possible for the chief law enforcement officer of the country to steal so much money? I shall return to this. I raised this question in my book, *Time to Reclaim Nigeria,* where I documented Tafa Balogun's exploit as a criminal mastermind.

Mr. Balogun became IGP in March 2002, and oversaw security during the April 2003 national elections. By the time Tafa Balogun was convicted in late 2005, he had over N5 billion ($33 million) of money meant for the police in his private accounts. With more than ten property around the world worth over N3 billion ($20 million) – property he acquired as a police officer – you won't be wrong to think that Mr. Balogun was an estate agent.

The former IGP was forced to resign in January 2005 after allegations of bribery, corruption and dalliance with corrupt politicians and criminal elements became public. In April 2005, Mr. Balogun was put on trial on a 70-count charge and found guilty of embezzling about N20 billion ($133 million) of police fund. After a plea deal, he was sentenced to six months in prison, part of which he spent at the Abuja National Hospital.

We can juxtapose these sweet deal convictions with the (in)justice for ordinary citizens. About the same time that Yusuf was walking home a free man with proceeds of his crime, someone was being sentenced to three years in prison, without an option of fine, for stealing a cell phone. In Abeokuta, Ogun State, a magistrate court headed by Idowu Olayinka sentenced 49-year-old Mustapha Adesina to two years in prison for stealing vegetables valued at N5,000 ($33) with an option of N10,000 fine ($66).

In Asaba, Delta State, a young man, Emmanuel Michael, was sentenced to five years in prison with hard labour by a Chief Magistrate Court for stealing gold earrings worth N25,000 ($166). In sentencing Michael, presiding Chief Magistrate, Sylvester Ehikwe, stated, "He does not deserve mercy as burglary is next to armed robbery". It was reported that Michael who had earlier pled guilty to the two-count charge preferred against him wept in the dock, saying, "I was hungry". There is the gut-wrenching story of a woman in Suleja prison in Niger State who has been awaiting trial for over two years, and is forced to live in prison with her six children, for stealing a goat.

It seems our prisons are meant for and are full of petty thieves while high profile criminals strut around and wine and dine in the presidency. What happens if our goat-stealing mother is later found not guilty? How much did it cost the government to prosecute John Yakubu Yusuf? I am not a learned fellow so I have left the legalese of these matters, particularly the cases involving Justices Abubakar Talba and Sylvester Ehikwe, to legal minds.

For me, the fundamental issue is the question I raised earlier: What kind of system makes it possible for public officers to steal so much of our collective wealth with impunity? The only answer I can come up with is that it is a system that lacks leadership; one in which the leadership would commit hara-kiri rather than let the public know what it is worth.

When you have a functional government and the man in charge not only "gives a damn" about fighting corruption but leads by example, then the tribe of John Yakubu Yusuf would be the exception rather than the rule.

---

36. The "risen" First Lady
February 2013

I join millions of Nigerians in giving thanks to God for the miraculous survival of the country's First Lady, Dame (Dr.) Patience Goodluck Jonathan. It is not every day you read such cheery news about a First Lady that rose from the dead. It is only befitting, therefore, that it should cost Nigerian taxpayers half a billion naira to celebrate her "death" and "resurrection".

Now that the First Lady is back, "hale and hearty", perhaps an apology might just be apposite; for the God of miracles is also a God that abhors lies and deception. Let's put in perspective the whole episode of the First Lady's disappearance, appearance, rumours and speculations about her whereabouts and her candour about going to the great beyond and returning to complete her work on earth, and maybe understand why the demand for an unreserved apology, even if not sufficient, seems to be the minimum penance acceptable.

For a visible First Lady, her noticeable absence from major public events last August was bound to stir a feeling of disquiet. After much speculation about her whereabouts, we were told she was "resting in Germany" following her hectic schedule hosting the African First Ladies Summit a month earlier. Then there was the secret visit by

President Goodluck Jonathan, accompanied by the chaplain of Aso Villa Chapel, Ven. Obioma Onwuzurumba. From TV footage of the visit, aired on national television, we saw a well-dressed First Lady asking to be allowed to "take picture with my husband". Dead people do not take pictures, do they?

All the while, the intrepid Saharareporters.com kept updating Nigerians about the true state of things with the First Lady in Germany. Enter Reuben Abati, the Special Adviser to the President on Media, Publicity, Dissimulation, Deception and other matters. The spin and dissembling went into overdrive. Abati alerted us that,

> "The video clip aired by the Nigerian Television Authority (NTA) was a confirmation that the President's wife was hale and hearty contrary to what some people wanted Nigerians to believe. The video has put paid to all the lies that people who play politics with almost everything have been spreading. It was clear from that video that the scene was not a hospital scene".

Knowing Abati, the public took his revelation with more than a pinch of salt. They wanted to hear it straight from the horse's mouth; the madam herself, not the "boy-boy". They waited patiently, hoping that in the end the truth would be revealed. When the First Lady returned to the country after almost two months of well-deserved rest, she was full of gratitude for those who prayed for her safe return and had nothing but curses for all those idle and godless Nigerians who wanted her dead. She thanked Almighty God for bringing her back safely to Nigeria and giving her a second chance. That was her own way of confirming what we already knew about her health. Only the initiated could have decoded the message.

For the unbelievers, the First Lady had this message:

> "Wherever there are good people, there are also bad ones. There are a few Nigerians that are saying whatever they like, not what God planned because God has a plan for all of us. And God has said it all that when two or three are gathered in His name, that He will be with them. And Nigerians gathered and prayed for me and God listened and

> heard their prayers. So, I thank God for that. God is wonderful and His mercy is forever. At the same time, I read in the media where they said I was in the hospital. God Almighty knows I have never been to that hospital. I don't even know the hospital they mentioned. I have to explain what God has done for me. I do not have terminal illness, or any cosmetic surgery much less tummy tuck".

That was the end of the matter. Nobody was to discuss why the First Lady spent six weeks in Germany unannounced. Anybody who dared was accused of the high crime of politicizing the First Lady's personal problems. We were reminded it should not be the case, after all the First Lady is not a public officer and is entitled to her privacy even though the public paid for her well-deserved vacation in Germany.

Fast forward to February 17, 2013. Venue: Aso Rock Chapel. The First Lady gathers thousands of people to share her tale of resurrection. She confesses to undergoing nine surgeries in one month in Germany. "I actually died. I passed out for more than a week. My intestine and tummy were opened. It was God himself in His infinite mercy that said I will return to Nigeria. God woke me up after seven days", the First Lady announced to her captive audience who would have intoned, "Hallelujah, Praise the Lord".

The Dame Patience Jonathan thanksgiving service was the place to be in Nigeria last weekend, not just for those who love the president and his wife, but for people that needed to endear themselves to the Presidency. The guest list included President Goodluck Jonathan; Vice President Namadi Sambo and his wife, Hajia Amina; former President of Ghana, John Agyekum Kufour; former Head of State, Gen. Yakubu Gowon; 18 state governors, and sundry VIPs.

Reports had it that several trucks bearing gifts from government officials and contractors lined the streets of the presidential villa waiting to deliver gifts to the First Lady. Clearly, anybody who didn't answer the roll call would have been tagged not just an enemy of the First Lady and amongst those who wanted her dead while she was in Germany, but an enemy of the state.

I would have loved the opportunity to partake in this lavish ceremony myself, not just for the food and drink, but to see firsthand what it looks and feels like coming face to face with a risen First Lady. Thanks to the efforts of one John Kennedy Okpara, the offering for the First Lady's thanksgiving service was a modest N500ml ($3ml). By any standard, it was a good outing for Dame Patience's chivalry.

Of course, this is Nigeria. The idle cynics have started wagging their tongues. They are questioning the First Lady's credibility. They want to know what has changed between late October when she claimed she was not hospitalized and now. They say the First Lady's case is emblematic of the credibility crisis of the Jonathan presidency.

What else is the government lying about (apart from President Jonathan's asset declaration) if it can look Nigerians in the eyes and blatantly lie about the health of the First Lady? But, aren't we are used to our government and its agents lying to us? There is nothing new about the double-speak, arrogance and disdain for truth by public officers in Nigeria. We saw it with the late President Umaru Yar'Adua and his First Lady, Turai.

Didn't Sullivan Chime, Governor of Enugu State, abscond for five months only to return and say he "owed nobody any apology for keeping them guessing throughout the period". To taper his mendacity about being hospitalized, he threw up these weasel words: "I started treatment and the treatment altogether lasted for twelve weeks. Throughout the period of my treatment, I was an outpatient. I was never admitted in any hospital. All my treatments, I took as an outpatient".

Back to the First Lady. We still do not know what she was treated for and we may never know. One thing is certain: we are not supposed to question her miraculous comeback. Not many people have the opportunity of experiencing death and coming back to life to tell the story. It is an experience money cannot buy. Which means for the First Lady her future will be committed to "doing things that will touch the lives of the less privileged".

Since the First Lady was sent back to Nigeria to complete her assignment in our god-forsaken nation, my only candid advice would be for her to invest the N500ml ($3ml) offering she collected during her thanksgiving in building a world-class hospital in Otuoke, Bayelsa State, so that she wouldn't need to abscond from Nigeria the next time she requires treatment.

◆

37. Orji Kalu's "Fake Degree"
March 2013

The war of attrition between Abia State governor, Theodore Orji, and his predecessor, Orji Uzor Kalu, took a bizarre turn two weeks ago when the Abia State University (ABSU) released a statement withdrawing the degree it awarded Mr. Kalu when he was governor. According to the university, "The admission and graduation of the former governor violated its extant rules and regulations". In a sentence, Mr. Kalu is parading a "fake degree".

Anyone looking for proof that governance in Nigeria is a sideshow need not look beyond the action of ABSU, and by extension the governor of Abia State. The only surprise here, for those who can afford to be surprised by the news that comes out of Nigeria every day, is that this action is coming, supposedly, from the citadel of learning. According to Mr. O. E. Onuoha, the registrar of ABSU, Mr. Kalu was stripped of his degree "after an emergency meeting of the university senate which considered the recommendations of an investigative panel which considered allegations of breach of the school's academic regulations by Mr. Kalu".

Mr. Kalu reportedly dropped out of the University of Maiduguri and enrolled at ABSU while he was governor of Abia State and, therefore, Visitor to the university. In the last two years, he and his former sidekick, the current governor, have been at each other's jugular in a state where governance has taken a backseat and citizens yearn for the dividends of democracy.

Mr. Kalu recently offered a *mea culpa* to citizens of Abia State for his malevolence in foisting his successor on them; a sad reminder of the malfeasance that is the hallmark of our brand of democracy. It sounds all too familiar. It was the same mindset that the Lord of the Manor at Ota worked with a few years ago. Nigerians are still waiting for him to show some grace and formally apologize as he bemoans the lack of credible leadership in the country. Not that an apology will serve any purpose really; but, at least, it will show that he can be taken seriously.

Back to Orji Kalu and his confessions.

> *"I made him a governor when he was incarcerated by the EFCC. I made him governor without his input even as much as to campaign for one day! Yet, he left and said he didn't know what he did to me. I think something is wrong somewhere. I did not quarrel with him except that I told him, 'Governor, you should work hard and get somebody to replace you because you can't win election again the way you are going.' That was after two years of his administration; the rating in Aba and Umuahia were very low. And he came to newsmen with the claim that I wanted to stop him from a second term in office. That was his grouse against me".*

That was the former governor speaking during a recent interview. It seems the chickens have come home to roost. Orji Kalu is reaping what he sowed; the only problem is that the good people of Abia State who are gnashing their teeth are also being made to pay the price of his perfidy. ABSU authorities say they withdrew Orji Kalu's "fake degree" "on the strength of the findings and recommendations of an investigative panel into allegations of breach of the extant Academic Regulations of Abia State University, in the process of the admission and graduation of Kalu Orji Uzor in the discipline of Government and Public Administration, of matriculation number 00/42226".

The senate said it based its decision on the following grounds, among others:

> *"The violation of the Academic Regulations of the univer-*

sity on Admission-by-Transfer, which rendered the offer irregular, ab initio; The non-completion of the mandatory six (6) semesters (i.e. three academic years of study), before he was awarded a degree of the university. He spent only two semesters in all". This decision, the senate maintained, "derived from the exercise of its onerous statutory responsibility to guard and maintain, at all times, the Academic Regulations of the University, its hard-earned reputation and the credibility of the certificates it awards".

Of course, ABSU senate reserves the right to withdraw any certificate or degree issued by the university. Accordingly, I do not have any problem with stripping Mr. Kalu of his degree if it is confirmed it was obtained fraudulently. My worry is that, in this case, it appears the fraud was perpetrated with the connivance of the university senate. If that is the case, then it means certain laws were broken and those responsible for the Orji Kalu admission racket, if we believe the claim of ABSU authorities, should be held to account.

Matters arising from this "fake degree" imbroglio are legion: Was it the same senate that admitted Orji Kalu to ABSU that awarded him a degree when he did not complete the mandatory six semesters? Was Mr. Onuoha, the current registrar, the registrar of ABSU when Orji Kalu was admitted to the university? Was he the same registrar that signed Mr. Kalu's certificate? What role did the VC then and Orji Kalu's dean play in this scandal? Did ABSU senate not see anything morally troubling to have the Visitor to the university double as a student?

The action of ABSU senate may cast doubt on the genuineness of the degree that Orji Kalu is parading, but it has also dented ABSU's image and calls to question the integrity of its senate and the thousands of degrees and certificates it awards every year. Who will take degrees awarded by ABSU seriously? How many other politically exposed persons also got degrees they were not entitled to during the eight years Mr. Kalu ruled Abia State?

This is an issue the National Universities Commission (NUC) should investigate. Unfortunately, there hasn't been as much as a whimper from the NUC on this issue. It is bad enough that our universities have become glorified secondary schools and can hardly compare with their counterparts on the continent; it is tragic that our academics have become the handmaiden of politicians, turning our universities into an extension of Government Houses across the country.

If Governor Theodore Orji compelled the senate of ABSU to withdraw Orji Kalu's certificate, let us hope, as someone observed, "he did not graduate from any state university where his political enemies are in charge".

38. IBB'S TWO-PARTY SOLUTION
March 2013

Ibrahim Badamasi Babangida, also known as IBB, must be a deeply troubled man; a retired general haunted by his past. There is no other way to explain his constant attempt to intrude into our national psyche after ruling the country for eight inglorious years. The former military president never misses an opportunity to show how relevant he is even though history cannot support that delusion. The recent merger of major opposition political parties to form the All Progressives Congress (APC) provided a good opportunity for him.

"IBB okays merger of political parties, insists on two-party system", was the headline in one newspaper a few weeks ago. The report seemed to have gone unnoticed by the horde of news junkies and commentators on Nigeria. It was expected. I do not know anyone out there who has not grown weary of IBB and what he has to say about the political and social trajectory of the country. For IBB, the merger talk is a vindication of his two-party philosophy which he believes "is the best political option for Nigeria".

> "When I introduced two-party system, you people said I am a soldier, now you have seen why I went for two-party system. I am happy for the emergence of APC. It is a wel-

come political development", IBB noted. The self-styled "evil genius" has since gone ahead to expand on his two-party theory. Though a founding member of the ruling People's Democratic Party (PDP), IBB said he had not made up his mind on the political party to vote for in 2015, and that he was leaning toward voting for the APC. "I have enough time to think and I am thinking and they will be anxious to come and see me", he boasted.

"I am a firm believer of two-party system and I also studied the emergence of political parties in this country immediately after independence and it shows that this country will be heading for a two-party system", IBB said in his familiar fit of self adulation. "When we were doing it in 1989, some of you wrote us in the media that, no it is going to be one Christian party, one Muslim party, then you say it is going to be one northern and one southern party and it did not work and everybody blended. The chairman of NRC was Chief Tom Ikimi, the chairman of SDP was Kingibe and everybody was in one or the other; you just have to have an accommodation".

If you have problems comprehending this balderdash, you are in good company. Finally, IBB reminded us that as a Nigerian he had "a right to vote any candidate of his choice," never mind the fact that he denied millions of Nigerians who voted on June 12, 1993, the benefit of their vote.

Asked why he orchestrated the return of Obasanjo to rule Nigeria again in 1999 IBB said, "The need to save Nigeria from looming crisis gave rise to bringing back Obasanjo". According to him,

"We have to simplify a lot of things without going back to what happened before; the emergence of Obasanjo came about as a result of what happened in the country; the country was in a very serious crisis and we had to find the solution to these problems and therefore we needed a leader known in the country, we did not believe in foisting some-

body who is not known; so, we looked for a man who has been involved in the affairs of this country, who held positions either in the military or in the cabinet and who has certain beliefs about Nigeria. Now, all of us that were trained as armed forces, there is one belief that you cannot take away from us; we believe in this country because this is part of our training. We fought for this country, so when you have a situation like that, you need a leader that has all these attributes and quite frankly, he quickly came to mind".

What IBB failed to mention was his role in the crisis that led to foisting Obasanjo on Nigerians. It is important we deconstruct IBB because we, as citizens, are central in understanding his newfound penchant for democracy and the rule of law. For those too young to remember and those who have conveniently forgotten, IBB was military president of Nigeria from August 27, 1985 to August 27, 1993. IBB claimed he overthrew the Buhari regime for its highhandedness even though, as Chief of Army Staff, he was very much a part of the regime.

IBB immediately embarked on a charm offensive by abrogating Decree 4, the anti-press law of the Buhari regime. He freed the two journalists that had been imprisoned under the decree. He also released from prison Second Republic politicians who had been jailed by his predecessor. He insisted on being called president. His desire was granted.

IBB launched a transition programme to return the country to civil rule. By the time he was through with the media and Nigerians in general eight years later, one editor, Dele Giwa had been letter-bombed to smithereens, scores of military officers executed, hundreds of anti-SAP and pro-democracy activists murdered, a presidential election annulled and the country left prostrate and polarized as never before.

IBB achieved notoriety for his transition, one of the longest, the most expensive (gulping over N40 bn at the time) and certainly the most convoluted political transition the world has witnessed. As a prelude, he set up a Political Bureau made up of some of the finest minds the country has produced. The bureau came up with a document which IBB tossed into the waste bin. He then set out to do things his own way, based on his fanciful study and knowledge of the two-party system.

He set up two political parties, the Social Democratic Party (SDP) and the National Republican Convention (NRC), the former "a little to the Left" and the latter, "a little to the Right"; built two national secretariats for the parties, two secretariats in each state and two secretariats in each local government. After banning those he termed "old breed politicians", he then proceeded to assign politicians to each party based on his whims. It was a grand vision, except that it was not meant to be. Today, those edifices, where they have not been taken over by "smart" Nigerians, are home to rodents and "area boys".

I have gone this far to show what IBB did when he had the golden opportunity to set the country on the right path. The high point of IBB's transition was the June 12, 1993 presidential election won by Moshood Abiola who was later murdered while in detention. On June 23, 1993, IBB, through his goons, announced the annulment of the election.

On August 27, 1993, exactly eight years after he seized power, IBB "stepped aside", leaving his evil alter ego, Sani Abacha, in charge. The rest, as they say, is history. June 12 this year marks the 20th anniversary of Babangida's failed diabolical two-party experiment. The country has come full circle. The remnants of that perfidious era, including David Mark, who now holds court as the Senate President of the Federal Republic, are in charge of our so-called democratic order.

IBB's recent outburst is a sad reminder of the true character of the Nigerian state; a state built on a feeling of entitlement. Two decades after he and his cohort annulled the sovereign will of Nigerians, IBB unabashedly tells us that they did it to save us from ourselves. This feeling of entitlement that makes IBB and his ilk think they have a divine right to rule or determine who should rule us is our greatest undoing as a nation. IBB, in his wisdom, handpicked Obasanjo without caring what majority of Nigerians thought or felt. After eight ruinous years, Obasanjo selected Umaru Yar'Adua to succeed him. Today, we are stuck with an oddity we never bargained for.

IBB's sins are numerous. It may be uncharitable to hold one person responsible for the problems of a nation; but more than anyone else, IBB ought to take the biggest blame for the current crisis facing the country. Someone should please tell him that the formation of the APC is not about Nigeria operating a two-party system.

It is about a much greater need which IBB does not and would probably never understand.

39. Please, Pardon President Jonathan
March 2013

Nigerians are justifiably outraged at the pardon of Diepreye Solomon Peter Alamieyeseigha, ex-governor of Bayelsa State. Alamieyeseigha was governor from May 1999 until December 2005, three months after he was detained in London on charges of money laundering. President Jonathan had served under Mr. Alamieyeseigha as deputy governor.

Instructively, in August 2005, a month before his arrest, Alamieyeseigha delivered a message, through his deputy, Goodluck Jonathan, at a seminar in Abuja on "Winning the War against Corruption". The self-styled Governor General of the Ijaw nation "commended government's stride with the establishment of the Economic and Financial Crimes Commission (EFCC) and the Code of Conduct Bureau, and urged the bodies not to ignore the private sector".

According to Alamieyeseigha who called for those with criminal records to be barred from elective office, "It is only in Nigeria where people who looted banks to a distress situation are allowed to use such loots to open their own banks or are given high political appointment". Alamieyeseigha's paper titled: "Corruption Reduction Through Government Policies: The Bayelsa Experience", highlighted "the various mechanism put in place by the state government to check corruption as it was inimical to national growth and development and as such, must be abhorred by all and sundry".

By the time Alamieyeseigha was arrested a month later in London, it was reported that the Metropolitan Police found about £1m in cash in his London home and later a total of £1.8m in cash and bank accounts. Alamieyeseigha jumped bail in December 2005 from the United Kingdom by allegedly disguising himself as a woman. He had hoped to continue in office as governor. Even though that hope did not materialise, it was a good judgement call. Remaining in the UK would have been calamitous. Today, we know why.

On July 26, 2007, the fugitive governor pled guilty to six charges of making false declaration of assets and 23 charges of money laundering by his companies. He was sentenced to two years in prison. The following day, July 27, just hours after being taken to prison, he walked home a free man. In our convoluted justice system, the period he spent in detention had served to compensate for the prison sentence.

Reuben Abati, then chairman of the editorial board of The Guardian and now presidential town crier had this to say about Alamieyeseigha in a 2005 piece titled, "Alami should go: It's over":

> *"By running away from England under the cover of the night, away from the British judiciary which was probing him on charges of money laundering, by taking evasive action from the law and communicating with his feet, Alamiyeseigha, a man who until now was known and addressed as His Excellency, has shown himself to be a dishonourable fellow, unfit to rule, unfit to sit among men and women of honour and integrity, unfit to preach to the people that he leads about ideals and values.*
>
> *"As for those persons who have been packaging Alami as a victim and who have been mouthing the asinine line: 'If Ijaw man thief Ijaw money, wetin concern Tony Blair inside', may the good Lord forgive them for they do not know what they are saying. All Ijaw must feel embarrassed for this is a difficult moment for them as a nation. They are being blackmailed emotionally to defend not a principled*

fighter, not a spirit of Ijawland, but an Ijaw leader who danced naked in a foreign land. The questions that would be asked are: what do Ijaws stand for? Where is the ancient and modern glory of the Ijaw nation? These are difficult questions. Alami must save his own people the embarrassment by stepping aside. Let him return to England and act like an honourable man".

Eight years later, nothing has changed, except that an Ijaw man is now President and Commander-in-Chief. "His Excellency, the (former) executive fugitive of Bayelsa State", as Abati once described Alamiyeseigha, remains a "dishonourable fellow, unfit to rule, unfit to sit among men and women of honour and integrity, unfit to preach to the people that he leads about ideals and values". What a difference eight years make. Today, thanks to his pardon, Alamiyeseigha is now "fit to rule, fit to sit among men and women of honour and integrity, fit to preach to the people that he leads about ideals and values".

Astonishingly, it is now Abati's job to repackage "Alami" as a victim and condemn those who accuse him of being an ex-convict and a danger to society. May the good Lord forgive all the idle Nigerians who are not only exhibiting "sophisticated ignorance", but want to destroy an Ijaw man for pardoning another Ijaw man for stealing money belonging to Ijaws for they do not know what they are saying.

To understand Alamieyeseigha's pardon is to understand the character of the Nigerian state. There is no case to make for his pardon other than to say it is what the doctors ordered. And by doctors, I do not mean the type our First Lady and sundry public officers scurry to in foreign lands. I refer to the ubiquitous marabouts and native doctors that have become an essential part of governance in Nigeria.

They are the ones goading President Jonathan and have convinced him that to secure a second term, he must of necessity pardon the Governor General of the Ijaw nation. That is the only way he can secure the support of the Ijaws. Evidently, in Nigeria, leadership is not about performance. What is uppermost now is that President Jonathan, the first president from the oily Niger Delta, has to, by any means necessary, complete his two terms of four years as the constitution stipulates.

A friend has likened President Jonathan's dilemma, if we can call it that, to that of a managing director of a failed company who wants to remain MD even when his company is in the red. He will do whatever he thinks will help him keep his job, including cooking the books and satisfying every interest, no matter how vile. Of course, President Jonathan is also a victim of the Nigerian tragedy. Alamieyeseigha was set free many years ago when we had a certain Umaru Yar'Adua as president. The pardon on March 12, 2013, was just the icing on the cake.

I do not think those who pardoned Alamieyeseigha thought or imagined that the tag "ex-convict" would ever leave him. Who cares really? Are we not witnesses to a senator wining election while on trial? A few days after his pardon, there were feelers signaling that Alamieyeseigha will run for senate in 2015. He does not need to do anything to emerge the next senator representing his district. Like that other exemplar of perfidy in Akwa Ibom State, all the governor of Bayelsa State, Seriake Dickson, needs to do at the behest of the president, is to remove the name of the winner and replace it with Alamieyeseigha's, if necessary, for his great service to Ijawland.

Alamieyeseigha will be in good company when he joins the senate in 2015. For me, that is the really troubling part of his pardon and why we must continue the quest to restructure Nigeria. Like Tafa Balogun, the rogue former Inspector General of Police, Alamieyeseigha will no doubt make a case for the return of his property "confiscated" by the state.

Alamieyeseigha believes he is entitled to be a senator and much more; after all, not many in the "hallowed" chamber can boast a superior résumé. Ours is a system that survives on cronyism. Alamieyeseigha may emerge as senate president if he so desires. He may even return to Bayelsa State someday to complete his second term as governor.

The structure of our country makes this unwholesome atmosphere possible. That is why President Jonathan deserves our pardon for his latest political blunder!

40. What does Obasanjo want?
April 2013

You couldn't miss the headline. I am referring to the conclave of gerontocrats that took place earlier in the week. It centred on former president, Olusegun Obasanjo.

"Anenih in secret meeting with Obasanjo", was how The Guardian headlined the event. If there was any doubt about the purpose of the meeting, Anthony Anenih, chair of the Board of Trustees (BoT) of the People's Democratic Party (PDP) and successor to Obasanjo in the very lucrative post of BoT chairman, dispelled it when he told reporters, "In 2015 we (PDP) will do what we know how to do best". Of course, we all know what the PDP knows how to do best. And we have Obasanjo to thank for that.

For whatever it is worth, Obasanjo is still held in high regard in the PDP family and he may well continue to direct the affairs of the party as long as he is alive. "I am here to see my leader (Obasanjo). I am here to pay my respect and indeed I am here with my colleagues, some members of the Board of Trustees of our party to discuss some issues that affect the corporate existence of this country," Anenih gushed after the meeting. "As you can see, we are all smiling, don't you see me smiling? And my leader too is smiling. So, we are quite happy about the outcome".

Unfortunately, the Nigerian crisis is no laughing matter. It would be tragic to leave the discussion about the corporate existence of Nigeria to the Obasanjos and Anenihs amongst us.

Chief (Gen.) Olusegun Matthew Okikiola Aremu Obasanjo, GCFR, is an enigma, in and out of office. I am sure he cherishes that role. Nobody, dead or alive, has had more impact on the course of post-independence history of the country than the retired general.

Obasanjo evokes different memories for different people. Academics and students in tertiary institutions in the late 70s would remember his assault on students, academics and education in general. Those in secondary schools also have memories of that era of despotism. In a remarkable show of defiance, Afrobeat icon, Fela

Anikulakpo-Kuti, withdrew his son, Femi, from Baptist Academy in Lagos State when Obasanjo deployed soldiers to secondary schools.

Like President Goodluck Jonathan, Obasanjo took charge of the Nigerian state after the death of his boss. It was in February 1976. The head of state, Gen. Murtala Ramat Muhammed, had been assassinated. That was when Obasanjo came into our consciousness. Before then, the much we knew about him was from the conflicting stories of his exploits during the civil war.

Ever since, Obasanjo has refused to go away. Through a combination of luck, guile and opportunism, he has managed to remain a constant figure in our political evolution. To his admirers, Obasanjo is the "father of modern Nigeria"; the "Mandela" of Nigeria. After all, like the legendary Nelson Mandela, South African anti-apartheid revolutionary, politician and president (1994 to 1999), he moved from prison to the presidency.

A few weeks ago, after my article titled "IBB's two-party solution", a responder had noted, "I always take the view that Obj (Obasanjo), IBB and Gowon – in that order – more than any of our ex-rulers had the best opportunities to set our country on a path to true greatness and all of them failed woefully. It is the enduring tragedy of our (potentially) great nation that the incumbent may yet surpass them all in terms of cluelessness and damage inflicted on our country".

Of course, this is not hyperbole. In 1979, Obasanjo had the chance to launch the country on the path of genuine democracy, but he bungled it. Twenty-eight years later, in 2007, after eight years as civilian president, he had the opportunity to make amends, but he squandered it in his characteristic devious manner.

If you do not know Obasanjo, you would probably mistake him for a global expert sent by the UN to oversee events in Nigeria. Ever since he reluctantly left power in 2007, he has never missed an opportunity to remind us of how ungrateful we are as a people for not recognizing his trailblazing role as the father of democracy in Nigeria.

Obasanjo has warned about revolution. He has talked about unemployment, corruption and what they portend for the country. "I'm afraid, and you know I am a General. When a General says he is afraid, that means the danger ahead is real and potent", he told the West African regional conference on youth employment in Senegal, earlier in the year.

"Today, rogues, armed robbers are in the State Houses of Assembly and the National Assembly", Obasanjo said not too long ago. Of course, he is right; except that he failed to take his share of the blame for the emergence of these scoundrels who have taken over our democratic space.

In a keynote lecture at the Agricultural and Rural Management Training Institute (ARMTI) in Ilorin, Kwara State, Obasanjo again warned, "We are sitting on a keg of gun-powder in this country due to the problems of unemployment of our youths. We have almost 150 universities now in the country turning out these young Nigerians but without job opportunities for them".

Recently, Obasanjo blamed poor leadership for the country's woes. He forgot to add that apart from his forgettable leadership (1976-1979 and 1999-2007), he orchestrated the poor leadership we had in 1979 and again in 2007. Fortunately for him, we have in President Jonathan a ruler who has redefined the meaning of poor leadership which in a way makes Obasanjo look like a messiah.

That is Obasanjo's modus operandi. As one writer noted, "In 1983 when the Shagari government started to wobble, he came out to play prophet". It was the same government he installed four years earlier. When the Babangida regime was at its wit's end and its demise looked certain, Obasanjo attacked the regime's disastrous economic policy dubbed Structural Adjustment Programme (SAP), arguing that the policy needed a "human face".

Obasanjo understands what democracy entails, but he does not have the moral courage to be guided by its rule. When Gen. Babangida annulled the June 12, 1993, presidential election won by Chief Moshood Abiola, Obasanjo told a bewildered nation that, "Abiola is not the messiah". Like an addict hankering after a fix, it was his way of saying he needed the job. It was that ambition that landed him in Abacha's prison after he reinvented himself and became a "born-again democrat". It's been twenty years since the annulment; and three disastrous elections (two supervised by Obasanjo in 2003 and 2007) after, we are still talking about Obasanjo.

In a 2008 piece titled "Obama's election and the needed change", Obasanjo, while congratulating then President-elect, Barack Obama, noted,

> *"The feeling of change that Senator Obama engendered through his campaign for the White House represents a significant theme of change we have all aspired and fought for in different areas, regions, cultures and historical times. The desire for change has never been the question nor has it ever been in question. It is the extent, the range, the tone, the quantity, the quantum and the sustenance of change that has always been the question.*
>
> *"Rooted in the achievements of Senator Obama is a far more significant theme for people aspiring to lead their communities, particularly for young Africans in Africa. It is the aspirations, the determination, the energy, the strategic thinking, planning and execution that Senator Obama and his campaign team have brought into what is being regarded as a movement. Entire generations have been roused and invited to bring about a change that they and the rest of the world desire".*

It is a measure of his hypocrisy that Obasanjo has remained the greatest threat to change in Nigeria. How can young Nigerians aspire to lead their communities when men who are almost 80 years old like Obasanjo and Anenih have sworn not to exit the political space? Clearly, in tackling the PDP and Jonathan in 2015, we must realize that we have to contend with the Obasanjo factor.

With all due respect, Mr. ex-President, you have earned the right to leave us the heck alone!

41. THE ACHEBE I KNEW
MAY 2013

"Indiscipline pervades our life so completely that one may be justified in calling it the condition par excellence of contemporary Nigerian society". – Chinua Achebe, The Trouble with Nigeria.

Prof. Chinua Achebe, literary giant, celebrated author, humanist and patriot par excellence, who was buried yesterday, was Nigeria's gift to Africa, and indeed, the world. Like most people, I first encountered Achebe through his numerous books before I met him in person. I shall return to the unforgettable encounter with him four years ago.

Anywhere you go around the world, there are certain things about Nigeria that feature prominently in conversations with those who want to know about the country: corruption, the various forms of advance fee fraud or 419 as it is known locally, ethnic/religious strife, football – when Eagles were really super; and of course, Chinua Achebe or *Things Fall Apart*, the literary classic that has sold millions of copies and has been translated into more than 50 languages.

A decade ago, I was in the tiny Caribbean Island of Haiti where I had gone to work with and report on people living with the dreaded HIV/AIDS. Amongst the first persons I met in the rundown capital, Port-au-Prince, was a Haitian dentist. Immediately I introduced myself as a Nigerian journalist, the first question he asked, to my utter surprise, was "Do you know Agbani Darego?" I had been away from Nigeria for some time and did not know much about Miss Darego (Most Beautiful Girl in Nigeria, 2001) though I had read a report of her being the first Black African to be crowned Miss World in 2001.

I answered my interlocutor in the affirmative. He gushed about how beautiful Miss Darego was and Nigerian women were in general. He said he had met a few while studying dentistry in the US. Next question, Chinua Achebe. Of course I knew Achebe. I had read

Things Fall Apart, but had not met its celebrated author. My friend then went on to tell me his Things Fall Apart story.

I have had many such encounters, the latest being during a study tour of Kenya in June 2012. It is a mark of the greatness of Achebe and the impact of his literary prowess. There are a few Nigerians I grew up admiring. Achebe was one of them. The others being the literary genius, Prof. Wole Soyinka, the iconoclast Prof Chinweizu, and my ideological mentor, Dr. Edwin Madunagu. I read most of their work and followed their activities closely.

For some reason, in my young mind, I felt Achebe was not "political" enough. Then I read *The Trouble with Nigeria*. It reminded me of my political bible, *The Communist Manifesto*. You could read it a million times over and it would appear fresh each time because of its eternal verities. Achebe believed in Nigeria. That much was evident in his statement that, "There is nothing basically wrong with the Nigerian character. There is nothing wrong with the Nigerian land or climate or water or air or anything else".

However, Achebe did not let his love for Nigeria blind him to the fact that,

> *"Nigeria is not a great country. It is one of the most disorderly nations in the world. It is one of the most corrupt, insensitive, inefficient places under the sun. It is one of the most expensive countries and one of those that give least value for money. It is dirty, callous, noisy, ostentatious, dishonest and vulgar. In short, it is among the most unpleasant places on earth".*

Three decades after Achebe wrote those words, Nigeria remains a country adrift, a soulless nation where rulers pervert justice and babies are bought and sold like commodities. Today, ethnic bigots, religious zealots and all manner of charlatans and imbeciles bestride our political, economic and social space.

Four years ago, my organisation, the African Centre for Media & Information Literacy, launched a project titled "Make Your Votes Count" as part of efforts to conscientize Nigerians, particularly our youth, on the need for active participation in the electoral process by voting and protecting their votes. We had gotten permission from some of the personalities we used in the promotional posters and banners, including Profs. Wole Soyinka and Pat Utomi. We needed to get in touch with Prof. Achebe whose image we had also used.

So when I received information that Brown University in Providence, Rhode Island, USA, was hosting the first ever Achebe Colloquium on Africa in December, 2009, I went in search of Achebe. I arrived New York City in early December 2009, in a whirlwind tour of the US which took me to Washington DC, Maryland, Boston and Providence, to promote our project. That was when the Turai Yar'Adua cabal in Nigeria was running amok.

Omoyele Sowore, the irrepressible publisher of Saharareporters.com hosted me. An interview at Saharareporters' studios was followed by a joint interview on the situation in Nigeria at the National Public Radio (NPR). I left Sowore to pursue my other programmes. We connected again at Boston's Logan International Airport a few days later on our way to the Achebe Colloquium.

We were joined in the one hour drive from Boston to Providence by Prof. Richard Joseph, the John Evans Professor of International History and Politics at Northwestern University, Illinois, USA. Known as the "father of prebendalism", Prof Joseph, an expert on African governance, political economy, and democratization, was at one time a lecturer in political science at the University of Ibadan, Nigeria, and University of Khartoum, Sudan.

Expectedly, our discussion focused on the situation in Nigeria; how a country with so much promise had been brought to it knees because of bad leadership. I arrived the Achebe Colloquium with so much foreboding. I didn't know if I would be able to see Achebe and present my "gift". I shared my apprehension with a former schoolmate, E.C. Osondu, an assistant professor of literature and resident of Providence who said he felt Achebe would like the poster we made in his honour. I also talked to Sowore who agreed to introduce me to one of Achebe's sons, Chidi. As it turned out, my worry was misplaced.

The introduction done, Chidi, who obviously was impressed with what I wanted to share with his famous father, asked me to wait for an opportunity to approach Achebe once the crowd around him had thinned out. Getting the crowd around Achebe to ease off was not going to be an easy task, but I was prepared to wait. Prof. Soyinka, Achebe's archenemy in the eyes of "literary hustlers and motor-park intellectuals", walked in and exchanged pleasantries with Prof. Achebe who was in a wheelchair at the back of the hall. Other dignitaries followed as participants trickled in.

I did eventually get a chance to introduce myself and my mission to Prof. Achebe. I told him how honoured we were to have his words and image as one of the faces of our electoral project. I presented the colourful posters to him and just as I was thinking of the right words to convey our apology for not seeking his permission, he looked up at me and in a measured tone said, "I like this. I'll keep it". I handed him extra copies which he placed on the table in front of him. He talked briefly about why we needed to get our electoral process right. I was elated. Of course, I didn't miss the photo opportunity, a request Achebe graciously granted. I knew how busy he was and I did not want to abuse the privilege. Mission accomplished, I took my seat amongst other participants.

The 2009 Achebe Colloquium on Africa with the theme "A Nation in Crisis and the Urgency of National Reform" was well attended and a huge success. Nigerians at the event included Prof. Okey Ndibe, Chief Odumegwu Ojukwu, former Senate President, Senator Ken Nnamani, Gov. Peter Obi of Anambra State, Prof. Bolaji Aluko, VC, Federal University, Otuoke, Bayelsa State and Emeka Ihedioha, deputy speaker of the House of Representatives. The communiqué at the end of the Colloquium noted that "elections in Nigeria have become progressively worse in quality over the years, and that this fact has gravely affected the country's international strategic significance".

I left the Achebe Colloquium fulfilled. Achebe was a dogged fighter. He taught us courage, sacrifice and optimism even in the face of adversity; he taught us love for country, not in the manner our rulers have debased the term and made us a laughing stock around the world. We should, therefore, celebrate Achebe in death rather than mourn him. While celebrating Achebe, we need to discover "where the rain started beating us" as a nation. We need to have a genuine and peaceful national dialogue which Achebe so eloquently espoused rather than the current monologue of threats and bombs.

I was thinking of approaching Achebe to write a blurb for my new book, *Nigeria is Negotiable*, when I received the news of his death. For Nigeria, Africa and humanity in general, Achebe's death is a huge loss. It is sad that many of those whom Achebe had nothing but contempt for while he was alive for the way they desecrated our nation are the ones crying loudest and lining the streets to honour him in death.

My utmost hope is that nobody will mourn all those who have brought us to this sad end; those who make our women die at childbirth and children from preventable diseases; those who have turned our young men to drug addicts, kidnappers, militants and terrorists and our young women to victims of the sex trade.

For those who have made a vocation of "explaining" why Achebe was not awarded the Nobel Prize and diminishing him in the process, I have just three words: shame on you!

SECTION THREE

MATTERS MISCELLANEOUS

A June Ago

A Busted Dance
For Kudirat Olayinka Abiola

By Chiedu Ezeanah

How with this rage shall beauty hold a plea whose action is no stronger than a flower? – Shakespeare, Sonnet 65

A June of polls gunned out of mind

left frozen lips
in the frozen wind.

Discontented she
too resisted the peace

somnambulating
into a dangerous pause.

She would add the streets'
scent of lead

upon her satin's
Parisian cologne?

Her bold march
blew an alarm.

Her bright eyes lit
the trampled town.

She made of the frozen winds,

the return of the heroine's love...

*Blasted out dead,
those eyes?*

*Blasted out dead,
those pearls?*

*A bereaved land
keeps seeing blood*

*in her bright eyes
blasted out dead.*

*Confronting curfews
in a General's void,*

*a mother's dance,
busted, turned to dread.*

*The dance of a mother
in the curfew is over.*

*She still dances in dew,
in dreams she's a flower.*

1. Appropriateness of pricing*
May 1993

Whether by June 1 or not; whether by the present military administration or the transition council, it has become evident with the propaganda being mounted by the Nigerian National Petroleum Corporation (NNPC) that the price of petrol, the "life buoy" of the masses of our country, would soon be increased.

Considering the amount it has spent on the campaign and the level it has reached, it is certain that the ruling elite is bent on this project it has embarked on. However, the issue of whether to increase prices or not cannot be isolated from the general feeling of ordinary Nigerians who will bear the burden.

Before now, the government used to inundate us with the gimmick of subsidy on oil. The argument then was that government was subsidizing oil for use by Nigerians (what is wrong with that?) thereby losing millions of naira that would have been used in other sectors. Now that the public has overcome the falsehood of this gimmick, government is resorting to the dubious propaganda of prices of petroleum products being "absurdly" low in Nigeria compared to other countries.

The NNPC, in its emotion-laden adverts, want the public not to be sentimental in viewing the options it has proposed. But it is the NNPC that is being sentimental. Rather than looking at the socio-economic situation in the country, the NNPC is busy comparing the prices available in Nigeria to those in other countries.

If we must follow the NNPC logic of comparison, we must not overlook the fact that petroleum prices in Nigeria are the lowest in Africa, just as life in Nigeria now is amongst the lowest in Africa. We need not even bother making reference to the fact that the disposable income of the average Nigerian cannot be compared to that of some of the most "backward" countries in Africa.

What the NNPC fails to realize is that as a nation on the throes of death, Nigeria cannot afford the luxury of using foreign indicators, ostensibly the dollar, in fixing the prices Nigerians should pay for such commodity as oil. With the perpetual depreciation of the naira, there can never be an end to correct pricing with the dollar as an indicator; it is all a ruse. The only meaningful prices are those that fall in line with our current economic and social predicaments.

There is the other argument also that with deregulation, the costs of machinery, spares and additives in the oil industry (all imported into the country) have moved up astronomically. Therefore, the prices of petroleum products must go up to reflect these changes.

One lesson from the on-going debate about appropriate pricing is the fact that our nation has not ceased to be an appendage of global imperialist onslaught. All the gibberish about correct pricing is nothing but a fulfillment of the IMF-imposed Structural Adjustment Programme.

The government and its agent, the NNPC, cannot convince Nigerians that they hope to achieve anything meaningful with the proceeds from the "correct pricing" of oil. Nigerians know better! Therefore, it will be politically expedient to let sleeping dogs lie.

Whatever gains the government expects from oil cannot vitiate the suffering of ordinary Nigerians from the increased "tax" on petroleum products. We must emphasize that any price increase that does not reflect the general poverty in the country would not be appropriate.

Evidence point to the fact that the oil industry, like every other sector, is in crisis not because of the "cheap" price of petroleum products or "inappropriate pricing" to use the new vocabulary of the government, but because of inefficiency, indiscipline and fraud in the oil industry in particular and the country in general.

The government and the NNPC have no moral justification to subject ordinary Nigerians to the untold hardship occasioned by international market "foxes".

- *This piece was done in collaboration with Isaac Osuoka, now Executive Director, Social Action, Nigeria.*

2. Towards a New Beginning
November 1993

It certainly would not be alarming to say that our beloved nation, Nigeria, is in the throes of death. The way those who have been decreed to rule us are going about their odious task, they seem to be saying let the blood of the people be on their heads and those of their children; they could not care less!

Presently, while the villains of yesteryear who stood in the way of the country's prosperity are trying to make themselves relevant and perhaps renew their villainy and treachery, we are witnessing the most ignominious and vainglorious pretensions to leadership. With distortions and deceit the new dictatorship is trying to brainwash the people into believing that it can squeeze water out of stone.

In the same vein, the so-called representatives of the people are basking in the euphoria of enthroning democracy when they have lost all claims to being the real representatives of the people. But, how long shall we bemoan this deception?

The answer can be found in Lenin's admonition that, "People always have been the foolish victims of deception and self-deception in politics, and they always will be until they have learnt to seek out the interests of some class or other behind all moral, religious, political and social phrases, declarations and promises". It becomes evident each passing day that the problems the country is facing can only be resolved between the forces of oppression and the oppressed.

When a nation degenerates so abysmally, when it is nigh impossible to make any progress in any field, no matter how minute, then we must look for solution somewhere else. We must seek a new beginning. Only those who understand the logic of ceaseless struggle in the progress of any society can appreciate the need for this new beginning. And they will always be consoled by the words of Kim II Sung that the oppressed in every decadent society should not bemoan its oppression, but raise the consciousness of the oppressed and ultimately its triumph.

Evidence point to the fact that the Nigerian reality of the 20th century is fraught with contradictions that go beyond party, tribe or creed. It must, therefore, be sounded clear to those who are dissatisfied with the perpetuation of injustice and suffering in this land, the epileptic supply of electricity, the chaotic transport system, the battered education system, the debilitating conditions of our hospitals, the accentuation of social vices, the general insecurity and disillusionment, the glorification of religion in the country to the detriment of its secularity and above all the anti-democratic culture, that the present system has to be recreated as a new foundation for the future.

This new foundation of progress can only be built and sustained if we understand the roles and positions of individuals and groups in the present political debacle; positions and roles which have vitiated progress. Nowhere in human history has progress been attained by people clasping their hands.

The vast majority of our countrymen and women who have been victims of oppression and injustice as well as the robbery and carnage perpetrated by the ruling class must understand the meaning of this political practice. Then, they will stop labouring slavishly and move to create that new beginning for the society in which there will be no room for exploitation and injustice.

In order to achieve victory, our people must show concern and doggedness. However, we must know what we fight for and why we fight. Interestingly, there are those who think the present political crises can be resolved in isolation; those who do not see the resolution within the interconnectedness of class relations; as a struggle of opposites not just in the realm of politics, but in the economic and social spheres.

Expectedly, it will not be long before we find out that the way our present taskmasters are leading us cannot propel the country to progress, cannot stop the impoverishment, the embitterment and weariness caused by the debauchery of our so-called political class. We must ponder very deeply over this new beginning for those who want to stop injustice and oppression must have the perseverance to try new methods, means and ways of struggle in order to achieve success.

In the end, it is this new beginning that will give us a democratic state in the true sense of the word; a state that shares the aspirations of the working and exploited people.

3. A Cycle of Rubbish
April 1995

It took place on January 15, 1966; the first bizarre event of our nationhood: the startling intervention of the military in our political evolution. And since then, the country has had to live with this nightmare for the greater part of its thirty-four-year history. Except, perhaps, the first military coup, all others have been comedies of vendetta and pillage.

Today, after twenty-five years of experimenting with the military, the country is enveloped in gloom and apologists of military rule are still wavering on the exit of the military. Of course, those who have made it their pastime to campaign for the military cannot appreciate the amount of injury they are causing our already frayed nerves.

What has been military rule in Nigeria if not dictatorship? Adventurism hiding under the cloak of messianism! And as the cycle continues, the people are daily groaning under the anvils of poverty and servitude. Everywhere you go, there is hunger and want. Nothing seems to be working or has ever worked. Depression, confusion and mass hysteria have always occasioned military rule in Nigeria. Undoubtedly, the resentment of this parody of governance is festering, not minding the hollowness of the battle cry to the contrary.

Gowon ruled for nine profligate years. It was an era of stupendous oil wealth and he left nobody in doubt that money was not the country's problem. He promised to return the country to civil rule few years after he took over power, but continued procrastinating until he was swept out of office. And when Obasanjo did keep his "promise", it was more out of expediency. Babangida ruled for close to a decade, casting dark shadows over the length and breadth of the country. The government led the people into believing it had the magic wand of freeing them from the various problems that confronted them. He launched a political transition that was, in the words of Wole Soyinka, "a transition to perdition". He set the stage for the perpetuation of military rule.

The military shares a greater blame for the morass in which we have found ourselves as a country. There are no indications that it wants to or is able to correct the situation. More than this, the military lacks the political and moral will to institute any kind of democracy. The present military government has succeeded in putting in place a constitutional conference, the opposition to the farce notwithstanding. Even at this, the government does not feel satisfied allowing the conference to chart its own "independent" course for this country.

The military government prides itself on being the bastion of national unity. Yet unity eludes the country. Never before has the nation been enmeshed in religious bigotry, ethnic chauvinism and regional mistrust. The military agenda fashioned for the country has shaken the equilibrium of our national existence.

The military has played an important part in the disintegration of the Nigerian economy. It has continuously undermined the political independence of the country while creating false hope for the people. Nigerians will continue to be the victims of the grand deception of the military until they learn to confront the military in its march of deceit.

4. The State and the People
May 1995

As the military regime waits confusedly for the outcome of the parody called constitutional conference, it is necessary we focus on the Nigerian state, as it is presently constituted, and the character of those who have run it since our flag independence vis-à-vis the future of the country and her peoples.

The latter, of course, for whom the present economic and social order hold no future, must understand that none of the factions, armed or unarmed, in power or trying desperately to grab power has any plan for the toiling and exploited people of this country.

Perhaps, we should concentrate less on this group of power mongers and pay more attention to the undue reverence the Nigerian state enjoys presently. Perhaps, we will then be better placed to understand this palpable national crisis and what is to be done to transform the contradictions in the country into a potent force for the dawn of a democratic, free and progressive Nigeria.

Of course, it is not enough to bemoan the collapse of the so-called cherished ideals in a society that is inherently hostile to itself; certainly, not enough to hope that the crisis can be wished away. No doubt, the economic and geo-political foundations of the country have been the major stultifying factors in our march to political, economic and social freedom.

The Nigerian state today represents an organized force serving exploitation and domination. That is why the issue of self-determination of nationalities is usually misinterpreted and not infrequently narrowed down to the issue of secession and defence of a bogus unity.

This is why people who are suffering national oppression in the most cruel, bizarre and savage forms are accused of impiety when they question the basis of their continued marginalization and deprivation in the midst of abundance. In the name of religion, the state is also able to obfuscate the reason for our underdevelopment and backwardness. Through such pernicious doctrines, it holds citizens hostage while finding divine undercover for its actions.

Independence for Nigeria did not mean much as to exclude the cultivation of archaic economic theories of development; it did not stop the omnipotence of feudalism where some people still look at Nigeria as one vast kingdom, neither did it seek to organise and strengthen our public life. As should be expected, the public sector has become a sinecure for government officials. And while the public sector has continuously witnessed a downward turn, the so-called organized private sector has fed fat on it.

It is clear that the Nigerian state has since inception joined in the "complicity of economic exploitation, social alienation and political domination". The Nigerian state reminds one of the devils in Ngugi's *Devil on the Cross* who commit murder then don their robes of pity and go to wipe the tears from the faces of orphans and widows; who steal food from people's store at midnight, then at dawn, visit the victims wearing robes of charity and offering them calabash filled with the grain they had stolen; who seize men's wealth, dress in robes of friendship and instruct the people to join in the pursuit of the villain who has robbed them.

Is it the corruption, graft, mismanagement and recklessness instituted by successive governments or the topsy-turvy transition programmes of various military regimes? Is it the omnipotence and lawlessness of a hegemonic few or the higgledy-higgledy pro-imperialist economic doctrines – SAP, privatisation and commercialisation? What has the Nigerian state not done to bring unmitigated catastrophe upon our people?

Let us give a graphic description of what makes up the Nigerian state. The Nigerian sate consists of those whose interests are diametrically opposed to the interests of those they claim to represent; the feudalists and internal colonialists who are touchy about the questions of restructuring the country. It also consists of the propertied class and its armed wing – the military – who have bled this country for thirty-five profligate years.

So, let the Nigerian state not tell us about democracy because it is undemocratic; neither should it promise us social justice because its structures are the direct antithesis of all the noble ideal it professes. The oppressed and exploited masses who have consistently cried out for freedom in their fatherland cannot rely on the Nigerian state to give them the overdue respite. It is illusory to think that the orchestrated efforts by the present military regime to enthrone democracy and enduring peace will materialize.

Let me state, at the risk of sounding monotonous, that the Nigerian state as the guardian and protector of our liberties cannot fulfill the democratic aspirations of our people. Therefore, the present alignment of political forces in the country represents for us an attempt to emasculate the sovereign will of the people and prolong the internal colonization going on in the country.

---

5. Far from World Order
May 1995

Watching rescuers evacuate victims of the April 19 bombing in Oklahoma City in the United States of America, one not only felt the agony of human suffering but the threat of a world at war with itself.

"Haters" of America would have been glad or too willing to give anything to claim responsibility for the carnage. And who knows, the world would have faced another blitz from God's own country. That singular event shook the American society to its very foundation. As an American journalist remarked, "For once, the most powerful country in the world stood helpless".

The concern here is not so much that the world is witnessing all these tragedies but the fact that these things are happening in an era of a New World Order. During his state of the union address in 1991, President George Bush had said:

> "It is a big idea, a New World Order where diverse nations are drawn together in common cause to achieve the universal aspirations of mankind, peace and security, freedom and the rule of law…only the United States has both the moral standing and the means to back it up".

With the supposed collapse of communism, the United States assumed the role of the undisputed leader of world politics. And counting on the moral standing and means of the United States, one would have thought that the threat to world peace would have been history. However, the world can hardly be said to be free or at peace. It only goes to show that there is more to world peace than the so-called snare of communism.

Baba Wey Agbeyangi in "How Conurbation will change the face of the Earth" states that,

> *"A new world order is in place yet old world habits of greed, domination and violence persist. There is more than enough food produced annually in the world today yet over half of the world's people, children, the old and the infirm included, go to bed hungry and rise with no prospect of where the next meal would come from. There is poverty in the midst of plenty."*

This paradox gets even more confounding when one looks at world politics, particularly Africa in the past five years: Liberia, Somalia, Ethiopia, Nigeria, Burundi, Rwanda, and Sierra Leone. The list is inexhaustible. These are supposed to be the beneficiaries of the New World Order.

The United States of America, as the executor of the New World Order, should see the convulsions in the nooks and crannies of the world, including America, as a signal that there is an organic relationship between genuine world peace and its presumed invincibility.

America's newfound posture as the policeman of the world will do nobody any good. There is no communism to stir the emotions of America. So she has nothing to worry about if she goes to intervene in any other country. However, that does not solve the question of internal crisis, the question of violence, of hunger, of freedom and of peace. We need to reorder our priorities and seek new initiatives in our desire for world peace.

A new world order of peace and détente is at variance with America's domineering status. For America to think that she only can negotiate world peace amounts to seeking the impossible. The West, with America at its head, created a "monster" in Boris Yeltsin. They watched him send armored tanks to sack the Russian parliament. Now that he is playing "Hitler" in Chechnya, they are screaming blue murder.

Last month marked the 20th anniversary of the inglorious end to an inglorious war in Vietnam. Of course, the effects of that war persist in the streets of Ho Chi Minh City (Saigon). The recantation of the United States' Secretary of Defense during that era, Robert McNamara, only goes to show how not to seek world peace.

It is evident, and we can only hope America comes to the realization, that the problem of the world is not communism. In this era of the new imperialism, the hysteria of a New World Order and the desire to enforce peace should be stripped hollow. Perhaps, the time has come for the United States to find a new approach to its foreign policy in order to contain the violence, carnage and destrution she is experiencing at home.

What it boils down to is that a genuine New World Order can only be sustained when nations and people are able to co-operate as equals; when nations and people are really free to determine what kind of progress they wish to pursue, what social and political forms best suit their quest for freedom, equality and development; when nations and people are under no obligation to follow a particular model of development that is not historically expedient.

---

6. THE TASK BEFORE THE YOUTH
JUNE 1995

"If law is of such a nature that it requires you to be an agent to injustice to another then break the law". – Henry David Thoreau

So much has been said about Nigerian youth and their role in nation building. A few days ago, the youth were the focus of attention as the country celebrated the children and youth day. It seems the Nigerian state is never tired celebrating the youth whom they claim are the leaders of tomorrow; a tomorrow that may never come considering the sordidness going on now under the guises of governance.

It has become imperative, therefore, to address ourselves not just to our historical role in the present debacle, but also to be wary of the diabolical signals that are capable of unmaking Nigeria. There is every need to put events in the country into proper perspective so that our responses can be articulated correctly; for we cannot hope to restore Nigeria to glory or anything near that if we do not make correct analysis of the debilitating crisis confronting her.

The necessity of this action stems from the fact that the military has become a fetter to any form of progress or social movement in the country. While other countries and people are moving forward, Nigeria is moving backward, gradually but consistently receding to barbarism and decadence, and turning into a country where the rule of law does not exist and the rule of force has taken over.

We must be wary of attempts by the military to foist a transition on the country. We must understand that its much-vaunted values about democracy are a sham. We must not forget that fascism and oppression are the same everywhere; the only difference is that in Nigeria they speak the local dialect. That is why the regime is always jittery and often forgets its high-sounding words about respect for liberty, democracy and the rule of law.

A particularly dismaying aspect of the mess the military and its civilian collaborators have thrown us into is the invidious plan to extend the tenure of the present regime indefinitely. The arbitrary decision taken by the so-called constitutional conference, though regrettable, is understandable. The lesson we must draw here is that class interest which is uppermost in the minds of those who are ever ready to maintain the *status quo* gains the upper hand when juxtaposed with the interest of the people.

As this task occupies our mind, we must not fail to understand the nature and character of the Nigeria state. We must not forget the chicanery, usurpation, corruption, confusion and the perpetuation of injustice in the country. The lesson here is that these things do not happen by chance. This regime, its predecessors and various collaborators are only behaving true to type. We must realize that the Nigerian state under which we subsist is essentially capricious and no amount of jabbering will change that.

We must make bold, therefore, to reject the present economic, social and political hierarchy in the country. We cannot tackle the issues of unemployment, absence of democratic freedom, free and qualitative education, free medical care, etc., except we understand the root cause.

Nigerian youth must not aspire to take over from those who have misruled this country for decades now. To attempt to do that will be to continue the way we are living. We must, therefore, be interested in replacing the present order – with its prejudices, cynicism, uncertainties and miseries – with a new social system.

As children and youth celebrate, it would be silly to think that the burden of life would become less. In the face of these glaring contradictions, we can only admonish ourselves not to waver. Fate has placed us in the centre of the present crisis. As Frantz Fanon said, "Each generation must, out of relative obscurity, discover its mission, fulfill it, or betray it".

We must not only fulfill this historic mission, but be ready to lay down our lives for our loyalty to our people. "Let people get angry and shudder at our resolve".

7. The Way We Live
July 1995

There is a way we live in this country which is not only cynical but suicidal. Not even the icon of social science, Karl Marx, would have been easily disposed to defining or characterizing our present dispensation. The legendary psychoanalyst, Sigmund Freud, would definitely be out of words for the Nigerian psyche.

You cannot talk about the organisation or discipline which capitalism pretends to uphold; neither can you talk about rationality which is the preserve of humans. It is even harder to talk about national consciousness or nationalism which every modern state cannot ignore. Everything in Nigeria is drowned in the sea of irrationality and insanity.

Already, the middle class has become extinct, thanks to the hopeless economic policies of successive regimes. Just as new avenues of wealth open up, new frontiers of despair assail us every day. Yet, we carry on as if nothing is happening. We live in the midst of so much confusion, executive lawlessness, inertia and the morbid fear of change.

Do our rulers really give a thought to how people live? How our citizens survive the pains of an underdeveloped, neo-colonial and parasitic economy like ours? The prices of goods and services – if they are available – keep rising on the hour, while salaries and wages remain same or keep depreciating. Life has become increasingly meaningless for the majority; our young men and women are daily groaning under the anvils of unemployment and insecurity of life.

As the citizens are tossed back and forth through the deceitful wiles of the rulers, the lives of the people *"keep rolling like one yeye ball wey one yeye wind dey blow from one yeye corner",* apologies to Fela. Living in Nigeria is like walking a thin and dangerous rope. Nothing in Nigeria works the way it should. The era of savagery cannot be compared to what we are experiencing in this country. Call it a primitive laissez-faire economy or society and you may only have succeeded in dressing the country in borrowed robes. Our rulers find it difficult to see the decay of the Nigeria state; cannot see the poverty in the streets. It is even doubtful if the people themselves really bother about their way of life; if they think things can ever be done right.

The nation has lost its soul; and the citizens, their morals and scruples. Time was when people found filth repulsive. Not anymore! Consumed by the quest for bread and butter, we couldn't care less. Raise the price of petrol today the Nigerian will adjust his mind attitude tomorrow. While the rulers, a minority in every sense, live in superfluous affluence, the majority live in poverty. We have never had it so bad. We now live in frenzy as if the world will end tomorrow. We have been transformed into a nation of money grabbers. Money has become the common index and makes all the difference between life and death. Money has become a magic wand which, under the present system, can transform itself into anything.

Yes, that is Nigeria for you; a place where everything has gone awry. The rulers are behaving as if they have no obligation to anybody. Perhaps, it is only in Nigeria that a police officer stops you; he has arms procured through your sweat and tax. He accuses you of wandering. You can only regain your freedom if you are able and willing to buy same.

What we are witnessing in the country today is institutionalized banditry. The politicians use their positions to acquire privileges for themselves. Those who possess arms maraud their way to power, daring anybody to challenge them.

A general today, a captain of industry the next day. Their goal is strengthening the reign of capital. That is how they have shamelessly run the country for almost four decades. As the reign of capital intensifies, stultifying any meaningful growth, the masses are wailing and gnashing their teeth.

The system, no doubt, has lost all it takes to humanise its citizens. Perhaps the end, the very end, is here.

---

8. Leftists and Transition Politics
July 1995

I shall use the term leftist in a very limited way; and for this purpose, it does exclude all those on the left who do not look beyond the Nigerian state as it is presently constituted and those who think that democracy in Nigeria, in whatever guise, whether "enduring", "lasting", or "genuine" can uplift the mass of our people from the throes of exploitation.

Since the country's unending transition programme started almost a decade ago, the left – the supposed bastion of the interest of the working people – has found itself playing certain unhistorical role. The general paralysis to which the left has fallen in the last eight years is traceable to a number of factors which the left, as a class that knows its own interest and how to defend it, should have been able to overcome.

To say that since the advent of the present transition, the left has witnessed a general complacency and towering degeneration unparalleled in the annals of leftist struggle in the country is like saying dawn will follow dusk. Not only has the left been unable to avail itself of any real programme, it has made itself almost irrelevant.

The past eight years have been so baleful that the duty of the left has been how to reconcile the working people with their exploiters; how to attune the suffering of the working people to the interest of the state. The quest for "bread and butter" which has worsened in the preceding years has engendered opportunism within the rank and file of the left and very little effort is needed to wipe out the vestiges of any articulate left posturing.

On the one hand, leftist intelligentsia lacking the moral courage to admit the indisputable contradictions in the transition programme succumb to the manoeuvres of the ruling class to form an alliance between the working people and their oppressors. Their criticisms, rather than being that of disdain for the latter, have tended to vitiate the position of the working class. It appears that the left cannot appreciate its own successes and little gains in the military junta's higgledy-piggledy transition programme. It will be asking too much from our leftists, therefore, to remember the need to enthrone the working and toiling people or to overthrow the state as it is presently constituted.

Today, our leftist scholars are not talking about the economic foundations of the state which is the cornerstone on which the massive exploitation of the working people rests or the relations of production which give insight into what can be done to stop the exploitation of the working class, without which we cannot accomplish any leap in social development. Hardly are there any critical essays about the philosophical and ideological foundation of the Nigeria state. Yes, that is the level to which cowardly opportunism has been elevated.

However, by far the singular event which has confounded the left and atomized it in the nebulous transition is the June 12 crisis. After about two years of prosecuting that struggle, it appears the left is at a crossroads. I have a feeling that if this crisis is not put in proper perspective, the left which is almost accustomed to failure as far as politics in Nigeria is concerned will fail gain.

The June 12, 1993 presidential election around which the present crisis whose solution appears not feasible within the context of one Nigeria, should be an elixir for the left in more ways than one. But it seems that is not the case. The significance of the election goes beyond the fact it was "free and fair"; it goes beyond the issue of it being a "sacred mandate". The significance is that it was revolutionary to an extent. It questioned the colonial geo-political malfeasance in the country.

Beyond June 12, there are just two options open to the left: transform the country quickly and immediately along revolutionary lines or participate in Abacha's transition. The prospects of the former, again within the context of one Nigeria, may not be feasible in the short term. And to adopt the second position while abandoning June 12 would amount to withdrawing halfway from a "victory" it has won.

What is to be done in the words of Edwin Madunagu, The Guardian, September 23, 1993, is, "To continue to demand that the winner of that election be installed as president and to intensify our struggle for a Sovereign National Conference (SNC) and hence a new constitutional order".

---

9. Market "Foxes" and the Rest of Us
August 1995

Over the years, economic theories have been put forward to save humanity – including majority of people from the developing world – from the clutches of poverty and underdevelopment, and enhance the frontiers of human freedom.

These theories, of course, have been in a life and death struggle with one another until very recently. With the supposed "fall" of Eastern Europe and by extension the "collapse" of communism and the emergence of a unipolar world that is systematically skewed toward the West, it is understandable that every sentence that spews out of the mouth of Euro-American ideologues, and their siblings in the colonies, is laced with the rhetoric of "free market", "market forces" and other jargons of capitalist emasculation.

Some of the concomitant of the preceding phenomenon include the Structural Adjustment Programme (SAP), debt-rescheduling, open market for finished goods, an end to any form of subsidy, privatisation and commercialisation, which we have pursued as a nation since independence and more vigorously implemented as a satellite economy since 1986.

Of course, we all know – well, except those who perpetrate these economic crimes against Nigerians – that the masses of our people are still groaning under the anvil of SAP that no amount of theorising can remedy the situation. Yet the apostles of Bretton Woods do not want to let go. They say SAP and other hopeless economic theories were necessitated by the deep and immutable principle which undergirds a free market economy. That it has failed, they claim, is more from the operators of the system than the system itself.

They go ahead to argue that, "Since man is born free, it is the free market system which engenders competition that best suits the traits of man because it draws the best out of him; it forces him to struggle, which is the basis of life". However, looking at our own peculiar economic situation, it will not be wrong to say you are free as far as those laws which are basically there to protect capital and property interests allow you to be free. Clearly, in a society full of class contradictions, if there is freedom for the exploiting class to exploit the working people, there is no freedom for the working people not to be exploited.

Man can only be free, therefore, in the arena of co-operation, not competition because competition through the so-called free market and "market foxes" contains the laws of its own destruction. It is planning through co-operation that can elevate man higher than other animals. It is only through such arrangement that man pulls together all his energies because he knows that it is going to benefit him since he is not exploiting anybody and nobody is exploiting or using his labour because he does not possess capital.

The increasing misery, despondency and lawlessness in our society can be attributed to the adulation of the present system of free market. The principles of competition and "market foxes" are principles of no-holds-barred. Those who exploit are free to exploit; just as those who rob are free to rob. Genuine freedom for man can only come about with the demise of the state, at least the way it is presently constituted. We know that the state is the greatest contrivance of capitalism to fetter humanity. The origin and emergence of the state and private property is well documented.

Of course, it is not the apostles of free market and "market foxes" who talk about the withering of the state. On the contrary, they insist on the state. It is strange, therefore, that a new phenomenon is emerging in the West – the concept of Limited Government – where multinationals are now taking over the functions of the state. It is only logical that they will seek to sack the state after using it. The effect, however, for humanity, particularly the developing nations, can only be imagined.

The reign of "market foxes", a major feature of free market economy has no room for decency, morality or fairness. It is the harbinger of anarchy. When "market foxes" ride roughshod over citizens, who sets the so-called laws and standards?

Conditions in Nigeria can change but not with the veneration of free market economy, particularly in the present dominant economic structures of the IMF and World Bank which have failed to confront the issues of integrated growth and development based on the principle of interdependency.

"Only the conscious organisation of social production", according to Friedrich Engels "in which production and distribution are carried out in a planned way can elevate mankind above the rest of the animal kingdom socially". Only this, I posit, can uplift the mass of our people from their unmitigated suffering and abate the crisis in the land.

10. LESSON OF WORLD REVOLUTIONS
AUGUST 1995

Every year, the cream of the Nigerian society, our rulers inclusive, gather to celebrate with the rest of the civilized world the anniversaries of their glorious dawn. At such occasions, they savour the warmth and felicity of people who are enjoying the dividends of democracy and are looking forward with delight to the challenges of the twenty-first century.

If they are not celebrating with the French and how they have enhanced the frontiers of equality, liberty, and freedom, they are felicitating with Americans and upholding their respect for the rule of law, democracy and freedom of expression. The lessons they are taught at such ceremonies include:

> "When the French revolutionary masses and peasants overthrew the monarchy at the end of the eighteenth century, when they made short work of their land owners in a revolutionary manner that was to shake the rest of Europe, they were able to put an end to many old evils".

They might be told that,

> "The event ended the privileges of the nobles and cleric. It ended feudalism and gave the middle class greater share in the running of the country. It created a fairer system of taxation, made all men equal before the law and provided education and other social benefits for the people".

If it is the United States celebrating, the Nigerian onlookers will also listen to eulogies about Americans and how through revolution they were able to create a society every American literally is proud of. The examples are endless. Paradoxically, more than two centuries after these illuminating pathways were created, back home in Nigeria the citizenry still groan under unemployment, diseases and poverty. "Neither the shantytowns nor the impoverished and miserable masses seem to have partaken in the prosperity and wealth which successive governments in the country have been exposed to".

Over the years, our rulers have completely alienated the people they claim to rule over and the nation is drifting slowly into anarchy. Luckily, they are not telling us to eat cake in the absence of bread as Marie Antoinette, the guillotined queen of France, did when the French were experiencing their worst food crisis.

However, the insensitivity of our rulers has not dimmed one bit. Today, Nigerians have begun scavenging the dustbins in search of bread as someone cynically predicted over a decade ago. The hungry faces on our streets, the destitute citizens that litter our roads and the political terror that pervades the air are just some of the many evils that confront the nation.

Presently, everything in the country bodes ill as it did in France over two hundred years ago. Nothing seems to be working. Each day, the country is faced with problems which are not insurmountable, but because of the avarice and insensitivity of a few, reminiscent of the role of the nobles prior to the French Revolution, the country can't move forward. The contrivance which decreed that, "The good things of life shall be retained as the exclusive right of a minority which reduced the majority to a position of servitude and subservience and which was the harbinger of the French Revolution" exists in Nigeria today.

With demagoguery, distortion and lies, the Nigerian nobility not only deludes the people that it has the magic wand of freeing them from their many scourge, it also finds spiritual undercover for its wiles. The traumatized masses are tossed back and forth. I wonder what lessons our rulers have learnt from history. Better still, when will Nigerians know liberty, equality, justice and freedom of expression? The military and politicians have proved incapable of providing leadership to the people in their struggle for emancipation.

Of course, we have come to a period in history when our ruling class should be confronted because satisfied with their gains in life, just like the French nobility, "they are touchy about criticism and skeptical about the call for change". But change is inevitable.

Beyond this, we must also realize that we have reached a point where we ought to face the possibility of a sudden change because the country has had its fair share of the morass of nationhood. And anybody who sees the internal contradictions in our society, "a society where the whole of man's energy is committed to keeping himself alive", will realize there cannot be a better time of throwing away this yoke.

---

11. BEIJING AND SUPERPOWER ANTICS
SEPTEMBER 1995

The Fourth World Conference on Women tagged Beijing '95, has come and gone. The memory, of course, will linger on for a lot of women who came to China with the genuine hope and feeling to address the multifarious problems confronting women; not so much for the fact that the conference may have addressed their genuine fears and aspirations, but the fact that for once in a long time world attention was focused on the plight of women.

With an apposite theme of peace, social justice and development, thousands of women had come from all over Africa and the developing world hoping to find an end to poverty, violence against women, political alienation and other injustices that have become the lot of women in a male dominated world. It is doubtful if they ever came close to achieving that. Of course, very few of them understood the battle of wits that preceded the conference and eventually spilled into the conference proper. And fewer still would have appreciated the import of the statements, manoeuvres, action, inaction and antics of the world's superpowers.

For African women and their counterparts in the developing world, their agenda was simply subsumed in the agenda of the West. Many women went to Beijing carrying anti-Chinese prejudices and in their naivety lost touch with the reality and what should be done to emancipate women.

It might take another decade, and perhaps in a more conducive arena, for the women of the world to rise up in unison in response to the prejudices against them. But, that will depend on the attitude of the superpowers and their willingness to confront the problems beyond the narrow confines of ideological and economic interest.

What we saw in Beijing was a replay of the Cold War between China and the United States. Of course, the lessons of the long drawn history of this war should not be lost on citizens, particularly women in Nigeria and by extension Africa. While the Sino-American diplomatic tussle raged, Mrs. Hilary Clinton, wife of the American president went to Beijing and slammed her hosts for alleged human rights and population control abuses. She was, no doubt, the woman of the hour for many delegates.

While Randal Robinson, leader of the Trans-Africa group was arrested in Washington for protesting the unspeakable human rights violation in Nigeria, a phenomenon the United States has shied away from or maintained doubletalk, Hilary Clinton was ready to march her army of supporters through the streets of Beijing in defence of women's rights. Of course, majority of the women at the conference came from countries whose human rights records, particularly against women, are no less grievous than the supposed Chinese experience.

Nigeria is one such country. The past one year has witnessed the most bizarre experience for Nigerian women. Detention and death arising from the loss of jobs, particularly for media practitioners, and emotional and psychological torture for those whose husbands and relatives have been incarcerated for months without trial.

The United States went to China with a very tall agenda. The sincerity of that agenda is what may be in doubt. Outlining US' goals for the conference, Ambassador Madeline Albright had said,

> *"We want to promote and protect the human rights of women. We want to end violence against women. We want to expand women's participation in political and economic decision-making. We want to assure equal access for women to education and health care throughout our lives".*

But, the problem of violence and discrimination against women in the economic political and social spheres is not just a Chinese problem. According to a United Nations fact sheet, one quarter of female gynecological patients in Norway have been sexually abused by their partners. One in five women in the United States has been raped. In Bangkok, half of all married women are beaten regularly, and in Peru, 70 percent of all crimes reported to police are of women beaten by their husbands. Using Beijing, therefore, as a showcase for the pursuit of punitive ideological end, does not serve any purpose. On the contrary, the generality of women are worse for it.

The continuing misery of women can be located within the context of a world economy manipulated by the superpowers. It is a historical fact that the position of women has changed, though not improved with each succeeding epoch: slave holding, feudalism and capitalism. It is not by chance that women have been reduced to simple articles of trade, subjected to the most gruesome form of back-breaking labour in farms and factories.

Of course, our women certainly deserve a better deal. There is more the superpowers can do to enhance the position of women across the globe. About two centuries ago, French philosopher, Charles Fourier, noted, "In any given society, the degree of women's emancipation is the natural measure of the general emancipation". According to Malcolm X,

> *"The level of a people was determined by the level reached by their women. If the women were conscious and educated, then the race would occupy the same level, where the women were oppressed, their oppression reflected the oppression of the entire race. Herein lies the essence of the global concern for women".*

It does appear, however, that beyond "opening up China", the Bamboo Curtain, to the "civilized" world, Beijing '95 was another wild goose chase.

12. Solving the Housing Question
February 1996

Adequate shelter – affordability, legal security of tenure and the availability of services, materials, facilities and infrastructure – like food is a basic human need. Just as they require food, people require a place to live. People require shelter just as they require medicines when they are sick.

Though the year 2000 when every person is expected to be housed is barely four years away, millions of people in Nigeria still roam the streets homeless, while millions more live in shacks, slums and houses that are far from being adequate for their dignity as human beings.

In tackling the housing question, we must first determine whether shelter falls within the purview of rights, a phenomenon that has been quite contentious. From various international conventions, it is clear that adequate shelter is a basic human right. What does the right to adequate shelter entail? Who should safeguard it? And why has it been almost impossible to maintain?

The right to adequate shelter states that everyone is entitled to live in decent structures. Put simply, everyone is entitled to live in conditions that promote his or her health and safety. It entails that, notwithstanding the type of tenure, all persons should possess a degree of security of tenure which guarantees legal protection against forced eviction, harassment and other threats.

It ensures that houses must contain certain facilities essential for health, security, comfort and nutrition, and that all beneficiaries of the right to adequate housing should have sustainable access to natural and common resources, potable drinking water, energy for cooking, heating and lighting, sanitation and washing facilities, food storage, refuse disposal, site drainage and emergency services.

It goes further to ensure that personal or household financial costs associated with housing should be at such a level that the attainment and satisfaction of other basic needs are not threatened or compromised; that the physical safety of occupants must be guaranteed through providing them with adequate space and protecting them from cold, damp, heat, rain, wind or other threats to health, structural hazards and disease vectors.

It also encourages a housing situation which takes into account disadvantaged groups and allows access to employment options, health care services, schools, child care centres and other social facilities.

Finally, it recommends that the way houses are constructed, the building materials used and the policies supporting these must appropriately enable the expression of cultural identity and diversity of housing. Beyond the issue of the right to adequate housing, however, is the vexed issue of who ought to safeguard this right. Some people believe that it is government's responsibility to safeguard the right to shelter; others suggest it is within the purview of individuals to make sure that they enjoy adequate shelter.

Whichever way we look at it, it does appear, however, that the greater responsibility of promoting the right to adequate shelter rests with the government. Why is this so? The International Covenant on Economic, Social and Cultural Rights which Nigeria is a party to, says that "State parties to the covenant recognize the right of everyone to an adequate standard of living for himself and his family, including adequate food, clothing and housing and to the continuous improvement of living conditions".

It goes ahead to recommend that state parties "take appropriate steps to ensure the realization of this right, recognizing to this effect the essential importance of international co-operation based on free consent". Since Nigeria is one of the many countries that have "ratified" this covenant, it has become, under international law, legally bound by it. That is, she is agreeing with the rest of the world that "We believe in the right to adequate shelter and we will do all we can to promote the realization of this right". Beyond this, the government must demonstrate to the world how it is working to promote the right to adequate shelter in Nigeria.

What is the situation on the ground? No doubt, there is a serious housing problem in the country which borders on shortage. The different housing programmes of various regimes in the country have failed to tackle the issue of availability of housing. In virtually all the major cities in the country, congestion resulting from shortage of housing is the norm. People living with their relatives, families sharing apartments in crowded and rather unhealthy and unsafe conditions, and squatters sprawling all over are a common sight.

This debilitating condition has led to increased homelessness, life under bridges and in shacks. The problem is further heightened by the economic situation which has made it impossible for people to afford even the available houses.

The rising cost of building materials and allied products is another problem. And since there is no stringent regulation or adherence to the laws protecting the housing rights of citizens, most house owners have assumed the posture of tin gods. Landlords evict their tenants at will. A lot of them are uncompromising and sometimes reckless in their relationship with tenants. In most cases, due to the contrivance of judicial officers, the law is not capable of protecting the rights of the affected tenants.

Worse still is the problem of large-scale eviction. For those who manage to secure a place to live, various local authorities have made it impossible for them to live in "peace" by forcibly evicting them, claiming the need to rid the society of "illegal structures". Of course, victims are not given any reprieve such as compensation or provision of alternative accommodation, even where such promises are made.

What can be done to ensure that people enjoy good living conditions rather than life in makeshift structures and inadequate houses? In answering this question, we must look at the totality of the problem. Firstly, the problem needs government's attention and concern. Building more houses for people to live in through its low cost housing schemes is one way the government can promote the right to housing.

There is also the need for government to make building materials cheaper by making them duty and tax free and, therefore, affordable so that more people can build their own houses. Government should also put in place legislations that will check the oppression and exploitation of tenants by their landlords.

The government should also go a step further to reaffirm the right of every woman, man and child to live in a secure place of peace and dignity by observing that the practice of forced eviction constitutes a gross violation of human rights, in particular the right to housing.

Government should take immediate actions, at all levels, aimed at eliminating the practice of forced eviction and seek to compensate or provide sufficient alternative accommodation to all persons and communities that have been forcibly evicted.

13. GLOBAL TACKLE FOR POVERTY
FEBRUARY 1996

Next to war, poverty is perhaps the greatest scourge that faces mankind. The world has witnessed numerous wars. Though wars persist today, the peoples of the world have sought practical ways of putting an end to wars and their attendant woes. Not so for the question of poverty.

Today, more than half of the world's population lives below the poverty line, a phenomenon which threatens the survival of humankind. From the Asian hinterland to Africa and the Caribbean, poverty extends its fangs, ravaging people like bush fire. The developed world, of course, is not spared. Reports have it that almost one in two African-American children is born below the poverty level. Europe also has pockets of impoverished inhabitants. Indeed, poverty is a global issue which seems to defy any solution.

Beyond its global nature, the crisis of poverty has been an age-long one. Not even the march of civilization and the advancement in science and technology seem to have made it possible to grapple with this scourge. What is poverty? And why has it become such a problem?

The cynical definition of poverty describes it as a "disease". Indeed, poverty is a disease; a disease far deadlier than the dreaded HIV/AIDS. Poverty is a disease which makes it impossible for those afflicted by it to live like human beings, to enjoy their basic rights. It cripples family ties, leads to social maladjustment, destroys its victim's psychology; in one sentence, it diminishes the individual. To be afflicted by poverty is to be "dead" while still alive.

Poverty is not the lack of riches, but the inability to meet primary needs. There are certain things which enhance living and whose absence will denigrate human existence. These include food, clothing, adequate housing that protects inhabitants from the rough elements or other structural hazards and disease vectors, and adequate medical services. Poverty is a product of lack of economic and social empowerment. Poverty manifests itself in prostitution, street life, unemployment, life in shacks, lack of access to good and qualitative education, and political inaction.

Since poverty is a global phenomenon that defies age, sex, colour or creed, it is evident that the solution must be sought on a global level. Expectedly, the United Nations has taken the initiative by declaring 1996 as the "International Year for the Eradication of Poverty". The Secretary General of the UN, Dr. Boutros Boutros-Ghali, launched the year on December 18, 1995, in New York.

According to him, "Persistent poverty is not only incompatible with social harmony and a durable political order, it is morally wrong. It is a major cause of violent crime, ethnic clashes and social disarray. Action to secure global peace, security and stability would be futile unless economic and social needs were addressed".

Of course, that was not the first time global attention would be drawn to the issue of poverty. In March 1995, in Copenhagen, Denmark, the UN Social Summit focused on the fight against poverty. The summit's final declaration on social development to curb poverty has yet to be fulfilled. Therefore, the question, "What panacea for poverty?" becomes imperative.

Clearly, we must change our traditional attitude to tackling poverty if the world is to be rid of its debilitating effect. The response hitherto has always been cosmetic. Why are more and more people around the world slipping into poverty by the hour? Is it that the world's resources cannot satisfy its population and its attendant needs?

If the answer is yes, then modernization has done nothing to change the world. However, this is not the case. Economic models are at the root of mankind's descent into poverty. The world's current economic trends are contributing in no small way to the emergence of both the rural and urban poor.

Poverty is a product of a dysfunctional market economy. It is the result of the war by minority of mankind that values speculation over production; a world that deifies "market forces". The present dominant neo-liberal economic development of global expansion (acquisition by multinationals), privatization and commercialization, and integrated growth and development not based on mutual interdependency are the harbingers of poverty.

By diverting resources that ordinarily would have served the indigenous population, we encourage consumerism and deprive people of essential resources to produce their basic needs. And by privatization, we undermine the distribution of wealth and expand the frontiers of profit. What we get in return are inequality, alienation, deprivation and all the effects of poverty.

In trying to tackle the question of poverty certain salient points must be taken into consideration. Poverty stems from economic and political malfunction. The world is so unevenly slanted in favour of the developed nations and to think of unrestrained fusion would create chaos.

Countries should be allowed, indeed encouraged, to pursue economic and social models which best suit their quest for development.

---

14. THE PARADOX OF LAW AND ORDER
MARCH 1996

Law and order, like democracy, has become a byword in the modern age as it strives for a new world order. Nothing so typifies its importance as the desire of modern states and governments to maintain it at any cost. There is the belief that it is essential for law and order to prevail for society to move forward.

The concept of law and order is indeed a universal one, rooted in the sociological thinking that without the former there cannot be the latter; and without the latter life will be "nasty, brutish and short". The idea becomes even more important as the modern state hinges its survival on it. It seems the world cannot do without law and order.

Unfortunately, the world has not witnessed order no matter how hard its rulers have tried. From Bosnia to Rwanda, down to West Africa, humanity has sunk into the lowest depths of disorder, barely escaping from its rabid claws of extermination. All too often, we are confronted with varieties of laws on different issues covering the social, economic, political and even religious spheres. Yet, disorder pervades the atmosphere, filling the air with its unrestrained flurry of conflicts, and overshadowing whatever good idea is left in society. This state of anomie raises the need to review the relationship between law and order.

Theoretically, it cannot be denied that the concept of law and order is a product of class rule; an instrument for the oppression of one class by another. And on the practical level, law and order is relevant in the quest for the state to play its historical role. The state must create order through its laws to be able to maintain its rule. This is how Karl Marx expressed the correlation: "It is the creation of order which legalizes and perpetuates the oppression of one class by another by moderating the conflict between the classes".

The relationship between law and order is one that has always proved sour at every juncture. Laws, in whatever guise have not been able to create the much-needed order. The laws of capitalist appropriation and exploitation cannot be far removed from the anarchy in production and the upheavals society has witnessed over the ages. It is only proper that disorder both in the socio-economic and political arena is the hallmark of the laws of free enterprise.

What this means is that order has a lot to do with the nature of law. South Africa under apartheid best describes this relationship. The Boers made a fetish of law and order. They even had a Law and Order Minister. For decades, various apartheid regimes kept rolling out laws. However, the more laws were made to sustain apartheid, the farther South Africa was enmeshed in violence and disorder.

Being unable to contain the violence and imminent disintegration of the country, the White minority rulers heeded the admonition of the American law historian, Henry David Thoreau, that, "If law is such a nature that it requires you to be an agent of injustice to another then break the law". The obnoxious apartheid law crumbled. The rest is now history. It is instructive to note that in less than half a decade after the fall of apartheid the Republic of South Africa is gradually emerging as one of the contending forces in world politics.

The gap between law and order is reflected in the relationship between the rulers and the ruled. It also means that there is a very thin line between law and disorder. The former is a harbinger of the latter, particularly where it is obnoxious. Social disorder is a sign that policies and laws so-called do not reflect the wishes and aspirations of the people. Today, Nigeria is sprinting toward self-destruction. Each day, our rulers keep manufacturing decrees and laws to bring amity and cohesion in the country, all to no avail. The wave of arrest and detention across the country is justified by decrees but the populace remains restive.

Nigeria is in dire straits. The unending violence in the country is a pointer to one thing: the economic, social and political laws in the country bear little or no relevance to the aspirations of the populace. It is not by chance that things have gone awry; that violence is rife. The very laws on which the country stands do not enhance justice. Rather than tackle the problems confronting the country, the government prefers to go after imaginary enemies.

NADECO, NALICON and human rights groups are not responsible for the poor living conditions of Nigerians brought about by hopeless economic laws. The injustices that manifest themselves in every sphere of our national life which have led to ethnic tension and distrust were not created by pro-democracy groups.

Clearly, there is a link between law and disorder. And unless Nigeria wants to self-destruct, there is an urgent need to look at the decrees under which we subsist, including those transiting us to democracy.

15. A Nation on Trial
June 1996

The charges are many. Count one: Nigeria is a mere geographical expression. Count two: she is a political contraption. Count three: she is a land of irreconcilable contradictions. That is the case against Nigeria, a land of over 200 ethnic nationalities, forced into a union by the British in 1914.

In the light of current events, the charges can go on *ad infinitum*. Ironically, the more charges that are brought against her, the more palpable is her guilt. The evidence of guilt weighs against her because the country, like many modern states, is a product of the growth of imperialism; the outcome of its gruesome encirclement through economic and military actions that took place in the last century. Of course, beyond geographical proximity, the various ethnic nationalities that would make up Nigeria had very little in common. This requirement was hardly enough to enhance the bond of nationhood.

The *Oxford Advanced Learners Dictionary* defines a nation simply as "large community of people, usually sharing a common history, language, etc., and living in a particular territory". From the foregoing, it is clear that some vital links were missing when the colonialists set up the political configuration called Nigeria. Though it is not necessary for all the factors to be present before a nation forges ahead, it is possible that the absence of one can unmake any potential nation.

This is the problem Nigeria, like most countries in Africa, has had to contend with since 1914 and more specifically since 1960. This same problem which has ravaged the whole of Africa has over the years assumed a monstrous dimension in Nigeria. Expectedly, the political class itself, being shamelessly entrenched in ethnic politics, rather than working to fix the union designed to satiate the economic and political whims of Britain, feels complacent and touchy about change.

Nigeria reels in contradictions. She looks at herself as the giant of Africa; a giant with clay feet whose tardiness is monumental. Nigeria is a super-rich country where the citizens not only feed on crumbs, but literally scavenge refuse dumps to survive; a greatly religious state that is in the grip of a moral crisis; a country where the masses are increasingly pauperized just as its fortunes grow; a state that wants to develop technologically, but treats its education system with contempt; a society that makes so much noise about democracy, yet majority of her citizens are disenfranchised and regimented by military dictatorship.

This is the true position of the country. Over the years, while the evolving nation reeled in self-destruction, opportunities have also presented themselves for the resolution of this endemic national crisis. The civil war, or rather the end of that ignoble war, presented one such opportunity. But, the ruling class was too obsessed belching the cliché "the unity of the country is nonnegotiable".

Unwittingly, the suspicion and ethnic distrust, rather than abating with the end of that war has exacerbated, confounding even the most optimistic patriot. Then came June 12, 1993. It appeared that what Nigerians could not achieve through arms, they resolved to effect through the ballot box. Again, ethnic chauvinism reared its head and that election was annulled. It is not out of place to aver the ethnic character of that annulment because those who caused it represented an interest far removed from the greater national interest.

Since 1993, the country has been enmeshed in an orgy of political tension and violence. The government on its part has put in place a transition programme as an alternative to the June 12 question. It has also set up a reconciliation committee which is more of a diversion since the regime is interested in hearing only its own voice. Of course, for a regime that rode on the crest of the June 12 crisis in its quest for power, the only genuine reconciliation would be to dialogue with the acclaimed winner of that election. But, the regime does not want to yield.

While M.K.O Abiola was detained by his captors, a bewildered nation woke up on June 4, 1996, to hear of the dastardly murder of Kudirat Abiola, the heroine of the June 12 struggle. Certainly, for now, no other event, in term of worsening the political crisis, parallels the murder of Kudirat Abiola. There is a worrisome dimension to the whole tragic drama. What is it that has made life so cheap in Nigeria? Why is it that assassins have become ten for a naira? Why are citizens no longer safe even with the massive presence of the military? These are questions that cannot be answered independently of the political crisis occasioned by the June 12 annulment.

It is now time to resolve the Nigerian crisis because I do not know how much more bloodletting we can afford. One is optimistic that Nigeria will survive. The optimism is borne out of the admonition of Hans Morgenthau in the *Restoration of American Politics* that,

> *"In the life of nations, as in life of individual a great crisis can be a boon if it reveals in the contours of the abyss, the stark and simple outlines of the eternal verities which men and women neglect only at their peril".*

The June 12 issue, and by extension the murder of Kudirat Abiola, has exposed the eternal verities of the country. Nigeria has offered all that it has to offer and nothing is left but the foul smell of a decaying corpse. We can only ignore the signs of an imminent catastrophe at our own peril.

Now is the time to pose the question of Nigeria's future. However, the question must be posed sincerely without any illusion about what it entails and a fearless disposition about its outcome.

16. SEASON OF BULLDOZERS
JULY 1996

For some time now, Lagosians have had to live with the threat of or actual demolition of their homes and sources of livelihood. Bulldozers have taken over the streets of Lagos, tearing down structures referred to as "illegal" and in their trail is an unmatched level of despair and anguish. It reminds one of locusts crossing a land.

The spate of destruction of goods and property worth millions of naira without recourse to law or due process should be of concern to civil society because ultimately it will have to deal with the multiplier effect of such actions. Of course, Lagosians are no strangers to the terror of bulldozers. It does appear that demolition and forced evictions form part of the "development" programmes of successive administrations in the state.

In 1990, more than 300,000 people who had yet to be resettled were sent packing from Maroko during the regime of Brig. Gen. Raji Rasaki. Today, the victims of that dislocation form the greater part of the large army of homeless people in the state. Six years after, there is no respite in sight for residents of Maroko. Ironically, what used to be Maroko, home for the "wretched of the earth" is presently an abode for the nouveau riche.

A distress message sent to the Administrator of Lagos State, Col. Olagunsoye Oyinlola, by the displaced inhabitants of Maroko conveys their pathetic story: "Today, thousands of people are seen sleeping in the open across Lagos State as vagabonds, thousands are still lurking around the old site, along the sea shores for lack of accommodation". Expectedly, there was a deluge of public outcry during the cannibalization of Maroko. The trauma and anguish was better imagined. But, Maroko did not stir the conscience of the government.

Nothing since the Maroko episode has hit Lagosians harder than the on-going demolition exercise embarked upon by the Ministry of Works and Housing. With the present onslaught, it is double tragedy for beleaguered Lagosians. It started with the demolition of stalls erected under fly-overs, and has extended to structures within 30 metres of federal highways.

Those affected did not get more than a week's notice; neither were there any plans to resettle them. Interestingly, most of the people now left to pick up the bits and pieces of their lives as vagabonds have no other source of livelihood. They have occupied the demolished locations for years, and in some instances even paying rents to various local authorities.

It does appear, however, that the ministry is not done yet. There are strong indications that over 250 families in Harvey/Moore Road area of Lagos State will join the band of homeless when the ministry's bulldozers visit soon. For a people who have lived the past 48 years at the settlement, the true aim of the ministry is questionable. And looking back at Maroko, there may be nothing to cheer in whatever promises made by the ministry.

Presently, there is no concrete plan to resettle the residents of Harvey/Moore Road in a suitable, alternative accommodation and the quit notice made it clear that the due process of law would not be followed, a phenomenon that is contrary to Nigeria's domestic laws requiring a proper notice to quit and resort to the judicial system for the recovery of possession of land or premises. It also contradicts Nigeria's obligations, freely entered under article II (1) of the International Covenant on Economic, Social and Cultural Rights.

More worrisome, however, is why forced eviction of groups and communities and demolition of structures have become a highlight of the activities of the Ministry of Works and Housing. And to imagine that these derogations are taking place in the year of the World Conference on Human Settlement (Habitat II). Beyond the foregoing, there are some important questions: Why Lagos? What makes the city provide this kind of attraction for bulldozers? What is the ultimate objective of those who unleash these monstrous machines on helpless citizens?

It may be true that the Ministry of Works and Housing has a right to protect property; but Lagosians also have the right to survive, and even more so in a country where the welfare of citizens is taken for granted by the government. As a developing nation, government's action should be seen to reflect the "developing" stage the country is passing through. To evict people from under flyovers or their homes and inadvertently increase the number of social miscreants and the rate of crime will serve no useful purpose.

Of course, one does not need to highlight the extreme futility of the Rambo-like action in dealing with citizens, particularly on issues that border on their livelihood. All what it reminds us is the militarization of our national psyche. But, it also raises the issue of democratising the polity so that the people can have a say in what affects their lives and future. The government is not building new houses while existing ones are in the state of decrepitude. The political climate has worsened the state of the economy so that people cannot build their own houses. Yet the onslaught goes on unabated.

As citizens of this country, Lagosians, and indeed all persons, deserve a secure place to live, both for their dignity and for their physical and mental development. That cannot happen when they are constantly hounded like refugees.

◆

17. ASUU AND OUR NATIONAL DILEMMA
JULY 1996

For some time now, the activities of the Academic Staff Union of Universities (ASUU) and by extension the crisis in our universities have occupied centre stage in public discourse. Recently, a cartoon in one of the national dailies not only stirred my interest in this war of nerves between ASUU and the military government, but also kept me musing about the future of tertiary education, and indeed, the future of Nigeria.

In a very captivating manner, the cartoon lampooned the tragedy of our education system. The setting is an employment bureau. A young man in search of job approaches a bespectacled employment officer and the conversation goes thus: Employment officer, "What can I do for you young man? Young man replies, "I am finding a job sir", and hands over his credentials. Employment officer: "I can see that you have a degree in English language", he queries the young graduate, peering in his file. The young man replies, "Yes sir, I got the best result in my class". Frustrated, the officer thinks quietly to himself, "Gosh! Another victim of ASUU strikes", and turns to the young man, "Please, remember to close the door on your way out…we'll get in touch with you later".

The above scenario may look comical, but it is the true position of the country's education system. Things have gone awry as far as education is concerned in Nigeria. We have never had it so bad. Many people, particularly parents, agree that educational standards have fallen drastically over the years. The general feeling is that standards have fallen because teachers are no longer dedicated to their job.

Very few people would want to see this social malaise as the product of a decrepit social order which has placed not just those who teach but those they teach in a very suffocating position. For a while now, students in tertiary institutions across the country have been on holiday due to the ASUU/government face-off. The students are, undoubtedly, tired of this unending holiday and are eager to be back to school. For many, the purpose is not to seek knowledge, but to acquire a certificate and join the rat race.

It is certain that life has been snuffed out of our ivory towers. Blaming ASUU for the current crisis would amount to giving a dog a bad name to hang it. Our universities today are a perfect reflection of the sorry state of the country. The crisis in the universities did not start today. It is the product of years of neglect, lack of planning and treachery of successive governments in the country. There are many areas in which various governments have not kept faith with higher education, including the issue of autonomy, funding and wages of lecturers.

Over the years, the erosion of the powers of our universities has manifested itself in the sacking of lecturers for "teaching what they are not paid to teach", the removal of vice-chancellors who do not acquiesce to government's position and their replacement with sole administrators. But, by far, the most serious problems facing the ivory towers are inadequate funding and debilitating wages for university teachers.

For example, according to National Universities Commission (NUC) figures, between 1985 and 1989, Nigerian universities requested N4.013bn. Though the NUC recommended N3.413bn, what the universities got was N2.083bn. Clearly, if the figures for 1990-95 are made available, no significant improvement would be recorded. Between 1989 and 1992, the budgetary allocation to the education sector of which the universities are the major stakeholders kept dwindling in this order: 4.28%, 3.59%, 2.18% and 4.22%.

Regrettably, the funds available to the universities have continued to deplete just as their needs have soared. The result has been an unfavourable learning environment. Lecturers share office without essential facilities and are deprived of the most basic teaching tools. For the students, crowded hostels and lecture rooms, scarcity of books and ill-equipped libraries are the norm. Just as university teachers grapple with poor infrastructure, they have had to contend with debilitating wages. Indeed, ASUU captured the sad situation in one of its numerous campaign posters which read: "My boss is a comedian; the wages he pays are a joke".

Notwithstanding this unwholesome situation, our academics are expected to squeeze water out of stone by graduating the best engineers, doctors and scientists that will propel the country to technological heights. Alternatively, the solution has been to undermine the lecturers' union, sack erring ones or close down the universities indefinitely. As a way out, some people have suggested handing the universities over to the states. But, we all know how terribly incapacitated the states are in a federation where the centre controls over 95 percent of the country's revenue.

Proscribing ASUU and allowing each university to negotiate with its lecturers will not serve any purpose. If anything, it will compound the anarchy in our education system. Are we to assume that the lecturers will accept the same paltry wages when they get back to their local universities? How will the decentralization improve the infrastructure in the universities to enable lecturers function effectively?

Perhaps, if we realize that we have made mistakes as a nation things might start to normalize in our ivory towers. It is interesting how we can afford to spend billions of naira maintaining ECOMOG in the name of peacekeeping while our universities are neglected.

It is even more perplexing when we spend millions of naira searching for a Technical Adviser for our national teams when most universities in the country do not have potable water or functional libraries. Recently, the Nigeria Football Association (NFA) was reported to have spent N3 million to host the Gabonese national team in a match that was aborted. Maybe, as a pariah nation, we live with the illusion that the momentary ecstasy and fame which football brings will provide the much needed international attention and respect. But this is mere wishful thinking. Nothing can lift a nation as the development of science and technology which comes through a functional education system.

In the heyday of Gen. Babangida's regime, military officers from the rank of major and above got a 504 Peugeot saloon car each. After severe public outcry, the regime claimed that the largesse was a loan. I do not know if our academics enjoy such patronage, and if they do, what it is worth. There are many lecturers who cannot secure loans to repair their cars, some of which are over twenty years old.

The following quotation from Dr. Pius Okigbo during a lecture on "Crisis in the Temple" at the University of Lagos in 1992 captures the crisis in the country's tertiary institutions and the lack of effort on the part of government in finding any meaningful solution:

> *"If the military administrations of this country have been eminent in nothing else in the twenty-two of thirty-two post-independence years, they have at least been eminent in their obstinate and mistaken belief in their superior patriotism and self-righteousness. Under their supervision these twenty-two years, we (especially in the universities) seem to have lost our soul; to have enthroned mediocrity; to have not only banished excellence, but also repudiated knowledge and experience. We have desecrated the Temple (of learning) and turned them from intellectual citadels to a purely political market place".*

18. THE PARADOX OF POWER
JULY 1996

As the world moves to the threshold of another century, social scientists and political watchers alike have an uphill task in appraising the concept of power. Power, in whatever form, is intoxicating. It not only corrupts, it places those who wield it in a position to decide the fate of men, women, children, and, indeed, everything within their reach.

Quite often, those who wield power never have enough of it. They rarely can let go, preferring to destroy even that which they control in order to maintain their position. However, the paradox of power as a concept is benumbing. The fluidity of power belies its seeming invincibility. In 1939, Europe was enmeshed in a civil war. During this period, Hitler, leader of the Nationalist Party in Germany, epitomized death. The fuehrer wielded power never again witnessed in modern history. He sought to rule or destroy those who did not acquiesce to his insatiable lust for power.

Hitler threatened to over-run Europe and the entire human civilization. Indeed, at a stage, he had the continent under his feet. Terror gripped Europe and Hitler basked in his omnipotence. Very few people dared defy his orders; fewer still questioned his method. He had the power of life and death and he left nobody in doubt what he could do with it. But when the end came, his power dissolved like an ice cube. Nobody seems to know how or where the remains of the historical freak were interred. Indeed, it is a paradox that with the power Hitler wielded, he was denied even the least honour in death.

Precedents notwithstanding, the quest for power has continued unabated. Ironically, power has not failed to consume those who abuse it. Africa, of course, has had its fair share of these schizophrenic psychopaths who see political power not just as a means of corruptly enriching themselves, but as a way of playing the messiah over the rest of us. We have had the Idi Amins, Bokassas, Marcias Nguemas and Mobutu Sese Sekos. But by far the most tragic example of the paradox of power is Gen. Samuel Kanyon Doe. In 1980, the gaunt 27-year-old master sergeant took over power in Liberia. Doe began his reign by assassinating his predecessor, William Tolbert, Jr. and his cronies.

Feeling surefooted, Doe went after the opposition. For him, power did not only provide an opportunity to be in control in the lives and actions of men, it provided a chance to show how vindictive those who wield it are. Slowly, but steadily, he eliminated his enemies, including those who set out with him. Doe perfected various strategies, including imaginary coup plots, in order to get even with the opposition. With the opposition decimated, Doe became the lord and master of Liberia. Liberians lived in awe of him while he rode roughshod over the small West African country. Nobody was beyond him to either imprison or execute.

Swiftly, he transformed himself into a civilian president in a higgledy-piggledy transition programme. As the "emperor" of Liberia, Doe demanded nothing less than slavish and total subservience of his fellow citizens. Of course, he got such groveling obedience from his own clan. Those who questioned his authority were not only killed, their regions were marked for extinction. And so began the war of attrition and ethnic cleansing that not only consumed Doe, but has left Liberia in ruins.

As leader of Liberia, Doe was least concerned about the economy, except perhaps how it benefited him personally. It did not bother him that Liberians were starving and the rising prices of food items made life increasingly meaningless. He savoured all the bounties of office and enjoyed power to its fullest.

However, power being what it is, "a perilous paradox", had a date with Doe. When the day of reckoning came, power proved to be an inconsistent and unreliable friend. Those who are familiar with Peter Enochong's film, "The Liberian Civil War", will appreciate the gist of the tragic end of one of the most despotic rulers in human history.

The all-powerful Doe who could order the execution of anybody he wished in Liberia, was transformed into a mere baby, sobbing uncontrollably, as death stared him in the face. Regrettably, Doe was consumed by power which he cherished and used to its fullest; but the chaos he left behind still haunts Liberia today.

Back home in Nigeria, we have also witnessed the reckless abuse of power. The cynical arrogance of those who wield power certainly does not take into cognizance the disastrous paradox of power. In 1985, a year many have described as Nigeria's *annus horribilis*, Gen. Babangida took over power in the country. And for eight years he held the country in his grip. Indeed, at the height of his parley with power, he did not mince words in telling a highly distraught populace that his regime was not just in government, but in power. He understood the efficacy of power. Perhaps, what he failed to realize was that power belongs to the people and that no amount of armoured tanks can stop a people determined to end oppression.

As a mark of his invincibility, Babangida annulled the June 12 1993 presidential election, not minding the risk to the nation. Expectedly, crisis trailed the annulment; but it also exposed the myth about the omnipotence of power. When the people resolved to protest the annulment, Babangida had to scurry out of office.

Today, the General who ruled Nigeria for eight years, controlling her vast human and materials resources and exercising the power of life and death over her citizens says he is afraid for his life. He was reported to have claimed that he dreaded Lagos, which was his seat of power for five years, and that he needed as much as N6 million every day to guarantee his safety. What a paradox! It is in this same Lagos, during his control of state power, that over 200 pro-democracy activists were mowed down without qualms.

Those who wield power presently live under the illusion that power is eternal. They may do well to learn from history. But learning from history is not a strong point for successive governments in the country. And as it is often said, "Those who do not learn from history are bound to repeat it". The wave of arrests, detention without trial and circumscription of our democratic aspirations will only serve to awaken our citizens from their reverie. The consequences are better imagined!

19. IN THE GRIP OF HISTORY
AUGUST 1996

In a matter of weeks, Nigeria will be celebrating thirty-six years of independence. Expectedly, attempts have been made over the years to "move the country forward". However, by a curious irony of fate, each attempt has been a crude rehash of earlier efforts. In one sentence, Nigeria is in the grip of history.

At every turn in Nigeria's political evolution, what we see is history repeating itself. Karl Marx in his great work, *The Eightieth*

Brumaire of Louis Bonaparte, did observe that history repeats itself, first as tragedy, then as farce. The observation holds true looking at the Nigerian situation. Regrettably, this sham permeates every aspect of our national life. As a people, we did not learn from the crisis of independence. Less than six years after, the animosities that preceded independence came to the fore again and we had a civil war. Not minding the bitter lessons the civil war brought, it has been difficult for us to learn.

In 1978, political parties were formed to herald the Second Republic. Both personages and events during this period were a replica of what we had during the First Republic. Fifteen years later, under the regime of Gen. Babangida, two parties were foisted on the people even though then Nigerians had over half a century experience in party politics. If that was absurd, I wonder what we can say of the fact that both parties were a farcical parody of parties of the Second Republic, themselves a tragic parody of parties that existed between 1959 and 1966.

Looking back at the country's history and the cycle of military rule, we can easily appreciate the fact that the crisis of military authoritarianism has succeeded only in moving Nigeria one step forward and two steps backward. A cursory look at the history of coups and counter coups, promises made and promises broken, will reveal how firmly Nigeria is in the grip of a twisted history.

Under various military regimes in the country, with their superior claim to patriotism, efforts have been made to unite the country, yet we have never been so divided. Even when it is certain that the road taken can only bring despair, and that it is a familiar but ungainly road, successive regimes have preferred to allow their actions complete the tragedy-farce theory. That is what you get when a country is in the grip of history. It is in the context of this historical parody that the present transition programme should be examined.

Let us start from the personages that are scheming to assume power. Of course, there is nothing worthwhile to say. In the majority is what literary critic, Odia Ofeimun, once described as a confederacy of jailbirds. In this regard, Dr. Umaru Dikko strikes one as a peculiar case. Here was a man who was almost crated back to Nigeria from the

United Kingdom in 1984 when the present military rulers were henchmen of the then military regime. He was to face charges for his role in the billions of naira fraud that rocked the Second Re- public. But, this is Nigeria. Today, Dikko is back. He is not just walk- ing the streets a free man, he has joined the band of kingmakers. The rest, as the saying goes, is history.

We never learn. Examine the institutional framework of the transition programme and you would discover the theatre of the absurd our political landscape has become; a farcical reminder of the tragedies of our past. Look at the gush of political parties even when it is certain that the requirements for party formation will hamper the evolution of democracy. Under Babangida, we had two parties, one a bit to the left and the other a bit to the right. Today, we have the National Centre Party of Nigeria (NCPN). For now, it is not clear how many parties will eventually scale NECON's hurdle. What is certain, however, is that the transition programme can be tinkered to suit the aspirations of those who initiated it. Vice-Chairman of the Transition Implementation Committee (TIC), Sam Grace Ikoku, has said this much.

Somebody should tell Ikoku that we have passed this road before; that this is only a replay of the film that was played less than three years ago of which he was a lead actor. What of the Bukar Mandara story? To imagine that his "Abacha Must Stay" campaign is coming at a time when the general disillusionment about the transition programme is growing tells so much about how history repeats itself in Nigeria. Of course, it is difficult to draw a line between Mandara's National Solidarity People's Alliance (NSPA) and the infamous Association for Better Nigeria (ABN).

Just as events make a comical rehash, the interpreters of these events themselves have not failed to show how in the firm grip of history they are. Walter Ofonagoro, our ebullient Minister of Information (and history), was reported to have said there was no annulment of the June 12 1993 election. According to him, "You cannot annul an irregularity. The court stopped the election before it was held". Quite unfortunate! The kind of history Ofonagoro is teaching the rest of the world, certainly not Nigerians, is the kind of history we were taught as primary school kids two decades ago: that Mungo Park "discovered "River Niger.

Against the backdrop of an Abeokuta High Court order nullifying the disqualification of an aspirant during the last local government election, Justice Minister, Michael Agbamuche, maintained that no court proceedings could vitiate the action of NECON. We all know this same script was written in 1993. However, since our professional historians who want to consign the June 12 election to the rubbish heap have found a way of standing logic on its head by claiming that the court stopped the election, we should expect that Agbamuche's treatise will be rewritten when the time comes.

It is difficult, however, to appreciate that we recognize and understand how impossible it is to move forward with this delusion, yet we prefer to play along like puppets. Like people in a trance, we have consigned our fate to the unknown. Of course, Chief Sumner Dagogo Jack, Chairman of NECON, may be a patriot. He may also be an altruistic and plain-hearted man, but so were professors Eme Awa and Humphrey Nwosu before him.

The reality is that when history is set to repeat itself, patriotism and plain-heartedness count for much less.

20. REQUIEM FOR THE STATE
DECEMBER 1996

> *"Democracy in Nigeria is dead – once and for all. No meetings are allowed. No expression of opinion may be made that does not reflect his government's opinion. Justice is dead. The courts are suspended. Arrest is automatic for the slightest misdemeanor. Detention is frequent, without trial".*

That was Chukwuemeka Odumegwu Ojukwu, head of state of Biafra, writing about the Nigerian state under Yakubu Gowon in a letter to a British Member of Parliament. That event took place on March 12, 1968. Today, 27 years after, nothing has changed; well, except, perhaps, the whimsies of the writer.

Against all expectations, the Nigerian state has gone ahead in recent years to replay the unprecedented horrors that accompanied the protracted and internecine civil war to the chagrin of even the international community. It is dismaying to see how issues that border on the survival of a people are attended to with contempt. It is even more painful to observe that repression or force and sometimes death seems to be the only solution the state can proffer.

Of course, there is no country when the state fails to serve the interest of the citizens. Historically, the duty of the state has always been to reconcile the interests of the former with those of the latter. However, even this token gesture, the Nigerian state has failed to grant.

Recent events in the country, particularly the hanging of the "Ogoni 9", go to show our inadequacies as a nation. After 35 years of independence, the rulers and the ruled appear not to be reconciled. And when rulers and the ruled cannot be reconciled, the state ceases to exist. Examples abound.

Fredrick Engels writes of the state as,

> "A product of society at a certain stage of development. It is the admission that society has become entangled in an insoluble contradiction with itself, that it has split into irreconcilable antagonism which it is powerless to dispel. But in order that these antagonisms, these classes with conflicting economic interests might not consume themselves and society in fruitless struggle, it became necessary to have a power, seemingly standing above society, that would alleviate the conflict and keep it within the bounds of 'order'".

However, the same cannot be said of the Nigerian state. Its idea of "order" has been to kill and make life unbearable for citizens. Such is Nigeria today; a death field where the state kills at will. The Ogoni situation will, of course, prove that it is illusory for the Nigerian state to imagine that it can restore "order" and bring about unity by armed intimidation and the summary execution of defenceless citizens.

What is happening now has happened repeatedly to those who do not learn from history. It is easy for the state to go on hounding her citizens, assuming unlimited powers and living with the illusion that it can maintain the *status quo* indefinitely.

A lot has been said and written about the hangings in Ogoni land and the culpability of the Nigerian state in the tragedy. Expectedly, some people have started drumming up support for the state while condemning Saro-Wiwa and his compatriots. However, one thing we cannot take away from Ken Saro-Wiwa, the charismatic leader of the Ogonis who was executed on November 10, 1995, is that he was a consistent fighter unto death.

The manner he rebuffed his executioners showed how convinced he was about his struggle. Faced with the threat of marginalization by the dominant Igbo ethnic group during the civil war, Saro-Wiwa stood up to the challenge and defended the right of his people. It is unfortunate that the struggle to free his people from the threat of domination coincided with the interest of the Nigerian state, a development which put Saro-Wiwa in the bad book of many Igbos.

For a man whose struggle was altruistic, he never flagged. And when it became necessary to take on the Nigerian state, he left nobody in doubt about his resolve. Undoubtedly, Saro-Wiwa made some mistakes which border on tactics. He underestimated the barbarity of the state and paid with his life.

Saro-Wiwa died a martyr and his name will definitely join the ranks of Amilcar Cabral, Franz's Fanon, Walter Rodney, Patrice Lumumba and others who dared the state and championed the cause of the oppressed.

His death has taught us to demystify the state. And once the people discover that the state is not sacrosanct or eternal then their liberation is near.

21. NIGERIA: OPEN SORE OF A CONTINENT
DECEMBER 1996

This heading is not original. It is the title of Wole Soyinka's recent work on the political crisis in Nigeria. The little book published some months ago gives a graphic account of the genesis of the Nigerian debacle, its implications for Africa and practical solutions to the political mess induced by a cabal of military adventurers. However, the title is even more relevant in the light of the renewed ego trip the ruling military regime which celebrated its third anniversary last week, precisely on November 17, has embarked upon.

Before I go on, a little digression. Wole Soyinka is a Nigerian, a professor of literature and the first Black man to win the Nobel Prize for literature. He achieved that feat a decade ago. At present, he is in exile, far from his motherland, a place he eulogised with these words some years ago: "I love my country, I no go lie. Na inside am I go live and die".

The Nobel Laureate evoked these fond memories about his country during the ill-fated Second Republic, when Nigeria was in a state of atrophy and the misrule by the politicians so-called was at its zenith. But, those were the "halcyon" days of petty stealing and party "politricks" by our pseudo democrats. It is a different story today.

Confronted with a regime that bares its fang at the slightest prodding, Soyinka had to seek refuge elsewhere. Soyinka represents a small fraction of the large army of Nigerians who are very patriotic, who have faith in their country, but who are gradually losing hope of any sincere and meaningful solution to the political crisis in the country, thanks to the machinations of our omnipotent military overlords.

This is what Nigeria, represented by a group of unperturbed harebrained soldiers, is doing to her sons and daughters, driving them to the farthest parts of the globe in search of protection, when their country ought to be a haven for them. No doubt, Nigeria's problems are manifold, but nothing threatens the already frayed threads that hold the country together than the supercilious arrogance of a military class whose claim to being the bastion of national unity is suspect.

It is pertinent to lay bare the lie that is being peddled by the military junta in Nigeria and its cronies that the military has the magic wand of moving Nigeria forward. Nigeria has had 36 years of flag independence. The military has been in control for 26 years, moving the country one step forward and two steps backward, conceiving and aborting democratic processes and creating a prostrate economy by a combination of corruption and nepotism.

Of course, it is clear that the only legacy which the military has left for Nigeria is a contorted political climatic which has turned the giant of Africa to a thing of ridicule. This has had its effect on the collective psyche of the citizens, particularly with regard to the question of national unity and ethnic domination.

Not too long ago, the military regime under Gen. Ibrahim Babangida supervised a political transition programme which was to put an end to almost a decade of misrule. Nigerians decided then to give the process a chance not so much because they had faith in that regime but the fact that they did not want to be blackmailed into giving the regime an open cheque to advance its onslaught on the people.

We would recall that the presidential election which climaxed that transition programme was annulled by the military dictatorship then even when it was adjudged free and fair by both local and international observers. Gen. Babangida annulled the election held on June 12, 1993, not because his whims took control of him or that he was at his wits' end. He was acting true to type because the military of which he was the head then was and has always been in the service of an oligarchy which has used the military as a rallying point to divide and rule Nigeria.

Naturally, Gen. Abacha's claim to superior patriotism and heroism would have been to correct the political *faux pas* of his predecessor. That was not done since Abacha himself was on a mission. We can see why nobody should be impressed with the glib argument that Nigerians should expect democracy in 1998.

There are enough reasons why Africa and the rest of humanity should be concerned about what is going on in Nigeria. In terms of size, economy and population, Nigeria occupies a strategic position in Africa. It is often reported that one in every five Africans is a Nigerian. Given its population, if Nigeria is allowed to self-destruct, the consequence would be the desolation of the African landscape.

Nigeria is the open sore of Africa as Soyinka aptly titles his latest book. Indeed, a very big sore which is festering with each passing minute. Whether the country will move forward or not depends on how genuine patriots articulate her present problem and the amount of effort they put in solving it, not minding the risk involved.

The bane of the Nigerian nation is not so much the war between the rich and the poor (a war which will be waged at the opportune time) as the need to balance the various geopolitical units politically and economically. The military in Nigeria has proved incapable of doing that. In fact, it has shown itself as a negation of genuine efforts to make this dream of national unity a reality. The recidivist politicians jostling to replace Abacha do not stand the nation in good stead. They are nothing but soldiers of fortune who are interested in democracy only to the extent that whatever exists serves to fill their pockets.

All hope is, however, not lost. Returning the winner of the June 12, 1993 presidential election, Bashorun M. K. O. Abiola, who is in his third year of detention, can induce a fit of hope and create the enabling environment for genuine peace and national reconciliation. But, that is if the present military czars have not imbibed Lord Acton's dictum that, "Power tends to corrupt, and absolute power corrupts absolutely".

22. A TALE OF TWO COUNTRIES
JANUARY 1997

Recently, Mr. Jerry John Rawlings was reported to have visited Nigeria – his first official trip outside Ghana after the December 7, 1996, presidential election in Ghana. The visit had set tongues wagging, coming on the heels of his electoral victory. Some curious observers wondered if Rawlings had not gone to brief his Nigeria counter part, Gen. Sani Abacha, on how his (Rawlings) brand of "militocracy" has worked in Ghana. That visit, we must understand, has its historical antecedent and must, therefore, be situated in its proper perspective.

There is a compelling corollary between Ghana and Nigeria, both English-speaking countries in sub-Saharan Africa. This similarity is noticeable by everyone, even a first time visitor. Historically, the semblance is there: Ghana and Nigeria were colonies of Britain. Both countries share a legacy of colonial distortions, degradation and misguided development paradigms.

The two countries provide a very cynical example of the manipulation of democracy. The political scene in both countries has witnessed a harvest of coups and senseless and spineless incursion by military adventurers. And there is little indication that the trend will change.

Indeed, in all aspects of life, the two countries share a social miasma that belies their claim to independence or an eye for self-emancipation. Majority of Ghanaians and Nigerians go about life with the despondency of a people sentenced to perpetual penury and atrophy. You can see it in the food they eat, the houses they live in and the kind of social infrastructure available to both people.

So many of the ordinary people in both countries have come to understand this brotherhood of poverty and human degradation which binds them, so much so that they are ever ready to extend a helping hand to each other and live on the hope of a better tomorrow. However, repeatedly, the twin problems of neo-colonialism and effete leadership serve to destroy whatever hope the citizens have left.

As you look at the gaunt faces in Accra and Lagos or in the numerous inaccessible villages and towns that make up both countries, you begin to wonder if the great gold and oil wealth respectively served any purpose other than quenching the insatiable appetite of successive leadership in both countries. At construction sites, markets and street corners, you see and feel this yoke, a product of an insensitive elite.

The gap between the rich and the poor in both countries is forever widening. Just as new sources of wealth emerge, new frontiers of poverty assail the common citizens. Deprivation and want stare you in the face everywhere you visit even as stupendous wealth serve to give a false sense of development and assuage the frayed nerves of the people.

In both countries, the majority suffer, bearing the burden of parlous economies and corrupt and inefficient leaders whose only claim to leadership is the fact that they are in control of the apparatuses of state power which have enabled them to sit over and mismanage the collective wealth. Over the years, these leaders so-called who were supposed to lead the people into a new dawn of self-sufficiency and economic development have placed them all in a cocoon of economic darkness and political chaos.

The effect of the neo-colonial economic pill called Structural Adjustment Programme (SAP) and other hopeless economic theories forced down the throat of the people of both countries by their governments are still bitterly felt by the people. With over seven decades of independence behind them, the citizens of both countries still survive on the fringe, living in a state of incertitude.

Relatively, Ghanaians and Nigerians alike are hard-working people. But, take a walk around the cities of Accra and Lagos and see how bestial the lives of the average hard working citizens have become. To say life in these places have become "nasty, brutish and short" would be repeating the obvious. For some reasons, both countries have the potential to self-destruct. In each case, the ruling class has played the ethnic card; not only to shore up distrust, but to divide and rule.

Every night, the same people in whose name our so-called leaders claim legitimacy retire to their shacks. Of course, that is for those who are fortunate. Many more who are not as lucky sleep on tabletops at market places or along the streets. Jobs do not exist while social services, health and education are a mirage.

The question that readily comes to the fore is: does economic development mean anything to those who have saddled themselves with the task of ruling over the rest of us? Saddled themselves! Yes, these are the right words because coups, counter coups and a caricature of democracy have been the vogue in both countries, leaving the help- less citizens with little or no chance to decide their destiny. Even where the leadership in question is supposedly a civilian regime, its agenda is still fraught with danger. At the end of the day, the interests it serves, politically and economically, are diametrically opposed to the wishes and aspirations of those it deludes itself that it is out to protect.

Both countries, therefore, share the tragedy of the African leadership crisis. The reason, of course, is not hard to discern. I personally do not know what propels African leaders, but in their attempts to remain relevant, they pander to the most insensitive political and economic construct that bears little relevance to Africa's developmental needs.

What Ghana, Nigeria, and indeed the whole of Africa, require are leaders who are inward looking. The treachery and chicanery going on at present under the guise of governance cannot take the African continent anywhere because it is difficult to see how long the respective governments can sustain a system which extricates the majority of the people or does not use their welfare as a yardstick for measuring development.

It is, therefore, not totally inexplicable when a Rawlings visits an Abacha. You can always draw a parallel.

23. Time to Snub Dictators
August 1997

Africa is certainly a continent out of tune. By some cruel irony of history, the African continent cannot come to grips with the democratic realities of the emerging millennium. All across Africa, signposts of militarism and dictatorship are being erected. Even though the Idi-Amins, Bokassas and Babangidas have made their ignominious exit, the Abachas, Mois, Eyademas and Jammehs have proved themselves worthy successors of these despicable species of African rulers.

None of these regimes has popular mandate; parroting democracy and transition, they usually end up as "mufti-presidents" and tyrants. And since they are not popular they cannot mobilize popular support to meet the aspirations of the masses in their various countries. They end up not only looting but also wrecking their nations.

In Nigeria, Abacha rules over a nation of more than 100 million people after he and his marauding band usurped power four years ago. With Abacha, of course, you can guess not only his intelligence, but also the most likely step in his mimicry of democracy. The idea of democracy is simply beyond him. It is not for him to be circumspect on national problems – which more often than not he does not understand.

He is simply an embodiment of brute force. Today, there are more political prisoners in his dungeon than there were from independence in 1960 up until he seized power in 1993. The economy is in ruins, law and order has broken down and the citizens are daily terrorized by the twin problems of poverty and militarization of their psyche. Indeed as the New York Times once observed, "Never before has Nigeria had a government as ruinous and oppressive as that of Gen. Sani Abacha".

Zambia under Chiluba is a veritable nightmare. While the rest of humanity is marching forward, the government is receding into barbarism. Though just six years in office, controversy, conspiracy and repression are the hallmark of his regime. The suppression of the media and the opposition is total. In Zambia, the Internet is banned.

In Kenya, dictatorship and terror form the cardinal principles of state policy. Since Daniel arap Moi came to power in 1978, he has left nobody in doubt about his disdain for opposition. Kenyans have been brutalized physically and economically by Moi who has ruled Kenya for 19 years. Moi, like all other dictators on the continent, manipulates the constitution to guarantee his stranglehold on power. In Moi's Kenya, there is no room for dissent. Any person who opposes him, in the words of Koigi wa Wamwere, "has been called either a communist or a violent plotter against the government". The solution: either throw him into jail or gun him down as happened to Kenyan university students.

Eyadema's Togo is another haven of dictatorship. For 34 long years, the general-turned-civilian president has held sway in the country, and the people have nothing to show for it other than impoverishment and the denial of their basic democratic and fundamental human rights. The list is indeed inexhaustible. If other notorious dictators have not been mentioned it is due more to space constraint than the benignity of their misrule.

Mobutu Sese Seko, "The all powerful warrior who moves from conquest to conquest and leaves fire in his wake", is now in exile, fading into history. After 32 murderous years as president of the Democratic Republic of the Congo (formerly Zaire), he became one of the world's richest men and his country one of the poorest.

It is intriguing that centuries after the demise of the divine rights of kings, Africa is still enmeshed in "one man rule"; that three years before the dawn of the 21st century, the fate of this continent would rest on the idiocy of some despots. In all of this, the masses are the losers. They bear the brunt not only of the damnable human rights records of these tyrants but their corruption, incompetence and megalomania.

As Africa moves languidly into the new millennium, there could not be a more opportune time to halt the dangerous drift towards despotism by questioning the continent's entrenched and nascent dictators, including the "mufti-presidents" who are running nothing but quasi-democratic empires.

Experience has shown that a better and easier way of guaranteeing peace and democracy on the continent is for the international community to stop giving support to dictatorial regimes. The African continent cannot develop as long as leadership remains in the hands of anti-democratic forces, megalomaniacs and brutes for whom power is the ultimate aphrodisiac.

All progressive and democratic forces on the continent must therefore continue to struggle until the vestiges of this antiquated breed are rooted out and their ignoble rule confined to the trash bin of history.

24. Exporting Terrorism
October 1997

Two weeks ago, the Central Intelligence Agency (CIA) of the United States marked its 50th anniversary. The organisation used the occasion to exhibit the tools (cameras, lipsticks, etc) of its five decades of murderous plots against the rest of humanity.

President Bill Clinton who opened the exhibition paid tribute to CIA's role in the demise of the Soviet Union. "You labour in obscurity by choice and design, serving with quiet patriotism that seeks neither spotlight nor praise", he told CIA personnel.

Certainly, there are enough reasons for Bill Clinton and the US to cheer about the activities and "success" of its prime spy agency. Between 1960 and 1970, the CIA was involved in eight government authorized plots to assassinate Cuban President, Fidel Castro.

In February 1966, the CIA plotted and executed the overthrow of Kwame Nkrumah, the first Prime Minister of Ghana. Before then, it had plotted the assassination of Congo's Prime Minister, Patrice Lumumba. Subsequently, it plotted the death of Dominican Republic's Rafael Trujillo, Ngo Dinh Diem, the first president of South Vietnam "and one of the most competent lackeys of the U.S" and President Allende of Chile.

This is just a tip of the iceberg in the orchestrated war by the US to remain the most potent political, economic and military force in the world. Just name it. Where hasn't the US been? Where hasn't its monstrous military machinery caused death and destruction?

In 1983, the US invaded the island of Grenada in its so-called war against communism. Today, more than a decade after, Grenadians have yet to overcome the trauma and hardship which that invasion brought to the country.

Three years later, the US attacked Tripoli and Benghazi, two cities in Libya, killing children and innocent civilians in an attempt to assassinate President Gaddafi. Subsequently the US made forays into Panama and abducted President Manuel Noriega and then Somalia where its forces roasted Somalia children alive.

Very few people would forget the activities of the US in Vietnam in the 60s. Even though there is an order signed by President Gerald Ford in February 1976 and strengthened by President Ronald Reagan in December 1981 barring the CIA and all other US agencies from any involvement in assassination anywhere – which confirms the fact that this has been an official policy of the US – the US has not ceased expanding its military octopus to the detriment of developing nations.

Since 1960, the US has maintained an economic blockade against Cuba, an island of about 10 million people. Not too long ago, against all laws of morality and international relations, the Clinton administration passed the Helms-Burton Law which forbids US overseas subsidiaries to trade with Cuba and further threatened to punish any country that traded with Cuba.

Such arrogance, highhandedness and lawlessness can only come from a country that glorifies in the illusion that it is the policeman of the world. Indeed, the US sees itself in that light. Recently while Madeleine Albright, US Secretary of State, was on a tour of the Middle East, the official White House propaganda was that the US was the only country in the world that could intervene and restore peace in that region. Such arrogance! What the US has failed to tell us is what efforts it is making to undermine peace in that region.

Evidently, the US remains the greatest threat to world peace and security with its renewed quest for arms and nuclear build-up in the light of the disintegration of the former Soviet Union. Just last week, the US declined to sign a global landmine treaty because, according to President Clinton, the treaty compromised US security interests. All Jimmy Carter, a former American president, could say was, "It's embarrassing to me to see a hundred other nations vote to eliminate landmines".

Embarrassment is certainly an understatement. The action by the US is callous, barbaric and murderous considering the effects of landmines in the countries where they are exported. But, what do you expect in a country where the Military Industrial Complex (MIC) – ever ready to appropriate profits at the cost of human lives – is the driving force?

Africans must begin to reappraise every policy and statement that comes out of the White House. The US has succeeded in bringing the whole of Europe into NATO which it controls. Now, the plan is to set up the African Crisis Response Initiative (ACRI) to tame Africa and create a permanent market for the US arms industry.

Of course, the US has nothing to offer the world except terror and its current initiatives are nothing but attempts at exporting terrorism.

25. WHERE IS RUSSIA GOING?
NOVEMBER 1997

Apart from ending the oligarchic rule of the czars and creating a just and equitable society founded on the principles of socialism, the Bolsheviks who came to power in the Soviet Union eight decades ago had other visions, one of which was to create a society devoid of the madness and racial bigotry that the world witnessed in Hitler's Germany. All that has vanished.

It is clear from reports coming out of Russia that Boris Yeltsin and his band of Coca-Cola democrats are set to put the last nail on the coffin they have made of the success of the Bolshevik Revolution. After throwing his country open to the economic vultures from the West in the name of free trade and liberalization, Mr. Yeltsin appears incapable of stemming the tide of hooliganism and criminal gang activities which are a direct result of the crisis in the Russian economy.

There are many reasons to be worried about the anti-social activities of Russian militiamen and skinheads who have unfortunately directed their action against Blacks. Blacks are molested daily in virtually all the major cities in Russia. Their crime: simply being Blacks. "Filthy Negro", "black monkey", "ape", "f...ing Negro", are some of the derogatory words hurled at Blacks both in the streets and even at their residencies. The harassment knows no limit and more often than not is followed by physical assault.

Last year alone about nine Africans were killed in Russia. These murders are usually racially motivated and some are carried out for very flimsy reasons like the 1992 murder of Zimbabwean student, Gideon Ghimsoro, for allegedly "showing cruelty" to a dog owned by a Russian, Andrey Fyodorovsky.

To date no action has been taken against Fyodorovsky. The inability of the Russian state under Boris Yeltsin to tackle the problem of racism is a serious indictment of a man whose democratic pretensions have remained suspect. It is not surprising that under Yeltsin, Russia is witnessing reverses in all that the country built in seven decades of socialism.

There is little doubt that Yeltsin is set to destroy what is left of the spirit of socialism in Russia in which people of every race and origin cohabited peacefully. For a man who sees nothing wrong in literally selling off his nation to Western imperialists, nothing much should be expected from Yeltsin in confronting the new social malaise in Russia.

The question is: why do Russian militiamen and skinheads have to direct their anger and frustrations against Blacks, majority of whom have lived and worked in Russia for years? Dr. Michael Waganda, a Kenyan historian resident in Moscow for the past 20 years, sums up the tragedy in an interview with West Africa magazine: "Russians have to survive the tragic economic consequences arising from their own post-communist reforms and political changes, but that's no reason to shift emotion, anger and dissatisfaction on to Blacks".

Where is Russia going? Evidently, what Mr. Yeltsin's "opening up" of Russia to the free world so-called has succeeded in doing is creating a soulless society; a society that does not place emphasis on human dignity and for that matter human life; a society that is surviving on the heroic struggles of its nationals in bringing peace and détente to the world yet destroying every link with that glorious past.

In Yeltsin's Russia, the world may yet witness Hitler's Germany once more. However, Blacks and Africans generally cannot be his guinea pigs. Yeltsin and his band of ethnic bigots really have no option unless they are ready to throw Russia into anarchy.

26. ANY RESPITE FOR MINORITIES?
December 1998

The human tragedy in Jesse, Delta State, Nigeria, in which about 1500 people were burnt alive, is a pointer to the enormity of the neglect and deprivation of oil producing communities who constitute a minority in Nigeria. The Niger Delta is the region of Nigeria close to the southern coastlines and includes such ethnic groups as the Ogonis, Ijaws, Itsekiris, Urhobos, Andonis, Isokos and Ishans. Its history is the history of oil exploration and its attendant denudation of the ecosystem.

Since Shell D'Arcy Oil Company (now Shell Petroleum Development Company of Nigeria) "discovered" oil in Oloibiri in the eastern Niger Delta in 1956, the oil producing communities have known only poverty and misery.

A 1995 World Bank report estimated that some 10% of the area's mangroves have been lost to deforestation occasioned by exploration and production activities of multinational oil companies such as Shell, Chevron, Elf and Agip. But the exploitation of the minority oil producing areas is not only carried out through the activities of oil producing companies. This exploitation has equally been perpetuated through revenue allocation formula in Nigeria which favours the majority groups because of their population and size.

Of course, the only way to maintain this imbalance is the heightening of repression both by the government and the oil companies. As you read this piece, armed soldiers are occupying a section of the Niger Delta, gas fire is burning on farmlands the local inhabitants depend on for livelihood, gas is being flared causing considerable health hazards to the people; oil leaks from oil wells and flow stations have taken over entire bodies of water; some swamp forest is in flames, thanks to oil spillage from a pipeline belonging to an oil company.

Last March, elders and community leaders of Omualaa/Omuamadi communities in Rivers State in a protest letter titled "Before We Perish" to the military administrator of the state noted about one of such fires:

> "Like we earlier informed his excellency in our 'Save our Souls' letter dated 6th February, 1998, this fire had destroyed several hectares of farmland, our ancestral shrines, agricultural products, economic tree, etc. It has also completely rendered the soil useless. Sir, you could imagine an impact of this type of unprecedented situation to a community whose only means of livelihood is farming... presently, we are in fear of total extinction because for now the solution to the problem is not yet in sight, particularly as the fire is still burning with impunity".

The doses of repression by successive military regimes in Nigeria have woefully failed to curtail the restiveness among the oil producing communities. Irked by the deterioration of their environment and economic conditions, these communities have over the years protested the desecration of their land by the government in collaboration with oil companies. Some months ago, according to the Niger Delta Alert, a bulletin of the Environment Rights Action which circulates news and information on key economic and political developments and campaigns for environmental rights in the Niger Delta,

> "Aggrieved youths from four communities in Southern Ijaw local government council of Bayelsa State stopped operations of the Nigerian Agip Oil Company at its Tebidaba oil fields flow stations".

Their demand, the organisation said, included employment and training of their indigenes, provision of potable water and payment of one billion dollar compensation for the massive oil spillage in November 1996. Indeed, in all the minority oil producing areas in Nigeria, no month goes by without a crisis arising from oil exploration.

The non-violent struggles and campaigns of the minority communities notwithstanding, the government has responded with increased violence, exemplified in the assassination of author and environmental rights activists, Ken Saro-Wiwa and eight of his compatriots three years ago, detention without trials, rape, and looting by soldiers of the Internal Security Task Force, a special military outfit set up specifically to check what the government has described as "treasonable activities" of the oil communities.

The complicity of oil companies in this reign of terror must also be acknowledged. Only recently, Pacifica Radio's daily national newsmagazine, Democracy Now documented for the first time Chevron's role in the killing of two Nigerian activists. In an interview with Democracy Now, officials of the San Francisco-based oil company acknowledged that on May 28, 1998, the company transported Nigerian soldiers to their oil platform and barge in the Niger Delta which dozens of community activists had occupied.

According to Pacifica Radio, soon after landing in Chevron-leased helicopters, the Nigerian soldiers shot to death two protesters, Jola Ogungbeje and Aroleka Irowaninu, and injured several others. During their imprisonment, one activist said he was handcuffed and hung from a ceiling fan hook for hours for refusing to sign a statement written by Nigerian federal authorities. This followed on the heels of reports that Shell paid and armed the soldiers that were deployed for the "wasting operations" in Ogoniland.

Recent protests in these oil-producing communities, many unreported, show that the issues on which Ken Saro-Wiwa and others hinged their campaigns and for which they paid the ultimate price have yet to be addressed. Increasingly, the Niger Delta, including the mangrove, rain forest, the local people and fauna, is being threatened by environmental degradation.

Oil spillage which pollutes farmlands, fishing streams and ponds and the indiscriminate flaring of gas which poisons the air and even affects the reproductive system of women have served to compound the lives of the inhabitants of these areas.

Worse still is the realization that the people of the Niger Delta do not receive any share of the oil proceeds obtained from their land, the bulk of which is appropriated by the Nigerian government as exemplified by the mindboggling revelation of stolen oil wealth by the regime of Nigeria's former military dictator, Gen. Sani Abacha.

What is the way out? How can the minority oil producing areas extricate themselves from this quagmire? To end the violence, the destruction of whole communities and natural habitats of disadvantaged groups, the government should respect the human, political, social, economic and cultural rights of her citizens to control their resources and manage them as best as they can, whether they are in the majority or not.

The oil companies operating in these areas must put an end to the ecological warfare on the people and their environment and desist from lending support to the government in its "fight" against the oil communities, as Shell did when it ferried the Nigerian military head of state, Gen. Abubakar, to the site of the Jesse carnage, a gesture which prompted the general to tag the victims as saboteurs.

Above all, the peoples of the Niger Delta deserve compensation for years of environmental degradation caused by the activities of oil companies in concert with the Nigerian government.

27. WHO WILL STOP AMERICA?
JANUARY 1999

There is little doubt that "savagery is the end result of capitalism in its imperialist stage"; for what monopoly capitalism has perpetrated in the Gulf in the past few weeks is nothing but savagery.

Sometimes, events in international politics and the studied silence of the international community so-called leaves one with very little hope for the survival of the human race. Reviewing America's atrocious onslaught in the Gulf, the question that easily comes to mind is: what moral justification has the US – forget Britain, she is just a cheerleader – to invade Iraq and unleash mayhem on defenceless women and children? The answer lies in the fact that in imperialism's quest for worldwide domination, morality counts for nothing; a confirmation of Lenin's thesis that imperialism has no law beyond its own interest.

There are some in the developing world who cling to the notion that the recent US savage attacks on Iraq were carried out essentially to tame Saddam whom they claim is a threat to his neighbours or meant to divert attention from the Clinton-Lewinsky sex imbroglio. They are very wrong.

The former theory certainly cannot explain the bombing of Iraq because the US has the world's largest nuclear arsenal, including an estimated 1,700 ton of VX nerve gas in Newport, Indiana. Coupled with this is the fact much of what Iraq has today, in terms of weapons of mass destruction, was either initiated or actually supplied by the US during Iraq's war with Iran. It is also too simplistic to assume that Clinton and his Joint Chiefs of Staff would attack Iraq just to divert public focus from the groin of Mr. Clinton.

America's limited war in Iraq can only be explained from one angle; that is, imperialism's desire to send one last warning to the world that it is effectively in charge and that its interests – selfish in the extreme – cannot be toyed with. America's terrorist acts against Iraq are an essential part of her foreign policy since the end of the Cold War. With the exit of the Soviet Union, the new bogeyman – Islamic fundamentalism which threatens the oil fields of the Middle East – has to be dealt with. Of course, Africa does not count yet in this post Cold War hangover, ostensibly because she does not pose any threat to American influence.

With the Soviet Union out of the scene, America's imperialist tactics which hitherto took into consideration its global military interest vis-à-vis the Soviet Union's took a dramatic turn. No consideration or consultation was needed before America invaded any country. It started with Iraq in 1991. Before the Gulf War (Operation Desert Storm) began in early 1991, just as she did in the latest wave of attacks last December, America had made up its mind to attack Iraq as shown by her large military presence in Saudi Arabia.

It was, therefore, not surprising when she pushed through Security Council Resolution 678 to justify the inevitable attack. Between then and now, the US has come a long way in its control of world affairs. After Iraq, there was Somalia in 1992 where US marines, under the cover of humanitarian mission, terrorized and brutalized Somalis.

"It's as if the US had a new vaccine they wanted to test. Now they have found an animal to test it on". That was how one UN observer described America's atrocities in Somalia. Last August, it was the turn of Afghanistan and Sudan. Their crimes: supporting terrorists and harbouring terrorist facilities. Again, the villains were the same people, Osama bin Laden and company, whom the US had once hailed as freedom fighters and supplied with weapons. This uni-polar superpower arrogance again best explains why before the world could come to terms with her sabre-rattling in the Gulf, America had started the bombardment of Iraq.

Of course, the larger game plan in the Gulf may not have been to overthrow Saddam even though the US would be glad to get rid of him. The US had the chance to do just that in 1991, but the fear that Iraq may become another Somalia and the fact that the new madman may not be able to tame Iraq's restive groups, particularly the Shi'a Muslims and the Kurds aborted such a move.

Such sinister manoeuvres – also aimed at protecting America's so-called strategic interest – should not be ruled out considering the position of Madeleine Albright, American Secretary of State, and her distant predecessor in office, Henry Kissinger. In the words of Kissinger:

> *"No creative Gulf policy is possible until Saddam is removed or made totally impotent...before embarking on such a course, we must make a cool evaluation of our capacities, either to overthrow Saddam or to weaken him to a point where patriotic Iraqis will overthrow him. An operation of a magnitude required to overthrow Saddam though labelled 'covert' cannot remain covert for long. And when it becomes overt, we must be sure that we are prepared to pay the price rather than abandon those we encourage to action – as we did the Kurdish leaders in 1996".*
> –New York Post, March 22, 1998.

I guess many people would have thought that at the turn of the 21st century, the world would have said goodbye to this kind of murderous hysteria and would not be grappling with latter-day

Hitlers. Clearly, what is happening today in the Gulf is worse than what happened about six decades ago when Hitler invaded Poland and precipitated World War 11.

The world indeed did exaggerate the bestiality of Hitler – at least, at the height of his madness there was no Security Council, no United Nations and the world did not have the hindsight of two calamitous imperialist world wars. Or how else can one explain the actions of Mr. Clinton in Iraq in the light of the sacrifices humankind has made in the last five decades to maintain world peace?

Nobody is counting the cost of America's inspired sanctions against Iraq and Libya – a phenomenon which has brought untold hardship to ordinary Iraqis and Libyans. This heartless pursuit of gunboat diplomacy, of course, flies in the face of reason considering the fact that the US never supported the imposition of sanctions against Apartheid South Africa, partly because, as she claimed, it would hurt Blacks more.

Unfortunately, the UN has assumed the role of a merry bystander in America's renewed international terror. When the US attacked Afghanistan and Sudan she, as has become the tradition, cited Article 51 of the UN Charter which has to do with a state being under threat and the possibility of consulting the Security Council is remote. From using the UN to enhance US interests, the US has moved to a position of total abandonment of the world body. In its latest attack on Iraq, to show how irrelevant the UN has become, America and her partner in crime, Britain, effortlessly by-passed it.

The only reason they offered to an incapacitated, but bewildered world was that they wanted to degrade Saddam Hussein's weapons of mass destruction as a way safeguarding his neighbours. The foregoing explanation which A. M. Babu aptly described as "beyond-the-war rhetoric garbage and the standard stock-in-trade of the imperialists when they enter any predatory war" must be seen for what it is: a facade for imperialism for world-wide domination.

According to Babu, "On the eve of every major imperialist war – add assault – the world has been bombarded with such high-sounding vision". George Bush's invasion of Iraq in 1991 was hinged on the principle of "New World Order", of free trade and unlimited market, which essentially meant a new power equation which gives the US unlimited power to protect "US national interest". The world has just begun to pay the price for acquiescing to America's vision of a "New World Order" and it is easy to predict where this madness called "New World Order" would end.

If the US claims her interest in the Gulf is to minimize Iraq's threat to her neighbours, the big question remains: as international monopoly capitalism enters its end phase of terror and savagery who will save the world from the US?

28. THE SHAME OF A NATION
MARCH 1999

Events in Nigeria, which at every turn "take heart-wrenching dimension, have a way of bringing tears to one's eyes". A few days after the February 27 political coup against Nigerians and one article expressing outrage at the fraud, I thought it would not be necessary to comment further on the infamy until May 29 when the country is supposed to rid itself of self-serving military goons.

I had hesitated, not because I thought Nigeria was beyond hope; far from it. I had hoped that, assuredly, the present contradiction would play itself out and then, at the opportune time, the forces that are the logical consequence of the political contraption that has been foisted on Nigeria would play their historical role. However, my resolve was broken too soon.

News that the former Chief of General Staff of the military junta that overthrew the Second Republic, Maj. Gen. Tunde Idiagbon (retd.), had died, at the age of 56, was received with the equanimity that he "tried" considering the fact that life in this part of the world has become generally brutish and short. However, that was not the last to be heard on the death of the unsmiling general. And when the news came that he had indeed succumbed to cholera, it was as revolting as it was incredible.

If memory fails you, Gen. Idiagbon was the second-in-command of the military junta that launched a "War Against Indiscipline" in 1984 after the collapse of the corruption ridden government of the National Party of Nigeria (NPN). That war included a campaign against economic sabotage – currency trafficking, money laundering and allied crimes. It, among other things, waged a fierce campaign to promote environmental sanitation, which would eventually lead to the setting up of a national environmental sanitation day.

Fifteen years after that war began, the ritual still goes on every last Saturday of the month. Meanwhile, Lagos, the commercial capital of Nigeria, is among the dirtiest capitals in the world and the general who was the chief prosecutor of that war has been eclipsed by a "common" disease like cholera at what is supposed to be one of the nation's best and leading hospitals.

Of course, Gen. Idiagbon's death from cholera at the University of Ilorin Teaching Hospital is symbolic in many ways. It shows the level the nation has sunk in terms of not only the parlous state of health delivery but also the collapse of infrastructure. For a general in the Nigerian army to be the victim of a disease which is looked upon as the burden of the wretched of the earth and the scourge of the illiterate, poor and undesirables in society shows that we are all at risk. It is simply emblematic of the level of decay of the country.

And to imagine that the world will be converging on Nigeria this week under the auspices of the FIFA Under 20 youth championships, the same competition which was denied Nigeria in 1995 due to, among several other findings, the outbreak of cholera, makes the matter even worse. I guess for the football world to have decided to come to Nigeria, it has made up its mind to tolerate the country and its intractable crises.

If the world cannot come to terms with the level of decay in Nigeria or has decided to close its eyes for reasons which border on self-flagellation, it must indeed be painful for many Nigerians who live with these problems daily to grapple with the nerve-racking puzzle of how a nation so richly endowed with both human and material resources which are the envy of many across the world can degenerate so rapidly that the lives of majority of its citizens are in jeopardy and the nation itself is teetering on the brink of a terrible catastrophe. Nigerians must be asking themselves questions about how to extricate themselves from this web of military dictatorship which has completely dehumanised them.

Is it not interesting that the self-abuse the military in Nigeria has subjected itself and the indignity it has heaped on Nigerians is beginning to manifest even at the very pinnacle of power? Undoubtedly, what this tells us all is that those who seek to preserve the current mayhem in Nigeria will sooner or later be consumed by it.

By many standards, Gen. Idiagbon was an officer and a gentleman, a soldier who lived up to the tenets of his profession; certainly, not the likes of Abacha who were scoundrels in uniform who flaunted their depravity. We may castigate Gen. Idiagbon for usurping power and undermining the constitution of Nigeria, but from his words and actions you couldn't deny the fact that he was light years ahead of his colleagues who have proved to be nothing but soldiers of fortune.

Many people will agree that it is a shame that Gen. Idiagbon was a victim of cholera. Perhaps, we really do not have to bemoan our national tragedy and the demise of another victim of the bloody fangs of this monstrosity; after all, this is Nigeria, a nation where rather than import drugs and other essential medical facilities, the head of state preferred to consort with imported prostitutes.

Can a nation sink lower than this?

29. Humanitarian intervention or US terror?
April 1999

"US President, Woodrow Wilson, entered World War 1 in 1917 with the declaration that the US intervention in the war would 'establish a new world of harmony', democ-

racy, and self-determination, secured by the League of Nations. We know what happened after that war! There was neither harmony, nor democracy or self-determination; only their opposites emerged with the advent of fascism and Nazism". – A. M. Babu

With the collapse of the Soviet Union and, supposedly, the threat of communism, one of the things that the US bandied about was that universal peace and détente would be the watchword in international politics. Not a few people bought this claptrap which was meant as a veritable cover for America's imminent world hegemony. Now they can see how very mistaken they were. Indeed, the decade (1991-2000) of the partial victory of international monopoly capital has turned out to be one of the bloodiest this century.

Events in the Balkans, one of Europe's hottest spots, and the tinderbox of World War 1, show that at no time in recent history has humanity faced greater threat and the possibility of a world-wide humanitarian catastrophe, thanks to two rookie statesmen who have proved more dangerous than all the maniacal dictators in the world put together.

Babu was right when he affirmed that at the beginning of every imperialist war, high sounding "visions" and demonizing catchphrases are employed to justify the barbaric and inhuman atrocities unleashed on the world. Only recently, we saw it in the military expedition in Iraq and the bombing of Sudan and Afghanistan. As it turned out, in the case of Sudan, the alleged terrorist hideout was the Al-Shifa pharmaceutical factory, while the United Nations' weapon inspection team in Iraq was nothing but a façade for the US to indulge in espionage.

If the spy mission had been to "detect" Iraqi military capabilities, the product of the treacherous activities of the US in the Gulf, it may not have stirred much interest; unfortunately, it was not. It provided a cover for the US to invade Iraq and ultimately enthrone a Pax Americana in the Gulf.

The effect has been the deaths of thousands of Iraqi people, particularly children who have become congenitally deformed due to depleted uranium used in the US missile warheads. Experts say that depleted uranium is one of the hardest metals in existence; that the effect of this highly radioactive material can be compared to the nuclear-bombing of Hiroshima and Nagasaki.

The US claimed it wanted to protect the Iraqi people and their neighbours from Saddam Hussein. Yet, among many other atrocities against Iraqis, there are reports that "hoof and mouth disease alone, a disease long eradicated in Iraq, has crippled at least one million sheep and cattle in the country and the lack of vaccines for the highly contagious disease is endangering the country's livestock". The effect is not only on Iraqis "since the virus clings to clothes and farming equipment and can drift as far as thirty miles into the air". Nobody cares. The US has what it wanted, and it is time to move on. Next stop, Europe.

Today, the targets are Slobodan Milosevic and defenceless Serbian women and children. Regrettably, the US and its cronies have moved from consulting the United Nations, even if they will not abide by its resolutions, to outright impunity in their quest to police the world for corporate capital.

We can be sure of one thing: once the bombs stop raining on Belgrade and its environs, Michel Camdessus, James Wolfensohn and their team of undertakers will be on hand to offer IMF/World Bank loans for the rebuilding of Yugoslavia. Of course, not before asking for the devaluation of the local currency.

Undoubtedly, the attacks on Yugoslavia have shown that it is capital that rules the world and there are no borders as it spreads its bloody fangs. Of course, there is nothing that binds the US and Britain together other than the defence of international monopoly capital. For those who are wondering why Messrs Bill Clinton and Tony Blair have become Siamese twins of sorts, the answer is that international capital speaks only one language – terror.

That is the only reason for Tony Blair's knee-jerk support of every murderous initiative of Bill Clinton. The talk that sovereignty has taken a new dimension with the New World Order and globalization orchestrated by the US is mere balderdash. It is another way of saying that you cannot stop international capital from garnering profit from any corner of the globe.

What are the facts of the matter in the US' latest military aggression against a sovereign state? The US and her murderous horde waffled about "degrading, demeaning, and destroying" Slobodan Milosevic's war machine with intent to "diminish" his threat to his neighbours. They claimed that Yugoslavia had failed to honour the Kosovo peace agreement, an agreement put in place at the behest of the US and her allies.

They quibbled about the potential humanitarian situation in the Balkan. Looking at the deaths and refugee situation among Serbs and Kosovo Albanians in the last two weeks of US-led NATO bombardment, it smacks of hypocrisy to claim that they went there, primarily, to avert a humanitarian catastrophe.

Nothing could dissuade them; not the fact that militarism would only exacerbate the already precarious situation; not even the fact that the whole of the Balkans is ravaged by byzantine politics; certainly, not the fact that military intervention has not worked anywhere and that only a political solution can bring peace to Kosovo Albanians considering their historical evolution.

With the latest development, the United Nations is doing what it knows best: crying over spilt milk. Suddenly the UN Secretary General is worried about the worsening humanitarian situation and the influx of Albanian refugees into neighbouring countries as if he did not see it coming.

Of course, the villainous air raids on Belgrade are contemptible to say the least; and the world, particularly Africa, cannot afford to be complacent because what it points to is the right to invade any country whenever the US deems it necessary. What then are the lessons from this despicable and vicious unwritten law for Africa and the whole of the developing world? Three issues must be addressed: Firstly, such myth peddling and conjuring up of reasons is just what it is: a ruse. There is nothing altruistic about the involvement of the US in Yugoslavia.

Looking at its record of humanitarian intervention or the lack of it, perhaps we should ask ourselves: what measures did the US take in Apartheid South Africa where foreign capital and corporate investments oiled the wheel of terror and millions of Blacks were decimated by white supremacists? In Somalia where US forces subjected Somalis to unimaginable horror? And in Rwanda, where it had foreknowledge of the gruesome massacre of Tutsis and moderate Hutus but did nothing to prevent it?

Secondly, when did the US become the enemy of dictators, considering that it has backed almost every tyrant the world has produced? The successful intervention of the US in Yugoslavia has confirmed its position as the most belligerent nation in the world, and as it did in Libya, Somalia, Grenada, Panama, and Haiti, sealed its right to intervene, without recourse to international laws, in any part of the world.

With the creation of the US-backed African Crisis Response Initiative (ACRI), the US has carte blanche the chance to invade the whole of Africa which may well become one big market for America thanks to its so-called Africa Growth and Opportunities Act.

Thirdly, the question of self-determination for Kosovo Albanians, an issue that appears to be very dear to the US, is a question that affects more than two-third of the African continent and is a direct product of international capital in its quest for market. Virtually every state in Africa is groaning under the problem of artificial boundaries which imperialism in the last century created in its attempt to build politically united territories for its market. Just like the Kosovo crisis, the crisis in Democratic Republic of the Congo, Sudan, Nigeria, Rwanda, etc., can only be solved through political settlement not militarism.

It is not in the interest of anybody, except of course international capital, that this problem created in the main by imperialism, be resolved by bombing nations. African rulers can do more than their current passivity in the light of the terror perpetrated by the US and the catastrophic effect on the human race.

30. This barbarity must stop
August 1998

Signs that the new military dictator in Nigeria, Gen. Abdulsalami Abubakar, would take his cue from his predecessor and even surpass him emerged very early at the inception of the regime. Beyond the commitment by words to defend the policies and programmes of the Abacha regime, Abubakar showed clearly that those looking for a practical and meaningful solution to the crisis in Nigeria had to look further afield.

On June 12, 1998, four days into his regime, which also marked the fifth anniversary of the June 12, 1993 presidential election, Abubakar's murderous machines prowled the streets of Lagos threatening death and destruction while sending home the lesson that the new maximum ruler would not brook any opposition. That action did not come as a surprise. Regrettably, Abubakar has followed up his action with even more vicious and highhanded policies which leave nobody in doubt that he is capable of surpassing his predecessor in infamy.

Those who were enthused about Abubakar's dismantling of the structures put in place by his predecessor have realized to their chagrin that there is no reason to celebrate. What Abubakar has done is to dismantle those programmes that were directly linked to Abacha as a person, programmes aimed at making him not just a civilian president but president for life. He has dissolved Abacha's political parties which were nothing more than a club of Abacha supporters. He has also ordered the release of journalists, pro-democracy and human rights activists, many of whom were arrested by Abacha's overzealous security surrogates for no apparent offence.

All other programmes which depict the Nigerian army as a predatory force that has little use except in the service of internal hegemony and neo-colonialism are perfectly in place. On foreign policy, Abubakar has done nothing to distance himself from Abacha's policies in West Africa; on the contrary he has demonstrated how unequivocally committed he is to Abacha's agenda for the sub-region, which he, as Abacha's Chief of Defence Staff, helped in implementing.

Currently, Nigerian soldiers, some of the best in an army that has largely become bankrupt, are still wasting away in Sierra Leone. "We are like sheep in the jungle", was how John Onovakpuri, a Nigerian soldier captured recently in Sierra Leone, described his plight and that of his colleagues in an interview with New Africa. And only recently, Abubakar organized the extradition of Corporal Foday Sankoh, leader of the Revolutionary United Front of Sierra Leone (RUF/SL).

It does appear really that the new military rulers in Nigeria, prodded by the West, have lost all sense of decency and respect for international principles and laws. What was the purpose of handing Foday Sankoh over to the authorities in Sierra Leone to stand trial? Was that action aimed at enhancing the peace process in Sierra Leone? The only reason that could possibly be adduced for this official lawlessness is that Abubakar wants to please the hawks who are supervising the so-called peace process in Sierra Leone and enhance the support he is getting from the West.

Historically, the present crisis in Sierra Leone dates back to 1991 when, like the present regime in Nigeria, the regime of Gen. Joseph Momoh scorned proposals for a meaningful democratic process, and ended up transforming himself into a civilian president. Sierra Leone had another chance in 1996 to work towards genuine national reconciliation, but the West wanted election at the cost of national reconciliation. Clearly, such a process could not engender peace.

It was in search of a way out of the impasse in Sierra Leone that Foday Sankoh went to Nigeria in March 1997. Abacha arrested him. First, the government denied he was there. Later, all manner of spurious allegations were levelled against him. He was accused of planning to buy arms and possessing weapons which he allegedly tried to smuggle into Nigeria illegally.

Rather than talk peace, Abacha decided to keep him under house arrest for more than a year. However, that did not in any way help the peace process in Sierra Leone. Abubakar, now acting under the spell of the US and Britain, has decided to throw a greater clog in the wheel of peace by trying to sideline one of the major stakeholders in the Sierra Leonean crisis.

It is unfortunate that Abubakar, desirous of international support, is slavishly pandering to those whose only interest in Sierra Leone, as in Nigeria, is to plunder resources. Certainly, there is no way these rapacious and self-seeking mediators can offer Sierra Leone peace. As Foday Sankoh notes in Footpaths to Democracy,

> *"We deem as more dangerous the quick-fix and prescriptive hidden agendas of self-seeking mediators. We have to be suspicious of those who have made careers out of Africa's plight. They invariably end up as meddlers in internal conflicts, prolonging the sufferings of our people".*

Interestingly, while Britain is working feverishly at seeking a "peaceful" solution to the ethnic crisis in Northern Ireland and the US and her NATO allies are threatening reprisals against Serbian forces in independence-seeking province of Kosovo, they are sending mercenaries to Sierra Leone to maim and kill innocent women and children. That is their idea of conflict resolution in Africa.

By extraditing Foday Sankoh, Abubakar, like his predecessor, is presiding over the collapse of peace in Sierra Leone. Sierra Leoneans have suffered enough and they should be allowed to sort out their problems based on their historical circumstances. We can only hope that the West, particularly Britain, will allow Sierra Leoneans enjoy peaceful negotiations in the present crisis.

The Nigerian army on its part has done enough damage in Sierra Leone, now is the time to bow out and end the barbarity.

---

31. THE NEW KILLING FIELD
AUGUST 1999

The carnage that swept through two Nigerian cities – first, Sagamu and then Kano – last month was overshadowed by an equally odious event, the case of the dishonourable Salisu Ibrahim Buhari, who, symptomatic of the rot that is Nigeria, sought to become Speaker of the House of Representatives through fraud.

Interestingly, the learned and honourable judge who decided Buhari's fate, in his infinite wisdom, argued that the plea by highly placed Nigerians on behalf of the disgraced Speaker and the public ridicule that deservedly trailed his action were enough to atone for his criminal actions. Well, ordinary and not so ordinary Nigerians for whom nobody would plead can kiss justice goodbye.

Undoubtedly, the Buhari conundrum proved a cruel diversion to what, if not checked, could sound the death-knell of the geo-political construct called Nigeria. Both events, the killings in Sagamu and Kano, left in their wake devastation and desolation beyond imagination. It was as if the murderous fiends that roamed Kigali and surrounding death camps a few years ago had taken up residence in both cities.

The chilling sights of people who had lived together for close to a century killing one another in such a macabre fashion painted a truly scary picture and made all the sound bite about "political regeneration" that was echoed at the exit of the military mere rhetoric.

The death of a Hausa woman who allegedly defied a traditional Yoruba rite reportedly sparked off the Sagamu tragedy. The revenge killings in Kano, though unnecessary, were highly expected. The killings were a reflection of how much faith the citizens have in the state and its agencies to address their grievances; a mark of how inadequate and futile it is for Nigerians to think that they can build a virile, purposeful and united nation through slogans.

As always, there is no shortage of explanation for the frenzied and terrifying violence that has seized the national psyche. Those who think they have something to gain by maintaining the *status quo* will conveniently gloss over the incident. For starters, we have been told that the gruesome attacks last month were the work of "evil people opposed to democratic government", the antics of unseen enemies who feel disfavoured by the so-called new order. This theory, perhaps, would make sense if what operates in Nigeria today can be called democracy. It is, therefore, imperative that attention is not diverted from an impending national catastrophe.

The conspiracy theory being bandied about is a simplistic way of looking at a grave problem. Sagamu and Kano are not isolated cases. They build into the general web of ethnic mayhem that has been an essential part of the Nigerian nation. Since independence Nigerians have been fighting mini-wars; fear and ethnic tensions have always been palpable and an intrinsic part of this tottering behemoth; ethnic cleansing has always been the norm rather than the exception.

Remember, if you will, the coup of January 15, 1966, and the countercoup six months later; the bloodcurdling horrors that were perpetrated a year later in the name of one Nigeria, a Nigeria that has refused to remain one ever since. Regrettably, some of those who supervised these acts of barbarity have become latter- day democrats and messiahs, without whom, we are told, Nigeria cannot move forward.

A few years ago, an outraged world witnessed the hanging of nine Ogoni leaders. That dastardly act was the high point of the death and destruction perpetrated in Ogoniland by rulers purportedly acting in the interest of Nigeria. Before that, the Hausa-Fulanis and Zango-Katafs, Tivs and Jukuns, all in northern Nigeria, had their share of the bloody feuds that stalk Nigeria.

For many years now, the Ijaws, Urhobos and Itsekiris in the Niger Delta have been locked in a battle of life and death. In between all this, the geo-political landscape is occasionally painted with blood of adherents propagating or defending one faith or another. As you read this, the Ijaws and Ilajes, in Southwest Nigeria are locked in a grotesque war over land just as another bizarre war is taking place between the Umuleris and Aguleris in the Southeast.

The renewed outburst of ethnic tension that has convulsed Nigeria, the murderous inability of Nigerians to coexist peacefully is indeed emblematic of a deeply troubled polity. This has flourished partly because those who have maintained a low intensity war of sorts, a war that can be felt even though the fighting is not visible, have refused to reckon with Nigeria's geo-political history.

This dilemma, of course, has not been made easy by the totalitarian military dictatorship that plagued Nigeria for many years. It was a period of gradual but consistent whittling down of all the indicators of nationhood. After more than three decades of bestriding Nigeria like a colossus, this dictatorship, which successfully destroyed federalism, has created a monstrosity that looks set to devour it. Old animosities bottled up for decades now find renewed expression. Now, more than ever before, the claims of marginalization fill the air. Even those who just a few months back controlled political power, and were fiercely pilloried for it, are complaining that the cards are stacked against them.

But, let's go back to the basics. If after almost a century of its creation and four decades of independence, those who call themselves Nigerians cannot live and feel secure in any part of the country; if only a few months to the next millennium, Nigerians can be so easily manipulated to unleash mayhem on fellow citizens; if after many years of propagating one nation, one destiny, Nigerians turn on each other at the slightest opportunity then Nigeria at best is a geo-political disaster.

Whatever reasons or motives people have to visit such orgy of violence on one another as the world witnessed last month, the bottom line is that Nigerians must begin immediately the process of redefinition of nationhood. Excuse my cynicism, but it is very easy to draw a correlation between the events of last month and those that precipitated the civil war in 1967; a war that three decades after it ended, there is just very little to show that there was "no victor" and "no vanquished".

The crisis may have ended, but the deep scars and their lingering effects should serve as a constant reminder that Nigeria is in dire need not so much of great leaders as a workable nation state. The present pseudo-democratic posturing of the current rulers in Nigeria who see no sense in the call for restructuring has the potential of turning Nigeria into the newest killing field.

Of course, Nigerians have everything to gain by resisting these warmongers who think they can only be relevant by using democracy to obscure a more sinister form of oppression.

32. Time to End Subsidy on Inefficiency
January 2012

President Jonathan's decision to increase the price of petrol on January 1, 2012, will go down in history as one of the most cynical decisions by a Nigerian president. Even though there is enough mistrust for the current government, very few people actually imagined that the president would decide to inflict so much pain on Nigerians during the season of festivities. Not when the government kept assuring the public that it was negotiating with stakeholders; certainly not when the minister of finance stated publicly that no date had been fixed for the so-called subsidy removal.

The more than 100% increase in the price of petrol, if not reversed, may turn around to haunt President Jonathan for the rest of his life. As I write, there are reports of thousands of Nigerians stranded in different parts of the country because of the astronomical rise in transport fares occasioned by the unconscionable increase in petrol price. Prices of food items have gone up, and soon landlords will be demanding higher rent. Add to this the mindless slaughter of innocent Nigerians by those who claim they want to propitiate Heaven and you have a recipe for disaster.

I have had reason to argue with my friends who say we should give President Jonathan the benefit of the doubt. My position is that the president cannot be trusted. So, I was not at all surprised by the announcement of the Petroleum Products Pricing Regulatory Agency (PPPRA) on January 1. I shall return to this. My position on President Jonathan is based on a simple, but fundamental issue: the president's asset declaration. Early last year, President Jonathan while campaigning for the April 2011 presidential election serenaded us about how he went to school without shoes. When he was sworn in on May 29, 2011, he promised a "transformation agenda" and to fight corruption.

The minimum standard for any president interested in transforming Nigeria and fighting corruption, one of the greatest problems confronting the country, would be a public declaration of his or her asset. If President Jonathan had done this, it would have enabled us to compare it with what he declared four years ago as vice-president after much public outcry. That would have been reassuring! However, he has refused to do so even when civil society groups have gone to court over the issue.

Why should we trust a president who finds it difficult to make public his asset? That is why I support the position of the Nigeria Labour Congress (NLC) and I hope it maintains it – that the only condition for discussion is for the government to revert to the *status quo ante*. The statement by the PPPRA announcing the price increase is quite instructive. The opening lines read, "Following extensive consultation with stakeholders across the nation, the Petroleum Products Pricing Regulatory Agency (PPPRA) wishes to inform all stakeholders of the commencement of formal removal of subsidy on Premium Motor Spirit (PMS), in accordance with the powers conferred on the agency by the law establishing it, in compliance with Section 7 of PPPRA Act, 2004".

According to reports, the Petroleum and Natural Gas Senior Staff Association has challenged the Executive Secretary of the Petroleum Products Pricing Regulatory Agency (PPPRA), Reginald Stanley, to tell Nigerians when the board of the agency met to decide on the adjustment in the pump price of fuel. The president of the union, Babatunde Ogun, maintains that the board of the agency has yet to be reconstituted and can therefore not meet on the hike in the price of petrol.

Clearly, the government needed the dialogue sessions and town hall meetings with so-called stakeholders to legitimize its position. The regime had made up its mind long ago. I hope our friends who insisted on "dialoguing" with the government have learnt some lessons. What the government did not reckon with, however, is the response of Nigerians from all walks of life. As one commentator put it, "The opposition to fuel increase will ultimately result in resistance to everything the ruling class represents in Nigeria".

Thanks to the resilience of Nigerians, the government has suddenly realize d it has to prune the cost of governance and cut back on the perquisites of government officials. To show that he feels our pain, the president, in his national broadcast on the eve of the planned nation-wide strike, said,

> "The basic salaries of all political office holders in the executive arm of government will be reduced by 25%". He also noted that he had "directed that overseas travels by all political office holders, including the president, should be reduced to the barest minimum. The size of delegations on foreign trips will also be drastically reduced; only trips that are absolutely necessary will be approved".

Great! But, he should go a step further. Let him and key functionaries of his government (the VP, the finance minister, the petroleum minister, the governor of the Central Bank, etc) declare their asset. I agree with the blogger who wrote that,

> "If they have decided to cut 25% of their salaries and reduce their travelling expenses to the barest minimum, if that can pay for the subsidy and repair our refineries, that will be fine, if not they should do more. All we want is for them to go back to N65. The masses have sacrificed a lot in the past. It's their turn now to sacrifice".

Where do we even begin to talk about cutting cost? The presidency plans to spend over a N1 billion ($6million) on food in 2012. The vice president will spend N1.7 billion ($11.3million) on trips and N1.3 billion ($8.6million) on office stationeries in 2012. This amount includes N12 million ($80,000) on books, N45 million ($300,000) on newspapers, and N9 million ($60,000) on magazines and periodicals. A breakdown shows that the VP will spend N723 million ($4.8 million) on local travels and N951 million ($6.3 million) on his international travels. For the president, just double or triple the amount for the VP. Can anyone tell me how many times Mr. Vice-president has travelled outside Nigerian since he was sworn in on May 29, 2011?

The average cost of newspapers in Nigeria is N150 ($1). Let us for the sake of argument raise it to N200 ($1.3). If the office of the VP buys 20 newspapers a day, it will cost him N4,000 ($26). Let us assume there are about 10 departments in the office of the VP. If we multiply N4,000 by 10, we'll get N40,000 ($266). So, on the average, the office will spend N40,000 ($266) everyday for newspapers.

Multiplied by 30 days, it comes to N1.2 million ($8,000) a month. In one year, the total amount will be N14.4 million ($96,000). Yet, the VP gets N45 million for newspapers. If we round it up to N15 million ($100,000), the government can save N30 million ($200,000) by cutting back on the cost of providing newspapers for the VP. We can do the same for magazines and periodicals.

There is a government directive that ministers, CEOs, and heads of government departments and agencies can only fly Business Class at government expense. Not a single minister or CEO adheres to this directive. They all fly First Class. Most times, with their family members, girlfriends, and concubines.

Depending on the airline, and the destination, the difference between Business Class and First Class could range from 5 to 8 thousand dollars or more. Let the smart people amongst us do the math, taking into consideration the number of ministries, government agencies and departments in Nigeria and how often our public "servants" travel overseas, for official (including medical checkup) and unofficial business.

If President Jonathan is looking for money "to ensure improvement in national infrastructure, power supply, transportation, irrigation and agriculture, education, healthcare, and other social services", he need not look any further. While we protest, we may do well to also show the government how it can save cost, apart from raising the price of petrol, since it appears clueless!

---

33. In Praise of Corruption
January 2012

One of the most frightening things about the Jonathan administration is the president's palpable lack of appreciation of the problems that confront us and "the fierce urgency of now". This phenomenon rears its head at every opportunity the president has to reassure Nigerians that he has the capacity to lead the country out of its current morass.

It is clichéd now to refer to the president's response when asked last June why he was unwilling to declare his asset publicly as a mark of his commitment to fighting corruption. The president told a bewildered nation that he did not "give a damn" about Nigerians not knowing what he is worth. That comment reverberated and still reverberates around the country, particularly whenever the words "fighting corruption" and "Jonathan administration" are used in a sentence.

Those who thought that was one presidential gaffe too many were surely mistaken. The president upped the ante during the 2012 Christmas service in Abuja when he said his government appeared to be slow because it did not want to make mistakes. "By human thinking our administration is slow; I won't say we are slow, but we need to think through things properly if we are to make lasting impact", the president said in his homily. "If we rush, we will make mistakes and sometimes it is more difficult to correct those mistakes".

Slow is an understatement. The president is simply telling us he does not know what he is doing. The truth is that there is no governance going on in the country. We all know the president is not circumspect or afraid of taking decisions, particularly when such decisions will benefit his friends in the oil industry. We witnessed that a year ago when, to the chagrin of the mass of our people, the president increased the price of petrol even when negotiations were ongoing with the Nigeria Labour Congress and civil society. Since then, the president has followed that insensate decision with numerous anti-people actions like spending N22.6bn of our collective wealth to offset bank loans owed by 84 rogue stock broking firms.

The major headline of the preceding week was not the hardship Nigerians had to endure during the holidays or the death and destruction that stalk the land. It was the pronouncement of President Jonathan in what appeared as an official endorsement of corruption during the funeral service of Gen. Owoye Azazi in Yenagoa, Bayelsa

State. Presidential aide, Reuben Abati, has admonished us not to take the president literally when he speaks. However, this is one time we have no option but to pay close attention to the president for "out of the abundance of the heart the mouth speaketh".

Bishop of Bomadi Catholic Diocese, Vicarage Hyacinth Egbebor, probably did not know he was stirring up a hornet's nest when he blamed the December 15 helicopter crash at Okoroba in Nembe Local Government Area, Bayelsa State, that killed the former National Security Adviser, Andrew Azazi, former Kaduna State Governor, Patrick Yakowa, and four others, on corruption.

> *"Corruption is the only underlying evil that is responsible for the air mishaps. If the military cannot guarantee the safety and security of their own, who else can they protect?"* Vicarage Egbebor noted in his sermon. *"If there is anywhere one looks for excellent performance, it is the military. Now we have compromised excellence for money. Money has taken over".*

An obviously peeved President Jonathan remarked in response to Vicarage Egbebor, "But most of these things we talk about corruption are not even corruption. It is true that most cases we talk about corruption as if corruption is the cause of most of our problems. Yes, we have corruption in this country, no doubt about that. The government is also fighting corruption". The president reminded us that, "Nigeria has more institutions that fight corruption than most other countries". His solution: attitudinal change on the part of Nigerians and concerted effort by at least half of the population to follow in the footsteps of the late Gen. Azazi.

It is a good thing that President Jonathan, while rejecting corruption as the problem, returned to the theme of attitude as the bane of Nigeria's development. As a result, the president apparently demonstrated the logic of rational analysis in locating corruption in the wider cosmic of attitude. In that context he is right to call for a change of attitude. Of course, Nigerians expect the change of attitude he preaches to begin with him. The only way to do this is for him to lead by example; to practice what he preaches.

President Jonathan should not expect the man on the street to heed the call to imbibe new ways of doing things when he himself is not demonstrating it. Unfortunately, he has refused to drive the process by, amongst other things, arrogantly failing to publicly declare his assets, apportioning over one billion naira to the Presidency for feeding and expanding the presidential fleet while saner countries are reducing theirs.

Unfortunately, the president failed to mention that the attitudinal change we need most is one that de-prioritises corruption as an ingrained culture of the Nigerian people. By so doing, he ignored the consensus among not just the dispossessed majority, but also in the circle of elites of which he is one, that corruption, contrary to what he believes, is the number one problem facing Nigeria today.

All the negative indices routinely ascribed to virtually every sector of Nigerian life are the consequence of widespread sleaze perpetrated by government officials and their collaborators outside government. As long as the *status quo* continues in the midst of rapid degeneration in the quality of life and infrastructure, corruption will continue to get the pride of place as the major cause of Nigeria's problem.

Though he never misses any opportunity to dish out rhetoric about his government's anti-corruption credentials, the president's mindset is one that places corruption at the lower rung of the socio-economic evils bedevilling the country. Thus, the will to confront it headlong does not exist. What exists is the impulse to nurture it in order to continue to sustain the plutocracy which he and the People's Democratic Party (PDP) have dishonestly sold to the people as democracy.

Evidence of this intent is the recent appointment of Tony Anenih, alias "Mr. Fix It", as the chairman of Nigeria Ports Authority, the cash cow which produces a large chunk of the money the ruling party uses to fund its political campaigns.

The president disregarded the mountain of allegations of corruption sitting on Chief Anenih's head to make the appointment. It is a mark of a president who is not only out of touch with the people, but one that does not "give a damn" about corruption and its deleterious impact on our society.

In a sense, I agree with President Jonathan. It is time to disband our anti-corruption agencies and set up an agency for attitudinal change, that is, if we cannot revive the National Orientation Agency (NOA). The first task of the new agency – the National Agency for Attitudinal and Behavioural Change – will be to get President Jonathan to change his attitude toward corruption. And the reason is simple. Corruption, regardless of the president's stance, is Nigeria's number one problem and it manifests itself in different ways whether the president sees it or not.

Martin Luther King, Jr. clergyman, activist and prominent leader in the African-American Civil Rights Movement, once reminded Americans about the "fierce urgency of now". In his "I Have a Dream" speech delivered almost fifty years ago on August 28, 1963, at the Lincoln Memorial, Washington D.C., he noted, "This is no time to engage in the luxury of cooling off or to take the tranquilizing drug of gradualism. Now is the time to make real the promises of democracy".

I think President Jonathan should read that speech if he has not done so. Even though its focus was race relations, its unifying idea was a warning for every people to frontally confront their national "demon" and "make justice a reality for all of God's children".

Corruption is Nigeria's "demon" and unless the president wants us to believe he is granting a national amnesty to corruption, now is the time to end the platitudes and confront it head on.

---

34. OF PRESIDENTIAL MEDIA CHAT AND ASSET DECLARATION
JUNE 2012

The highlight of President Goodluck Jonathan's media chat today was his response to the question about his asset declaration. I watched the event online and I missed his answer to this all-important question because of disruptions in the Channels TV streaming.

If reports from online journals about the president's response are anything to go by, then there is little hope for the country. According to one report, asked why he had not declared his assets, President Jonathan replied, "I don't give a damn" about declaration of assets. He said he had gone to late President Umaru Yar'Adua to caution that,

> *"We should not play to the hands of some people (by openly declaring their assets)", adding, "That is a matter of principle and I am not going to declare. It is not the president declaring his asset that will end Boko Haram".*

The president went on to say whether he is criticized from "head to toe" he would not declare his assets.

The president's response raises a number of issues, including trust, integrity, the rule of law and respect for the Constitution of the Federal Republic. Maybe, I am missing something! It is important to see what the Constitution says vis a vis the president's response.

THIRD SCHEDULETHIRD SCHEDULE

> *Paragraph 3, Part I of the Third Schedule of the Constitution of the Federal Republic of Nigeria provides that the Code of Conduct Bureau shall have power to: (a) receive declarations by public officers made under paragraph 12 of Part I of the Fifth Schedule to this Constitution; (b) examine the declarations in accordance with the requirements of the Code of Conduct or any law; (c) retain custody of such declarations and make them available for inspection by any citizen of Nigeria on such terms and conditions as the National Assembly may prescribe.*

FIFTH SCHEDULEFIFTH SCHEDULE

Paragraph 11 of Part I of the Fifth Schedule to the Constitution provides that:

> *Subject to the provisions of this Constitution, every public officer shall within three months after the coming into*

force of this Code of Conduct or immediately after taking office and thereafter – (a) at the end of every four years; and (b) at the end of his term of office, submit to the Code of Conduct Bureau a written declaration of all his properties, assets, and liabilities and those of his unmarried children under the age of eighteen years.

SEVENTH SCHEDULESEVENTH SCHEDULE
Oaths
Oaths of Allegiance

I, ...Goodluck Ebele Jonathan...Do solemnly swear/affirm that I will be faithful and bear true allegiance to the Federal Republic of Nigeria and that I will preserve, protect and defend the Constitution of the Federal Republic of Nigeria.

So help me God

Oath of Office of President

I, ...Goodluck Ebele Jonathan...do solemnly swear/affirm that I will be faithful and bear true allegiance to the Federal Republic of Nigeria; that as President of the Federal Republic of Nigeria, I will discharge my duties to the best of my ability, faithfully and in accordance with the Constitution of the Federal Republic of Nigeria and the law, and always in the interest of the sovereignty, integrity, solidarity, well-being and prosperity of the Federal Republic of Nigeria; that I will strive to preserve the Fundamental Objectives and Directive Principles of State Policy contained in the Constitution of the Federal Republic of Nigeria; that I will not allow my personal interest to influence my official conduct or my official decisions; that I will to the best of my ability preserve, protect and defend the Constitution of the Federal Republic of Nigeria; that I will abide by the CODE OF CONDUCT (emphasis added) contained in the Fifth Schedule to the Constitution of the Federal Republic of Nigeria; that in all circumstances, I will do right to all manner of people, according to law, without fear or favour, affection or ill-will; that I will not directly or indirectly communicate or reveal to any person any matter which shall be brought under my consideration or shall become known to me as President of the Federal Republic of Nigeria, except as may be required for the due discharge of my duties as President; and that I will devote myself to the service and well-being of the people of Nigeria. So help me God.

---

35. President Jonathan's One Child Policy
July 2012

The outrage that greeted what looked like a one-child policy of the Jonathan administration is understandable. Beyond the fact that the country's population is its selling point, the theory that the level of poverty in a country is somehow related to the size of its population has proved patently untenable. But, the bigger question is: how do you legislate on what happens in people's bedroom?

The president's emergency response to our so-called population crisis was reeled out late last month at the swearing-in of newly appointed chairman and commissioners of the National Population Commission (NPC) at the Presidential Villa, Abuja. The president said the Federal Government was considering a bill to regulate the country's population and that the government would not wait until it became uncontrollable before facing the menace.

"Before enacting the laws controlling birth and population, however, the government would carry out enough sensitization", the president said, adding,

> "First and foremost is the personal consciousness that people should get the family they can manage. Sometimes

you get to somebody's house living in a well-furnished duplex, the husband and wife there may have two, three, four children. The man guarding them has nine children. That is the scenario you have. That means there is a segment of the population that knows that you must get a number that you can manage, but the other segment of the population doesn't".

"If you are used to military barracks, you see that the officers, General this, Major General this, Brigadier this, Colonel this have three, five children but those that have no rank have eight, 12. This is the scenario. The people up, probably because of their level of education, know that they must control their population. But, the people down, because of the level of exposure and education, are still not aware that you must control your population. So, first and foremost, before government comes up with regulations, guidelines or laws, Nigerians must be made to know that we cannot continue to procreate and procreate, even though we know children are God's gifts".

Why the president thinks the way to deal with wanton procreation is enacting a law to curb it, is difficult to comprehend. Expectedly, the issue has veered off the radar of national discourse.

We have quickly moved to other issues. As I write, nobody, not the newly appointed chairman of the NPC, not the commissioners, not even related ministries, like health and national planning, will remember anything President Jonathan said, much less act on it. But, I digress.

Two weeks after President Jonathan's quick fix to the country's population problem, on July 11, 2012, world leaders, development partners and health and population activists met in London for a global summit on family planning. The summit, put together by the UK Government and the Bill and Melinda Gates Foundation, in partnership with the UN Population Fund (UNFPA) and several national governments aimed to "make affordable, lifesaving contraceptive information, services and supplies available to an additional 120 million women and girls in developing countries by 2020 as well as prevent over 200,000 women dying in pregnancy and childbirth".

Coming 18 years after the 1994 International Conference on Population and Development, in Cairo, Egypt, which emphasized the right of individuals to determine freely the size of their families and highlighted the role and importance of women in the population debate, the London Summit was groundbreaking in many respects. Nigeria was represented at the summit by Dr. Muhammad Ali Pate, minister of state for health. Dr. Pate said all the right things, even though it was difficult to reconcile his claims with the situation on the ground in Nigeria.

Surprisingly, no reference was made to President Jonathan's pet idea of birth and population control law. "We are fully committed to reducing our currently unacceptably high maternal and child mortality rates. In this context, we are committed to enhancing access to, and utilization of essential, basic life-saving interventions, including the unmet need for family planning. This will be done in an integrated manner within the framework of primary health care approach", the minister noted. "Within the context of our desire to enhance maternal and child survival, as well as accelerate our demographic transition, we are committed to achieving the goal of a contraceptive prevalence rate of 36% by 2018".

The minister added,

> *"In addition to our current annual commitment of US$3 million for the procurement of reproductive health commodities, we are now committing to provide an additional US$8,350,000 annually over the next four years, making a total of US$33,400,000 over the next four years. This additional amount will be programmed within the existing projection for the Subsidy Reinvestment and Empowerment (SURE) Programme funds for Maternal and Child Health. We will use the funds to procure the commodities through UNFPA on the platform of an already existing agreement".*

It was a bold statement, except that the SURE programme the minister alluded to has since been discarded by the government. Add to this the fact that countries like Bangladesh (with a predominantly Moslem population) and Nicaragua, the poorest country in Central America (with a predominantly Christian population) currently have about 50% and 70% contraceptive prevalence rate respectively, then you begin to understand how unserious Nigeria (currently at 14%) is about reproductive health issues.

Ahead of the London Family Planning Summit, I tried to access the website of the National Population Commission (NPC) to no avail. The message that popped up each time was that the site had been taken over by "hackactivists". A week after the summit, I returned to the site. This time around, it was up except that it contained no information about Nigeria's commitment at the London summit. Beyond the scanty two-page National Population Policy, there was nothing to show what the country was doing in the area of reproductive health. Surprisingly, President Jonathan's statement at the inauguration of the new leadership of the NPC was conspicuously missing.

A visit to the website of the ministry of health yielded no result. There was no mention of the London summit and no information about the pledge Dr. Pate made on behalf of the Federal Government. In the midst of this chaos, however, the real troubling aspect of Nigeria's population programme is the clear disconnect between President Jonathan and the managers of our population policy.

The London summit put women at the heart of the reproductive health agenda and highlighted the link between family planning and development. It emphasised the fact that family planning is a human right. It affirmed that access to family planning services and information is perhaps the best way to deal with the population issue.

It showed that millions of women who want to delay or avoid their next pregnancy can exercise that right with modern contraceptives; that countries need to invest in families, in education for girls and boys, and reproductive health; that religion and culture should not be barriers to contraceptive security; and that the ability of women to choose when to get pregnant and how many children to have is empowering for women and essential for safe motherhood.

If the Nigerian government is interested in understanding how to deal with its imagined population crisis, it necessarily must take a few lessons from the outcome of the London Summit on Family Planning.

---

36. Murder Incorporated
July 2012

It was not until weeks after that I realize d I had lost a former colleague in the Dana Air crash of June 3. It was sad enough that score of innocent Nigerians from all walks of life died in such a gruesome circumstance; it was even sadder with the realization that someone I knew and had worked with was a victim. But, in the end, are we not all victims? I shall return to this.

The jury is still out on the direct and remote causes of the Dana crash. If and when the cause is known and it is evident that it was a result of negligence by the airline and complicity on the part of regulators, I do hope that the authorities will, for the sake of the precious lives lost on that fateful day, ensure that those found guilty are punished accordingly.

Very few incidents have drawn the collective angst and empathy of Nigerians as the Dana Air crash. Perhaps it had to do with the profile of the passengers in the ill-fated aircraft and the numerous human-interest stories that they provoked. Perhaps, it had been long we witnessed a plane crash after the spate of crashes in the early and mid 2000s. Soon, all the hue and cry will die down; the matter forgotten and interred in history like the mangled bodies of the Dana Air crash victims.

We are inured to death. Life is cheap in Nigeria, and death, even of the most gruesome kind, has become "one of those things" we have to live with. Just the other day, an electricity pole collapsed in Ibadan, Oyo State, killing seven people. Nigerians have died in their hundreds scooping kerosene and fuel from petrol tankers and damaged pipelines. Every day, scores of Nigerians die in bomb blasts and road accidents. Women die in their thousands every year from childbirth. For millions of Nigerian children "the future is a child-size coffin because they lack access to basic vaccine".

According to experts, at 47 years, life expectancy in Nigeria is the lowest among West African countries. Recently, Dr. Abdulsalam Nasidi, a professor of human virology and biotechnology and Project Director, Nigeria Centre for Disease Control (NCDC), noted, "One out of every five children dies before the age of five years due to polio and other infections. Nigeria is one of four countries where polio is still an on-going epidemic".

Clearly, we are all victims; victims of a state that has institutionalized murder. One of the most interesting analyses I have read of the Dana crash is "Crash as Symptom" by Prof. Pat Utomi. The thrust of Utomi's analysis is that "the (Dana) crash was only a symptom of a very deep malaise, which like cancer in metastasis has spread through every aspect of our national life. The trouble in Nigeria is our living in denial regarding the failure of the Nigerian state".

It is sad to say, but the reality is that the Nigerian state has collapsed. And when a state fails, like in Somalia, the last thing to worry about are rules and regulations. We only need to look at our everyday life to appreciate this breakdown of law and order. Some people get uncomfortable when Nigeria is compared with other countries.

I do not share such discomfiture and I shall do exactly that here because with the human and material resources that Nigeria is blessed with, there is no reason for the country to be where it is today. It does appear that our dear country is holding the rest of Africa and the Black race back.

Recently, I was on a study tour of Kenya under the auspices of the International Reporting Project of the Johns Hopkins University School of Advanced International Studies (SAIS) and the Bill & Melinda Gates Foundation. The trip was instructive in many ways. Kenya and Nigeria share a lot in common, including corruption, political violence, terrorism, and deep ethnic and cultural divisions. But, Kenya is a society that realize s that it has problems and seems genuinely committed to addressing them.

I spent an afternoon looking for generators in Nairobi and my Kenyan guide, an editor at The Nation, East and Central Africa's largest newspaper, could not contain his disbelief. My guide told me that power failure was not an issue in Kenya and, therefore, there was no need for generators. When I told him of the situation in Nigeria, all he could mutter was, "My friend you should sack someone".

If only he knew that our power problem goes beyond sacking someone. I learnt a few things about Kenya that further strengthened my position about the theory of the collapse of the Nigerian state. I was informed that if power would go off for as short a period as one hour, residents would be notified.

I did not hear the sound of sirens throughout the ten days I spent in Kenya because the law permits only the president of Kenya to use siren. The other groups that are permitted this privilege are ambulances and emergency vehicles like fire trucks. This is the first lesson Kenyans are taught in driving school. In Nigeria, it is hard to keep up with the brutalities citizens suffer or the number of deaths from all manner of convoys driving at breakneck speed.

The president of Kenya, Mwai Kibaki, was recently conferred with an honourary doctorate degree from his alma mater, Makerere University, Uganda, where he graduated with a First Class Honours Degree in Economics in 1955, but he does not parade his "doctorate". In Nigeria, every buffoon who can afford it is "Dr. this and that".

Mr. Kibaki flies commercial planes, including Kenya Airways, one of Africa's leading airlines with flights to almost 60 destinations worldwide. In Kenya, streetlights work, roads are motorable; yet, corruption is rife. The difference is that when politicians and public servants steal public fund in Nigeria, they steal as if there is no tomorrow; as if they are colonisers.

Even though English is the official language, there is a national language (Kiswahili) in Kenya and a brand new constitution that seeks to address the many challenges of the Kenya society, including ensuring 35% gender representation. Kenya exports tea and flowers. It depends on tourism and Kenyans have managed to make the best out of this. Nigeria, on the other hand is a major oil producer, yet it imports refined petroleum products because the county's four refineries are comatose.

By the time my guide and I had finished our comparison of Nigeria and Kenya, his conclusion was that, "Even in Africa, we are different", meaning we may all be "developing countries" in the eyes of the West, but some countries have moved way ahead. I couldn't agree more. Kenya is a modern state and for me the indicator is that it is a society with rules of engagement between citizens and between the government and the governed.

We cannot say the same for Nigeria. You have to have a functional state to make that assertion. In the 2011 budget, for example, the cost of maintaining the Nigerian Presidential Air Fleet was N18 billion ($120 million), while the budget for the entire aviation industry was N20 billion ($133 million). Is it surprising, therefore, that very little attention is paid to regulations in the aviation industry? I recently came across a National Universities Commission (NUC) document that lists 44 "fake universities" in the country. That is about a third of the total number of "genuine" universities. Only in Nigeria!

I think it was the Cuban revolutionary, Fidel Castro, who once said that "In a lawless society, it is illegal to be law abiding". Nigerians seem to have imbibed that saying. Our president says he does not" give a damn" about publicly declaring his asset or the right of Nigerians to know his worth even if such harmless gesture can enhance transparency and transform the way we deal with corruption.

As it is in education so is it in the health sector. Even with NAFDAC, reports have it that between 70-80 percent of all the drugs sold in Nigeria are fake. It was not too long ago that we were regaled with stories of how some Indian "doctors" operating high-end clinics in Abuja, the capital city, scarred and scammed Nigerian women who were "diagnosed" with fibroid.

If there are fake hospitals and fake doctors parading our streets without hindrance, it follows therefore that there are fake lawmakers, teachers, policemen, judges, contractors, civil servants, etc. The bottom line is that there is no governance going on and there is no institution, from the presidency to the local government, that functions in Nigeria.

> When a state neglects and murders its own citizens, it is nothing but a failed state.

❖

37. The N5,000 Note Déjà Vu
September 1012

Those who are sounding jubilant and triumphant over President Jonathan's decision to "suspend" the introduction of the N5,000 note should read and reread the report in The Guardian (Friday, Sept 21, 2012). It is déjà vu all over again!

According to The Guardian, "The Senate yesterday expressed displeasure over the way the Executive arm handles the resolutions of the Upper Chamber, saying it threatens the mutual respect and understanding with which the two arms of government are expected to perform their constitutional duties for the progress of the country.

"Essentially, the lawmakers decried the statement credited to the Minister of Information, Labaran Maku, in the media to the effect that the Senate resolutions concerning the controversial N5000 note were not binding.

"Coincidentally, the government disclosed that it was stepping down the introduction of the N5,000 note by the Central Bank of Nigeria (CBN). Presidential Spokesman, Dr. Reuben Abati, responding to inquiries last night, said 'the introduction is being suspended for now to enable the CBN do more enlightenment on the issue'.

"He further said: 'Yes, President Jonathan has directed that the implementation of the new N5,000 note be suspended for now. This is to enable the apex bank to do more in terms of making Nigerians understand why it proposed it in the first place. So, for now, the full implementation is on hold".

It is important that we read between the lines. The government has not said it is abandoning its harebrained decision to introduce the N5,000 note. What it is saying is that Nigerians, in their typical slow way of appreciating government policies, need time to be educated on why they should understand this particular government policy with all its detrimental effect. So the new note is "being suspended for now to enable the CBN do more enlightenment on the issue".

For Nigerians, an idle and angry bunch, distracted by Facebook, Twitter and Blackberry, whose favorite pastime is to oppose anything the government says, a few extra billion on mass enlightenment by the CBN won't be a wasted effort.

That process of enlightenment started yesterday via Reuben Abati's pronouncement. Who says the government cannot turn around and introduce the note by October 1, 2012, and if not, by January 1, 2013? Its action of January 1, 2012, is still fresh in our memories.

"Eternal vigilance is the price of liberty".

38. THE FUEL SUBSIDY CONUNDRUM (1)
NOVEMBER 2012

If you are confused about the assurance by President Jonathan during his recent media chat that "Subsidy stays in 2013", you are not alone. A few days before the presidential media chat, the frightening headline had been, "Total fuel subsidy removal is a must". That headline was attributed to President Jonathan.

The story is that on Thursday, November 15, 2012, while receiving the report of the graduating participants of the Senior Executive Course 34, 2012, of the National Institute of Policy and Strategic Studies (NIPSS), Kuru, Jos, President Jonathan told his audience, "Only the total removal of subsidy on petroleum products would attract investors to the oil sector and put an end to the importation of petroleum products as it is currently being done". Waxing rhetorical, the president asked, "Why is it that people are not building refineries in Nigeria despite that it is a big business?" His answer: "It is because of the policy of subsidy, and that is why we want to get out of it".

Just as the president and his team did last year before the increase (from N65 to N141 and later to N97) in the price of petrol on January 1, 2012, an action that precipitated days of massive nation-wide protests under the aegis of Occupy Nigeria, the president sought to allay our fears by "rubbing mentholatum" on our severely frayed nerves, noting, "While the total removal of subsidy could be painful to Nigerians, they would be happier at the end if they could bear the initial pains".

Assuming the position of surgeon-in-chief, the president went a step further to clarify his position for the benefit of millions of unintelligent Nigerians. "To change a nation is like surgery", he averred.

> *"If you have a young daughter of five years who has a boil at a very strategic part of the face, you either as a parent leave that boil because the young girl will cry or you take the girl to the surgeon. So you have the option of just rubbing mentholatum on the face until the boil will burst and disfigure her face or you take that child to the surgeon. On sighting the scalpel of the surgeon alone, the child will start crying. But if she bears the pain and does the incision and treats it, after some days or weeks, the child will grow up to be a beautiful lady. There are certain decisions that government must take that may be painful at the beginning and people must be properly informed so that they will be ready to bear the pain".*

For good measure, the president added that Canada has 16 functional refineries and Nigeria has four that are struggling to refine at 30 per cent of installed capacity because all the refineries in Canada are privately owned.

Some people have joked about the president being a quack; that before a doctor performs surgery, the patient would have to be given anesthetics to ease the pain. With Doctor Jonathan, all the patient requires is to be "properly informed so that they will be ready to bear the pain".

This joke would have been amusing if not that our situation is really tragic. First, there is something troubling about the president's "young girl with boil" analogy. The problem with the oil and gas sector, and indeed the country, cannot be likened to a boil. It is more like cancer that has metastasized.

A few days later, when the president had the chance to make a categorical statement, including what concrete steps he had taken to deal with those involved in the subsidy scam, he decided to obfuscate. "If we are going to remove subsidy from January, as you are afraid we will do in January, we couldn't have made provisions for it in the 2013 budget. We have made provisions from January till December", the president said during his media chat.

There is really nothing reassuring by the president's doublespeak. You could read more from what he did not say than from what he said. The president's assurance that subsidy stays in 2013 and his silence on a possible increase in the pump price of petrol says a lot. And it is this obfuscation that has led to speculation and the long queues at petrol stations across the country. The artificial shortage has led to increases in price of petrol ranging from N100 to N150 per litre. The president's response?

> *"This situation can manifest in different areas, some people may have the product and decide to manipulate the system so that they can get more money. I am asking Nigerians to bear with us".*

Expectedly, Nigerians are heeding the president's advice. We are gradually getting used to the situation. The government's strategy this time, it appears, is to increase the price of petrol without linking it to subsidy, which in the president's reasoning makes his argument about keeping subsidy 2013 valid. What the president fails to realize is that there can't be any justification for an increase in the price of petrol. Certainly, not with the insight Nigerians have about the rot in the oil and gas sector and those responsible.

Going by his antecedents, President Jonathan's attempt to repudiate his earlier comments about the removal of so-called oil subsidy leaves a bad taste in our mouths. Clearly, the price of petrol will go up and it is just a matter of time. It's almost a year since that insensate action that saw the price of petrol rise from N65 to N97 per litre with its attendant mass suffering.

We all know that the president had vowed during the last discussion on subsidy that he would consult widely and would not take a decision without the input of Nigerians. Even though Nigerians vehemently opposed the planned increase, the president still went ahead to effect the increase on New Year's Day. That cold-hearted decision caught Nigerians unawares, and left millions who had gone on holiday stranded. The president also promised then that Nigerians would benefit from the proceeds accruing from the increase; that our refineries would start working again; and that he would rein in those involved in the subsidy scam.

None of these has happened. Rather, the president confirmed last week that his friends in the oil industry are holding the rest of the country hostage and that he is helpless. "I got the report from the (Aig) Imokhuede committee on Friday, an advance copy of the report. The arguments by the marketers is that it is government that is owing them. The preliminary report we have indicates that they owe the government", the president told a not-too-surprised nation.

> "They (oil marketers) are businessmen; they could decide to manipulate the system to get more money. I got a copy of the report. We will look into it. Experts are being brought in to do forensic audit. The human element is there, and we have our own challenges. I believe that by the time we finish sanitizing the oil sector, the issue of fuel queue will be put behind us for good".

How reassuring! On whose side really is President Jonathan? Certainly, not on the side of the working and toiling people of Nigeria.

---

39. THE FUEL SUBSIDY CONUNDRUM (2)
NOVEMBER 2012

I ended the first part of this piece last week by asking on whose side President Jonathan was on the fuel subsidy debacle: the Nigerian masses or his oil-marketers friends? I had barely finished sending out the piece when I read the troubling headline in The Punch, "Unpaid subsidy: Diezani, NNPC report Okonjo-Iweala to Jonathan". I shall return to the sordid details of what is gradually turning into an albatross around the president's neck.

Two weeks ago, President Jonathan had said "Total fuel subsidy removal is a must". A few days after that statement, he reversed himself, noting, "Subsidy stays in 2013", while remaining silent about the prospect of an increase in the price of petrol. There are many issues arising from the fuel subsidy imbroglio and there is no better place to start than the president's own argument.

The thrust of President Jonathan's argument is that we need to attract investors to the oil sector and the only way to do it is for government to end so-called subsidy and privatize our refineries before they can become functional. Of course, the president's argument falls flat in the light of current reality. As one commentator noted,

> *"It is not the removal of oil subsidy on petrol products that will attract investors to the oil sector; it is the government having zero tolerance for corruption, fraud, waste and abuse; prosecuting and jailing anyone found guilty of any felony".*

There is very little to add here, except to note that it is not enough for the government to wish for investors; it has to create the environment for investments to thrive. In the last one week, Nigeria has moved from being the most fraudulent country in Africa to the worst place for a baby to be born. KPMG, the global audit and financial advisory firm, recently rated Nigeria as "the most fraudulent country in Africa, with the cost of fraud during the first half of 2012 estimated at N225 billion ($1.5 billion).

According to reports, the firm's Africa Fraud Barometer, instituted this year, measures fraud on the continent and assesses the FRAUD RISK THAT CONFRONTS COMPANIES (emphasis mine) in their operations. A few days before that not-too-shocking revelation, it was reported that "Nigeria came last of 80 countries researched in a recent study by the Economist Intelligence Unit, as the worst place for a baby born in 2013".

Do we really need these meddlers to define us? We know Nigeria is one of the worst places on earth to do business. As the Halliburton bribery scandal revealed, even our presidents are not left out of official bribery and the wheeling and dealing when it comes to doing business in the country. So, what investors are we really hoping to attract under the prevailing business environment?

The president referenced Canada as having 16 functional refineries because they are privately owned. It appears when it is convenient for our rulers they make reference to other countries. While the president was on the issue of Canada, he should have talked about Canada's public health system which provides near universal coverage to all Canadians and is a reference point around the world. He should have also mentioned Canada's infrastructural advances, social security system and the fact that working parents are entitled to a full year of maternity leave.

Perhaps, the president needs to be informed that at the height of the US invasion of Iraq after the 9/11 terror attacks in the US, Canadian taxpayers received bonus cheques from their government because the country earned extra oil revenue from the rise of oil prices occasioned by the 2003 invasion.

Let us forget the Canadian diversion for a minute and come back to our own reality. The president says our refineries are struggling to refine at 30 per cent of installed capacity because they are publicly owned. Since we cannot manage our refineries, the way out is to sell them off. But, if there is one thing that has failed woefully in more than five decades of independence, it is the Presidency. I have yet to hear our rulers make a case for outsourcing the Presidency.

There are four African countries, including Nigeria, that are members of the Organisation of Petroleum Exporting Countries (OPEC). Almost all the refineries in these countries are state-owned. Algeria has five refineries. One is run by the China National Petroleum Corporation, while four are run by Sonatrach, a state-owned company. Angola has two. One is run by Chevron Corporation; the other, run by Sonangol Group, is state-owned. Libya has five refineries. All five are state-owned. Three are run by the National Oil Corporation

(NOC) while the other two are run by the Arabian Gulf Oil Company (AGOCO).

It seems that the corruption which permeates the oil industry for which some people are making the asinine argument for the privatization of our refineries is the issue here. Just last week, The Nation newspaper reported of "disquiet in the Presidency over a 'close' relationship between a serving minister and Pinnacle Contractors Limited, an unregistered firm which was indicted for N2.7 billion ($18 million) phony oil subsidy deals".

Before this latest revelation, we had been alerted on how subsidy claims shot up from N300 billion ($2 billion) to N2.3 trillion ($15 billion) under President Jonathan. Many of the culprits in that unprecedented pillage are currently trying to plea-bargain their way out of jail. That corruption has rendered the oil sector comatose should not be a case against public sector-driven oil industry. But, it is not just corruption that has dogged the oil sector and the subsidy business. The confusion and incompetence is mind-boggling. On November 22, The Punch reported: "The Nigerian National Petroleum Corporation (NNPC) had alerted President Jonathan to a looming acute fuel shortage if the Federal Government failed to pay N1.13trn ($7.5 billion) subsidy owed it (NNPC).

> *"The NNPC top management, led by the Minister of Petroleum Resources, Diezani Alison-Madueke, and the corporation's Group Managing Director, Mr. Andrew Yakubu, reportedly made this known to Jonathan at a recent meeting", the newspaper said, adding that the team told the President that the Minister of Finance, Mrs. Ngozi Okonjo-Iweala, had failed to pay the debt. Alison-Madueke and her cash cow, the NNPC, hinged their "capacity to continue the importation of fuel on the payment of the debt which had accumulated over the months".*

Interestingly, three days later, on November 25, The Guardian reported that, "The Federal Government is apparently set to recover about N1.3 trillion ($8.6 billion) owed it by the NNPC and other multinational oil companies". The newspaper quoted the president at the retreat for new members of the NEITI as saying the recovery task team would comprise high-ranking government officials as well as government agencies that are saddled with either the responsibility of collecting or managing Nigeria's oil and gas revenue. If you are confused, so am I!

So, what really is the subsidy argument? The government's position which is self-indicting is that the country cannot refine enough petrol for local consumption because our refineries are not functional. The government has to export crude oil and import refined petroleum products. In an attempt to address the problem, the government set up the Kalu Idika Kalu-led National Refineries Special Task Force.

The committee's report says that Nigeria, with Africa's third largest refining capacity with its 445,000 barrels per day installed capacity, has only 18 per cent capacity utilization and efficiency. This contradicts President Jonathan's claim that the country's refineries are operating at 30 per cent of installed capacity. What really is the exact figure? According to the committee, Egypt (Africa's largest refiner of petroleum) with 774,900bd capacity has 81 per cent efficiency level.

The committee also highlighted the massive corruption associated with the Turn Around Maintenance of the refineries which is not surprising. Unfortunately, Kalu Idika Kalu and his team fell into the privatization trap by calling for the sale of Nigeria's refineries. It is interesting to note that Egypt has nine refineries, with the tenth one under construction. All the refineries are run by the state-owned Egyptian General Petroleum Corporation (EGPC).

Clearly, the subsidy scheme is a ruse. If we can get our refineries working again, we can put an end to this subsidy palaver, provide employment for thousands of Nigerians, and create and expand local industries. I agree with Prof. Asisi Asobie that,

> "A government that is transformative should not say it cannot run the refineries; what it can do is to change the way the refineries have been run in the past. The culture and values of doing things must change and the government must find the necessary political will to make that

change happen. Cultures and values are the hallmarks of a transformative government and not a government that derives pleasure in creating committees. Committees will not change the country for the better, but taking actions that produce results".

It is heartwarming that civil society has fired the warning shots against any increase in the price of petrol as we head into the first anniversary of the Occupy Nigeria protests. President Jonathan has a choice: either to allow dubious private businessmen hold him hostage or govern in the interest of the people.

40. THE NIGERIA POLICE FORCE AS A METAPHOR
JANUARY 2013

The media buzz last week was President Jonathan's "unscheduled" visit to the Police College Ikeja (PCI), Lagos. As a public relations stunt, it was a huge success. But, beyond the razzmatazz, TV cameras and punditry lies the need for a deep national reflection on not just the collapse of infrastructure and institutions across the country, but also the absence of a reformative national ethos.

Unfortunately, this collapse and lack of a reformative national ethos finds expression even outside Nigeria. While the debate on President Jonathan's visit to the PCI was still on, I spoke with a friend at Georgetown University, Washington, DC, U.S.A, who is organizing a colloquium on war crimes and genocide.

He told me he went to the Nigerian Embassy in Washington, DC, to inform embassy officials about his event and was dispirited at the sight of the tattered Nigerian flag at the embassy flying at half-mast. To think we have an ambassador who goes into the embassy every morning and leaves at the close of work. To any curious foreigner, there couldn't be a better glimpse of how dysfunctional the motherland is.

How much does a flag cost? How much pride and faith do we

the roadside, he told me that was the standard price. I told him it was unfair "charging" me the equivalent of 10 percent of the minimum wage for a file. He reminded me that the minimum wage had been increased.

However, this shouldn't be the story of the Nigeria Police. Its duty is to serve not to service itself. This story, of course, is by no means peculiar to the Nigeria Police. It is the same with the military, customs, immigration, prison, university lecturers, civil servants, legislators and judges. The list is endless. It appears the police is a greater menace because we come in contact with police officers every day and everywhere we turn.

Clearly, the depressing condition of the PCI is not likely to improve anytime soon considering the official position on the issue. The president was quoted as saying the documentary by Channels TV which exposed the living condition at the PCI was a calculated attempt to damage the image of his government.

In a remarkable show of indifference, the president reminded us that, "The Police College, Ikeja, is not the only training institution in Nigeria". Then came the opportunistic response of Usman Kumo, Chairman of the House of Representatives Committee on Police Affairs, whose committee is supposed to provide oversight for the PCI, who described the president's visit as "meaningless", adding, "Who does not know that all police colleges in Nigeria are in a dilapidated state and uninhabitable?"

Beyond the outrage, the president, if he is serious about trans- forming the Nigeria Police, needs to query the Inspector General of Police and the Minister of Police Affairs. From Tafa Balogun, a former Inspector General of Police, we learnt that much of the money meant for the welfare of the police ends up in private accounts or is laundered through phony companies. After that, the president should sit down and look at the reports of various groups, including the Network on Police Reform in Nigeria (NOPRIN) that have done great work exposing the inhuman living and service conditions of police- men and women. Considering his very busy schedule, this would save the president many more trips to police installations across the country.

This is important because whether we like it or not, the state of the Nigeria Police Force would have a direct impact on the election of 2015.

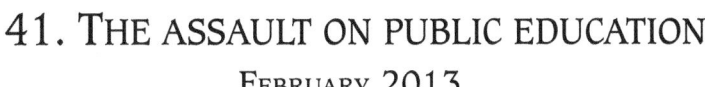

41. THE ASSAULT ON PUBLIC EDUCATION
FEBRUARY 2013

There has been a hue and cry about the collapse of public institutions and infrastructure in Nigeria, particularly since the visit to the Police College Ikeja (PCI) by President Goodluck Jonathan. Gradually, as it always happens, the pictures will soon fade from our memories, and we will move to other matters. Those who are hoping that things will improve at PCI, or that someone would actually be held responsible, would wait in vain. The most we can expect is the "retouching" of the college and things will return to the *status quo ante.*

Of course, nowhere has the vicious attack by Nigeria's ruling elite against the citizens, and everything we hold sacred, impacted more than in public education. Public education in Nigeria is in free fall. I am talking about a collapse so mind-boggling that it is actually threatening the very foundation of the Nigerian state. It seems our ruling elite understand too well that the moment you deprive the citizens of education, you deprive them of everything, including their dignity, and ability to reason and defend themselves. The outcome is that they are powerless and vulnerable and therefore amenable to control.

Last December, I received a picture via an Internet group. The picture left me despondent and has etched on my mind ever since. It provided the impetus for this piece. It was a picture of a group of secondary school students in a ramshackle classroom with some of the students visible in the picture sitting on disused car tyres while taking lesson.

Another row of students behind sat on what looked like a bench with their laps serving as desks. This is not an isolated case. While we have seen many state governors showcase new and modern school buildings (mostly in urban areas), the scenario above paints a vivid picture of the state of most public schools across the country, even in the so-called highbrow public schools in Abuja, the Federal Capital Territory (FCT).

A few months ago, the minister of state for education, Nyesom Wike, inspected schools in the FCT. The minister was "shocked" that some of the schools in the FCT, including those that have the incongruous tag "Government Secondary School", did not have chairs and desks. Some schools had converted whole classroom blocks into toilets. So, apart from not getting quality education, the students are also at risk of contracting diseases in the name of going to school. It was a good photo opportunity though for the minister and it provided the necessary sound bites. It would be interesting to go back to those schools and see what, if anything, has changed.

It is in the same FCT where the minister, Bala Mohammed, appropriated N4bn ($26m) in the 2013 budget for the building of the First Ladies Mission office. Before that, Mr. Mohammed had drawn public ire with the approval of an additional N2bn ($13m) for the ongoing construction of the residence of the vice president. Just as the debate on the appropriateness of such mindless spending of public fund was going on, the Sun newspaper carried a story titled, "In Abuja school, pupils attend classes under tree…share 'classroom' with welder".

According to the paper,

> "Pupils and teachers of Wuye LA Primary School, Abuja, located just two kilometres from Utako District and six kilometres from the administrative block of the Federal Capital Territory Administration (FCTA), have been completely abandoned by the authorities. Since the government demolished the temporary structure put up by the school's Parent-Teacher Association (PTA), the pupils and their teachers have moved their 'classroom' under a dangerous locust beans tree located in the compound of the Federal Government Boys' College, Wuye".

"When the Commissioner of the FCT Public Complaints Commission (PCC), Hon. Obunike Ohaegbu, led a team of journalists and staffers of the commission to the sight, what the team met on ground was horrible. Beyond the pathetic situation of receiving classes under a tree, the 'school' also shares the little space with a welder. The artisan's work tools seemed to pose more danger to the pupils and their teachers than the tree itself. Electrical appliances used by the technician were seen scattered around with the sound of the power generator, located in the same place, disrupting the classes.

"Speaking to Daily Sun, the headmaster of the school, Mr. Muhammed Kolo, revealed that education inspectors had visited the school under the tree, lamenting that no one expressed any concern. He added that the teachers had no teaching boards to use. Some teachers, who didn't want their names mentioned, said no serious academic activity had taken place since they were displaced".

There you have it, apologies to Prof. Bolaji Aluko, vice chancellor of the president's hometown university in Otuoke, Bayelsa State. It is a long way from Otuoke to Abuja. It is a journey that will take weeks, if not months, on foot. Not so the journey from the presidential villa – where we have a president whose resume includes the trauma of walking to school without shoes – to Wuye LA Primary School.

How did we get here? Many of us went to public schools and they were functional in terms of infrastructure and learning. Most of those parading themselves as governors, ministers, honourable this and that, are products of public schools. I do not know any of them that would send his or her goat to what passes as public schools these days. What kind of learning do we really expect students to get from schools like Wuye LA Primary School?

How are the students expected to compete globally? How can the future leaders of this country – as if we really expect leaders to emerge from such schools – get valuable information and knowledge? What we end up doing is grooming delinquent citizens in the name of education rather than producing active and conscious citizens who are not only able to ask questions but are aware of their rights.

In an apparent response to criticism of the Jonathan administration's handling of the education crisis, Oronto Douglas, the president's Special Adviser on Research Documentation and Strategy, noted last September,

> "After Mr. President convened the National Education Summit in December of 2010 and initiated the Bring Back the Book initiative in the same month, he declared that it was his desire to return academic excellence to our citadels of learning. What followed thereafter was that the Education Sector got the highest sectoral allocation in the 2011 Appropriation Bill and the second highest allocation in the 2012 Appropriation Bill. And what has been the result? Today, the National Examination Council (NECO) has released the 2012 June/July Senior Secondary Certificate Examination (SSCE) result with over 50 percent credit and above pass levels in basic subjects as against 22 percent average pass last year".

This, basically, encapsulates the education policy of the Jonathan administration. Of course, the over 50% percent credit and above pass level may be the effect of the ubiquitous "Miracle Centres" and the money-for-marks phenomenon. We have yet to see how the huge sectoral allocation – which is way below the 26 per cent of total expenditure for education specified by UNESCO – has translated to real changes on the ground for schools across the country. Beyond infrastructure, what is the policy on the quality of teachers, instructional materials and training?

The result of this decay, of course, like everything Nigerian, is the migration to private education with its attendant limitations as the solution. Our young men and women, the greatest resource of the country, are now at the mercy of traders posing as educationists. People who have no business running primary schools much less universities have become those pushing the education agenda of the country.

I have said this before, but it is worth mentioning again. The truth is that public education in Nigeria, just like public health, is in crisis because those who oversee it have options. It is either their sons and daughters are in the best international schools in Nigeria or some elite school outside Nigeria.

Nigeria is courting disaster. While the efforts of old students in addressing the infrastructural decay in public schools are commendable, they cannot replace the duty and responsibility of the state to citizens. I hope this neglect does not come back to haunt us. That is if it is not already too late.

This is for you, Olufemi Oyinade Tunde-Oladepo, as you turn 18 tomorrow. You are the best daughter any parents could wish for. As college beckons, may all your dreams come true and may education not just be a meal ticket, but an opportunity to cultivate your intellect and contribute to humanity.

42. The "fake universities" syndrome
April 2013

Last July, shortly after the horrific Dana Air crash that killed over a hundred Nigerians, I did an article titled "Murder Incorporated".

The thrust of the piece was that the government ought to take the larger blame for the incident. Why? Because ours is a country of "anything goes".

There are laws, but people break them with impunity and no one gets punished. That really is what separates us from the rest of the so-called developed world. The lack of respect for laws by citizens and the inability of government to uphold the rule of law make all the difference between a stable and prosperous state and one poised to fail.

While working on the article referenced above, I came across a National Universities Commission (NUC) newsletter that had a list of 44 "fake universities" in the country. That piece of information was meant as a cautionary note for students and parents as well as the public. It is hard to say how many of those concerned saw and benefited from the NUC alert. From all indications, not many.

Just last week, close to a year after the NUC highlighted the issue of "fake universities", I visited the NUC website only to discover that the list had grown to 49 and counting. It is either that, in response to the country's glorification of paper qualification, business is thriving for "fake universities" or those who are supposed to rein in these illegal entities are not doing what is expected of them.

That the NUC had to issue another warning recently is a pointer to how menacing the issue has become. The latest information about "fake universities" and "degree mills" in the country came via a public announcement signed by Prof. Julius Okojie, Executive Secretary, National Universities Commission.

> *"The National Universities Commission (NUC) wishes to announce to the general public, especially parents and prospective undergraduates that the underlisted 'Degree Mills' have not been licensed by the Federal Government and have, therefore, been closed down for violating the Education (National Minimum Standards, etc) Act CAP E3 Law of the Federation of Nigeria 2004",* Prof. Okojie noted.

The list of "fake universities" included such incongruous names as Christians of Charity American University of Science & Technology, Nkpor, Anambra State; University of Industry, Yaba, Lagos; Blacksmith University, Awka; UNESCO University, Ndoni, Rivers State; The International University, Missouri, USA, Kano and Lagos Study Centres; Pilgrims University operating anywhere in Nigeria; Kingdom of Christ University, Abuja; Acada University, Akinlalu, Oyo State; Fifom University, Mbaise, Imo State; Atlantic Intercontinental University, Okija, Anambra State; Olympic University, Nsukka, Enugu State; and Federal College of Complementary and Alternative Medicine, Abuja.

According to the NUC,

> *"In addition to the closure, the following 'Degree Mills' are currently undergoing further investigations and/or ongoing court actions. The purpose of these actions is to prosecute the proprietors and recover illegal fees and charges on subscribers: National University of Nigeria,*

Keffi, Nasarawa State; North Central University, Otukpo, Benue State; Christ Alive Christian Seminary and University, Enugu, Enugu State; Richmond Open University, Arochukwu, Abia State; West Coast University, Umuahia, Abia State; Saint Clements University, Iyin Ekiti, Ekiti State; Volta University College, Aba, Abia State; illegal satellite campuses of Ambrose Alli University, Ekpoma, Edo State".

For good measure, Prof Okojie added,

"For the avoidance of doubt, anybody who patronises or obtains any certificate from any of these illegal institutions does so at his or her own risk. Certificates obtained from these sources will not be recognized for the purposes of NYSC, employment, and further studies. The relevant law enforcement agencies have also been informed for their further necessary action. This list of illegal institutions is not exhaustive".

How reassuring! It is heartwarming that the NUC appears to be tackling the menace of "fake universities" frontally. But there are many questions begging for answers. What type of "investigations" is the NUC conducting? Universities are not daycare centres. How did these "Degree Mills" start off? Is there a "cabal" behind these "fake universities"? Are there no regulations/requirements before universities are accredited? Did the NUC accredit the universities it is investigating?

The NUC has a list of legally recognized universities in the country and any institution that purports to be a university that is not on the list should be closed down immediately and its proprietors prosecuted. That is the easiest way to put an end to this scam. In this regard, does the NUC have the support of the government and its relevant agencies to prosecute the proprietors of these illegal universities?

Coming on the heels of the federal government's appointment of Salisu Buhari, discredited former Speaker of the House of Representatives, to the governing council of a federal university, it is easy to see the kind of support the NUC would get from the government. For those who need reminding, Mr. Buhari was the first Speaker of the House of Representatives when the Fourth Republic took off in 1999. He came to that position having lied about his age and qualification. He claimed a degree from the University of Toronto, Canada, which he never earned.

When Buhari bowed to public pressure and tearfully tendered his letter of resignation to the House, claiming to be motivated by his zeal to serve his country, he received a thunderous applause from his fellow honourable colleagues who agreed to pardon him. That pardon did come eventually through his mentor, then president, Olusegun Obasanjo.

The other day, I watched presidential spokesman, Reuben Abati, on Channels TV trying laboriously to defend the appointment of Buhari. According to Abati, "The thing about pardon is that it turns you into a new man. Out of 251 persons appointed to governing council of federal universities, I don't think we really have to worry ourselves so much about one man".

Perhaps, in tackling the problem of "fake universities" the government needs to borrow a leaf from its own playbook. Only recently, through one of its agencies, the National Film and Video Censors Board (NFVCB), the government banned the airing and distribution of the documentary, "Fuelling Poverty". The 30-minute film documents the corruption in the country's oil industry, its impact and the response of Nigerians to the waste and obnoxious policies it has engendered.

The NFVCB says the documentary "is highly provocative and likely to incite or encourage public disorder and undermine national security". It warned the film maker and his associates about the consequences of violating the order, saying, "All relevant national security agencies (including the Department of State Services and the Police) are on the alert". I would think the menace of "fake universities" is a greater threat to us than a 30-minute film that merely documents what Nigerians already know.

We look forward to the outcome of the NUC's "investigation" and hope that at the end of the day, we actually see people punished for violating the Education (National Minimum Standards etc) Act CAP E3 Law of the Federation of Nigeria 2004.

43. President Jonathan as "Big Brother"
May 2013

Typical of the Jonathan regime, it took the effort of investigative journalists – this time, the reporters at Premium Times – to alert Nigerians about the planned assault on our civil liberties.

The latest deal, involving an Israeli company, Elbit Systems Ltd., is for the supply of the "Wise Intelligence Technology (WiT) System for Intelligence Analysis and Cyber Defense". That we have not heard from presidential spokespersons, Reuben Abati and Doyin Okupe, is a tacit acknowledgment that the contract, as reported last week, is indeed real. We can bet they are busy cooking up an "appropriate" response.

Elbit describes its system as "a highly advanced end-to-end solution (which) supports every stage of the intelligence process, including the collection of the data from multiple sources, databases and sensors, processing of the information, supporting intelligence personnel in the analysis and evaluation of the information and disseminating the intelligence to the intended recipient". In simple terms, it means the government is engaging Elbit to undermine the privacy of citizens and spy on the close to 50 million Internet users in the country.

It is a measure of the lack of transparency that is the hallmark of the Jonathan government that the WiT contract went ahead without due process. After all, it is not as if the appropriation for the contract was not documented. According to Premium Times, "The administration had indicated in the 2013 budget that it would procure a Wise Intelligence Network Harvest Analyzer System, Open Source Internet Monitoring System and Personal Internet Surveillance System at a cost of N9.496bn ($61.26 million)".

Elbit on its part, announced the contract award in a global press release on April 24, 2013, claiming "it was awarded an approximately $40 million contract to supply a country in Africa with the Wise Intelligence Technology (WiT) System for Intelligence Analysis and Cyber Defense".

It would be interesting to know, as Premium Times observed,

> "Now that the contract has been awarded to Elbit for about $40 million, if the National Assembly will raise questions as to what becomes of the extra $21 million earmarked for the project".

We are also informed by the online publication that,

> "In awarding the contract to the Israeli firm, no tenders or calls for bids were made just as there were no public announcements. The contract was awarded following a proposal from a single vendor who dictated the contract sum and the terms of the contract".

"The manner of award directly contravenes the 2007 Public Procurement Act," the publication noted. "While the Act gives room for single source contracts, the Elbit contract met none of the requirements under which such special contracts could be awarded. Section 47 (3) (iii) of the 2007 Act stipulates that single source contracts are to be awarded in emergency situations such as "natural disasters or a financial crisis".

Beyond the issue of due process is the fundamental question of the appropriateness of this contract. Of course, there are those who will question the angst of civil libertarians and say the government needs this kind of "intelligence" gathering in light of the monumental security breaches across the country. But, what guarantee is there that Nigeria will get value for its money?

It is troubling enough that we have to hand over our national security to a private company in a foreign country. The two-year WiT contract comes with a proviso that should concern anybody interested in where our country is headed. According to Joseph Gaspar, Executive VP and CFO of Elbit,

> *"This press release contains forward-looking statements (within the meaning of Section 27A of the Securities Act of 1933, as amended and Section 21E of the Securities Exchange Act of 1934, as amended) regarding Elbit Systems Ltd. and/or its subsidiaries (collectively the Company), to the extent such statements do not relate to historical or current fact".*

"Forward Looking Statements are based on management's expectations, estimates, projections and assumptions. Forward-looking statements are made pursuant to the safe harbor provisions of the Private Securities Litigation Reform Act of 1995, as amended. These statements are not guarantees of future performance and involve certain risks and uncertainties, which are difficult to predict.

> *"Therefore, actual future results, performance and trends may differ materially from these forward-looking statements due to a variety of factors, including, without limitation: scope and length of customer contracts; governmental regulations and approvals; changes in governmental budgeting priorities; general market, political and economic conditions in the countries in which the Company operates or sells, including Israel and the United States among others; differences in anticipated and actual program performance, including the ability to perform under long-term fixed-price contracts; and the outcome of legal and/or regulatory proceedings".*

I have a feeling some "smart" Nigerians must have convinced the government that if it invests $40m, it would be able to keep a tab on opponents and "troublemakers". How does the WiT project fit into the country's existing intelligence programme and security initiatives? We know how ill-trained and ill-equipped our security agencies, particularly the police, are. Their lack of coordination has become a national embarrassment.

A few months ago, President Jonathan visited the Police College, Ikeja (PCI), Lagos, and was justifiably alarmed at the state of the country's premier police training institution. During the president's visit, we got to know that the situation at PCI was just a tip of the iceberg of the monumental rot that is characteristic of police colleges across the country. We can only imagine the kind of security police officers trained at PCI and allied colleges will provide and how amenable they will be to intelligence gathering.

The quality of personnel is an integral part of any effective security and intelligence operation. Rather than frittering millions of dollars on a bogus, illegal and clearly dangerous project, the government should pay a bit more attention to the internal crisis within the country's security agencies.

Saturday Punch, April 27, 2013, reported that the federal government had blocked the installation of 10,000 security cameras in Lagos. The scheme, under the Lagos Safe City Project, according to the paper, aims at "providing 10,000 solar-powered closed circuit cameras all over the metropolis".

"In an information technology-driven world, we have to be counted as one of those states and communities which will adopt best practices. Cameras, sensors, tracking devices are the nerve centre of these facilities that would assist men and officers of the police force, fire service among others to do their duty much more effectively", the governor of Lagos State, Babatunde Fashola was quoted as saying about the project that was initiated in 2009.

A federal government that is interested in the security of its citizens should not be seen to be engaged in this kind of faceoff over an issue that states can handle.

There are many factors to take into consideration in dealing with insecurity in the country. What, for example is the state of the National ID project? How effective is the country's driver's licence system? In a country where people can claim who they are not and transform to anybody they want in a minute; a country where people can move in and out through our numerous porous borders without any form of documentation, it would take more than a $40 million sweet deal and the not-too-reassuring words of a foreign company to keep Nigerians safe.

Of course, the government would do well investing in the lives of citizens through the provision of quality education, effective healthcare, creation of the enabling environment for the economy to thrive and facilitate job creation for millions of unemployed university graduates.

That, ultimately, is the best defence against insecurity.

SECTION FOUR

NIGERIA IS NEGOTIABLE

A Poem For My Country

By Chiedu Ezeanah

Country of hisses, country of debris
Country of sweet barbarities

Country of memories that flow
like ghosts out of Tutuola's scrolls

Country where handshakes pilfer groins
Country of amulets and chest incisions

Country masked behind whose smiles
savage thirsts hide with knives

Country whose famous sagas
reinvent Dr. and Madam Bandas

Country of Trickster-Generals and Presidents
Country of kolanut-peddlers chanting: "Let's join them"

Country swarming with football and fleas.
Country stranded among stranded corpses.

Country of ballot-robberies
Country that topples and bleeds

Country that aborts Children's Day
Country of beauty queens who can't spell Achebe

Country as glorious as corpulent fugitives
Country scarier than Becket's absurdities

Country of delicious taboos
Country of imperiled at golden jubilee

Country of grief and gun-bursts,
why don't you dream anymore?

Inconsolable country that I solemnize
in couplets traumatized-

I hardly dream in you, dear:
my dreams stir inside me, everywhere

until you translate more hopes in maidens
by the hearthstone of night's yearnings

Country let voices be voices, the dreads left to play,
freely to plait tents, freely to plait years

with compassion naming, healing the heart...

1. Postponing the Evil Day
October 1995

> *"The difference between a patriot and a traitor depends on who is in power".* - Sidney Sheldon, *Sand of Times*

Indeed, very few people would have been surprised at the Independence Day broadcast by Gen. Sani Abacha. And it was not by chance that the address took that format. For a regime that is sinking, nothing but a bold-faced assault would have worked.

Suddenly, the regime appeared to have woken from its slumber to address the country's political and social woes; to take her to some Eldorado of sorts. It raised hope of a quick return to "true and enduring democracy" so that the country will move forward. The citizens are, therefore, expected to be part of this effort by acquiescing to the plans of the regime and allowing it to decide how the way forward will be constructed.

We all saw the pressure our esteemed general was under to declare his regime innocent by declaring that the judiciary had the final say on the June 12 issue; a judiciary that has been incapacitated and rendered prostrate by ouster clauses and other jargon of military dictatorship.

As I said earlier, people are not surprised one bit. The regime must justify its existence. Even though majority of Nigerians have become cynical and disillusioned about the talk of democracy and the prospect of the military quitting the scene considering its culpability in the misgovernance of the country, the regime is digging in assuredly and claiming it has the wand to do the magic.

The Abacha regime, rather than addressing the main issues which led to its unfortunate emergence, issues which remain pivotal, has decided to play the ostrich, preferring to hide its head in the sand. Of course, there is nothing to cheer about in the speech considering the antecedent of those who have saddled themselves with the task of determining our future and who think they have the prerogative to move the country forward.

Clearly, the next three years will be as baleful as the past two years which have served to strengthen the hands of the regime in its quest to control every aspect of our lives. The past two years have been a period of rude awakening for Nigerians. We have witnessed human rights abuses, illegal arrests and detention and debilitating social conditions. To say that Nigeria is indeed heading for a hard time, and that no amount of posturing can save that, would be repeating the obvious. Abacha's October 1 broadcast dimmed all hope about a meaningful resolution of the country's political crisis.

Despite a thriving oil industry that produces more than two million barrels a day, the quality of life of Nigerians has continued to decrease. Inflation has remained on the high side in the past two years and the people have been living under fear with the greatest level of uncertainty. That is not likely to change. Our roads have remained deplorable in the past two years with social services almost grinding to a half. There is no end in sight.

The October 1 speech was not different from the many hope-shattering speeches made in the past which have served to maintain the grand illusion that the military can move the country forward. Unmistakably, the regime tried to use the occasion to assuage our frayed nerves through such vaunted talk about "economic reconstruction", "genuine democracy", "rule of law", and "peace and unity". Of course, Nigerians know better.

On the contrary, we may slip back to fascism, as it is not likely that the total repression embarked upon by the regime will abate. This has really proved attractive to the regime as the only way it can move the country forward. It has become evident that Nigerians cannot get a reprieve from a regime that sees political and press freedom as threat to national security; a regime that scorns public opinion and upholds the travesty of justice; a regime that believes in naked force since it cannot rule by any other means.

The riot act the regime read on October 1 when it also launched its own transition programme will serve no purpose. The country needs to look beyond the speech in its search for a new beginning.

And to the regime, the general disillusionment notwithstanding, it must be wary of the danger when people are dissatisfied.

2. THE MASSES AND THE DRAFT CONSTITUTION
SEPTEMBER 1995

Ordinarily, it would have been unnecessary to dignify the action of members of the constitutional conference by commenting on the draft constitution, but political practice teaches that you can give your opponent credit or compliment if the need arises. This thesis, therefore, aims at warning the masses and working people who are always the victims of the country's political power-play by situating their position within the context of the emerging scenario.

The major plank of the draft constitution is the rotational presidency clause. Expectedly, opinions are divided on whether to support or to oppose it. Those who support it invoke democracy, arguing that it will enhance the country's unity and give every section a sense of belonging. Its antagonists also invoke democracy, claiming that it will be undemocratic to determine beforehand where the president should come from.

Both arguments are understandable considering the character and background of those who make them. There is one thing common to both arguments. None of those who want the presidency "rotated", or the *status quo* to remain, is interested in what happens to the masses and working people when they attain power. Watching the Nigerian state and its crisis of identity, it is not difficult to decipher the tendencies which are markedly parochial. Beyond their parochialism, our ruling elite are consciously or unconsciously exacerbating an issue which has remained recurrent in our polity and is trying to tear the country, and even the radical movement, apart: the national question.

My position, which stems from the foregoing and the interplay of forces in the country's political arena, is that the hegemony exercised by sections of the country is real. If the bourgeoisie and ruling elite in Nigeria had a national outlook, even while pillaging and bestriding the nation's political environment, it would still have been able to "move the country forward". Unfortunately, that is not the case.

Of course, no one can doubt that ultimately the class question is central and crucial in resolving the country's political impasse; but only to the extent that it is not used to obfuscate the simple proposition that nations precede ideologies. Back to the situation of the masses and working people under a "stationary" or "rotational" presidency. The position of the masses and working people, their alliances and support, must be conditioned by their proletarian class interest; interest that is not only diametrically opposed to that of the ruling elite, but also superior to it.

What is this all-important proletarian class interest? It is an interest that goes beyond the narrow confines of bourgeois electioneering, and by extension democracy. Certainly, it goes beyond the muddled and truncated military induced transition the country has been enmeshed in for a decade now. It means the masses and working people aspiring to govern themselves!

We saw how Babangida and his ilk supplanted the sovereign will of the people under the guise of democracy. Of course, when we consider and reflect on the antics of the present military government, including its antecedent, it is not difficult to see that a people's democratic state which the masses will benefit from is a mirage. Of course, it is only a people's democratic state that the working people and exploited masses of the country, should aspire to; a state conceived, not under the jackboot of military dictatorship and the tutelage of recidivist politicians, but actualized through political consciousness that promotes the interest of the working people.

That interest also serves to make sure that the majority of the working people and masses labouring feverishly across the country overcome the inhumanity and degrading conditions they are experiencing; overcome unemployment, social misery, exploitation and other such disasters that accompany bourgeois democracy.

Collaboration in any form will only serve to undermine the position of the masses and working people under the present dispensation because the myths about enduring democracy and transition to civil rule only serves to buy time for the regime while it continues its onslaught against citizens.

It is important, therefore, to address the class interest of the masses and working people, not from the standpoint of the draft constitution which really is not different from the 1979 and 1989 constitutions that only contributed to worsening the plight of Nigerians.

The way of addressing such a question should not be abstract, lest we succumb to another bogus and treacherous transition. It must conform to the historical role of the downtrodden masses and working people as the only people who can usher in a new and better society. This will entail resisting any attempt by this regime to force its will on the people.

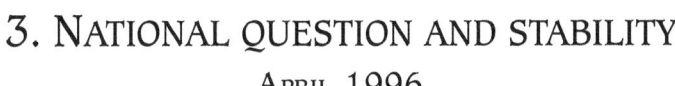

3. NATIONAL QUESTION AND STABILITY
APRIL 1996

The greatest problem facing the Nigerian state as it embarks on another bogus transition to civil rule is the crisis of identity. What is Nigeria? It has become imperative to answer this question if we must move forward. Beyond the problem of democracy, the scourge of military rule and the travails of a dilapidated neo-colonial economy which has further dampened the hopes of citizens, lies the deeper and vexed issue of nationhood.

The problem has always been there, but successive governments have worsened it. Even though independence was pursued on a pan-Nigerian basis, the various groups which were autonomous and independent prior to the coming of the colonialists could not agree on the structure of the country at independence.

So while a section was calling for independence, another was proclaiming unpreparedness. At independence so-called, "When our rulers found it inexorable to enhance the frontiers of national unity, a phenomenon which had been debased by the colonialists, they were too obsessed carving out spheres of domination for themselves. It did not occur to them – well, they saw no reason for it – that they had to create a nation out of the contraption imagined by the British; that they had to develop a new system to suit the country. The emergent ruling elite and local bourgeoisie which the colonialists created had no idea – in fact, were unable in the least – to bring about any radical political economic or social changes that could enhance nationhood.

The reason for this is simple. Those who were in the forefront of the struggle for independence – the radical pan-Nigerian elements – for one reason or another were shoved aside, which meant their concept and idea of a new Nigeria could not materialize. Many people have argued that such a concession was necessary to enhance national unity and safeguard the emergent nation-state. It is doubtful if the choice has served any useful purpose.

Of course, neo-colonialism played an important role in this grand design to gradually alienate the people and undermine the unity of the country through its policy of divide and rule. After all, since the various ethnic groups were "conquered" individually and later brought together there was the need to maintain such individual authority while assuming to be ruling them collectively so that the emergence of a unanimous struggle against neo-colonial forces would be difficult.

The result was that political unity was taken for granted, while the lopsided colonial structure were accepted or defined as God-given. And since the ruling elite lacked political will, it could not mediate in the unfortunate condition the country found itself. With this development, social and political cohesion in the country became almost impossible and the differences – religious, language and cultural – in the country only served to complement it.

Certainly, the foregoing analysis is necessary as it provides a prelude to understanding the present crisis in Nigeria. It is interesting how history works on the psyche of those who tend to undermine it. Years ago, it would have been difficult – indeed, it was seen as a taboo even among radical elements – to discuss the future of the country, particularly the issues of autonomy of the various units or what has been referred to as the national question.

What is the national question and why has its resolution become the primary issue in Nigeria's political evolution? Its resolution will answer those who are worried about the anarchy in the educational sector, the parlous state of our healthcare system and the general deprivation, disillusionment and instability that pervade the polity.

The historical solution to this dilemma as we can see lies in the structure of the polity. Nigeria is a nation-state, which means a country made up of ethnic nationalities. Due to the interplay of political forces buoyed by the colonialists, these ethnic nationalities, before and after independence, sought to form themselves into various power groupings or what is called power bloc. That is, they tried to organize themselves politically. The fall-out of such organisation was that each group sought to control power not just in its area of dominion but also in the entire nation, if possible.

Naturally, to achieve this end, there was bound to be domination of one group by another. It is this struggle, for domination and the desire not to be dominated, by the various ethnic nationalities that is referred to as the national question. As stated earlier, to make certain their aims, the ethnic nationalities formed themselves into power-blocs based on pre-colonial socio-political groupings.

It is, therefore, untenable as Dr. Bala Usman argues that, "The Nigerian polity is not an amalgam of ethnic and religious blocs which can be separated and set up as new states". Regrettably, at independence, these ethnic amalgamations manifested themselves. Even at that, they had always been there. Introductory history teaches that these entities existed long before the coming of the British. They ran their own governments, had systems of adjudication and defended their territories. The only relationship that existed, if any, was in commerce and sometimes war because of the desire of the "stronger" groups to conquer the "weaker" ones.

Again, Dr. Usman's assertion that, "With the British conquest, the hitherto sovereign territorial rights of the citizens and governments of the pre-colonial polities of Nigeria were revoked" cannot stand for all time, since with the "exit" of the British in 1960, an "annulment" of the conquest could be assumed to have taken place. Therefore, we can evoke the right of the "sovereign territories" to revert to their pre-colonial states.

Except, of course, Dr. Usman holds the British conquest sacred or eternal.

4. Before We Democratise
April 1996

Dr. Bala Usman, erudite scholar and historian was at his vintage best last week. The occasion was the 1996 Vanguard Annual Lecture at the MUSON centre. He was frank and consistent. At the end of his lecture, the radical history teacher from Ahmadu Bello University, Zaria, illuminated the path of Nigeria's historical evolution.

His contention that the crisis in Nigeria stems from the inability of the right class of people to run the affairs of the country is a pointer to his conviction that the country's political instability is not caused by the structure of the polity and that voting those with the capability to run the economy and the country will do the magic.

The distinguished lecturer delved into history and concluded that the question of "restructuring" the country will only magnify Nigeria's problem in the emergent federations, which in turn could lead to civil wars between the various units. Expressly, what Dr. Usman has succeeded in doing is to deny the nationality question and by extension the right of ethnic nationalities to self-determination.

I submit that the primary contradiction in the polity today is the national question, not democracy, not the chicanery of our so-called politicians, not the scourge of military rule. Who can deny the fact that the national question is real and alive in the country? When the national question is raised, the issue is not the unity or otherwise of the various nationalities in the country.

As a measure of the relationship between various nationalities, the national question defines the power equation; and in a "primitive" capitalist and neocolonial entity like ours, power is paramount as it appropriates and allocates resources, in this case crude oil.

The national question has been with us since independence. However, it has been intense in the past decade because of the strengthening of ethnic bias conditioned by the debilitating economic crisis since 1986. It manifested itself in 1966. The 1992 Zangon-Kataf crisis was a fall-out of the national question. It came to its height with the murder of Ken Saro-Wiwa on November 10, 1995. Expectedly, Saro-

Wiwa's death has removed whatever illusion people had about the character of the Nigerian state.

Dr. Bala Usman contends that Nigeria's struggle for independence was done nationally and not on the basis of ethnic forces. This assertion holds true. However, history has shown us that Nigeria's independence was hijacked by ethnic forces who have over the years nurtured and exacerbated the ethnic crisis. Through their activities, these ethnic bigots who have a divine concept of power developed structures which can be defined as power blocs.

These power blocs exist in the East, the West and the North; and they are made up of members of the armed forces for the West and the North and comprador capitalists, merchants, commission agents, bureaucrats, academics and religious leaders for all the three blocs.

Ask some people why democracy or political stability has failed in Nigeria. The answer would be the ineptitude of the political class. How do we democratize a deeply-troubled polity? According to Prof. Claude Ake, "Nigeria cannot be held together by the arithmetical majoritarianism of liberal democracy. We need to recognize the reality of being a federation of ethnicities and nationalities".

It is ironic when those who should know try to obfuscate political reality either consciously or unconsciously. Dr. Usman's thesis that there was no Hausa-Fulani, Yoruba, Igbo, Ogoni, Kataf or Efik polity before colonialism which can be resurrected to form a confederal Nigeria, is tenable. What the learned historian has done is to dim the struggle of ethnic nationalities, particularly the minority groups.

Unwittingly, Dr. Usman has succeeded in strengthening the internal colonization going on in the country under the guise of governance. For, even though ethnic nationalities were not prominent before independence, they grew at independence, matured and took root after independence. Since the dominant power bloc knows the meaning and reality of state power within the Nigerian context, it would continue to maintain the *status quo*.

The ruling class – civilian and military, including the present – cannot solve the question of democracy, political instability or good governance. Restructuring the polity by decentralizing the instruments and institutions of power is a sure way of meeting these ideals. Such restructuring is not meant to dismember the polity, but to create room for viable and healthy co-existence. We cannot institute democracy without addressing the national question. Any analysis that undermines this reality is illusory.

5. The Nigerian tragedy
July 1996

The Nigerian situation looks like a well-rehearsed tragedy interspersed with comedies. And it seems, beyond the whimsicalities of the comedians, this tragedy is going to play itself out. Let us go back to the beginning. We must remind ourselves that eight decades have gone by since a paper bridge was build across what is today called Nigeria; and thirty-four years have passed since the colonialists took a tactical withdrawal.

Throughout this period, nothing has changed. By the 1960s when our rulers found the inexorability of making concrete this bridge, they were too obsessed with their new status as an independent state to do anything. Rather, clannishness and primitive accumulation began to burgeon. Basking in the euphoria of independence which meant the opportunity to acquire what was not possible under the colonialists, it did not occur to them that they had to "create a nation out of the contraption imagined by the British". We can rightly say that in the beginning there was no country. And if there was, it did not make sense; and it makes much less sense today.

Of course, as the country gropes from one crisis to the other, the prospect of keeping it together gets dimmer and dimmer. What is keeping Nigeria one is not so much the fact that its obsequies cannot be performed as the fact that the various nationalities that constitute it are still disposed to living together, though for various reasons and clearly on different terms.

Therefore, we should not take this disposition for granted. We can only do so at our peril. For those who romanticize this unity, it will be naïve to think that the military and the idealists who never cease talking about the need to protect the unity of the country can be of any use in this regard.

Military interventionism has provided the comic relief for this consuming tragedy. Of course, this cannot be taken in isolation. It must be situated within the context of power struggle and the structure of the country. It is convenient for us to say that the military is riding roughshod over the rest of the country without taking into cognizance the indolence of a political class which itself is far from being nationalistic. If we understand and appreciate the above phenomenon, then we can understand the June 12 crisis and the various responses in terms of support and opposition and what can be done to really move the country forward, to borrow the cliché of the military junta.

The argument has been on for a long time whether to pursue the country's problems from a purely class angle instead of the "ephemeral" military must go posture. Those who support the former view appreciate the fact that only a class solution can put an end to the mess the country is witnessing. Proponents of the latter view – this does not include our pseudo-democrats – believe, and rightly too, that getting rid of the military ought to be the first task of all revolutionary democrats.

I have been in support of the argument against those who would want to use class analysis to obfuscate our present crisis. But, watching members of the constitutional conference grinning from ear to ear and applauding intermittently at the presentation of the draft constitution, I began to wonder what a post-military rule Nigeria would look like. It appeared our politicians had an indissoluble agreement with the Nigerian military.

When Nigerians protested almost a decade of murderous rule by the Babangida administration, our politicians unabashedly saw it differently. They saw it as an attempt by "disgruntled elements" to cause disaffection and undermine the unity of the country. During the Interim National Government, they were at their fawning best. Today, they know no other way of moving the country forward other than Abacha's transition. Of course, if there is a change of guard at

Aso Rock tomorrow, our politicians would be singing a different tune.

This provocation by the political class, military and civilian, portend only one thing: a precipitation of war, an ethnic conflagration that is beyond the imagination of anyone. The Liberian and Rwandan tragedies are still fresh in our memories. However, we must rise in reprobation of war; not because we are averse to all wars, but because the present war drums being sounded aim at strengthening a cabal and offer fresh opportunity for exploitation and oppression.

Those who are fanning the embers of war by their action and inaction, by their perpetuation of injustice, should put aside the illusion that Nigeria will always be there. They must appreciate the fact that the unity of the country can only be meaningful when the state which claims to be an embodiment of that unity is just.

The present repressive state is merely buying time. Soon, it will find out that it is much easier to "unmake" Nigeria than it took to "make" her.

---

6. NIGERIA: DIVIDED WE STAND?
JULY 1998

Does this title sound cataclysmic? If it does, the reason is simple. Each day, the inanities of a bankrupt and moribund ruling class place the country on the brink and accentuate the inevitability of a return to the *status quo ante*. Some have questioned the rationale behind looking back. But, why shouldn't we, even if it "offends the sensibilities of a super race, discomfits the expectations of scions of empire builders or thwarts the imperialist illusion of the monarchs at Buckingham Palace".

Eighty-four years ago, a contraption was created by the British colonialists in what was the culmination of more than a century of brigandage. That act was the official seal to legitimize not just colonialism but to stamp the imprimatur of international capital on the conquered territory. Since then, the different nations that constitute this rogue territory have spent their time trying to undo one another while at the same time struggling hard to maintain the contraption within the orbit of global capitalism.

Just as they were when the colonialists, and before them the slave merchants, first set foot on the African soil, the rights of the various nationalities were ignored completely in the effort to build an empire out of their territorial conquest. The economic foundation and prosperity of colonialism was the underlying factor in building the paper bridge that was bound to collapse soon afterwards. Looking back now, only a totally deranged and perfidious conqueror, beaming with imperial arrogance, could have welded the disparate nations together in the manner that the British did.

Of course, the resultant crisis was not so much the fact that the various nations were brought together in such a carefree manner than the fact that built-in mechanisms for chaos, like the disproportionate sizes of the component units and the systems of governance adopted, were instituted. As they did everywhere else, the British created and foisted on the territory a ruling elite whose primary loyalty was to the imperial motherland and burgeoning monopoly capital.

This elite, comprador in every sense, was completely oblivious of the underlying current that the Nigerian nation was a product of British imperialism. Because of its feudal and aristocratic disposition, it could not even do what was least expected of it; that is, build a politically united territory and develop national ethos in line with the demands of modern capitalism. Some may argue that the fault is not really theirs but the necessary outcome of colonialism.

Whatever explanation we accept, clearly, the patchwork called Nigeria was not meant to succeed; and if it did, it was not designed to fulfil the aspirations of those who inhabit the geographical space, but meet the demands of those who conquered it. If discontent mounts in the country today, it is simply because we built on a negative past. Expectedly, many theories have been put forward on how to resolve this impasse, some bordering on the reasonable; yet others, completely inane and provocative.

Not surprisingly, the ruling class has preoccupied itself with how to share or control political power, which essentially is about how to control Nigeria's vast oil resources. Indeed, since 1960, when independence was granted, an act spurious in the extreme, Nigeria, a country of diverse nationalities has been enmeshed in an orgy of bloodletting all in an attempt by those who claim they want to maintain the country's unity, that is, keep Nigeria "one indivisible entity"; and partly by those who think the concept of Nigeria which Chief Obafemi Awolowo, one of the main pillars of Nigeria's independence struggle described as "a mere geographical expression", is indeed, a ruse.

What then is the way out of this *cul-de-sac* if not to come to terms with the realities of nationhood? The argument whether the various ethnic nationalities have a right to make demands on the Nigerian nation, or better still, whether they have a right to self-determination has been the source of conflict particularly among academics and radical political activists in the country.

Those, like eminent historian, Dr. Bala Usman, who use history – suitably distorted – to obfuscate the problem have argued repeatedly that such a right does not exist. According to Usman, once the various nationalities that were merged to form Nigeria succumbed to British conquest they ceded their rights to separate nationhood. To him, those who now talk of restructuring Nigeria are nothing but "nation wreckers".

Undoubtedly, this is one of the most cynical and bigoted comments to come out of Nigeria and it is flawed in so many ways. First, many of the pre-colonial nations did not gleefully give themselves up to the British; they engaged the British in very bitter wars. But, since they were "defeated", they, of course, became victims of the idiotic arrogance of the conquerors.

Second, if the British wanted to create as many as, say, ten nations after the conquest of the geographical area that later became Nigeria they would have done so. The merger was purely for their administrative convenience and the need to have a close-knit market. Third, and most important, is the fact that Usman's argument is an endorsement of colonialism. By making colonialism sacrosanct, he is saying essentially that it is heretic to undo the "damage" that the colonialists did.

Usman's "nation wreckers" bogeyman, certainly an unwarranted diversion, also finds expression in his belief that since independence was won on the platform of a pan-Nigeria political movement, nobody has the right to question the lopsided nature of political structure that was bequeathed to us at independence. Of course, it was necessary to form such an alliance if the different nations saw the British as a common enemy.

Clearly, if some of the nations had tried to confront the colonialists alone, the latter would have sought the help of the pliant nations to subdue those who may have had a different idea about being part of the Nigeria project. However, the quest for independence was by no means a "united" one as those who prefer to dig the gutters of history would want us to believe. Up until 1957, that is, three years before independence, there were those who still believed they were not ready for self-government.

Flowing from Usman's diatribe are two fundamental questions: what is a nation? And when can people demand their right to self-determination? Of course, nations are "geographical expressions". However, a nation goes beyond mere geographical construct to embrace such other elements as "common language, culture, religion, economic and social life".

If we accept this simple definition, then we can conveniently say that pre-colonial Nigerian societies were nations on their own. Whether these nations now have the right to self-determination depends on the conditions of their amalgamation, and whose interests it serves.

Because of the absence of a national bourgeoisie and the underdeveloped nature of capitalist infrastructure in Nigeria – the West has long put an end to independent capitalist development – the tendency is that the major disagreement in Nigeria, at least on the national level, is not that between the bourgeoisie and the working class, but that between ethnic nationalities.

Therefore, not even the knowledge that nationalist agitation – which could go on ad infinitum – cannot, for example, end class exploitation can deter us from seeking an end to oppression based on ethnic, religious or even geographical hegemony. Should the slogan "One Nigeria" then be of interest to radical forces or the immediate priority of those who are concerned about building a society based on social justice? Clearly, it should not.

There are those who stick to the illusion, for obvious reasons, that Nigeria must remain one even where such a spurious contention means that some nationalities have to be oppressed. This feigned concern for national unity and the rhetoric that the "unity of the country is nonnegotiable" are only a facade to hide the oppression of ethnic nationalities.

Undeniably, the central issue in Nigeria today is whether the national aspirations of all or even majority of the nationalities can be realized within the concept of one Nigeria. To call for self-determination is not to support the territorial ambition of various bourgeoisies but to create a basis on which the working people can begin to address not just working class unity but its control of political power.

Of course, only a working class revolution can upturn national injustices and create national equality. However, the prospect of such a revolution in Nigeria is dim. It is difficult for the working people of this country to unite as long as national injustices persist; for no matter how far we stretch the argument that workers are workers everywhere and the masses suffer the same exploitation in every part of Nigeria, the dominant position and the hegemonic character of each local bourgeoisie rubs off on their kin. In a sentence, even among the workers and masses of this country, there are those whom the present imbalance in the country has favoured and those it has not favoured.

It is commonplace to hear words such as "north-south dichotomy" "ethnic imbalance" and "ethnic domination". Depending on who is telling the story, the opinion is usually one of domination or being the dominated. To address the monstrous nature the national question has assumed, sectional bourgeoisie are calling for "power shift".

What they hope to achieve is to replace one hegemonic rule with another. What is at stake, however, is not the unity of the country but the destruction of nations, and the denial of their inalienable right to exist and survive. There is no law in favour of the unitary political structure in Nigeria which cannot be questioned; nothing that says a nation is not a nation because it is not economically viable; except, of course, the oil law which makes it easier to forget the "dreary labour" of cocoa, groundnut and palm oil plantations.

The case for restructuring the Nigerian nation is simply a product of historical expediency. While demanding this, we cannot share the illusion that ethnic self-determination on its own will solve the problems of the working people. Having said that, we must go back to history to help us understand Abubakar's regime and its messianic pretensions. Of course, relying on this regime to address the problems of Nigeria is like "relying on a virus to find the cure for a disease".

The greatest trickery of Abubakar's transition is that elections have gone ahead without the constitution. The next stage in this charade will be to design the constitution based on the outcome of the December 5 election. It is understandable. Abubakar must fulfil the historical role of the military as the armed wing of the hegemonic bloc in Nigeria. This military, which seizes every opportunity to pose as the Nigerian military is ready to go to war once the interest of the class it represents is threatened.

This phenomenon best explains why the June 12, 1993 election was annulled and till date the culprits are still roaming the streets and talking glibly about their crimes. It also explains why Abacha cannibalized Nigerians in his self-succession drive without as much as a whimper from the so-called Nigerian military. A truly patriotic and national force would have objected to such brutal and senseless manoeuvre which had the potential of tearing Nigeria apart.

However, because Abacha's efforts were in line with its broader game plan, it could not oppose it. It is for the same reason that Abubakar cannot address the agitation for self-determination. Abubakar, just like Babangida and Abacha before him, assumes that his regime will be the last military regime in Nigeria. Of course, the so-called Nigerian military, a subclass enmeshed in thievery, will intervene whenever it feels the "unity of the country is threatened". That is the major reason it has given each time it usurped power.

Clearly, the way Nigeria was designed, and is being run, it cannot survive for too long. What Abubakar needs to hang on to power is to invoke the melodious tune "We cannot compromise the unity and survival of our nation". Our nation, indeed!

But, we shouldn't harbour any illusions; for nowhere has the exploiter class given up its privileges freely; nowhere has self-government been granted on a silver platter.

---

7. Charter of demands for a new Nigeria
January 2012

> *"The administration would do well to ponder the principle that a government which refuses to submit to the will of the people, its sovereign, is a rebel government and, by its own rebellion, legitimizes and invites upon itself the rebellion of the people".* – Chinweizu

To say that the Occupy Nigeria protest which enters its second week on Monday, January 16, 2012, has exposed the bankruptcy and dirty backside of the ruling class in Nigeria is an understatement. It has become clear that public service in Nigeria is not about service to the public. If it were, our roads would not be death traps; there would be steady power supply to support our local industries; our educational institutions would be functional and we do not have to go to Ghana to educate those we expect to run our country in the years ahead.

Public service in Nigeria is about whose "Mercedes Benz (read bank account) is bigger" at the end of the day. Public officers in Nigeria see their position as prayer answered by the good Lord and an opportunity to "come and chop". I say this in light of the allegations against the attorney general of the federation and minister of justice, Mohammed Bello Adoke, who was recently accused by iReports-

Ng.com of maintaining several bank accounts running into billions of naira. The minister is also alleged to have investments in about 25 blue-chip companies in Nigeria. The "honourable" minister has denied the allegations.

Though he confirmed the said accounts, he noted, however, that the "balances" were "nowhere near the outrageous figures quoted in the publication". This is part of the defence put up by the minister, according to his chief press secretary, Ambrose Momoh,

> *"We wish to categorically state that while the attorney general maintains accounts with Diamond Bank and First City Monument Bank, the balances in those accounts are certainly nowhere near the outrageous figures quoted in the publication. It is instructive to note that Mr. Mohammed Bello Adoke, has been a legal practitioner for 26 years and was in recognition of his achievements elevated to the rank of Senior Advocate of Nigeria (SAN) in 2006. As an investment lawyer, he made careful investments which yielded good returns. At the time he was invited to serve as Attorney General of the Federation, he was by the grace of God, a successful legal practitioner, by every standard".*

Regrettably, the minister deliberately refused to comment on his links to Oando Oil and Eterna Oil, companies alleged to have benefited more than N230 billion between January and August 2011 from fuel subsidy funds. The minister did not deem it necessary to disclose how much he really has in the said accounts to debunk the allegations.

Of course, it will be foolhardy for Mr. Adoke to make his asset declaration public when his principal has refused to do so. That is Nigeria for you. Everything about our rulers is shrouded in secrecy. We do not know how many wives and children our president has. Can any agency provide information about who and how much was contributed to Jonathan's presidential campaign?

Does it surprise anyone, therefore, that there is a serious trust deficit in the country? We do not trust our rulers, not because they are not

Nigerians, but because they have shown they are not trustworthy. When the price of petrol was increased under Obasanjo, it was the same Ngozi Okonjo-Iweala who told a skeptical nation that the proceeds will go into education, infrastructure, stemming the tide of maternal mortality and other problems confronting the country.

I am amused each time I hear Mrs. Okonjo-Iweala talk about maternal mortality like she did recently during an interview with Al-Jazeera, when she kept repeating the mantra that it is unconscionable to watch thousands of mothers in Nigeria die during child-birth. Madam minster, what is unconscionable is for you to continue lying to us. Between you and me, by the end of the Jonathan administration, at the rate the government is going with its policy of impoverishment, maternal mortality rate would have doubled.

It has been noted that under Obasanjo, a regime that was scandalously corrupt, the government spent N300 billion ($2 billion) per year on fuel subsidy. Today, it is estimated that the administration of Goodluck Jonathan spends N1.3 trillion ($8.6 billion) which is the fanciful figure being bandied about by Western media and disingenuous analysts. No one, not the loquacious governor of the Central Bank of Nigeria, Sanusi Lamido Sanusi, who thinks petrol is a luxury item; not our queen of bling, the minister of petroleum resources, Diezani Alison-Madueke, has been able to offer an explanation of how we arrived at this mind-boggling figures.

The bejeweled minster never fails to remind us that petrol costs more in neigbouring countries, a statement that ought not to be dignified with a response. Government and its spokespeople are just content peddling figures. Nobody knows the exact amount that is paid on subsidy. We do not know the exact amount of petrol Nigerians consume every day. We do not know the quantity of petrol our four refineries produce even at 25% capacity.

The insensate increase in price of petrol may turn out to be a blessing in disguise for the mass of our people. Never in the history of this country, at least not in my own lifetime, have Nigerians been more united against our rapacious ruling elite. And we have just begun! No matter how this ends, and I hope it ends in favour of the Nigerian people, the country will not be the same.

I believe this is a once-in-a-life-time opportunity. We must seize it to demand accountability from our rulers. This struggle has to go beyond the increase in the price of petrol. While demanding that the government maintains the former price of N65, the Nigeria Labour Congress (NLC), the Trade Union Congress (TUC), and their civil society allies must develop a charter of demands that the government must accede to.

That is the only thing that can give legitimacy to this government in the eyes of Nigerians. If in the months ahead, for example, there is justifiable reason(s) to increase the price of petrol, all stakeholders must agree that the increase is necessary and not because of corruption or inefficiency of government.

I have been scouring the Internet since the NlC/Occupy Nigeria protests began on January 9, 2012, and I shall attempt to briefly summarise the demands of Nigerians which should form what I call the Charter of Demands for a New Nigeria. There are so many things wrong with the Nigerian nation which cannot be corrected unless we have a new constitution which ought to emanate from a conference of "we the people".

The faulty constitution aside, we can still demand certain things from our rulers. They are supposed be to be our employees, and if they cannot do the job on our terms, they are free to resign. This is my charter and everybody is welcome to contribute to the list.

1. The government should tell Nigerians its plans for the country's four refineries and how soon they will be operational. There should be no reason for the country to import petrol by January 1, 2013.
2. There should be steady power supply across the country by the end of June 2012.
3. A 50% reduction in the salaries and allowances of political office holders until May 2015 (if they do not like it, let them resign, after all they claim they are serving us). This should take immediate effect.
4. Prosecution of those found guilty in the oil subsidy scam and immediate resumption of other cases of grand corruption.

5. An independent ombudsman that can receive complaints from Nigerians about the government, companies, and institutions, and forward same to the relevant prosecuting agencies. The ombudsman should also have the power to investigate and make public its findings.
6. A clearly defined programme to implement the Freedom of Information Act which will ensure transparency in the way government operates.

Nigeria belongs to all of us. Nobody has a greater stake or right to the country or its resources than any other Nigerian, not Goodluck Jonathan, not Lamido Sanusi Lamido, not Mohammed Adoke; certainly, not Ngozi Okojo-Iweala and not Diezani Alison-Madueke!

8. Was There a Country?
March 2012

Two compatriots have commented publicly on the title of my book, *Time to Reclaim Nigeria*. At the public presentation of the book in Abuja on December 15, 2011, the special guest, Governor, of the State of Osun, Ogbeni Rauf Aregbesola, in his presentation, "In Search of True Federalism", noted,

> *"This mission to reclaim Nigeria however is a little bit problematic. To attempt to reclaim something suggests that it was in your possession ab initio. Beginning from the forcible amalgamation in 1914, the despotism of colonial rule leading to independence in 1960, the hegemonic conspiracy of post independence military dictatorship, civilian interregnum of 1979 to 1983, the return of the military and the new era of civil rule in 1999, Nigeria has hardly ever belonged to Nigerians. To attempt to reclaim what you never had therefore is a misnomer".*

In a five-part review of the same book, eminent columnist, Edwin Madunagu, had this to say,

> "To reclaim, as I understand it, is to take back. I am aware that this ideological slogan, together with Occupy Nigeria, is now popular with radical patriots, democrats and human rights activists in Nigeria. But I doubt if the Nigerian masses had, at any time since Nigeria was created in 1914 and especially since independence in 1960, owned Nigeria".

I agree with the two positions above that the Nigerian masses have hardly owned the country. But, there is also another side of this debate about reclaiming Nigeria, which is whether we actually have a country in the true sense of the word. That is what I intend to address in this essay.

My preliminary comments about this poser is that nominally there is a country called Nigeria. That is, Nigeria meets the internationally recognized definition of a country. It has "internationally recognized boundaries, has a government, has external recognition", etc.

The *Chambers Combined Dictionary and Thesaurus* defines a country as "the land of any of the nations of the world". Going by this definition, a country presupposes a nation. The same dictionary defines a nation as "the people living in, belonging to, and together forming, a single state". Wikipedia, the online dictionary gives a more elaborate definition of a nation as "A tightly-knit group of people which share a common culture. Nations are culturally homogeneous groups of people, larger than a single tribe or community, which share a common language, institutions, religion, and historical experience".

From the preceding definition, it is clear that Nigeria is not a nation. It is also not a nation-state as some people erroneously argue. When Nigeria was created in 1914, it was not a union of the different "nations" that made up the geo-political space that came to be known as the Colony and Protectorate of Nigeria, but a merger of the two areas (the northern and southern protectorates) that had been under colonial administration for many years. In essence, the country was not created on the basis of the distinct "ethnic nationalities" in Nigeria.

What this tells us is that we needed to build a nation out of the contraption that was created in 1914. Nigeria in 1914 was like an "arrangee" marriage. Such marriages are not meant to work beyond the financial and other benefits that necessitated the union. If on the other hand, the spouses find out that they "love" each other and actually have something in common, they can build a purposeful and lasting relationship. The survival of such unions cannot be taken for granted. Those involved have to make conscious efforts to make the marriage work for it to survive.

This is exactly the position Nigeria has found itself almost a century after its creation. Beyond the fact that, to some extent, the different groups in Nigeria share a common historical experience, there has not been any conscious effort to develop a common ethos, if not a common culture or language. This phenomenon is aptly captured by Maduabuchi Dukor, Professor of philosophy at Nnamdi Azikiwe University, Awka, Anambra State, in his contribution to the Sovereign National Conference debate. According to Dukor,

> *"The concept of Nigeria since 1914 amalgamation of the north and south has phenomenologically waned socially, politically and economically. Social, religious, and ethnic conflicts constitute a life style; the political pond is characterized by the interplay of the forces of disunity where the end justifies the means; and the fiscal and economic policies of successive governments are theoretically and practically against the poor (about 75 per cent of Nigerian population)".*

Essentially, what we have witnessed since that forced marriage in 1914 is an exacerbation of the fault lines in Nigeria. It led to a military coup barely six years after independence, and a civil war followed soon after. It worsened when crude oil, because of the ease of the return on its investment, took over as the only source of income for the Nigerian state.

Today, the politics of oil looks certain to rip the country apart.

State governments and sundry groups across the country are at each other's jugular over who should get what or who controls what. But, it shouldn't be so and hasn't always been so. Agreed that the politics of oil is fundamental to the current crisis, but we will be mistaken to think that it is the only issue that threatens the survival of Nigeria because even before the commercial exploitation of oil, the country could not be said to be united any more than it is today.

Over the years, bad leadership and the attendant impoverishment of the Nigerian masses have devalued what it ought to mean to be a Nigerian. The belief of Nigerians in their country has waned considerably, not minding the occasional bout of nationalism, as for example, when the country won the gold medal in football at the 1996 Atlanta Olympics, or recently when South Africa kicked us in the gut by deporting over 100 of our citizens for allegedly possessing fake immunization papers.

Majority of Nigerians do not feel an equal possession of the space called Nigeria. The structure of Nigeria is so lopsided such that injustice, be it political, economic, or social, has become the rule rather than the exception. Statesmen are in short supply, whether we are talking about those who managed the country immediately after the civil war or those who have ruled the country as military or civilian presidents.

That explains why Generals Ibrahim Babangida and Abdulsalami Abaubakar, two ex-rulers of Nigeria, have become regional champions, spearheading a regional dialogue when they ought to be in the forefront of a national dialogue to save Nigeria.

It appears the only dialogue they want to have is a monologue.

9. Before Nigeria Implodes!
March 2012

In Sunday, February 19, 2012, The Guardian carried a frightening story with the headline "S'East, S'South, Middle Belt form Alliance". It was a report of a meeting attended by youth from the three zones and led by Alhaji Mujahid Dokubo-Asari, leader of the Niger Delta People's Volunteer Force (NDPVF).

According to the report,

> "Members of a coalition, comprising ethnic nationalities and groups from the North Central, South East and South South geo-political zones of the country, yesterday converged on Enugu to hold an all-night vigil and chart the way on how to retain political power even beyond 2015...leader of Niger Delta People's Volunteer Force (NDPVF), Asari Dokubo, led the gathering into sending a red signal to the core north, which has ruled the country for the greater part of its existence, saying the core north will no longer smell power in the capacity of a president in the nearest future".

Dokubo-Asari's strong rhetoric, we are told, is in response to "the core northern part of the country, which believes it is born to rule the country". According to him, "The plan of the coalition (Coalition of National Organisations of Nigeria) is to ensure that the leadership of the country will be retained within the three zones until the core north people who think Nigeria is for them to rule perpetually would beg to leave". With the wave of the hand, Dokubo and his cohorts contrived to excise sections of the country. If this is not a declaration of war, I do not know what else is.

What could be driving the likes of Dokubo-Asari? Perhaps, he believes he can resolve the current crisis by replacing "Hausa-Fulani hegemony" with "Ijaw-Niger Delta hegemony". It is the height of political naivety to think that because an Ijaw man is the president of the country, Dokubo-Asari and his group have the prerogative to determine which individuals or groups will or will not rule or should be part of Nigeria. Regrettably, there was no official response to these comments which the government would have termed treasonable if they came from some other groups.

In light of the tragic events of the last one year, the mayhem and mindless violence that have enveloped the country, that report was a wake-up call. We cannot afford to dismiss Dokubo-Asari. His assertion is a pointer to the danger that stares us in the face and, therefore, the need for true patriots to do something, and urgently too, not necessarily to keep Nigeria one (that task will depend on all Nigerians), but to prevent the impending tragedy.

There is no denying the fact that Nigeria has some fundamental problems. Add to these problems, the inability of our rulers to rise to the challenge of nationhood. All these have deepened the contradictions in the country and created the need for an alternative resolution mechanism such as the Sovereign National Conference (SNC).

I believe in the need to restructure Nigeria through a Sovereign National Conference, as a minimal approach to addressing the "complaints" of the various interests groups, including ethnic nationalities, that make up Nigeria. But, before we proceed, it is important that we debunk a few myths about the SNC. This has become necessary because the dominant voice for or against the SNC has been that of people who do not offer hope to the mass of our people.

Myth: The clamour for a Sovereign National Conference (SNC) is a call for the disintegration of Nigeria. **Fact:** The clamour for SNC is a response to an immediate threat that confronts us as a country. But, we can't say for certain that at the end of the day Nigeria will remain "one indivisible" country. That decision will be taken by "we the people".

Myth: Proponents of the SNC are sour election losers who seek relevance by subterfuge. **Fact:** While it is true that there are those calling for SNC because of what they can "chop", there are proponents of SNC who are genuinely interested in saving Nigeria from itself.

Myth: The National Assembly can take care of all the needs of the SNC. **Fact:** It cannot. The National Assembly itself is subject to the SNC. Nigerians have the right to determine, through the SNC, whether an entity which is famous for its inefficiency and profligacy is worth preserving.

Myth: The SNC is about ethnic nationalities that make up Nigeria and will lead to the formation of new nations like Oodua Peoples Federation, Biafra, Arewa Republic, Lower Niger Republic, Middle

Belt Federation, etc. **Fact**: It is not. As Edwin Madunagu has noted, "Nigeria is not, and has never been, the arithmetical sum of ethnic nationalities".

Myth: The constitution can take care of the needs of those calling for the SNC, especially now that there is an on-going constitutional review. **Fact**: It cannot. A nation is more than its constitution. It is only when a nation has resolved or "settled" certain fundamental issues that a constitution is put in place to take care of the details of those resolved or "settled" issues.

Now that we have laid some of the myths about the SNC to rest, let us be reminded that neither threat and arrogance nor deception and denial are helpful in this debate. When I read the report of the Dokubo-Asari-led meeting, I was reminded of the comments by that other exemplar of perfidy who told us not too long ago that he was not only ready to put on his military garb once more to go to war to defend "the unity of Nigeria", but that certain fundamental issues about Nigeria were "settled" and, therefore, not subject to discussion.

Clearly, this is not the kind of rhetoric we need at this time. To avert the imminent chaos, we necessarily must go back to the drawing board on the Nigerian project. Space won't permit me to detail the issues that have the potential of tearing the country apart, whether it is the division of the country into 19 northern states and 17 southern states, the clamour for "equitable" sharing of oil money, the link between poverty and the current state of terror, the quest for true federalism, and the desire to create pockets of theocracies in a section of the country.

The duty of progressive elements, therefore, is not to gloss over these issues, deny people the right to raise these issues or impose their own answers to the resolution of these issues. What then should be the attitude of progressives? Their attitude should be to maintain that the SNC is not a silver bullet. But, it is, short of a revolution, in the words of Madunagu, "the only viable historical option" under the present circumstance.

Genuine democrats can help negotiate the new Nigeria if they can stop charlatans and opportunists from "hijacking" the SNC debate.

That is the least they can do to prevent the imminent implosion, unless of course they are willing to be the handmaiden of tribal warlords in the not too distant future!

---

10. THE MORAL IMPERATIVE OF A SOVEREIGN NATIONAL CONFERENCE
MAY 2012

It is evident that Nigeria has been so abused to a breaking point, that the only thing that seems plausible now is a national dialogue in form of a Sovereign National Conference (SNC).

The alternatives to this national dialogue are better imagined than experienced. If there appears to be a consensus on the unity of Nigeria because it is "difficult" to split it along "ethnic" lines without resorting to wars, which I am sure no "ethnic" group is ready for, the question then becomes, how do we live peacefully in harmony so that we can build a prosperous nation, pull 99 percent of our population out of poverty, and become a global contender?

We can distinguish four strands of opinions in the SNC debate. There are those who argue that the outcome of the SNC should be, as a minimum, the splitting of the country into at least four parts. What this group is pushing for in reality is a Conference of Ethnic Nationalities (CEN) because a Sovereign National Conference in Nigeria cannot be reduced to a conference of ethnic nationalities. To use Edwin Madunagu's "wall" analogy, a wall is not the sum total of the blocks used in erecting it. If you take the wall as Nigeria, and the blocks as the different ethnic nationalities in the country, you realize that you need more than blocks to erect the wall, and once the wall has been erected, it becomes almost impossible to retrieve the individual blocks in their original state.

The next group is made up of those who like to bury their head in the sand. They argue that the unity of Nigeria should be taken for granted. They talk glibly about the indivisibility of Nigeria. They fail to realize, or refuse to accept, because it suits their immediate interest, that Nigeria is a country in name only; that what holds the country together is the state and its instrument of coercion.

The third group, made up of genuine patriots and democrats, argue that the way out of the current political, social, and economic quagmire is the quick convocation of an SNC, taking into account all the contending interests in the country. The major issue before this group is the procedure for convoking the SNC.

The fourth group on the SNC debate consists of those who argue that the problem of Nigeria is that of corruption and bad leadership. That if we tackle these problems, we will be able to eradicate poverty and would not have the kind of centrifugal pull that threatens to rip the country apart. While I agree in principle that the twin evils of corruption and bad leadership are about the greatest problems we have in Nigeria, my point of departure is that to take this position is to presume that we have a nation and it is functional.

My response to those pushing this mantra of corruption and bad leadership is that they are putting the cart before the horse. Whether we like it or not we can't deny the fact that ethnic, religious, political and social tensions exist in Nigeria. They have always been with us even though they have been heightened by poverty and underdevelopment.

It is too simplistic to argue, therefore, that once we are able to conduct "free and fair" elections, we are on our way to building a prosperous nation. While it is correct to posit that we cannot have good politics and build sustainable democratic institutions in an underdeveloped nation, it is equally important to note that the "new" leaders we envisage will not fall from the sky.

So how do we create the environment for these leaders to emerge? The answer is that as a nation, we have to develop workable and acceptable rules of political, economic and social engagement. Today, even though the constitution talks about states and geo-political zones, the country is still divided along the same fault lines that have made unity impossible and development unattainable.

Now that it is apparent that a Sovereign National Conference is one of the very few realistic and "safe options" to the "clear and present danger" facing the country, the next step is how to achieve it. Genuine democrats and progressives have the key to unraveling this mystery. Of course, it is going to be a long and arduous road. For them, political openings have been few and far between. There was an opening in 1999, unfortunately they failed to take advantage of it.

Afraid to go for power, they allowed all manner of political miscreants to take over the political space. That miscalculation set the radical movement many years backwards. Today, those mass organizations that were used as platforms for mobilization – Democratic Alternative, CDHR, United Action for Democracy, JACOM, Campaign for Democracy, etc., – have all but collapsed. If progressives had their structures in place, the oil subsidy/Occupy Nigeria protests provided a veritable opportunity for genuine democrats and humanists to attain political power and change the course of our nation's history. This shortcoming notwithstanding, the protests showed the willingness and readiness of the mass of our people to be mobilized for change.

The question is no longer whether, because the alternatives are too dire, but when and how? For those who genuinely believe in resolving the problems of the country through an SNC rather than wars, this is the time to begin to organize and mobilize. The quest for the control of the political space, to save Nigeria and bring about change, will be a difficult task because power, especially of the conservative and reactionary hue, will not concede anything.

Those who have suddenly found themselves in power are not thinking of using same to better the lives of Nigerians. Their only interest is how to consolidate and perhaps perpetuate themselves. And they will do anything to achieve their aim and ultimately imperil the nation.

We cannot continue to patch up our problems. Now is the time to reclaim Nigeria as a civic space, and humanize it. These times call for a progressive movement that confronts problems frontally.

The focus of this movement should be threefold: (1) hasten the convocation of the SNC by any means necessary (2) define the role radical patriots, genuine democrats, progressives and popular masses would play at the conference (3) define the shape of the New Nigeria we envisage.

11. Nigeria is Negotiable
August 2012

Two retired generals and former heads of state stirred the hornet's nest recently when they proffered solutions to the growing insecurity and hopelessness in the country. Coming on the heels of a war of attrition between them, there was enough reason for Nigerians to be guarded about the intervention by Olusegun Obasanjo and Ibrahim Babangida who ruled Nigeria cumulatively for 19 years.

The periods that these generals ruled (1976-79; 1985-93; and 1999-2007) were about the most glorious of the nation's history, not in terms of development or genuine attempt to redefine the future of the country, but in terms of hope and desire on the part of Nigerians to lift up their country and make it a global contender. As it turned out, Obasanjo and Babangida made sure they were the years of the locust. Obasanjo and Babangida orchestrated perhaps the greatest plunder of Nigeria, its wealth as well as its human and material resources.

Obasanjo and Babangida talked about the greatness of Nigeria and Nigerians, but they did everything possible to undermine the country and its people. They had the opportunity to write their names in gold as true statesmen, but they botched it. Of course, on the personal level, both Obasanjo and Babangida have received adequate response to their unwarranted intervention so I shall not dwell on that. I shall focus on the thrust of their intervention.

> *"Nigeria's existence not negotiable – OBJ, IBB"* was how one newspaper headlined the intercession of the retired generals the morning after. The paper reported Obasanjo and Babangida as saying that, *"The worrying trend emerging from the violent attacks, bombings and mindless killing of innocent Nigerians was creating room for doubt about the end of the carnage, but the continued unity of this nation is not only priceless, but nonnegotiable".*

I wonder what our rulers really mean when they say the "unity of

Nigeria is not negotiable". If you hear this glib talk from people who actually did something to advance the unity of Nigeria, then it is understandable. It becomes worrisome when those who advance this proposition are those who have done everything possible to undermine the unity of the country. In simple terms, "negotiable" means "open to discussion; not fixed, but able to be established or changed through discussion and compromise". Considering the current state of the nation, the social and political upheavals that go to the very core of national existence, only a masochist will deny that this is time to "negotiate" Nigeria.

A nation is usually united around a common national ethos, a set of values and principles that are abiding. Not so in Nigeria. For the ruling class in Nigeria, the only unifying factor is corruption, as one of their own, Governor Babangida Aliyu of Niger State, eloquently espoused in his speech at Chatham House, London, in June. For majority of Nigerians, the unifying factor is a life of grinding poverty and hopelessness. No country sustained by corruption and the poverty and hopelessness of its citizenry can survive for too long.

In a sense, therefore, the real threat to the unity of Nigeria has come from those who have succeeded in dividing Nigerians through their pillage and misuse of our patrimony. Our rulers know that the country is not working because of massive corruption and that we cannot sustain the current system for too long. Yet, because our elite, and in some cases ordinary Nigerians, seem satisfied with the proceeds of corruption, they are blind to the danger we are all entrapped in.

While we are nibbling at the seams of the nation, we wilfully assume that the country will still hold together and that things will get better. It is this same false hope that led us to the London Olympics after just three months of preparation. As I write, the London games are about to end without any medal hope for Nigeria. Anybody who understands Nigeria will not be surprised that this may yet be our worst Olympics.

Regrettably, our youth on whose shoulders the survival of this nation rests, appear to have imbibed the worst examples of the "wasted generation" before them. That is the real tragedy of our situation.

Just last week, the African Centre for Media & Information Literacy (AFRICMIL) held a lecture to mark the 2012 International Youth Day.

It was meant as a sober occasion for our youth, the greatest resource of our nation, to reflect on their role and contribution to national development, as well the responsibility of the government to the youth. Many of the so-called youth leaders that came for this event arrived with much fanfare, with retinues of aides in tow. All someone close by could mutter was, "If these people ever come close to power, they will do worse than our current crop of rulers".

When I look at corruption in Nigeria, our dismal showing in London, the attitude of our dehumanized and traumatized youth, and the war-mongering going on, it all makes sense to me. The conclusion I have arrived at is that it is necessary but not sufficient to do critiques of sectoral deficiencies of our problems as a nation.

Nigeria has collapsed. It is imperative, therefore, that the systemic dysfunction in Nigeria is confronted and changed to cater to all in a truly law governed country. And the only way to do this is to "negotiate" Nigeria through a Sovereign National Conference (SNC), not just of so-called ethnic nationalities, but also of marginalized and pauperized people of Nigeria.

Part of the reason corruption thrives so much in Nigeria is the structure of the country. Political violence is rife, states and ethnic nationalities are threatening secession, yet there are people who still insist that it is forbidden to question the *status quo*. Those who are concerned about Nigeria and genuinely fear that the country will break up if it goes the route of SNC, as opposed to those who mouth "The unity of Nigeria is nonnegotiable" should rest assured that it won't happen without a very bloody war or wars.

It is not exactly clear which ethnic nationality wants to embark on that futile journey. The greater prospect now is that of anarchy (as in Somalia) or the rise of fascism through what Edwin Madunagu describes as "a coalition of the most unlikely bed-follows".

What Nigeria needs now is a radical change that will redefine the country and create a new national ethos. It is for this reason that all those who have bled the country and brought it to its knees should be wary, not just of social media, but also the street anger of Nigerians.

This street anger must fester and yield positive results if we are to achieve a national renewal and end what a colleague has described as the "hackers' paradise" called Nigeria.

12. How not to Build a Nation: Reflections on Nigeria @ 52 (1)
October 2012

Except in the eyes of the extremely naive and incurable swindlers in the corridors of power, this country has already collapsed; only that the horror of its probable disintegration would be difficult to face".

This fascinating quote by journalist and activist, Godwin Onyeacholem, truly captures the Nigerian reality today. It has been 52 years in the making.

On October 1, 2012, the Nigerian State under the supervision of President Goodluck Jonathan will perform the ritual of celebrating the country's independence. It is noteworthy that the Jonathan administration has decided not to go for the pomp and circumstance associated with such celebrations which really would have added insult to our collective injury. Typical of our ruling elite, the planned sombre celebration is just another ruse, meant to pave way for a more elaborate, yet misguided, multi-billion naira celebration in 2014 to mark the centennial anniversary of the creation of Nigeria in 1914.

By every standard one decides to judge Nigeria, it has failed woefully as a nation. It is worth repeating because there are those afflicted with eternal delusions about, to use the weasel words of our politicians, "moving it forward", the way it is presently constituted. It is mere wishful thinking. No amount of fancy talk or transformational balderdash can alter the fact that Nigeria is a full-blown "kleptocracy", a state ruled by thieves, in the words of Prof. Niyi Osundare, on the way to imminent implosion.

It has been said that Nigeria is a country of great potential and promise. It remains just that after 52 years: a country of great potential and promise. The reality, to quote Chinua Achebe is that,

> *"Nigeria is not a great country. It is one of the most disorderly nations in the world. It is one of the most corrupt, insensitive, inefficient places under the sun. It is one of the most expensive countries and one of those that give least value for money. It is dirty, callous, noisy, ostentatious, dishonest and vulgar. In short, it is among the most unpleasant places on earth".*

That was almost three decades ago. We have since raised the stakes. "Today, rogues, armed robbers are in the State Houses of Assembly and the National Assembly", former President Olusegun Obasanjo – a man who ought to stand trial for his unqualified misgovernance of Nigeria – said a few months ago. Obasanjo should know. He, more than anyone else, facilitated the emergence of these scoundrels who have taken over our democratic space.

Very few countries in the world can take the unrepressed pillage, outrageous abuse and unmitigated violation which the self-acclaimed giant of Africa has received and remain standing. David Cameron, British PM, has been quoted as saying,

> *"If the amount of money stolen out of Nigeria in the last 30 years was stolen in the UK, the UK would not exist again".*

There are many figures in the public domain about how much our leaders have siphoned from the country since independence.

From Nuhu Ribadu, former Chairman of the Economic and Financial Crimes Commission (EFCC), we learnt that the amount is "more than six times the total sum that went into rebuilding Europe in the aftermath of the Second World War via the famous European

Recovery Programme, ERP programme or Marshall Plan". The ERP programme was $13billion. Interestingly, Germany, the choice location for medical care for our leaders, was one of the beneficiaries of the Marshall Plan.

We can spend the next few weeks cataloguing the problems of Nigeria and we would not have scratched the surface. Where do we start? Is it something as basic as education where it has been revealed that, "Nigerians commit about N160 billion ($1 billion) to the education of their children in Ghanaian universities every year".

A recent newspaper report quotes the Chairman, Committee of Pro-Chancellors of Nigerian Universities, Dr. Wale Babalakin, as saying "The cost excludes huge amounts also spent on education of Nigerians in other countries such as the United States of America, the United Kingdom, Canada and Malaysia".

From Dr. Babalakin we also learnt that there are about 75,000 Nigerian students in Ghana, a country which, in the last decade, has been spending up to 35 percent of its annual budget (far beyond the UNESCO recommendation of a minimum of 26 percent) on education.

Let us take a minor issue like polio eradication. Just recently, the Independent Monitoring Board (IMB) of the Global Polio Eradication Initiative (GPEI) issued a report which noted that, "Of six global sanctuaries for the poliovirus (which stand against the anticipated eradication), Nigeria's Kano and Bornu States are the most problematic".

> *"Apart from Afghanistan, Nigeria's northern region specifically constitutes major concern for global polio fighters, who now worry over the quality of local personnel and efforts. Although Kano, Bornu and four other global (problematic) spots represent a relatively tiny proportion of the earth's land surface area, the Monitoring Board had hinted that they pose disproportionate risk to the likelihood of success for the entire globe", the report noted.*
>
> *"There are now just six countries with persistent polio*

transmission. Afghanistan, Nigeria and Pakistan have never interrupted transmission. Angola, Chad and DR Congo have 're-established' polio. Nigeria has slipped back in a quite alarming way. Afghanistan's programme is consistently performing at a reasonable level".

This is a snapshot of the sorry story of Nigeria. We are not just the poster child for corruption. Whether we are talking about education, maternal or infant mortality, security, justice and rule of law, we rank at the very bottom and are constantly in competition with the world's most retrograde countries.

❖

13. HOW NOT TO BUILD A NATION: REFLECTIONS ON NIGERIA @ 52 (2)
OCTOBER 2012

The failure of Nigeria is essentially the failure of leadership. For some strange reason, it appears, we have been cursed with bad leaders right from the moment the colonialists departed 52 years ago. Unlike in places like Ghana and Tanzania, our post-independence rulers, rather than building a new nation and an egalitarian society, were more eager to replace the departing colonizers. They subsequently initiated a more malicious brand of internal colonialism from the contraption that was handed over to them.

Over the years, the quality of leadership has degenerated, breeding various vices and entrenching unparalleled corruption which has now become a directive principle of state policy. There are those who accuse "ordinary" Nigerians of complicity in this rot. A typical example would be to point to the police officer at a "road block" and conveniently say corruption is a Nigerian and, therefore, there is nothing we can do about it. I disagree. If the man on the street is corrupt, it is simply because the country's leadership has not led by example.

Where is the incentive for the policeman to be upright? Is it that his take-home pay can take him to and fro work in a month? That his children can get basic education or that his family can afford adequate medical care when they need it? Never mind that he is more likely to buy his own uniform and other paraphernalia of policing. That's after he must have paid around N200,000 ($1250) to middlemen to join the police. Meanwhile, his Inspector General is the proud owner of numerous housing estates and companies and would rank amongst the richest men in the country.

Can a people really rise above the leadership they are confronted with? Leadership is everything! Since my encounter with Chinua Achebe's book, The Trouble with Nigeria almost three decades ago, I have found it a constant companion. Achebe's book goes to the heart of the Nigerian problem. But, it is also a book that gives us hope that Nigeria is redeemable and we shouldn't give up on the country.

At his pedagogic best, Achebe wrote:

> *"The trouble with Nigeria is simply and squarely a failure of leadership. There is nothing basically wrong with the Nigerian character. There is nothing wrong with the Nigerian land or climate or water or air or anything else. The Nigerian problem is the unwillingness or inability of its leaders to rise to the responsibility, to the challenge of personal example which are the hallmarks of true leadership. Leaders are, in the language of psychologists, role models. People look up to them and copy their actions, behaviour and even mannerisms. Therefore if a leader lacks discipline the effect is apt to spread automatically down to his followers".*

Nigerians are good followers. So it is only proper that if our leaders have shown themselves to be lawless, Nigerians have learnt not to be law-abiding. Achebe talks about indiscipline on the part of our leaders. I would add impunity. Ours is a system built and sustained by impunity. Our leaders know they can do anything and get away with it.

It is their despicable philosophy of "there is no going back", "no shaking", "I dey kampe" that has brought us to where we are today. As someone noted on one of the ubiquitous social media sites, we have failed repeatedly to win any form of medal in the Olympics of leadership. And the reason is evident: Our worse eleven have always emerged each time the opportunity rears its head.

However, there is no use lamenting our leadership deficit. There is no chance things will change until the Nigerian people rise and take charge of their destiny. A little over a year ago, a "transformation train" predictably destined for disaster took off from Aso Rock, the seat of power. If Nigerians thought they had been taken for a ride by their leaders in the past, this is one bumpy ride – no pun intended – in a "One Chance" transformation bus. Every action provokes an unsurprising feeling of *deja vu*.

It has been a month since the First Lady went AWOL. There has not been any coherent or intelligent explanation from the Presidency or Bayelsa State, her official workplace. It says a lot about a regime that rode to office on the back of a president that went AWOL for months. And for those who have been hoodwinked into believing that the First Lady is not a public official, let's be reminded that she is also a permanent secretary in Bayelsa State.

For all we know, we may have a putative dictator on our hand.

> *"The demonstration in Lagos, people were given bottled water that people in my village don't have access to, people were given expensive food that the ordinary people in Lagos cannot eat. So, even going to eat free alone attracts people. They go and hire the best musician to come and play and the best comedian to come and entertain; is that demonstration? Are you telling me that that is a demonstration from ordinary masses in Nigeria who want to communicate something to government? I am hardly intimidated by anybody who wants to push any issue he has. I believe that that protest in Lagos was manipulated by a class in Lagos and was not from the ordinary people."*

That was President Jonathan – a man who came to power two years ago on the strength of public demonstrations on his behalf –

responding recently to the nationwide protests in January against the removal of so-called oil subsidy. That insensate action was premised on the theory that there was an oil cabal that was ripping off the country through the oil subsidy scheme. As it turned out, this cabal so-called is an integral part of the current administration and the ruling People's Democratic Party (PDP). Is it surprising, therefore, that nine months later, no one has been brought to justice for the billions the government freely paid out to its dubious partners in the private sector?

---

14. How not to build a nation: Reflections on Nigeria @ 52 (3)
October 2012

Having taken a critical look at Nigeria, I have also come to the conclusion that the problem of leadership which Achebe so brilliantly espoused in *The Trouble with Nigeria* is due in part to the structure of the country. 52 years after independence, we are still talking about the unity of Nigeria and whether we are one nation or not. It is this ambivalence about Nigeria – the structure and power relations – and what it means to different people and interest groups that has created a fertile ground for the large-scale plundering currently going on across the length and breadth of the country.

In essence, we do not have a nation and that is our greatest undoing. Maybe we used to have a nation, not any more. A nation is made of people with shared interests and vision. Someone commenting about Nigeria not winning an Olympic medal at the recently concluded games in London had remarked morbidly, "There used to be a country called Nigeria. For some reasons no one loved her and after hanging on desperately for resuscitation gave up the ghost. Ghosts do not compete in Olympics".

At the risk of sounding repetitious, let me state that Nigeria cannot continue on this wobbly part for too long. Something has to give. Those who had predicted 2015 as the tipping point may not be too far off the mark considering the fraud being perpetrated in the name of governance.

This rudderless government has created room for a political frenzy that portends only one thing: a serious threat to the survival of Nigeria. But, the problem is not so much the fault of the present administration. It is really about the structure of Nigeria and who controls power at the centre because that person or group controls everything.

Of all people, one of those who have played no small part in bringing Nigeria to this sorry state, Atiku Abubakar, perhaps in a momentary fit of catharsis, voiced complaints at a recent function in Abuja about the scandalously limitless powers wielded by anyone who occupies the presidential seat in Nigeria. He referred specifically to President Jonathan as the most powerful president in the world.

With the scales now cleared from his eyes, the former vice president says there is something wrong in a system that preserves this aberration. It is doubtful if he would have publicly expressed this same sentiment were he in Jonathan's shoes. In spite of the messenger, this reaction is a measure of the growing irritation with power relations and the structure of governance in the country.

Everybody is jockeying for the presidency. The South-south insists it deserves a second shot at the presidency in 2015. For the Southeast, the presidency in 2015 is nonnegotiable; and for the north, the region must produce the president in 2015.

Add to this the declaration of independence and secession by various groups as well as the political and religious violence and banditry that are routine across the country and you have a recipe for disaster. But, this is just a snapshot of the political power play for the soul of Nigeria as we inch towards 2015. And it is because of one thing: oil. Everyone wants their share and they would do anything to get it.

Remove oil and the party is over. Everyone will go home. The corruption and mind-boggling looting and primitive accumulation currently going on will cease. If our governors had to tax their citizens or generate fund internally to sustain their states, chances are that they will not so easily and freely loot their state treasuries.

And, of course, if there isn't excess money accruing from states to the federal government, the president, first lady, ministers, senators, reps and sundry political office holders, will have very little to steal from. Oil and the "free" money accruing from it is the reason our leaders are so distant from the people.

Unfortunately, the people themselves have taken a "siddon look" approach. We really do not see the billions stolen everyday as our money because it is not coming directly from your pockets. We talk about corruption and the theft of our patrimony so distantly. "Let them continue to steal oil money, one day the oil go finish", is the common refrain.

Of course, our leaders are too glad to brazenly help themselves to the "national cake". The only time there is a problem is when the quarterly allocation does not come on time. Like bandits, the other concern is the sharing formula. You will never hear them talk about revenue generation.

It is for this same reason that politics has become the only real job in Nigeria today. Nobody who comes near government wants to leave. A minister today, a senator tomorrow; a governor today, a senator or presidential candidate tomorrow. Once you steal enough money as a councillor, you aspire to be a local government chairman.

Once you make it big as a chairman, you aspire to the state assembly or house of representatives. From there, you steal enough to make you emerge as a senator/minister with an eye on the governorship of your state. And when you steal enough to emerge as governor, you empty the state treasury to enable you run for president or better still stash it overseas.

Of course, I can relate with people who are frustrated with President Jonathan and are looking for the next person to fix our problem. But, as I noted earlier, our problem goes beyond President Jonathan, even though a bit of sincerity and some action on his part can help.

When a car has a bad engine, I do not think the preoccupation should be how to find a good driver. What this points to is that the Nigerian society is overdue for a social and political revolution to redefine its future.

Nothing in Nigeria today works according to any logic of a modern society. Virtually every sector of the Nigerian society – National Assembly, tertiary education, judiciary, law enforcement, etc., – has collapsed. The greater tragedy is we don't even realize it.

Perhaps, the problem is that we expect too much from professional politicians and the current crop of leaders so-called. We still have hope and expect them to give us good roads, health care, quality education, security, etc. They simply will not do it. It is just not on their radar, even when they see and enjoy these amenities in other countries.

15. How not to Build a Nation: Reflections on Nigeria @ 52 (4)
October 2012

As a nation, a couple of possibilities stare at us. One is the possibility of a military takeover. As much as we hate it, the prospect looms large. However, it is one option, no matter how tempting, that Nigerians should not condone. Understandably, Nigerians are going through a lot and anything but the present order will do.

As Edwin Madunagu cautions, we should be wary of the emergence of a fascist movement (it could come to power "legally", by "electoral means" or some other means) that deceptively looks like radical populism and whose historical mission is to block a genuine revolution of the people. It will ride on the "deteriorating socio-economic situation, widespread poverty, social divisions, insecurity (physical and economic) and mass discontent".

Another possibility is that the country could descend into anarchy and witness an implosion. Neither option serves the interest of the mass of our people whose sweat and blood have largely sustained the country so far. If it is clear that we do not have a nation and that the options open to us are very few, how then do we begin the process of creating a nation – a land of freedom, justice, and opportunities – before it is too late.

Short of a Sovereign National Conference (SNC), I do not see any other realistic option that can save Nigeria. Our so-called lawmakers have nothing to fear about the word SOVEREIGN. The conference will not rob them of their redundant, freeloading status as "distinguished senators" and "honourables". The envisaged conference will be sovereign only to the extent that its resolutions will not be turned over to the legislature or the presidency or any other body for that matter for approval.

That way, the Nigerian people would have spoken about how they want to be governed. And those who hold the levers of power, to whom the responsibility of governance is entrusted, are not to act contrary to the people's expectation. This, in my view, is the first step towards truly creating a Nigeria of everyone's choice. There are those who have talked about political reform and a new constitution. These are mere cosmetic changes that do not get to the heart of our problem. As Prof. Chinweizu noted,

> *"Many of the deadly problems plaguing Nigeria are maintained by the provisions of the constitution as well as the structures it has set up. Therefore, tackling many of Nigeria's problems would require a comprehensive critique and gutting of the constitution in which they are rooted".*

Essentially, political reform and a new constitution would emerge after there has been a national consensus on the structure of country and the power relations between different groups and interests.

I believe in the territorial integrity of Nigeria and I think it would be foolhardy to tamper with it. I also believe in justice and equity which are sorely lacking in Nigeria today. We may not have been the same "tribe or nation" from the outset as some people have noted, but living in and travelling across Nigeria has shown me that the things that unite us are far greater than those that divide us; that after living together for almost 100 years and going through a bloody civil war, we can build a country of shared opportunities and vision, a perfect union, if we can isolate and defang the ethnic chauvinist, religious bigots and political swindlers in our midst.

We can't take the unity of the country for granted. That is why I believe the SNC still offers the best possible way out of the current imbroglio. I do not think many of those clamouring for the SNC have a problem with the geographical space called Nigeria. Their desire is that the relationship between those who inhabit it be negotiated and agreed upon. It is important that we do this to ease the fear, tension, anger, frustration as well as political and religious violence that stalk the land.

While we clamour for the SNC, we must necessarily distinguish it from a conference of ethnic nationalities because, in the words of Edwin Madunagu, "Nigeria is more than the sum total of its ethnic nationalities". We can distinguish two broad opponents of the SNC: those who want to main the *status quo*. They are the first to mouth the slogan, "The unity of the country is not negotiable".

For many of them like Gen. Ibrahim Babangida whose misrule precipitated the current crisis, any discussion about SNC amounts to talking about the disintegration of Nigeria, never mind that the country is already on the brink. Then, there is the other group that appears genuinely concerned about Nigeria, but worry about such inconsequential details as, "How do we convoke the SNC?"

Ideally, in a sovereign conference of the people, there should be no "no go areas"; nothing is sacrosanct! But I shall go ahead and propose a compromise position if only to reassure those who are genuinely concerned about Nigeria but worry that the SNC could lead to its disintegration. Before we go into the conference, we can, without prejudice to the resolutions that will emerge, agree on three fundamental things: maintain the territorial integrity of Nigeria; ensure its secularity; and guarantee equal citizenship rights to every Nigerian wherever he or she may be in Nigeria.

Once we agree on these fundamentals, we should go into the conference with an open mind to discuss everything else, including the vexed issues of revenue sharing/allocation and the political structure of the country. My take on the revenue problem is simple: states should keep 50% of the revenue accruing from their states from natural resources, taxes, etc. 30% should go to the national government and

20% to a special fund (jointly supervised by all the states) for emergency/crisis situation anywhere in the country.

On the political structure, it seems we have a very tidy arrangement with the current geo-political structure. My only addition will be that for balance and equity, every geo-political zone should have seven states for a total of 42 states. We should dissolve the 774 local governments and allow states to create their own councils as needed. I support the call by former governor of Lagos State, Asiwaju Bola Tinubu, for the scrapping of the Senate. The unicameral National Assembly should be made up five representatives from each state (42 states) for a total of 210 members, who will operate on a part-time basis. The states would have to decide how to elect their representatives.

As for representation for the conference, here is a sample arrangement: two representatives from every ethnic nationality, not withstanding its size and population; one representative from each senatorial district; two representatives from each recognized professional body: NMA, NBA, NLC, NUJ, TUC, NUT, etc.; five representatives from the National Youth Council of Nigeria (NYCN); five representatives from the National Association of Nigerian Students (NANS); five representatives from the National Council of Women Societies (NCWS); five representatives from civil society/NGOs; five representatives from Nigerians in Diaspora, etc.

These organizations are to decide how to choose their representatives. All that is required now is for these groups to start educating their members about the inevitability and benefits of the SNC and how they will be represented effectively.

One last thing: instead of subjecting our children to learning every language in vogue (Chinese for now), the conference should explore the possibility of developing a national language to create a truly national identity.

These suggestions are not inviolable. They are meant to spur a national conversation on the future of our country. Suffice to say that for those who genuinely want to save Nigeria, time is running out!

16. Piracy as Democracy
November 2012

For those who know the level of graft, not only in our oil industry, but also the gamut of the Jonathan administration, there is nothing surprising about the report of the Nuhu Ribadu-led Petroleum Revenue Special Task Force. What is surprising is that it took so long for the committee's report to be made "public". If anything, the report confirms what we already know: that our brand of democracy is nothing but plain-faced piracy.

Considering the contradictory views from the government, chances are that if the report did not come to us through Reuters, it may not have seen the light of day. Now the government, through its handlers, has gone into overdrive in its effort at damage control and convince us that there was no attempt at cover-up.

The government headlined its response through its spokesperson, Reuben Abati, an attempt to embarrass the Presidency, as if anything could embarrass the Jonathan administration. Except, of course, the government is complicit in the damning indictment as contained in the committee's report, I do not know how the report of a committee set up by the government to review the activities of a particular sector, should constitute an embarrassment.

It appears the government is more concerned about managing the so-called leakage than the findings of the committee's report. Abati said the excerpts from the report could not be taken as an official document because the committee had not formally submitted its report to the appropriate authority. I agree with him. But, he went ahead to expose himself by saying "as far as the Federal Government was concerned, the report in the public domain was suspicious". What makes it suspicious? Is it because it was revealed by the media?

According to Abati, "It is strange that government will set up a committee, that report has not been submitted to the authorities that set up the committee and the report will be found on the pages of newspapers". There is nothing strange about this. Abati is a newspaperman and he ought to know better.

When the President's Senior Special Assistant on Public Affairs, Doyin "the-attack-lion" Okupe, weighed in (no pun intended) he offered this explanation,

> "What appears to have been irregularly released prematurely to the media is a draft copy which still requires full assent of all members of the committee and clarifications and due process from the originating ministry before the official handing over to the Presidency".

And to clear any doubts, he reminded us that,

> "President Jonathan's resolve to fight corruption and dig out all the rot in the system should not be misconstrued or politicized by the opposition as if it is his administration that is guilty of corruption, rather, he should be commended for taken the bold step that will ultimately sanitize the polity and the system".

Much earlier, the country's controversial Minister of Petroleum Resources and de facto vice president, Diezani Alison-Madueke, while reacting to the publication by Reuters had described the report as a draft and that a committee had been set up by the Ministry of Petroleum Resources to look into the "differences in perspective on the Ribadu committee report" and make an "input". Alison-Madueke who acknowledged receiving the same report last month and failed to act on it, said the new committee "will complete its work and submit a comprehensive report in the next 10 days".

Interestingly, Alison-Madueke's "next ten days" coincides with Friday, November 2, 2012, the day the President directed that the Ribadu committee report be submitted to him. We eagerly await the version of the report that will be submitted to the President: the real report or the one with "input" from the Minister of Petroleum Resources.

The Ribadu committee report, amongst other things, revealed that $183m signature bonuses from seven discretionary oil licences awarded by petroleum ministers between 2008 and 2011 were missing. Three of these "sweetheart deals" occurred from 2010 when

Alison-Madueke was appointed Minister of Petroleum Resources.

The report also noted that multi-national oil companies, Shell, Total and Eni, made "bumper profits from cut-price gas", at the expense of Nigerians "while Nigerian oil ministers handed out licences at their own discretion".

Writing on this issue, under the title: "Looting Nigeria to Death: Piracy as Democracy", social activist, Jaye Gaskia, noted,

> *"It is important to emphasize that there is no way this scale and scope of corruption could have been perpetrated and perpetuated without the connivance and collaboration of officials of state institutions, including ministries, departments and parastatals.*
>
> *"It is inconceivable that the current Minister of Petroleum Resources and chairperson of the board of NNPC is still in office, not sacked and facing prosecution along with the NNPC board after all these revelations! It is unthinkable that all the previous petroleum ministers over the last 10 years have not yet been arrested and are not facing prosecution along with all previous Group Managing Directors and boards of the NNPC! How can any government and any political elite be comfortable with the loss of over $100bn in 10 years to corrupt practices, if such a regime and political elite is not complicit in the fraud in the first place?"*

Gaskia's intervention, in a sense, explains why nothing will come out of the Ribadu committee report. This regime and our political elite are complicit in the unmitigated piracy that has left Nigeria comatose. Asking the Jonathan administration to act on the Ribadu committee report is simply asking it to indict itself. It will not happen!

To hazard a guess, the President will receive a version of the committee's report on November 2, and in his usual belaboured response to such revealing probes, thank the committee for doing a great job. He will promise vainly, in line with his fuzzy transformation agenda, that the committee's recommendations will be addressed. And then, pretending commitment to due process, he will set up a committee to produce a White Paper on the report. A committee will then be set up to review the findings of the White Paper.

The report will then be submitted to the Senate Committees on Petroleum (Upstream) and Gas for further investigations. The Chairman, Senate Committee on Gas, Nkechi Nwogu, has already expressed her committee's interest in looking at the report "to find out the true position of things as contained in it". Her committee's report will then be submitted to the Senate Committee on Anti-corruption, a committee whose members parade a rap sheet that will put the legendary Lawrence Anini and his sidekick, Monday Osunbor, to shame. Depending on their inclination, the report will then go back to the Presidency or any of our anti-corruption agencies for safekeeping.

Damn the opposition for playing politics with a serious national issue. Now, we will never know those responsible for this mess much less get them to account for their misdeed!

17. NIGERIA WON'T BREAK UP
JANUARY 2013

How many times have we heard the expression "Nigeria won't break up"? This clichéd expression has become the chorus of Nigeria's ruling elite; an elite that will not raise a finger to defend the territorial integrity of Nigeria if it becomes necessary to do so.

Like every bankrupt ruling class, ours never ceases to find an opportunity to proclaim its commitment to the country and her unity. One such opportunity offered itself a few days ago during the Inter-Denominational Church Service to mark the 2013 Armed Forces Remembrance Day Celebrations at the National Christian Centre in Abuja.

The Armed Forces Remembrance Day, also known as Remembrance Day, was celebrated on November 11 to coincide with the

Remembrance Day for veterans of World War II in the British Commonwealth of Nations. The date was changed to January 15, in commemoration of the surrender of Biafran troops to the Federal troops on January 15, 1970, an action that ended the Nigerian Civil War.

January 15 is also remembered for another important event in Nigeria's tortuous road to democratic governance and nationhood. It was on that day, 47 years ago, that the first of many military coups took place, ending the country's First Republic.

It is understandable, therefore, if presidential emotions run high on Remembrance Day. While lauding the Armed Forces and other security service for their efforts to "keep the nation one and in peace" the president assured Nigerians that the country would not break up. "Some people talk about disintegration of Nigeria, now even at political levels some people take it as a weapon…when they want to discuss politics. But my conviction and I believe that of most people here and those listening to us, is that Nigeria will continue to remain a united nation", the president averred.

Two months ago, at the height of the debate about another petrol price increase, the president had likened the pains Nigerians were experiencing to a boil on the face of a five-year-old girl. Then, he had suggested surgery for the little girl with an assurance that, "If she bears the pain and does the incision and treats it, after some days or weeks, the child will grow up to be a beautiful lady". The president was saying in essence that Nigerians should be ready to bear the pain of his government's agonizing policies.

This time around, President Jonathan likened Nigeria to a 100-year-old marriage, which, in his wisdom, is indissoluble. "Nigeria will not disintegrate…I know Nigeria will remain one", the president assured his audience.

> *"In 2014 we will celebrate our centenary, 100 years in existence. It will only take two mad people to stay in marriage for 100 years and say that is the time you will divorce and we are not mad. If there are issues that have been brewing over the period and we have been managing, we will continue to manage".*

I wonder why the president keeps coming up with these crude comparisons. First, there are not many people in the world who live up to 100 years and there are even fewer who are married for that long. Even if we assume that the president was speaking metaphorically, there is no law that says people who have been married for so long cannot go their separate ways. You do not have to be mad to divorce after being married for a long time. Sacrifice, yes, but marriages survive based on trust, love and respect, not because of how long. No marriage can survive for too long if it is based on abuse, neglect and deprivation.

Mr. President, we cannot continue to manage after over five decades of independence and almost a century of amalgamation and billions of dollars in earnings. Every Nigerian, including those whose actions have brought the country to its knees, has become a professional "manager". No country can survive if it continues patching rather than fixing the long-term structural problems that continue to hold down its progress.

Waxing patriotic, President Jonathan had this to say about the motherland:

> "I always say that Nigeria is great not because of our oil, because we have people that produce more oil than us but we are appreciated and still reckoned with because of our size and diversity both for human beings and environment. These are areas we should exploit for unity and development".

Mr. President, I hate to be the bearer of bad news, but the reality is that Nigeria is only great in our imaginations. Nigeria is big for nothing! We are not respected in the comity of nations; our citizens are mistreated around the world, sometimes because of their actions, and other times simply because they have a green passport. What is there to respect? Even with the abundance of human and natural resources, we have one of the highest maternal mortality rates in the world.

We are ranked amongst the most corrupt nations in the world and we are in competition with Afghanistan, Chad, Angola, DR Congo and Pakistan, for countries with persistent polio transmission. To our eternal shame, while Afghanistan's polio programme has been described as "consistently performing at a reasonable level", Nigeria's "has slipped back in a quite alarming way".

That President Jonathan – like those before him – has to use every opportunity to proclaim "Nigeria won't break up" is reflective of the state of our union. Forty-three years after the civil war ended, we have a virtual war on our hand. The same issues that existed before the civil war began are still with us, except that today they have grown worse.

The president is unable to visit certain parts of the country; fiends are murdering at will in the name of religion; militancy has become profitable; armed robbers and "freelance assassins" prowl the country while kidnapping has become a lucrative profession; poverty, anger and disillusionment are rife; and our corrupt public officials have graduated from 10% to 150% kickback.

What this means is that our rulers, and their collaborators in the private sector, have become so brazen that contractors are guaranteed to receive full payment for a contract that was never started, much less completed. And they are entitled to an additional half of the total contract sum after a review of the contract in line with the rate of inflation.

Indeed, we are witnessing a scenario worse than the country breaking up. The real fear should not be the country breaking up because that is a harder and much longer route to travel. The real fear is the possibility that anarchy will envelop the country and we will go the route of Somalia, the poster child of failed states.

The president admonishes "us all (to) stand up and condemn those who say otherwise about our unity. Those who call for our disintegration or who make similar statements should be condemned by all Nigerians". I agree with the president. Now also is the time for all Nigerians, including the president, to rise up in one voice and condemn those ills that breed terrorism, anger, disillusionment, poverty and threaten the unity of the country. Ills like corruption, abuse of power and suppression of the rule of law.

Ultimately, Nigerians would have to take control of their destiny and decide the shape of things to come. If in the end the country survives the doomsday prophesy, it will not be because the present administration has done anything to stem the slide.

SECTION FIVE

2015 And all that jazz

1. 2015 And all that jazz
May 2012

Shortly after President Goodluck Jonathan was sworn in on May 29, 2011, I noted that his government should at best be a transitional regime and that unless something was done, and urgently too, Goodluck Jonathan would be the last president of Nigeria. One year into the administration, I am even more convinced about my proposition. My conviction hinges on the mad struggle for 2015 that has enveloped the nation.

Let me say from the outset that I have a problem with those who are obsessed with "overthrowing" President Jonathan and taking over in 2015. It shows two things: a lack of understanding of the quandary we are in as a nation; and the lack of forthrightness to confront our problems. The bashing and loathing of the shoeless lad from Otuoke who has made it all the way to Aso Rock is troubling to say the least. Troubling in the sense that it distracts us from the current task which is how to reclaim Nigeria.

This piece is not a defence of President Jonathan and the reason is simple: no matter how hard you try, you will find it impossible to conjure something in praise of the current administration. The president himself has rightly admitted that the problems of the country did not start with his government. That he reminds Nigerians of this is a subtle way of saying he is helpless and that we should look for the solution somewhere else.

As we draw nearer to 2015, the apocalypse as some have described it, we need to take a step back and understand "where the rain started beating us", to quote Prof. Chinua Achebe's popular proverb. The stakes are being raised each day. The battle for the soul of Nigeria is on. If the recent statement credited to Chief Edwin Clark, the president's alter ego, is anything to go by, then we can conclude that President Goodluck Jonathan will contest the 2015 presidential election. The argument is not in favour of the teeming population condemned to a life of poverty under the current system; it is simply that the country's ethnic minorities are also entitled to two-terms of four years.

Gen. Muhammadu Buhari (retd.) the presidential candidate of the Congress for Progressive Change (CPC) in the 2011 election has warned that there will be "trouble" if the 2015 elections are rigged. Of course, the elections would be rigged. There is no possibility of free and fair elections in Nigeria just yet. The Independent National Electoral Commission (INEC) is neither independent nor committed to credible elections. INEC under Professor Attahiru Jega has become a huge joke and an embarrassment and nothing but the handmaiden of the ruling party, the People's Democratic Party (PDP), notorious for election rigging.

Our regional gladiators are at their atavistic best. In late 2010, Alhaji Lawal Kaita, a founding member of the PDP, responding to the possibility of President Goodluck Jonathan emerging as the presidential candidate of the PDP in the 2011 election, had remarked: "The North is determined, if that happens, to make the country ungovernable for President Jonathan or any other Southerner who finds his way to the seat of power on the platform of the PDP against the principle of the party's zoning policy".

Alhaji Lawal Kaita has upped the ante. Only recently, he told his audience: "We hear rumours all over that Jonathan is planning to contest in 2015. Well, the North is going to be prepared if the country remains one. That is, if the country remains one, we are going to fight for it. If not, everybody can go his way".

Alhaji Kaita was, perhaps, speaking the mind of the so-called northern establishment. Following on the heels of that provocative and treasonable statement, the amorphous group known as the Northern Governors' Forum (NGF) rose from its meeting in Kaduna and declared through its spokesperson, Gov. Babangida Aliyu of Niger State, that, "The North would not allow the 2015 presidency to elude it".

> "We must be united more than ever to go into the 2015 elections as one entity with the aim of producing the President", Gov. Aliyu vowed on behalf of his colleagues. While the northern governors are salivating at the prospects of one of them becoming president in 2015, a section of the North, specifically the Middle Belt, says if the presidency

must come to the North it should come to them, thus betraying the seeming "unity of the North".

For the President-General of Ohanaeze Ndigbo, Ambassador Raph Uwechue, a president of Igbo extraction in 2015 "is not a favour waiting to be granted, but a logically due and legitimate political right justly accruing to it (Ndigbo) within the Nigerian family in a true 'federal character' setting".

Regrettably, in the midst of these geo-political permutations, the ordinary citizen is lost and forgotten. But, as President Jonathan has shown, the problem of Nigeria is not where the rulers come from. No matter the zone the next president comes from, if there is no serious effort to tinker with the structure of the Nigerian federation, we will only be moving one step forward and two steps backward.

Just as I was rounding off this piece, I came across an interview Mallam Nasir El-Rufai, former minister of the Federal Capital Territory and stalwart of the CPC, granted Premium Times, an online journal. El-Rufai took a swipe at the Jonathan administration as usual and predicted that the country might not "get to 2015 unless those in power change their strategy". Some people have taken the former minister to task on his recent posturing. Their argument is that he was an integral part of the shenanigans of the Obasanjo era, including the massively rigged elections of 2003 and 2007 that brought us to this sad end.

It is hard to fault this argument. However, the former minister raised a fundamental issue in the interview which we can't ignore no mater our disposition toward the messenger. He averred that Nigeria is a federation only in name; that a federation means having federating units that are strong and independent of the centre. He went as far as saying that we should revert to the era (1963 constitution) when states (sic) controlled half of the revenue that accrued to them internally. Well said! My only addition would be that El-Rufai and other members of the ruling class who share his forward-looking view should put their money where their mouth is, and really support the clamour for true federalism.

The cacophony of voices we hear about 2015 can be linked to the structural defect of the country. If states stop depending on handouts from Abuja, nobody will be interested in who presides over the country. How do we strengthen the federating units of the federal republic so that they can contribute to the centre, rather than depend on it?

Governors are clamouring for a review of the revenue sharing formula while very little attention is paid to how their states can generate revenue to be self-reliant. But, it is not just the politics of revenue (specifically petroleum) sharing that oils the current crisis. Equally troubling is the secularity or lack of it of the Nigerian federation.

These are the two issues genuine patriots and democrats should be fixated on as we head towards 2015. Nigerians need to prioritize and choose between our fixation on 2015 and hoping against hope that the 2015 election will be free and fair and building a strong, diverse, and united federal republic. Whether we want to achieve it through a Sovereign National Conference or a new constitution of "we the people", the urgent task before all true patriots is to look beyond the current regime if they want to save Nigeria.

I believe in Nigeria, but I also share the illuminating view of my friend and colleague, Godwin Onyeacholem, that, "Except in the eyes of the extremely naive and incurable swindlers in the corridors of power, this country has already collapsed; only that the horror of its probable disintegration would be difficult to face".

---

2. In defence of President Jonathan?
September 2012

First, a caveat: I agree with Reuben Abati. President Jonathan "is a grossly misunderstood President".

It is understandable though if the shoeless and homeless mass of our people who voted for him last year expect a lot from him. That is the least they should expect from a man who claimed he was once like them, but whose presidency has become a nightmare for majority of Nigerians. Having said that, I must also note that I seriously want to "wean" myself from criticizing President Jonathan and his administration and I shall explain why.

Sometime last year, I had predicted that considering the bumbling character of his presidency, President Jonathan may well be Nigeria's last president. A few months ago, I did an article titled "2015 and all that Jazz" which sought to address those I thought were fixated on 2015 to the detriment of the fundamental challenges facing our nation.

After the piece appeared in the papers, a friend and former colleague, an assistant professor at an American university, sent me this thoughtful response:

> "I found your Guardian piece illuminating as usual. Allow me to disagree with you on one of the finer points in an otherwise very thoughtful piece, which is about what our collective attitude towards GEJ and his administration should be. You are right indeed that we need to be more attentive to substantive issues like our steadily eroding federalism, and the creeping loss of basic secular guarantees in the constitution. I don't know of any right thinking Nigerian who will dispute that.
>
> "But I disagree with you that GEJ himself ought to be ignored because, as you argue, he is merely a transitional figure. There are at least two problems with this. One is that GEJ hardly sees himself as a transitional figure. He may have all the bumbling rhetoric of one, but his performances and politics are those of someone who actively yearns to be in power. Second, GEJ is our president right now, and for good or ill, his actions are determinative of our economic and political trajectories for the foreseeable future.
>
> "These are two of the many reasons why GEJ, transitional or not, ought to be taken quite seriously and engaged with. He is the president of Nigeria at one of the most interest-

ing conjunctures in the country's history, yet there is nothing to give an assurance that he really understands the rudimentaries of governance, apart from the kind of shallow and demeaning politicking that the Nigerian political class, emblemized by the PDP, has perfected.

"This is my cent's worth. Rest assured that I do not hold GEJ responsible for all our country's problems. That one needs to always enter that caveat these days is itself evidence of the depths to which public discourse in our country has fallen. My point is that since the man craves the office so much, the least that we can do is hold him accountable to its loftiest expectations. Congrats on a great piece".

This was my reply:

"Thanks for your mail and sorry for the late response. Been busy with the programme of tributes for our friend, Olaitan Oyerinde. Where do I start? I agree with you completely that Jonathan should be held to account. I was a bit concerned doing this piece; even the Jonathan people might construe it as 'support' for them.

"I don't have any problem with some of us who criticize Jonathan because we are sincere about our criticism. Where it gets a bit unnerving is when the criticism comes from those (and they are in the majority or better still they are more vocal) whose only interest is to take over from Jonathan. And it is to those people that the part of the piece you referenced is addressed. By all means, let's criticize Jonathan (and he deserves all of it and more) because his government has been tragic to say the least.

"But at the same time, we shouldn't fall into the trap of hoping that any of these charlatans who are getting ready *for 2015 will do any better than Jonathan. Our strategy, therefore, should be twofold. While we must hold Jonathan accountable as the president of the country, we should not lose sight of the fact that the structure of the country is flawed fundamentally. And until the restructuring takes place, for me, any government that emerges can only be transitional at best!*

"Of course Jonathan doesn't see himself as a transitional leader because, 1) he does not understand his role in the current scheme of things; 2) he does not have the capacity or presence of mind to appreciate the enormity of the problems facing us; and 3) he and his cronies are too preoccupied with looting to want to give up and they are ready to drag us all down.

"My worry, therefore, is that if we get consumed in "chasing" Jonathan, we may all sadly end up abdicating the urgent task before us which is to save this country. Jonathan can't save Nigeria and if we are not careful, it will disintegrate before our very eyes. When that happens, Jonathan and his Dame will jump into any of the numerous presidential jets to an undisclosed location.

"The other side of this argument which will buttress my point is the argument that the military should take over. Some people (including those in civil society) have started making the call. As enticing as this appears (if it will get rid of all these rogue politicians), it does not help us in any way. I see it as a shortcut to arriving at the solution.

Even though shortcuts can be useful sometimes, this particular shortcut is strewn with landmines. It simply means taking power from one rapacious group and handing it to another. At the end of the day, we would have given up our rights to govern ourselves. I guess what I am saying is that we need to address the question of power! Thanks my brother for finding time to reflect on my piece. Let's continue the discussion".

That was four months ago. Nothing has changed. It seems to me that until we devise ways to frontally confront this rogue state called Nigeria and those who superintend it (for now President Jonathan), we will continually be derided as "idle and idling, twittering, collective children of anger, distracted crowd of Facebook addicts, BBM-pinging soap opera gossips of Nigeria, who seem to be in competition to pull down President Goodluck Jonathan".

Thank God for President Jonathan. His incompetence and incapacity has brought to the fore and further exacerbated the national question. There couldn't be a better time to bring down this house – by any means necessary!

---

3. 2015: Let the Race Begin
January 2013

If there was any lingering doubt that campaigns for the 2015 presidential election have started in earnest, that doubt was erased with the emergence last week of the Jonathan 2015 campaign posters. The audaciousness of that action and the feeble response from the Presidency to the effect that the president is "pre-occupied with working to fix Nigeria and did not want to be distracted by undue politicking about 2015", are all too typical of the People's Democratic Party's brand of democracy.

For those who cringed and raged about the appointment a few weeks ago of octogenarian, Tony Anenih, a man who ordinarily should be in an old people's home, as chairman of the board of the Nigeria Ports Authority (NPA), that selection is beginning to make sense.

President Jonathan has said publicly that he will not think about

2015 until next year. This disclaimer comes even as his aides keep reassuring us that, "The wonderful performance of Jonathan at the end of the tenure would make most Nigerians to compel him to run in 2015". That was the decisive argument.

It does not matter whether the president thinks about it now or in 2014, "Nigerians are going to applaud him and even if he does not want to run for election, Nigerians are going to force him to run again because of the level of performance". That is according to Doyin Okupe, the Special Assistant to the President on Public Affairs.

In the last few months, President Jonathan has had occasions to trumpet his democratic credentials, all with an eye to the 2015 election. After the governorship election in Ondo State on October 20, 2012, Reuben Abati, the president's spokesman, reminded us that,

> "The President would naturally have wanted his party, the PDP, to win the governorship election in the state, the fact that he has never abused the enormous powers of the Presidency to influence the outcome of elections shows that he is a man of his words, a committed democrat and a President who believes in the rule of law and the supremacy of the will of the people".

Shortly before the US presidential election on November 6, 2012, Abati wrote,

> "This should mean something to us in Nigeria, and in the larger African community, for it is at the centre of President Goodluck Jonathan's Transformation Agenda. It is the same electoral ethic that President Jonathan has insisted upon since his assumption of office as President. Nigerians, long used to a political situation in which the privilege of incumbency confers all powers have seen under President Jonathan's watch, a completely different arrangement. It used to be the case in this land, that all that was required of an incumbent in the position of a President or Governor was to sit back and assume that incumbency will confer automatic re-election, and if the incumbent

managed to stir at all, he did so with so much arrogance. Most of the time, this worked. The incumbent bullied and forced his way through to a second term".

Beyond this rhetoric, however, there is nothing the Jonathan administration has done to advance the integrity of the electoral process in Nigeria. Recall that after the 2007 presidential election that saw the selection of Umaru Yar'Adua as president (and Goodluck Jonathan as vice president), President Yar'Adua was humble enough to acknowledge the electoral heist and travesty that brought him and his deputy to power.

Three months after he was sworn in, on August 28, 2007, he set up a 22-member Electoral Reform Committee (ERC) headed by retired Justice Muhammadu Lawal Uwais, to "examine the entire electoral process with a view to ensuring that we raise the quality and standard of our general elections and thereby deepen our democracy".

The ERC made far-reaching recommendations aimed at guaranteeing the independence of the Independent National Electoral Commission (INEC) and safeguarding the electoral process. Rather than addressing the salient issues raised by the ERC, as a first step toward deepening our democracy, President Jonathan has conveniently discarded the report and left the electoral process to run on autopilot.

Shortly after the 2011 presidential election, in an article titled "When Democracy Insults", I took Jonathan's INEC to task on its avowed commitment to free and fair elections. I wrote,

> *"When a court ruled that INEC was the only body with the authority to fix the order of election, after President Jonathan had colluded with the National Assembly to subvert that power, why did INEC appear helpless? The lame excuse the commission offered was that ballot papers had been printed, as if that had any bearing on the date the election would take place".*

That action which amounted to holding the electoral process to ransom – and the massive infusion of fund, way beyond anything Nigerians could have imagined – led to "victory" for President

Jonathan and the PDP. It is the same confidence of their ability to manipulate the electoral process that President Jonathan and the PDP will ride on to contest the 2015 election. The scenario above, minus the money factor, may not be the trump card this time around, but rest assured they have their plan well laid out.

It is in this context that we should view the mysterious appearance of the Jonathan 2015 posters described as the work of "mischief makers who want to deceive Nigerians". That statement actually fits the PDP because that is exactly what the party has done since 1999. I have brought this up to show that Jonathan and the PDP will do anything to remain in power, not minding what Nigerians want. It also comes as a warning to the opposition. It is with this in mind that the opposition should approach 2015 knowing that they are not fighting against "flesh and blood".

As I write, there is a suit at the Federal High Court, Abuja, presided by Justice Adamu Bello, where President Jonathan through his counsel, Mr. Ade Okeaya-Inneh, has made a case that he has the right to run in 2015. The question is no longer why or whether President Jonathan will run in 2015. He will. As a layman, legally speaking, I believe he has the right to run. Does he deserve re-election? The answer, of course, is a resounding no.

The question, therefore, is how do we defeat President Jonathan and the PDP in 2015? The opposition should stop behaving like the kid whose toy was taken away by the unruly neighbourhood bully. If they truly share a common vision for Nigeria, and if that vision is altruistic, then it should not be difficult for them to unite in this urgent task of national reclamation.

So, I say, let the race begin. Now is the time for those outside the PDP who have expressed interest in the 2015 race or have been linked with it one way or another to come out and present their agenda on what is to be done. Many names have been bandied about. Here is a shortlist, in no particular order: Muhammadu Buhari, Nuhu Ribadu, Bola Ahmed Tinubu, Pat Utomi, Abubakar Dangiwa Umar, Nasir el Rufai, Babatunde Fashola, Adams Oshiomhole, Olisa Agbakoba, Ibrahim Shekarau, Mathew Hassan Kukah and Jubrin Ibrahim.

The issue should not be where you come from or "it is the turn of this region or ethnic group". As we have seen, to our eternal regret, the politics of "it is our turn" has failed us repeatedly. President Jonathan says we should wait until 2014 for his position – a position we already know. That should be the standard for an opposition that seeks an alternative, a new Nigeria.

It is never too early to prepare for victory. The opposition needs to stop watching President Jonathan's body language and concentrate on its most urgent task: rally behind a nationally acceptable and credible candidate.

The public presentation of "2015 Manifesto of Nigerian Opposition Politics" in Abuja on Tuesday, January 15, 2013, is a great platform to kick-start this agenda.

4. CAN APC CURE NIGERIA'S HEADACHE? (1)
APRIL 2013

As the merger of the country's major opposition parties crystallized a few months ago into a mega party known as All Progressives Congress (APC), I received an email from my friend, Richard Mammah, who wanted to get my opinion on the new party. "Is the new mega party in Nigeria a marginal improvement over where we are coming from?" Mammah asked pointedly. My immediate response was emphatic: "It is (if it succeeds). It is important that genuine democrats and progressives find a way to key in as soon as possible".

Since then, there have been debates (among progressives) about the desirability of "joining" the new party. Expectedly, the ruling People's Democratic Party (PDP) responded to news of the merger with disdain. "No merger will succeed against us in 2015" was the party's official position through its former national secretary, Olagunsoye Oyinlola, who spoke to journalists in Abuja. Oyinlola dismissed the merger as "gang-ups".

"We don't think we are threatened by what we would call

gang-ups", said the former governor of Osun State who was sent packing by the court in 2010 before he could complete his second term. "In those days when the National Party of Nigeria (NPN) and Nigerian Peoples Party (NPP) closed ranks, it was called an accord. When the Unity Party of Nigeria (UPN) and Great Nigeria People's Party (GNPP) did the same, they called it a gang-up".

Oyinlola went on,

"Honestly speaking, ganging up is an indication of some weaknesses. Why can't a party stand on its own and contest elections if it is sure that it would be acceptable to the people? You don't need to gang up. If you are ganging up then you don't have the strength. The only true national party today that cuts across every nook and cranny of the Nigerian federation is the PDP. Gang up has never succeeded; it will not succeed".

Oyinlola's diatribe was upped by Governor Sule Lamido of Jigawa State who described the opposition parties as "inventions of the last two years". "They are the invention of pain, agony and anger", Lamido said, adding, "They thought PDP is like them. We have political party history from 1998 when they were not in existence. Those who were talking in ANPP, ACN and CPC were formally PDP members that were flushed out in the field by the party (PDP)".

Bamanga Tukur, the national chairman of the PDP, in his now infamous reaction to the merger described his party as the "Messi of Nigerian politics". "If you go for a contest, you have the striker. You know Lionel Messi (Barcelona and Argentine football star)? PDP is Messi in that contest. They (opposition) are no threat at all. It is better, it inspires PDP to action. In that contest, tell them Chairman said PDP is the Messi". Football lovers in the country must feel insulted and incensed by this laughable comparison.

Of course, the PDP is grandstanding and its disdain for the APC is borne out of fear more than anything else. I can understand the position of the Oyinlolas, Lamidos and Tukurs. It is one that demands no response. For them, there is no meaningful job other than being in the corridors of power. And that has to be done by any means necessary. I felt differently, however, when I read a response on the merger from a much younger former colleague, Ohimai Amaize, who "joined" the PDP by way of political appointment about three years ago.

In his piece, "The APC, is it a merger or 'maga'?" Amaize asked, "What is the core ideology of this new contrivance? What is its blueprint for Nigeria's regeneration? An existing manifesto or some consultants are still working on it? When will it be ready? Perhaps, a few months to the next general elections! And this is part of the problem. Contrivances don't work". According to Amaize,

> *"The assumption by some of our youth that Nigeria will be transformed simply because some 'big guns' within the political class have assembled under the toga of a new opposition party remains nothing but an illusion. The notion that a group of recycled politicians uniting against the ruling PDP in the name of 'opposition' will present an already-made change, is at best, a hasty journey to a land of frustration. It is not that simple. There is nothing like already-made change. Nirvana does not exist. We must humble ourselves, bury our pride and work under existing political platforms no matter how educated and enlightened we think we are".*

Amaize admonished Nigerian youth to be wary of the APC. "When this new opposition party was being formed, what was its agenda for the youth?" Amaize wondered.

> *"Is there any or will it hurriedly cook up one within the next few days? Which of the pro-APC youth activists on Twitter can confidently tell us the youth agenda of their new party? How many of my fellow Twitter busybodies were consulted to share their ideas for this merger before it was hatched? None! Because as far as they are concerned, you are not important in the scheme of things and do not exist".*

These are legitimate questions from a very "concerned" young Nigerian knowing Amaize's antecedent before he joined the "transformation" wagon. However, the analysis shows a shallow and opportunistic reading of history. It presupposes Amaize is "happy" with the way things are in the country and if ever there is any talk of change, it can only take place "under existing political platforms". And by this I am sure he means the PDP.

Of all the arguments in support of the emergence of APC, or what the response of genuine democrats should be to the new party, two stand out. In his piece, "APC and the continuing crisis of Left politics in Nigeria", Adagbo Onoja concluded that, "As long as there is no Left party or a broad-based democratic coalition in Nigeria, comrades would have no options than spread to whichever platform they find space to continue the struggle in whatever ways possible".

In his article, "Reflections on party combinations", The Guardian, March 7 & 14, 2013, Edwin Madunagu noted, "The announcement of a merger of the leading opposition parties in Nigeria is a development which no serious political formation or tendency in the country can ignore or dismiss with cynicism of the type: 'they always do this whenever a major election approaches'".

> *"Yes, 'they' always announce coalitions, alliances, mergers, working agreements, etc, and the more uncharitable commentators may also remind us that they almost invariably fail to achieve their minimum post-announcement objective, that is, to actually deliver a living (and not a still-born or mortally sick) child",* Madunagu wrote. *"When we have granted the cynics and pessimists their due, we may still insist that we are confronted with a development, which rules out the option of 'Siddon look'".*

These two arguments speak for themselves and capture, to a great extent, what the response of radical and progressive elements, particularly youth and students, should be with regard to the APC as we head toward 2015.

5. CAN APC CURE NIGERIA'S HEADACHE? (2)
MARCH 2013

I have no illusions about the challenges (some of which are beginning to manifest) and limitations of the new mega party being proposed by the country's main opposition parties. The reality is that the All Progressives Congress (APC) can only go so far in the quest to lift our people from poverty, disease, unemployment and other problems associated with a neo-colonial capitalist economy like ours. The reasons are quite clear.

However, it is important to state that in the midst of the general chaos that has enveloped the country and the rudderless leadership of the ruling People's Democratic Party (PDP) which threatens the very survival of the country, there are very few options open for us to push back the country from the brink.

In general, there are three likely scenarios that could play out in the next two years. None of the scenarios is capable of addressing the urgent crisis confronting the country. What are these scenarios? One, the opposition abdicates the political space and allows the current charade to run its full course. Two things are possible here: first, the implosion of the PDP which seems quite imminent could prove even costlier for the nation. Second, President Jonathan is "reelected" in 2015. By 2019, he, like his predecessors, hands over to a governor of his choice and the cycle continues while we groan and complain ad nauseam.

The second scenario is the military option. This option looks menacingly real and tantalizing for some. Many of the people who would lampoon the effort to confront the PDP and its despicable rule are salivating at the prospect of a military coup. They are readying themselves, like their forebears, in the spirit of "service to the nation" to be part of the process. It does not matter to them that such action will take us a one step forward and twenty years backward.

The third scenario, which looms large, is anarchy or civil war. The mindless bloodletting and general insecurity in the country could get out of control and precipitate anarchy or civil war; and like Somalia, the country could become the poster child of failed states. These scenarios should not be viewed lightly.

So what is the way forward? In this regard, two scenarios appear feasible. One, the prospect of a social revolution or what Edwin Madunagu, "The Hugo Chavez Revolution", The Guardian (March 28, 2013) describes as "a fundamental, non-sectarian and mass-engineered rupture in the structure and content of the Nigerian state". Even though the objective conditions are present and the fact that in most cases such "mass-engineered rupture" do not "give notice", Gov. Rotimi Amaechi of Rivers State, a chieftain of the PDP, in his wisdom, has ruled out this option because according to him, "Our elasticity (for suffering) has no limit".

The last option would be a popular and broad-based coalition to unseat the PDP in 2015. This is where the APC comes in. Of course, the APC is not necessarily the only option here. The Labour Party/National Conscience Party coalition, as a friend suggested, is another. However, if the opposition is really serious about unseating a behemoth like the PDP, it will do well to close ranks.

These are the only viable options. Every Nigerian would have to decide where he or she fits in. There is no room for vacillation or "siddon look". How then do we get out of the current *cul-de-sac*? Which of the preceding options is meaningful and achievable (before things get out of hand) within the context of the current bourgeoisie "democratic" order? I would say the last option.

I understand the "fierce urgency of now" in relation to ending the suffering and deprivation of citizens. At the same time, we need to save and secure the country before we can move forward. Unfortunately, the PDP which has been in power since 1999 has foreclosed any meaningful debate about the future of the country and the possibility of change. For us to start any real discussion about the future of the country, we need to get rid of the PDP which has elevated misgovernance to a religion.

The PDP is in the throes of death and it looks like it wants to drag the rest of the country with it. With the PDP, we are dealing with a collection of megalomaniacs. Currently, we can identify three centres of powers within the party: The Presidency, the Nigeria Governors' Forum, and the Northern Governors' Forum. The ambition of the men who control these centres of power, President Goodluck Jonathan, Gov. Rotimi Amaechi of Rivers State and Gov. Babangida Aliyu of Niger State, as well as that of other tangential gladiators will, undoubtedly, sink the party.

The question is: do we want to sink with the PDP? Now is the time to confront the arrogance and egregious folly of the PDP. When former president, Olusegun Obasanjo, and national chairman, Bamanga Tukur, say the PDP will rule for 100 years, we should not see it as mere political-speak. The PDP cares for this country, to paraphrase American political journalist, DeWayne Wickham, in much the same way that pimps care for their whores: just what they can get out of them.

How do we defeat President Jonathan and the PDP in 2015? There is no other way than for the opposition to come together and show that it is capable of this urgent task of national reclamation. If the APC succeeds, and I hope and pray it does, it will be "a marginal improvement over where we are coming from". If the country can once in its history have a leader elected by popular will – not installed by the incumbent or the military – it is a step forward.

I shall end this piece by going back to Edwin Madunagu who noted in his piece "Reflections on Party Combinations", The Guardian, March 7 & 14, 2013, "Someone has referred to the newly-formed APC as the "new" SDP. Yes, there are a couple of elements in common. But there is at least one more requirement for the APC: It has to show that not only is the status-quo totally bankrupt (which is the case), but also that the APC is a historically progressive way forward at this moment, and that it is the only one".

This is the battle progressives in the APC have to wage in the weeks and months ahead.

6. Let's negotiate Nigeria
May 2013

> *"There is nothing exclusive in the term unity; unity for Nigeria holds out the best chance for progress when that unity is a unity of purpose rather than the present hollow approach to unity for sake of unity. For unity to be meaningful, it has to be creative, not the unity of Jonah in the whale but the unity of holy matrimony. The first can only lead to defecation, the second to procreation".*
> – Chukwuemeka Odumegwu Ojukwu

I have just finished work on a new book titled *Nigeria is Negotiable*. Its release is scheduled to coincide with the 20th anniversary of the June 12, 1993 presidential election won by Chief Moshood Abiola. Many of us know how that experiment under the gap-toothed dictator, Gen. Ibrahim Babangida, ended. But that is a topic for another essay.

It is the title of the book that is of interest here. I chose the title deliberately, to stir debate; but it is also a reaffirmation of my conviction about where our dear country is headed and what needs to be done. At no time since I became politically conscious more than three decades ago have I been as worried as I am today about Project Nigeria.

What is worrying is not so much the demands of various groups who seek to tear the country apart, but the hypocrisy and half-hearted response of those who are in a position to save the looming calamity. That we are still debating whether there is a nation, almost 100 years after the country was created and 53 years of political independence is emblematic of a country mired in deep crisis.

I take that back. There is really no debate about the future of our country. What we have are platitudes, threats and a presupposition that one way or another, things will work out. If we had any meaningful debate, perhaps we would have come to the inevitable conclusion that there is so much wrong with Nigeria and that if we do not deal with the cancer of disunity, it will metastasize and consume the country.

President Jonathan, like all rulers before him, has had occasions to talk about the vexed issue of national unity, the most recent being in September 2012 during the national summit and rally for peace, unity and development, organized by the Nigeria Labour Congress (NLC).

"I agree with other speakers that we cannot talk about cannibalizing and balkanizing Nigeria", the president said.

> *"I think those who are thinking that way want to be kings in tiny islands, because I believe from the little I know that Nigeria is still rated as a country to look at globally. It's not because we produce oil and some people think it's because of our oil. One small country with less than 10 million population produces more oil than Nigeria. So it is not the oil, it is not the vast land. What is the land space of Nigeria compared to Sudan? So any person who feels that they just want to stay as one nation, just want to be king without hard work. They will not get it, because Nigeria will not divide".*

How many times have we heard the glib talk "Nigeria will not divide" or "the unity of the country is nonnegotiable"? Of course, if it were as simple as the president imagined, we would not spend valuable time and space on the issue. It seems people talk about the unity of Nigeria the way it suits them. For many, it is the unity of Jonah in the belly of the whale.

It is our inability to confront this unhealthy unity that is our greatest undoing. There is something troubling about the structure of Nigeria which explains why we cannot achieve much no matter how hard we try to "move the country forward", to use the weasel words of our politicians.

While not excusing corruption and the perfidy of the ruling class, we can conveniently argue that the monumental corruption going on in the country, the violation of human rights, the contempt for rule of law and widespread injustice are all tied inexorably to the structure of the country. So we need to go back to basics. In a sentence, we need to negotiate Nigeria. This has become imperative in the light of the "clear and present danger".

Every day, we hear war drums, threats and counter threats. A few days ago, leader of the Niger Delta People's Volunteer Force, Alhaji Mujahid Dokubo-Asari, while reacting to the faceoff between President Jonathan and Governor Rotimi Amaechi of Rivers State vowed that, "There will be no peace, not only in the Niger Delta, but everywhere, if Goodluck Jonathan is not the president by 2015, except God takes his life, which we do not pray for".

> *"Jonathan has uninterrupted eight years of two terms to be president, according to the Nigeria constitution," Dokubo-Asari added. "We must have our uninterrupted eight years of two tenures. I am not in support of any amendment to the constitution that will reduce the eight years".*

If this is not a declaration of war against the Nigerian state, I do not know what is. That is the nature of our democracy. Our votes do not count; they have never counted. I do not know which constitution Dokubo-Asari is referring to, but the 1999 constitution which President Jonathan swore to uphold does not guarantee an automatic "uninterrupted eight years of two tenures" for any Nigerian, no matter where they come from.

In the past, we talked about the hegemony of the three dominant ethnic groups in the country. That is no longer the case. If you thought Dokubo-Asari was merely being mischievous, perhaps you missed the memo by the Special Adviser to the President on Niger Delta, and chairman, presidential amnesty programme, Kingsley Kuku, who last week warned of "dire consequences in the Niger Delta if President Jonathan is not re-elected".

Speaking at a session with officials of the U.S. State Department led by the Deputy Assistant Secretary of State (Bureau of African Affairs), Donald Teitelbaum, Kuku was reported to have said, "Only Mr. Jonathan can guarantee peace in the restive region and hence, the compelling need to persuade him to seek re-election in 2015.

However, if we allow anything to hurt the peace in the Niger Delta, Nigeria's economy will be endangered and energy security in Nigeria and even America will not be guaranteed. The attention and interest of the U.S. in Nigeria must remain the stability of the Niger Delta and the easiest way to ensure this is to encourage President Jonathan to complete an eight-year term".

What kind of president instigates war against his own people? It is only a president that does not have faith in the country he governs. Of course, if we uphold the right of one group to wage war against the state, we cannot, for any reason, deny same to other groups. That is why the planned trial of members of the Movement for the Actualization of the Sovereign State of Biafra (MASSOB) for treason must be resisted.

We may dismiss Dokubo-Asari, but it is difficult to fault his assertion that, "The 2015 general elections would 'define and decide' the existence of Nigeria". That much was confirmed by the statement credited to Farouk Adamu Aliyu, a former member of the House of Representatives and the 2011 Congress for Progressive Change, (CPC) governorship candidate in Jigawa State, who warned a few days ago that, "It is either a Northerner as president in 2015 or there will be no more Nigeria".

> *"Let me also use this opportunity to say on behalf of us in the north that nobody has monopoly of violence and that on behalf of the people of northern extraction, there shall be no one Nigeria if a northerner is not elected president of this country, because politics is a game of numbers and the Ijaw people are not up to one million or two million or even five million",* Aliyu said.

In "response" to Dokubo-Asari, Aliyu put forward a faulty argument which is as cynical as it is troubling. The fact that the "Ijaw people are not up to one million or two million or even five million" does not in any way vitiate the right of an Ijaw man to emerge as president of Nigeria or reelected as president of Nigeria. What about other Nigerians who are not Ijaws or Northerners? Are they not entitled to be president of Nigeria?

Before now, we heard from people who promised to make Nigeria "ungovernable" if President Jonathan won the 2011 election. Clearly, our problem as a nation is much graver than we are willing to admit.

Rather than worrying about reelection in 2015, President Jonathan can etch his name in history and save Nigeria by facilitating a process for "we the people" to have a meaningful debate about the future of Nigeria.

The president seems fortunate to be in charge when the country celebrates 100 years of amalgamation. What an auspicious moment to negotiate Nigeria. Forget corruption, forget electricity, forget infrastructure. You need to have a nation for these things to work.

I hope it is not asking too much!

APPENDIX 1

July 2012

"President Jonathan is a product of a very corrupt process". - Dr. Adunbi

Dr. Omolade Adunbi is a political anthropologist and an Assistant Professor at the Department of Afro-American and African Studies (DAAS), University of Michigan, Ann Arbor, Michigan, U.S.A. In this interview with **Chido Onumah**, he examines corruption, the national question and political violence in Nigeria, amongst other national issues.

CO: What is your assessment of the current situation in Nigeria?

OA: Nigeria is in a state of rot. A rot caused by being held hostage by a cabal that is bent on destroying the country. A lens through which to see Nigeria is that of a sick person who suddenly found himself in a hospital. At the hospital, he was given wrong diagnoses and of course wrong prescription. Each time the patient takes his medication, his condition keeps getting worse and the physician keeps conducting tests upon tests without the patient realizing that the physician is actually not a trained physician but a fraudster parading himself as one.

This is the situation in which Nigeria, a country rich in human and natural resources has found herself today. In spite of the abundance of those with the right expertise to tackle Nigeria's problems, the cabal that has held the country hostage will not allow Nigeria, the sick patient, to be treated by a trained physician. Until the patient frees himself from this fraudster, he will continue to fall sick while his peers are making their lives better. This is my assessment of Nigeria of today.

CO: To what extent are you worried that the unsettled question of nationhood continues to dominate public discourse in Nigeria?

OA: Am I worried that the national discourse today is about the unsettled question of nationhood? Any patriotic Nigerian should be worried about this. I am worried because after more than 50 years of nationhood and almost a century of having an entity called Nigeria, we ought to have moved beyond questioning our ability to stay together. Some will say, if you have been married for over fifty years and the marriage is still enmeshed in discord, then you are not compatible. But, the issue is not that of incompatibility here but that of social inequality. When there is an increase in social inequality, people tend to look for ways of fending for themselves and the process of doing this often lead to discord with a capacity to degenerate into what some might call ethnic divide.

When this happens, many will begin to call into question the idea of Nigerian nationhood itself. The other way to reflect on the question itself is to argue that Nigeria has never been a nation, so there is no point talking about whether the discourse of nationhood is dominating the political landscape or not. The question then will be why is Nigeria not a nation? Nigeria is not a nation because it is an imposed entity.

This may not suggest that it does not have the capacity to become a nation, but after over 50 years of independence, it is yet to clearly demonstrate that it has that capability of becoming a nation. What we see today is a situation whereby people continue to see themselves not as Nigerians but more importantly as Birom, Igbo, Hausa, Fulani, Ijaw, Ibibio, Yoruba, etc. People continue to cling on to their ethnic cleavages rather than clinging on to the idea of Nigeria as a nation.

If you look critically at the history of formation of many of these ethnic groups, it is not as if they all started through a process of homogenization. Many can be considered as a hybrid of many traditions, cultures and practices, but living together over the years and with the right leadership, many began to see themselves as one. For example, if we look at the Yorubas of Southwest Nigeria, the development of Yoruba orthography helped in shaping a Yoruba identity.

Prior to the development of Yoruba orthography, many would either see themselves as the Oyos, Ifes, Owos, etc., with a common ancestry which can also be interrogated or questioned but developing a Yoruba orthography helped in making people believe that they are at once a Yoruba person before being an Oyo person.

Same thing can be said for the Igbos, the Hausa/Fulanis and others. So, nations are formed through commonalities and unfortunately, the only thing we have in common in Nigeria today can be categorized into two. Those who are extremely rich because of their access to our commonwealth. This group constitutes less than 1% of the population. The second category is the more than 99% of the population who are extremely poor and continually pushed to the margins by the less than 1% of the population. The tragedy of the whole situation is that this group, who for many years have been told that they are different and compartmentalized into being Yoruba, Hausa, Igbo, Ijaw, Birom, Zango-Kataf, etc., do not see their destiny as being tied together. Rather they see their destiny as being tied to a representative of the less than 1% within their community.

That is why when that person who has been co-opted into the less than 1% group comes home to talk about marginalization, those who should chastise him will be the same people who will be ready to die for him not knowing that he is in fact one of their oppressors. Therefore, the less than 1% of the population who constitute the oppressing cabal have succeeded in manipulating and transforming what ordinarily should be a national psyche into a local, ethnic or communal psyche. Such is the tragedy of the Nigerian situation and this is why the question of nationhood keeps coming up because there is no nation.

CO: Recently the National Assembly called for memos for the review of the constitution. Do you think this is the right way to go? If not, how should Nigerians go about fashioning a workable constitution for themselves?

OA: I have thought about this severally and I am beginning to think that the constitution might after all not be the problem. We have been fashioning constitutions since the 1900s and here we are in the 2000s and we still have not been able to fashion a workable constitution for ourselves. We have had what I will call a pseudo democracy for over 13 years now and every four years the National Assembly sets up a committee to review the constitution but what have we got from this?

We are fast becoming a nation of committees. Committees that help in the process of siphoning our commonwealth instead of designing appropriate policies and programmes that will help uplift our people. If we must have a workable constitution then my suggestion will be that it should be done through a democratic process. Let all Nigerians elect their representatives to a constitution drafting assembly and let the outcome be a subject of a referendum to either approve or reject the new constitution.

The election of representatives must be conducted by a genuine and transparent electoral commission put in place not by the present government but by an independent body.

CO: How would you rate President Jonathan's fight against corruption?

OA: Is President Jonathan fighting corruption? I am not sure he is. Jonathan is a product of a very corrupt process and such a person lacks the capacity to fight corruption. In Nigeria, corruption has become an institution and it is highly destructive. Corruption as an institution will make sure that other institutions that could help strengthen the nation are weakened. This is the only way it can thrive.

Of course you also have the beneficiaries like Jonathan and others who might feel threatened if there is a serious war on corruption. The bottom-line is that if we succeed in fighting or destroying institutional corruption, then we could say we are on our way to strengthening institutions of the state. As things stand today, we do not have a state but what we have is Nigeria in name and not a Nigerian state. Strong institutions are what make a state and not name recognition.

So, Nigeria is just hanging on to name recognition and crying for serious help and Jonathan does not have the capacity to render the kind of help that Nigeria needs.

CO: What's your view of his decision not to publicly declare his assets in the face of continued public anger against corruption in the top echelon of his administration?

OA: Jonathan's view that he does not "give a damn" about asset declaration stems from the fact that he is not representing the Nigerian people. The institution he represents is comfortable with his not declaring his assets, so he feels he does not owe the rest of the country anything. Jonathan can only be worried if the cabal who put him in office becomes uncomfortable with him.

After all, votes do not count in Nigeria, so he really does not need our votes to remain in office. Until votes begin to count and Nigerians are able to freely elect their representatives, we will continue to have leaders such as Jonathan. So, we need to move beyond procedural democracy that we currently have to more inclusive and transparent democratic practices.

CO: Can this administration be trusted when the president says those found guilty in the oil subsidy report will be prosecuted? What do you make of the faceoff between Messrs Femi Otedola and Farouk Lawan over bribery allegation?

OA: We have had several probes in the past and nothing happened. The administration of Jonathan has set up several committees since its inception and nothing has come out of those committees. I remember when Obasanjo left office, there was a power probe committee set up by the National Assembly and nothing came out of the committee's report. So, you can expect that the same thing will happen to the oil subsidy committee too. I think the National Assembly and its leaders have become what I will call a 'craftimanipulative' institution if I am permitted to use a word like that.

What I mean by this is that they are schooled in the art of distracting the general population from the main issues of social inequality. So, when you hear that there is an oil subsidy or power project probe, the expectations of citizens are immediately raised, thinking that finally, something is going to be done about their plight. The period of the probe will become theatrical where the so-called leaders who may think the idea of shame is foreign will expose their 'secret dealings' for a few weeks for Nigerians to see. Ordinarily, such public expositions should be a mobilizing tool for Nigerians but it is not.

If you remember where I started from, the less than 1% have succeeded in manipulating the population to believing that the reason why there is social inequality is because of the other person who is not from their ethnic group. Again, what such probes do is to turn the light towards ethnic witch-hunting as the reason why things are the way they are. Thus, Femi Otedola and Farouk Lawan are products of the same corrupt institutions and I will not be surprised if tomorrow people start to think that Farouk Lawan is being witch-hunted because he is Hausa/Fulani.

The fact is no one is asking questions about Otedola's sudden wealth. How did he suddenly become a multi-millionaire? What is his background? Where did he get his initial capital to start a business? The truth is both Otedola and Lawal are beneficiaries of a corrupt institution called Nigeria.

CO: How would you assess the problem of insecurity and what it portends for the future of the country?

OA: The truth is that Nigeria is currently at war. It is only those who are delusional that will say Nigeria is at peace and that what is going on are pockets of violence here and there. The tragedy of the Nigerian situation is that a time bomb placed at the centre of the country several years ago is beginning to detonate. Unfortunately, those who can help stop the degeneration are not in a position to do so.

The problem of insecurity ties neatly into the problem of social inequality and the continued marginalization of the majority of the population. When you have a population that is highly pauperized by the few elites, the dignity of the person becomes bare through a process of Darwinism. Survival becomes an uphill task and the resultant effect is the recourse to ethnic or religious chauvinism. Religion then turns to opium of the people and those who cannot stand the double marginalization hide under the cloak of fighting for a God's kingdom to further traumatize the aggrieved population.

It is in this context that I see the level of insecurity in the country. Just pumping money into national security cannot solve the problem. The only solution is to address the marginalization of the majority of the population by addressing issues of access to education, health, roads and rural infrastructure. When the so-called Boko Haram says it is opposed to Western education, it is because it equates Western education with the institutionalization of corruption in Nigeria.

I see their cry as the cry for equity, justice, access to education, healthcare, good roads and over all development of the country. I see them as wanting to be part of an inclusive process that will address social inequity in the Nigerian state. Their grievance is not in any way different from the unannounced grievance of Nigerians out there who are disgusted about the decay in their country.

CO: What do you make of the clamour for 2015 in light of the crisis of the Nigerian state?

OA: Politicians will always jostle for office whenever the opportunity presents itself. Those who believe Jonathan will not run in 2015 need to re-examine their minds. Jonathan will run in 2015 and the question is whether the opposition will be able to put their acts together and give him a run for the Nigerian money that he is spending.

More importantly, it is hard to see if the salvation of Nigeria lies in the current political system. If the Nigerian people can rise up and fight, they may be able to change the system and install a more durable democratic system in Nigeria. We need to rekindle the fighting spirit of the 1970s, 1980s and 1990s when Nigeria was the leading light in democratic struggles. What Nigerians need to do is to create an enduring process that will shield the popular struggle from the rampaging elite who might want to take advantage of it and reinstall themselves in office.

This is exactly what happened in the 1990s when the elite hijacked a genuine movement for democratic change and installed what is presently in place. To guide against that, Nigerians need to rally round an organisation that will be all-inclusive and ready to take the fight to the elite and rescue the Nigerian nation. It is when this happens that Nigeria can move away from being a nation recognized in name only to that of a Nigerian state that will be democratic, where justice and equity will reign supreme.

CO: What role can Nigerians in the Diaspora play in the effort to reclaim Nigeria?

OA: The role I see for Nigerians in Diaspora is to be more involved in the process of reclaiming Nigeria from the marauding elite that has taken Nigeria hostage. Nigerians in Diaspora can liaise with those in Nigeria to help shape the form and character of whatever organization will be put in place to rescue Nigeria. This category of Nigerians may need to take a cue from other Diasporas who have helped to shape the future of their countries in the past.

There are several examples to draw from. Within the African continent, history of democratic struggle in South Africa where those in the Diaspora supported those at home still lingers in our memory. We can also draw from various countries in Latin America, and the Middle East.

APPENDIX II

❖

Chronology (1960-2013)*

The Federal Republic of Nigeria is a federal constitutional republic comprising 36 states and the Federal Capital Territory, Abuja.

The country is located in West Africa and shares land borders with the Republic of Benin in the west, Chad and Cameroon in the east, and Niger in the north. Its coast in the south lies on the Gulf of Guinea, on the Atlantic Ocean.

The name Nigeria was taken from the Niger River running through the country. It was coined by Flora Shaw, the future wife of Baron Lugard, a British colonial administrator, and first Governor General of Nigeria. In 1914, two British colonies: the Protectorate of Southern Nigeria and the Protectorate of Northern Nigeria were merged, to form a single territorial unit known as Nigeria. This territory was administered by the British until 1960 when the Union Jack (British flag) was lowered for the Nigerian flag to take its place.

Nigeria is the most populous country in Africa, the seventh most populous country in the world and the most populous Black nation in the world. Nigeria has a total area of 923,768 km2 (356,669 sq ml), making it the 14th largest country in Africa and the world's 32nd-largest country (after Tanzania).

The highest point in Nigeria is Chappal Waddi (in Taraba State) at 2,419 m (7,936 ft). The main rivers are the Niger and the Benue River which converge and empty into the Niger Delta, one of the world's largest river deltas and the location of a large area of Central African Mangroves.

On January 15, 1956, Shell Darcy "discovered" oil in commercial quantity at Oloibiri, Bayelsa State. Nigeria is the 12th largest producer of petroleum in the world and the 8th largest exporter. It has the 10th largest proven reserves. The country joined OPEC in 1971.

Petroleum plays a large role in the Nigerian economy, accounting for 40% of GDP and 80% of government earnings.

KEY DATES:
- October 1, 1960: Nigeria (35 million people) gains independence from Britain with Sir Abubakar Tafawa Balewa as the first and only prime minister. Six days later, Nigeria is recognized by the United Nations as its 99th member.
- November 16, 1960: Dr. Nnamdi Azikiwe, becomes the first Governor-General of Nigeria.
- October 1, 1963: Nigeria becomes a republic with Dr. Nnamdi Azikiwe as first president.
- December 30, 1964: First parliamentary elections after independence are held. The elections are marred by violence. Sir Abubakar Tafawa Balewa is re-elected Prime Minister. Elections were not held until 18 March, 1965, in some constituencies in the Eastern Region, Lagos, and Mid-Western Region due to a boycott in December 1964.
- January 15, 1966: A coup d'état led by Major Kaduna Nzeogwu leads to the death of Prime Minister, Abubakar Tafawa Balewa, Sir Ahmadu Bello, Premier of Northern Nigeria and Samuel Akintola, Premier of Western Region, as well as some top military officers. Major General Johnson Aguiyi-Ironsi becomes the first Nigerian Head of State after the coup.
- July 29, 1966: Another military coup takes place. General Aguiyi-Ironsi is killed and Lt. Colonel Yakubu Gowon emerges head of state.
- May 27, 1967: Yakubu Gowon divides the country into twelve states.
- May 30, 1967: Colonel Odumegwu Ojukwu, Military Governor of Eastern Region, declares a secession of the region, naming it the Republic of Biafra.
- July 6, 1967: A civil war officially breaks out.
- January 13, 1970: Colonel Ojukwu's deputy, Philip Effiong, surrenders to the Nigerian government.
- January 15, 1970: The civil war officially comes to an end.

- July 29, 1975: General Gowon is ousted in a bloodless coup. Brigadier General Murtala Ramat Muhammed becomes head of state.
- February 3, 1976: A new capital city, Abuja, is created. Seven new states are created, bringing the total to 19.
- February 13, 1976: Gen. Muhammed is killed in a bloody coup led by Colonel Bukar Sukar Dimka. General Olusegun Obasanjo, Mohammed's second in command, takes over.
- October 1, 1979: General Obasanjo hands over to a civilian government led by Alhaji Shehu Shagari to begin the 2nd Republic.
- October 1, 1983: Alhaji Shehu Shagari is sworn in for a second term after a disputed presidential election.
- December 31, 1983: Brigadier Sani Abacha announces the overthrow of the 2nd Republic. Major General Muhammadu Buhari takes over as head of state with Major General Tunde Idiagbon as his deputy.
- August 27, 1985: General Ibrahim Badamosi Babangida leads another military coup that ousts Maj-Gen Buhari.
- March 5, 1986: General Babangida orders the execution of Major General Mamman Vatsa, his childhood friend, for allegedly plotting to overthrow him.
- October 19, 1986: Prominent journalist, Dele Giwa, is assassinated via a parcel bomb.
- December 8, 1986: Professor Wole Soyinka delivers a lecture, "This Past Must Address Its Present" in Stockholm, Sweden, after being awarded the Nobel Prize for literature, the first African to be so honoured.
- September 23, 1987: General Babangida creates two additional states.
- May 23-31, 1989: Anti-Structural Adjustment Programme (SAP) riots sweep the country. Over 100 people killed by security forces.
- April 22, 1990: Major Gideon Orkar-led bloody coup (excising a section of northern Nigeria) does not succeed in ousting General Babangida.
- July 27, 1990: 48 soldiers, including Major Gideon Orkar, are executed for their roles in the April 22 coup.
- September 13, 1990: 27 soldiers, previously freed during the April

22 coup trial, are executed after their conviction by a reconstituted tribunal.
- August 27, 1991. General Babangida creates 9 new states.
- November 14, 1991: General Babangida relocates to Abuja, officially making it the new capital city of Nigeria.
- June 12, 1993: Presidential election holds after ten years of military rule. Chief Moshood Kashimawo Abiola of the Social Democratic Party (SDP) emerges winner defeating Bashir Tofa of the National Republican Convention (NRC).
- June 23, 1993: General Ibrahim Babangida annuls the result of the June 12 presidential election which was declared Nigeria's freest and fairest presidential election by national and international observers.
- August 12, 1993: Anti-government protests disrupt commercial activities nationwide.
- August 26, 1993: Babangida appoints Chief Ernest Shonekan as Head of the Interim National Government (ING).
- August 27, 1993: General Babaginda "steps aside".
- November 9, 1993: The Interim National Government (ING) increases fuel price from 70 kobo to N5 per litre.
- November 11, 1993: Lagos High Court with Justice Dolapo Akinsanya presiding, declares the ING illegal.
- November 15, 1993: Workers start nationwide protest over fuel price increases.
- November 17, 1993: Shonekan "resigns", paving the way for General Sani Abacha.
- May 15, 1994: The National Democratic Coalition (NADECO) is formed by a broad coalition of Nigerians. It calls on the military government of Sani Abacha to step down in favour of the winner of the June 12, 1993 election, M. K. O. Abiola.
- June 11, 1994: Moshood Abiola declares himself president and is charged for treason by General Sani Abacha. Abacha offers N50,000 reward for information leading to Chief Abiola's arrest.
- October 2, 1994: Abacha's government raises fuel prices by 400 percent.
- March 13, 1995: General Olusegun Obasanjo arrested. After sev-

eral days, he is released and placed under house arrest.
- July 1995: Generals Olusegun Obasanjo and Shehu Yar'Adua are sentenced to death by a military tribunal for allegedly plotting to overthrow the regime of General Sani Abacha. 40 others, including rights activist, Dr. Beko Ransome-Kuti, receive various jail sentences. Four editors: Kunle Ajibade, George Mbah, Ben Charles Obi and Chris Anyanwu are sentenced to life imprisonment for being "accessories" in the coup plot.
- October 6, 1995: Alfred Rewane, philanthropist and financier of the National Democratic Coalition (NADECO) is assassinated in his bedroom in Lagos.
- November 10, 1995: Author and environmentalist, Ken Saro Wiwa, and eight other Ogoni activists are executed by the Abacha regime.
- June 4, 1996: Kudirat Abiola, wife of the winner of the June 12, 1993 presidential election, M.K.O. Abiola, is assassinated in Lagos.
- October 1, 1996: General Abacha creates six new states.
- December 8, 1997: General Shehu Yar'Adua dies in prison.
- December 20, 1997: General Oladipo Diya, Abacha's deputy, is arrested for an alleged coup plot.
- June 8, 1998: General Abacha dies in office.
- June 9, 1998: General Abdulsalami Abubakar takes over as head of state.
- June 16, 1998: General Olusegun Obasanjo is released from prison.
- July 7, 1998: Moshood Abiola dies while in custody of the Nigerian government.
- February 27, 1999: Olusegun Obasanjo "elected" president on the platform of the People's Democratic Party (PDP).
- May 29, 1999: Olusegun Obasanjo is sworn in as president, marking the beginning of the 4th Republic.
- May 29, 2003: Olusegun Obasanjo is sworn in for a second term
- May 29, 2007: Umaru Yar'Adua is sworn in as president, after a very contentious election. It is the first civilian-to-civilian transition in Nigeria.

- November 23, 2009: Umaru Yar'Adua leaves the country for treatment in Saudi Arabia. He was never again seen in public.
- December 25, 2009: A Nigerian, Umar Farouk Abdul Mutallab, 23, attempts to blow up Northwest Airlines Flight 253, en route from Amsterdam to Detroit, Michigan, USA, with 289 people aboard using a bomb strapped in his underwear.
- February 9, 2010: The National Assembly declares Goodluck Jonathan acting president following months of uncertainty about the health of President Yar'Adua.
- May 5, 2010: President Yar'Adua dies in the presidential Villa amidst controversies.
- May 6, 2010: Goodluck Jonathan takes oath of office as president following the death of President Yar'Adua.
- October 1, 2010: A car bomb goes off during the Independence Day celebrations in Abuja killing 12 people. The Movement for the Emancipation of the Niger Delta (MEND) claims responsibility.
- May 29, 2011: Goodluck Jonathan is sworn in as president following the April 16, 2011 presidential election.
- June 16, 2011: A car bomb goes off at the police headquarters in Abuja. Six people die in the attacks. A radical Islamic sect, Boko Harm, claims responsibility.
- August 26, 2011: A suicide bomber sets off a bomb at the United Nations headquarters in Abuja. Over 20 people are killed. Boko Haram, claims responsibility.
- November 4, 2011: Several bombs go off during the Eid-el-Kabir celebrations in Damaturu and Maiduguri, North-east Nigeria, killing over 100 people. Boko Harm, claims responsibility.
- November 11, 2011: Police disrupt a youth protest under the auspices of the National Youth Council of Nigeria (NYCN) over planned removal of fuel subsidy by the federal government.
- January 1, 2012: President Goodluck Jonathan announces the removal of "fuel subsidy". The pump price of petrol is increased to N141 from N65. The price was later pegged at N97 after many days of protests by Nigerians.
- January 2, 2012: Occupy Nigeria protests against removal of fuel

subsidy begins across the county, including in the cities of Kano, Lagos, Kaduna, Ibadan, Abuja and Nigerian Embassies in London, Ottawa, Washington DC and New York.

- January 20, 2012: Channels TV reporter, Eneche Akogwu, is killed while covering terrorist attacks in Kano, North-west, Nigeria.
- May 5, 2012: The Principal Private Secretary to Edo State Governor, Mr. Olaitan Oyerinde, is shot dead in his home in Benin City, Edo State, South-south, Nigeria.
- June 3, 2012: Dana Air McDonnell Douglas MD-83 Flight 992 making a scheduled commercial passenger flight from Abuja to Lagos, crashes into a furniture works and printing press in the Iju-Ishaga neighbourhood of Lagos, killing all 153 people on board. It also caused approximately ten deaths and an unknown number of injuries to people on the ground.
- July 3, 2012: President Goodluck Jonathan forwards the name of Justice Aloma Mariam Mukhtar to the Senate for confirmation as first female Chief Justice of Nigeria.
- July 14, 2012: Adams Oshiomole is re-elected governor of Edo State under the Action Congress of Nigeria (ACN).
- October 5, 2012: Four students of the University of Port Harcourt: Ugonna Obuzor, 18; Lloyd Toku, 19; Tekena Elkanah, 20, and Chiadika Biringa, 20, are lynched and burnt to death by villagers in Aluu, Rivers State, South-south, Nigeria.
- October 17, 2012: Nigeria's First Lady, Dame Patience Jonathan returns to Nigeria from Germany where she was hospitalized for about two months for an undisclosed ailment.
- October 20, 2012: Olusegun Mimiko is re-elected Governor of Ondo State under the Labour Party (LP).
- December 15, 2012: Kaduna State Governor, Patrick Ibrahim Yakowa, and ex-National Security Adviser, Gen. Patrick Owoye Azazi (retd.), their aides, pilot and co-pilot die in a helicopter crash in Bayelsa State, South-south Nigeria.
- February 10, 2013: Nigeria's Super Eagles beat the Stallions of Burkina Faso to lift the Africa Cup of Nations for the third time.
- March 12, 2013: Diepreye Solomon Peter Alamieyeseigha, convicted ex-governor of Bayelsa State is pardoned by President

Goodluck Jonathan, amidst nationwide opposition.
- March 18, 2013: Terrorist attacks at New Road bus station, a popular luxury bus park in Sabon Gari, Kano, North-west Nigeria, claim more than 70 lives. Boko Haram claims responsibility.
- March 21, 2013: Author of Things Fall Apart and acclaimed writer, Prof. Chinua Achebe, dies in Boston, Massachusetts, United States, at 82.
- May 23, 2013: Prof. Chinua Achebe is buried in Ogidi, Anambra State, South-east Nigeria.
- May 24, 2013: Nigeria Governor's Forum (NGF) election ends in a stalemate as two chairmen emerge.
- June 12, 2013: Nigerians from all walks of life celebrate twenty years of the June 12, 1993 presidential election.

- *This chronology was compiled from different sources by Elor Nkeruwem and Kehinde Adewole.*

INDEX

❖

A

Abacha 6, 10-1, 13-20, 23-4, 26, 28, 30-32, 34-37, 39, 41-44, 47-50, 53-4, 56-7, 68-9, 78-103, 107-122, 125, 127-8, 131-3, 139-43, 146, 150-1, 155, 157-8, 204, 211, 237, 266, 271-273, 275-6, 284, 291, 296-7, 349-50, 359, 365
Abacha denies Nigerians 18
Abacha-for-president campaign 80
Abacha for president campaigners 87
Abacha junta 90, 92-93, 142
Abacha presidency 50, 97
Abacha regime 14, 17-8, 83, 85, 87, 94, 107-8, 118, 128, 143, 296, 349, 440
Abachaism 86, 88
Abacharite democracy 83
Abacha's court 47, 82
Abacha's criminal inclinations 91
Abacha's democracy 13-14, 89
Abacha's dungeons 95
Abacha's government 439
Abacha's megalomania 43, 142
Abacha's military 19
Abacha's military tribunal 150
Abacha's Minister 96, 99
Abacha's Nigeria 13
Abacha's presidency 87
Abacha's regime 82, 96
Abacha's transition 15, 18, 39, 48, 50, 68, 86, 97-99, 140, 237, 359
Abati 159-60, 166-8, 181, 195, 206-7, 254, 304, 320-1, 341, 396, 408, 413
Abia State 198-200, 339
Abia State University *see* ABSU
Abiola 18, 20, 24-26, 28-9, 31-35, 43, 46, 51-2, 64, 77-78, 85, 90, 94, 98, 100-1, 105, 115-6, 119, 122, 125, 140-143, 157-8, 204, 211, 219, 254-5, 272, 423, 439, 440
ABN (Association for Better Nigeria) 85, 87, 189, 266
ABSU (Abia State University) 198-201
ABSU senate 198-9
Abubakar 31, 34, 37-46, 53-8, 61, 106, 117-22, 127-8, 130, 132-5, 138-40, 142-4, 155, 190, 193, 285, 296-8, 365-6, 390, 415, 437, 440
Abubakar regime 55, 133, 143
Abubakar's transition 39, 40, 46, 56, 58, 106, 117, 132-3, 135, 138-40, 144, 365
Abuja 84-5, 87, 96, 101, 107, 141, 163, 175, 181, 187, 190, 193, 205, 306, 312, 319, 331, 334-5, 338, 370, 390, 399, 408, 415-6, 436, 438-9, 441-2
Abuja High Court 84-5
Academic Staff Union of Universities *see* ASUU
academics 123, 131, 148, 201, 209, 260-1, 357, 362
accommodation 202, 247-8, 256-7
accountability 112, 167, 184, 188
accounts 193, 206, 331, 332, 367
 bank 206, 331, 367
 private 193, 332
ACE (Alliance for Credible Elections) 330
Achebe 213-7, 347, 384, 387, 389, 405, 443
Achebe Colloquium 215-6
ACN (Action Congress of Nigeria) 442
ACRI (African Crisis Response Initiative) 280, 295
administration 41, 52, 66, 83, 97, 101, 159, 162-4, 170, 179, 182-3, 185, 199, 221, 256, 261, 279, 305-6, 312, 334-6, 341, 359, 366, 368, 371, 383, 389-90, 396-8, 403, 405, 407, 409, 414, 432
Africa 19-24, 26-7, 36, 41, 44-5, 59, 72-4, 84, 99, 102, 111, 113, 136, 140, 150, 156, 183, 189, 194, 210, 211-217, 221, 230, 240, 243, 251, 252, 253, 262, 263, 270, 271, 290, 291, 312, 313, 320
African continent 21, 24, 275, 277, 295, 435

African Crisis Response Initiative (ACRI) 280, 295
African revolution 72-5
AFRICMIL 179-81, 382
agencies 177-8, 181, 183, 279, 299, 305, 308, 330, 339-40, 343-4, 370, 399
agenda 9, 25, 43, 144, 118, 120, 135, 158, 181-2, 226, 242-3, 275, 296, 298, 302, 315, 336, 399, 413, 415-6, 418
Alamieyeseigha 192, 205-208, 442
All Progressives Congress *see* APC
allegations 177, 182, 193, 198-9, 297, 308, 367
Alliance for Credible Elections (ACE) 330
amalgamation 27, 52, 128, 131, 355, 363, 370, 372, 401, 427
ambition 37, 80-1, 94-5, 101, 121-2, 125, 142, 154, 174, 187, 211, 364, 422
political 41-2
America 20, 21-4, 31-6, 43, 59, 75, 91, 108, 115, 140, 145, 149-50, 153, 155, 188, 229-31, 238, 240, 252, 255, 279, 285-9, 292, 295, 309, 315, 330, 338, 385, 409, 422, 426, 428, 435,
American century 149
American dream of democracy in Nigeria 34
Americans 31, 188, 240, 309
Anenih 209, 212, 308, 412,
annulment 19-20, 24, 27, 29, 35, 53-4, 66-7, 76, 85, 95, 109, 122, 141, 157, 187, 204, 211, 254-5, 264, 266, 355
anti-democracy 124-5
Anyaoku 17-18, 114, 133
APC (All Progressives Congress) 201, 416, 420
argument 17, 24, 42, 58, 82, 168, 172, 189, 221-2, 271, 304, 323-5, 327-8, 351, 359, 362, 364, 405 407, 411, 413, 419, 426
assassination 94, 278-9, 283
asset declaration 179-81, 183-5, 197, 302, 309, 367, 432
president's 181, 184, 302
assets 180-182, 184-5, 191, 206, 308, 310-1, 431, 432,
Association for Better Nigeria *see* ABN
ASUU (Academic Staff Union of Universities) 79, 258

B

Babangida 9, 13, 20, 25, 28, 29, 35, 37-9, 44-5, 47-8, 53-4, 57, 69-70, 80-1, 85, 87, 99, 102, 109, 114, 118, 124, 127, 131, 139, 141, 143, 146-9, 156-8, 186, 201, 204, 211, 225, 261, 263-6, 271, 275, 352, 359, 365, 373, 380-1, 394, 406, 422-3, 438-9
Babangida/Abacha regime 87
Babangida Aliyu of Niger State 381, 406, 422
Babangida and Abacha 57, 69, 118, 131, 365
Babangida plans 148-9
Babangida regime 20, 28, 45, 69, 85, 211
Babangida transition cost Nigerian taxpayers 13
Bala Usman 355-7, 362
Bayelsa State 192, 198, 205, 207, 208, 216, 283, 307, 335, 388, 436, 442,
Beijing 242-4
bill 179, 187, 312
Blacks 280-1, 288, 295
Blair, Tony 17, 149, 206, 293
blocks 334, 377
borders 117, 149, 246, 293, 344, 436,
bridge 358, 361
British 17, 23-4, 52, 55, 104, 104-5, 127-9, 131, 176, 206, 253, 268, 330, 353, 358, 360-3, 384, 400, 436
British and American International Schools in Nigeria 330
BS 166
budget 171, 173, 176-7, 319, 323, 331, 334, 341, 385
Buhari 47, 69, 118, 153-5, 203, 299, 339, 340, 406, 415, 438
Buhari regime 203
building materials 246-7
business 11, 18, 33-4, 41, 88, 100, 117, 137, 147, 166, 305, 321, 326-7, 336, 338, 433

C

Campaign for Democracy (CD) 76, 379
Canada 32, 322, 326, 340, 385
candidate, presidential 391, 406
capacity, installed 322, 326, 328

capital
 international 236, 36, 59, 293, 295, 360
 international monopoly 23, 36, 289, 292-3
CBN (Central Bank of Nigeria) 170-2, 320-1, 368
CCB (Code of Conduct Bureau) 179-81, 183, 205, 310-1
CD (Campaign for Democracy) 76
Central Bank of Nigeria *see* CBN
Central Intelligence Agency *see* CIA
certificates 200, 339
Challenges for Nation-Building in Nigeria 177
change 6, 16, 22, 40, 66-67, 86, 114, 160, 212, 230, 232, 234, 239, 241, 249, 250, 253, 273, 307-9, 322, 328-30, 350, 359, 379, 382, 388, 406, 407, 418-9, 421, 426, 434
 attitudinal 307-9
charges 77, 79, 190, 192, 205, 206, 253, 266, 338
children 83, 113, 161, 165, 177, 180, 191, 193, 217, 223, 230-1, 233, 248, 261, 278, 285, 292-3, 298, 309, 311, 313, 315, 317, 367, 385, 387, 395, 412
Chima Ubani 76, 78
Chinua Achebe 213, 384, 443
CIA (Central Intelligence Agency) 21, 35, 278-9
citizens 6-7, 32, 59, 61, 69-71, 75, 79, 83, 95, 106-7, 111, 113, 129, 160, 170, 176-7, 179, 187-9, 193, 198, 198, 203, 227, 234-5, 239, 241, 243, 247, 254-5, 257-8, 263-4, 268-9, 271, 273-6, 285, 290, 299, 301, 318-20, 333, 335, 337, 341, 344-5, 349, 352-3, 355, 373, 390, 401, 421, 432
civil rule 10, 23, 48, 54, 80, 129, 203, 225, 352-3, 370
civil servants 88, 137, 170-1, 319, 332
civil service 165, 170-2, 176, 190
civil war 12, 16, 28, 40, 50, 54, 70, 125, 129, 134, 210, 254, 262, 263, 265, 268, -9, 301, 372-3, 393, 400, 402, 420, 437
civilian presidents 23, 81, 124, 373
claims responsibility 441, 443
Class Struggle in Africa 74
Clinton 20, 35-36, 44, 91, 115, 149-50, 243, 278-9, 286, 288, 293
Code of Conduct 179-81, 183, 205, 310-1
Code of Conduct Bureau *see* CCB
colonial Nigeria 104, 128
colonialists 27, 29, 52, 73-4, 127, 149, 228, 253, 353, 355, 358, 360-1, 363, 386
commission 45, 55-6, 84, 85, 89, 91, 176, 335, 357, 414, 431
committee 25, 163-5, 167-9, 176, 254, 324, 328, 332, 396-9, 432
Committee of Pro-Chancellors of Nigerian Universities 385
committee's report 162-3, 169, 328, 396, 398-9, 432
communism 21, 36, 59, 229-31, 237, 278, 292
communities 212, 248, 257, 282-5, 344, 371, 385, 421,
 producing 282-4
companies 23, 130, 151, 206, 282-3, 284-5, 327, 332, 367, 370, 387, 398
complaints 38, 41, 56-8, 123, 139, 370, 375, 390
concept 22, 47, 239, 251, 261-2, 354, 357, 362, 364, 372
conference 8-9, 17, 20, 45, 47, 55, 80-1, 86, 98, 172, 178, 182, 211, 226, 232, 242, 343, 351, 359, 369, 377, 379, 382, 393-5
Congo 21, 45, 277, 295, 386, 401
Congo crisis 45
Congress for Progressive Change *see* CPC
constitution, draft 86, 98, 162, 351, 359
constitutional conference 8, 9, 81, 98, 226, 323, 351, 359, 431,
contest 47, 60, 80, 92, 97, 101, 121, 125, 140-1, 143, 158, 405-6, 415, 417
context of one Nigeria 237
contract 174, 192, 341-2, 402
contradictions 8, 10, 39, 45-6, 51, 70, 74, 125, 145, 148, 149, 224, 227, 233, 236, 238, 242, 253, 375
conviction 116-7, 136, 191, 356, 400, 405, 423, 439
corporate existence 25, 28, 66-7, 116, 209
corruption 92, 119, 153, 163, 169, 176, 179, 181-6, 188, 192-4, 205, 210, 213, 228, 232, 271, 277, 290, 302, 305-9, 319, 327,

328
  fighting 90, 178, 182, 194, 300, 302, 306-9, 317-9, 325, 327-8, 330-1, 340, 369, 378, 381-2, 386, 390-1, 397-9, 402, 424, 427-8, 431-2, 434
country hostage 39, 324, 428
country's problems 129, 359, 410
country's unity 7, 351, 362
county 442
coup 14-15, 21, 28-9, 44, 53, 76, 86, 100-1, 112, 120, 134, 142, 150-1, 225, 262, 289, 300, 372, 392, 400, 420, 438-40
  counter 28, 53, 265, 273, 275, 425
court 6, 47, 69, 82-5, 107, 141, 191, 193, 204, 266-7, 303, 338, 414, 417
credible elections 98, 406
crisis 8, 11-12, 16,-28, 30, 38, 40, 42, 45, 49, 53, 57, 86, 90, 105, 120, 128, 131, 132, 134, 135, 137, 139, 144, 145, 149, 150, 152, 155, 156,162, 163, 189, 197, 202, 203, 205, 209, 216, 222, 227, 230, 232, 233, 236, 248, 254, 259, 265, 270, 275, 280, 295, 298, 301, 312, 316, 335, 336, 342, 356, 358, 374, 394, 419,
crossroads 2, 64-5, 236

D

DA (Democratic Alternative) 26, 30, 76, 379
death 7, 29, 32, 37, 46, 52, 56, 62, 70-2, 89, 95-6, 107-9, 111, 113, 116, 122, 126, 128, 130, 132, 141, 149, 158, 188, 191, 194, 197, 210, 216-7, 221, 306, 316, 357, 366, 421, 437, 440-2
decay 234, 290, 330, 336-7, 434
declarations 180, 184-5, 223, 310
defeat President Jonathan 415, 422
degree 94, 146, 155, 198-200, 244-5, 258, 318, 338, 340
democracy 4-5, 7-11, 13-4, 16, 19-22, 24-26, 28, 33-8, 40-1, 43-50, 54-5, 59-62, 67, 69, 76, 78, 79-83, 85-6, 88-9, 91-6, 98, 102, 108-9, 111-3, 115-20, 122, 124-5, 129, 131-6, 138, 141-2, 150-2, 154-5, 158, 173, 175, 186, 198,-9, 203, 210-1, 223, 226, 228, 232, 235, 240, 250, 250, 254, 264, 266, 271-3, 275-7, 292, 296, 299, 301, 308-9, 349, 350-4, 356-8, 396, 412, 356-8, 396, 412, 414, 425, 431-2
  downplay 20-1, 83
  travesty of 19, 21, 36
democratic 10, 13-5, 20, 25-6
Democratic Alternative see DA
democratic forces 24, 42-3, 277
democratic governance 128, 131, 399
democratic government 34, 112, 299
  elected 10, 47, 95-6, 99, 100, 149
democratic order
  new 45, 154
  so-called 59, 135, 204
democratic process 61, 121, 134, 274, 296, 430
Democratic Republic 21, 45, 279, 2951
democratic rule 37, 47, 111
democratic struggles 434
democrats, genuine 376, 379, 416, 419
deputy 13, 85, 171, 173, 175, 205, 216, 414, 425, 437-8, 440
detention 32-3, 58, 76-7, 79, 85, 90, 94, 113, 141, 204, 206, 243, 252, 264, 267, 272, 284, 350
Diaspora 395, 435
dictatorship 19, 21, 26, 70, 86, 90-2, 94-6, 100, 124, 126-7, 133, 135, 137, 146, 148, 223, 225, 254, 271, 275-7, 291, 300-1, 349, 352, 370
disorder 68, 251, 340
disputed presidential election 438
doctors 31, 90, 161, 207, 260, 319
Dokubo-Asari 374-6, 425-6
dollars 33-4, 41, 50, 71, 167, 305, 344, 401
domination 27, 49, 51, 227-8, 230, 269, 285, 288, 253, 355, 364

E

Economic and Financial Crimes Commission see EFCC
Economic Community of West African States (ECOWAS) 81
ECOWAS (Economic Community of West African States) 81
education 145, 207, 237, 240, 255, 270, 300, 308, 310, 314, 328, 330-2, 335, 378, 424
EFCC (Economic and Financial Crimes Commission) 162-3, 168, 199, 205, 384

elected president 11, 14, 16, 18, 48, 91, 96-7, 99-100, 113, 426, 440
  democratically 11, 18, 48, 91, 96-7, 99, 100
election 5-6, 8-9, 11, 13, 16, 18-20, 24-5, 27-9, 33-6, 42, 47, 49, 51, 53-6, 58-60, 66-7, 76-7, 80, 83-5, 89, 91-2, 94-9, 101, 109, 113, 116, 121, 122, 125, 132-3, 135, 138-43, 145, 147, 157, 187, 199, 203-4, 208, 211-2, 237, 254, 264, 266-7, 271-2, 296-7, 302, 333, 365, 375, 405-6, 408, 412-5, 419, 423, 425, 427, 431, 438-41, 443
  fair 36, 55, 140
  governorship 413
electoral commission 37, 45, 55-6, 84-5, 89, 91, 101, 406, 414, 431
electoral process 40-1, 141, 214, 216, 414-5
Electoral Reform Committee (ERC) 414
elite, political 5, 88, 398
embarrass 164, 167, 396
employment 177, 211, 246, 258, 283, 328, 339
entitlement 170, 172, 204
equity 393, 395, 434
ERC (Electoral Reform Committee) 414
ethnic nationalities 27, 111, 145, 253, 355-7, 362-4, 372, 374-7, 382, 394
ethnicity 25, 27, 30, 116
exploit 40, 192, 238, 239, 401
exploitation 25, 59, 224, 227-8, 235-6, 247, 251, 282, 352, 360, 364, 373

F

fairest presidential election 439
faith 34-35, 61, 180, 259, 270-1, 299-300, 329, 426
family planning 313-6
FCT (Federal Capital Territory) 172, 334-5
FEC (Federal Executive Council) 172, 174
Federal Capital Territory *see* FCT
Federal Executive Council *see* FEC
federal government 97, 125, 167, 168, 312, 315, 327, 334, 338, 344, 391, 396, 441

Federal Republic of Nigeria 180, 310-2, 436
federation 52, 54, 70, 85, 127, 133, 134, 165, 171-, 260, 338, 341, 357, 366-7, 375-6, 407-8, 417
Federation of Nigeria 338, 341
Fifth Schedule 180, 310, 312
fight 6, 24, 26, 45, 156, 169, 178-9, 181-3, 185, 224, 249, 285, 302, 307, 397, 406, 431, 434
fight corruption 169, 178, 181, 302, 397, 431
First Lady 195-7, 207, 388, 391, 442
Foday Sankoh 16, 86, 297-8
FoIA (Freedom of Information Act) 178-81, 183-5
eviction 245, 247-8, 257
foundation 10, 60, 69-71, 73, 83, 100, 105-6, 108, 146, 179, 224, 229, 236, 313, 317, 333, 361
freedom 8, 12, 14, 18, 31, 59, 61, 77-8, 81, 90, 95-6, 106, 117, 123, 134, 178-81, 183, 185, 188, 190, 227-31, 233, 235, 237-41, 287, 350, 370, 393
Freedom of Information Act *see* FoIA
friend 4, 17, 101, 153, 156-7, 175, 208, 214, 263, 318, 329, 331, 408-10, 416, 421, 438

G

gas sector 167, 169, 323
GEJ 409-10
Gen. Abacha 13-6, 18-20, 69, 79, 82-3, 110
General Abacha 440
General Babangida 438-9
General Olusegun Obasanjo 438-9, 440
General Sani Abacha 439-40
generals 3, 44, 65, 82, 102, 111-4, 133, 1, 30657, 347, 373, 380, 440
Germany 16, 159-62, 185, 194-6, 262, 280-1, 330, 385, 442
Ghana 21, 23, 80, 83, 172, 196, 272-3, 275, 278, 366, 385-6
GNPP (Great Nigeria People's Party) 417, 448
God 48, 52, 95, 101, 121, 122, 131, 137, 160-2, 176, 194-7, 311-2, 354, 367, 412,

Goodluck Jonathan 159, 172-4, 181-, 194-6, 205, 210, 333, 368, 370, 383, 405-6, 412, 414, 422, 425, 441-3

governance 36, 52, 91, 100, 112-3, 124, 128, 132, 138, 160, 162, 173-4, 179, 183, 185, 198, 207, 215, 225, 231, 275, 303, 306, 319, 357, 361, 390, 393, 400, 410, 447

government 5-11, 17, 29, 32-5, 41, 43, 48, 52-3, 56, 66, 72, 80-1, 83-6, 88-90, 97-9, 101, 104, 106, 110, 113, 116, 119-20, 122-3, 125, 136, 139-41, 157, 159, 163-4, 167-74, 177-9, 181, 183, 188, 191, 193-4, 196-7, 199, 201, 204-5, 211, 221-2, 226-7, 239, 246-8, 250, 254, 256-9, 261, 263, 267, 276, 278, 282-5, 290, 297, 299, 302-8, 312, 313, 315-6, 319-22, 324-30, 332, 334, 337-44, 352, 359, 363, 366, 368-71, 374, 382, 388-91, 394, 396, 398, 405, 410-11, 431, 437-41

  civilian 85, 122, 438
  elected 48, 88
  interim 29, 53, 86, 116
  local 11, 56, 83, 88-9, 101, 139, 170, 188, 204, 267, 283, 307, 319, 391, 450
  present 9-10, 431
  transitional 10, 116

government agencies 177, 181, 305, 328
government of national unity 41, 90, 106, 116
government officials 17, 167, 191, 196, 227, 303, 308, 328
government policies 205, 320
governor 100, 170, 174, 177, 192, 197-9, 201, 205-8, 304, 307, 344, 368, 370, 381, 391, 395, 413, 417, 420, 425, 436-7, 442
Great Nigeria People's Party (GNPP) 417
groups 27, 43, 46, 49, 52, 55, 76, 79, 85, 87, 89-90, 94, 97, 117, 119, 122, 125, 141, 174, 224, 246, 252, 257, 282, 285, 287, 303, 318, 332, 353, 354, 355, 357, 371-5, 389-90, 393, 395, 425-6, 429
  pro-democracy 76, 122, 141, 252
Guardian 51, 68, 157, 206, 209, 228, 237, 320, 327, 373, 409, 419, 421-2
Gulf 22, 154, 285-9, 292, 327, 436

H

harbinger 4, 25, 44, 154, 239, 241, 252
headline 201, 209, 305, 321, 325, 373
health 32, 111, 160, 162, 195, 197, 243, 245-246, 274, 282, 290, 313-314-315 319, 326, 336, 392, 434, 441
hegemony 49-50, 73, 138, 140, 292, 296, 351, 364, 374, 425,
help 18, 21, 27, 77, 141, 153, 177, 208, 275, 297, 311, 312, 363, 365, 376, 391, 411, 431, 433, 435
history 10, 13, 16, 18-19, 22, 28, 30, 33, 36, 40, 47- 48, 54 - 55 – 56, 68 – 69 – 70, 76, 82, 84, 86, 108 – 109 – 110 – 111,118, 122 – 123, 127 – 128, 131, 133, 138, 143, 149, 157, 165, 175, 201, 204, 209, 215, 224 – 225, 229, 241, 243, 252 – 253, 626 – 263 – 264 – 265 – 266 – 267, 269, 275, 277, 282, 292, 300, 302, 316, 354 – 355 – 356 – 357, 362 – 363, 365, 368, 379, 80, 410, 417, 419, 422, 427, 429, 435
  country's 7, 70, 108, 129, 139, 149, 190, 192, 194, 211, 216, 223, 225, 235, 258, 260, 261, 265, 293, 312-313, 328, 338, 340, 343-344, 349-50, 351-2, 356, 359, 362, 369, 383, 386, 397, 400, 405, 410, 416, 420
  grip of 10, 12, 114, 141, 254, 263, 264-266
  national 4-5, 7-8, 16, 25-6, 28, 30-2, 37-8, 41, 45-47, 51, 53-55, 58, 61, 70, 72-3, 76, 80, 84, 86-87, 90, 92, 101, 103, 106, 111-3-116-7, 123, 127-8, 130, 139-41, 144-6, 148, 151-2, 154, 157, 159, 170-1, 173-5, 177, 179-80, 185, 187, 190-93, 195, 200-1, 204-5, 211, 215-7, 221, 226-227, 233, 237, 252, 254, 257-59-60, 265-266, 270-72, 276, 284, 289-91, 297, 299, 304-5, 307, 309-10, 312-3, 315, 317-9, 321, 326-31, 336-38, 340-44, 350-51, 353-6, 358-9, 361, 363-5, 372-5, 377-8, 381-4, 391-5, 398-9, 406, 408, 412, 414-7, 421-2, 424, 428-33, 439-42
  nation's 379, 380
history of colonial Nigeria 128
history of Nigeria 18, 40, 111, 123
Hitler 17, 110, 137, 230, 262, 288
homosexuality 187-9

hospitals 89, 224, 290, 319, 330
housing 245-9, 256-7, 387
human rights 6, 7, 10, 12, 14, 19-21, 76, 78-9, 81, 83, 85, 91, 93, 94-5, 98, 100-3, 108, 112, 123, 141-2, 156, 188, 243, 248, 252, 277, 296, 350, 371, 424
humanity 121, 187-8, 217, 237, 239, 251, 271, 276, 278, 292, 337
humiliation 5, 38, 45, 57, 144
hunger 28, 225, 230
husbands 243-4

I

IBB (Ibrahim Badamosi Babangida) 124, 126, 156, 201-5, 210, 380
Ibrahim Badamosi Babangida *see* IBB
Idiagbon 47, 69, 118, 289-91, 438
Ijaw nation 144, 205, 207
Ijaws 207, 282, 300, 426
illusion 6-8, 36, 39-40, 47, 49, 70, 105, 108, 118, 135, 150, 152, 255, 260, 264, 269, 279, 350, 357, 360, 364-5, 418
image 7, 10, 41, 64, 82-3, 176, 182, 184, 200, 215, 216, 332
IMF/World Bank 22-3, 36, 74, 124, 293
imperialism 23-4, 31, 38, 43, 74, 115, 149, 231, 253, 285, 288, 295, 361
incumbent 210, 413-4, 422
independence 12, 25, 27, 52-3, 56, 73, 98, 129, 202, 209, 226-7, 238, 261, 264-5, 268, 271, 273-4, 276, 298, 300-1, 326 349, 353, 356-7, 364, 382-3, 428
Independent National Electoral Commission *see* INEC
INEC (Independent National Electoral Commission) 37, 45, 55, 406 414
inequality, social 429, 432-3
information 66-8, 80, 84, 178-81, 183-5, 214-5, 266, 283, 315, 320, 335, 337-8, 341, 344, 367, 370, 382, 439
infrastructure 89, 162, 172, 174, 245, 260, 273, 290, 305, 308, 329, 330, 333, 335-6, 363, 368, 427, 434
injustices 40, 130, 242, 252, 364
 national 364
institutions 89, 123, 148, 185, 209, 259, 261, 307, 329, 330-1, 333, 339, 357, 366, 370-1, 378, 398, 431, 433

Interim National Government 5, 7, 53, 80, 140-1, 359, 439
international community 17, 20, 31, 40, 58-9, 71, 93, 102, 114, 116, 120, 135, 140-1, 152, 268, 277, 285
investigations 338-9
Iraq 285-8, 292-3, 326

J

Jonathan 184-5, 194-7, 205, 207-8, 210-2, 302-3, 305-15, 320-2, 324-5, 327, 329, 331, 333, 335, 336, 341, 343, 368, 370, 383, 388, 390-1, 396, 398, 400-2, 405-16, 420, 422, 424-28, 431, 441, 442-3
Jonathan administration 159, 164, 170, 179, 185, 305-6, 312, 366, 368, 383, 396, 398, 407, 414
Jonathan government 174, 341
junta 11, 13-4, 79-80, 82-3, 90, 92-4, 101, 113, 142, 271, 289-90, 359
justice 4-6, 8, 62, 70, 72, 80, 95-6, 100, 103, 115, 117, 131, 145, 149, 190-3, 206, 214, 228, 241-2, 252, 267, 299, 309, 350, 364, 366, 386, 389, 393, 414-5, 434, 439, 442
justification 81, 98, 137-8, 222, 285, 232

K

Kano 104, 298-300, 338, 385, 442, 443
Kudirat Abiola 77, 94, 119, 254-5, 440

L

Lagos 14, 84, 110, 210, 255, 256-7, 261, 264, 273-4, 290, 296, 329, 338, 343-4, 388, 395, 437, 439-40, 442
Lagosians 110, 255-8
laws 4, 6, 33, 74, 84-5, 92, 114, 148, 154, 179-85, 187-8, 192, 203, 206, 229, 231-2, 240, 246-7, 250-2, 255, 257, 276, 279, 285, 294, 303, 310-4, 317-9, 337-9, 341, 350, 365, 382, 386, 387, 392, 401-2, 413, 424
 international 246
leaders 13, 17, 20, 40, 50, 55, 82, 95, 117, 160, 173, 177, 231, 274-5, 282, 287, 300-1, 313, 330, 335, 357, 378, 382, 384, 385, 386, 387-8, 391-2, 432
 so-called 324-5, 423
leadership 32, 61, 99, 137, 151, 175, 194,

199, 207, 211, 215, 223 241, 273-5, 277, 315, 373-4, 378, 386-9, 420, 430
lecturers 147, 259-61, 332
lesbians 185, 187-8
Liberia 82, 107, 114, 146, 150, 230, 262-3
liberty 31, 35, 117, 131, 232, 240-1, 321
livelihood 151, 255-7, 282-3
Local Government Council elections in Nigeria 56
local government election 11, 83, 101, 139, 267
love 44, 64-5, 147, 161, 190, 196, 214, 216, 220, 270, 331, 372, 401

M

Madunagu, Edwin 68, 214, 237, 371, 376, 382, 392, 394, 419, 421-2
march 5, 7-10, 20-1, 44, 82-3, 89, 102, 115, 117, 135, 155, 192, 198, 201, 205, 208, 219, 226-7, 243, 248, 249, 250, 268, 282, 287, 289, 297, 370, 373, 419, 420-2, 437-9, 442-3
marriage, same-sex 187, 189
masses 7, 23, 25, 26, 28, 67, 74-5, 103, 116, 192, 221, 228, 235, 238, 240-1, 254, 276-7, 304, 325, 351-3, 364, 371, 373, 379, 388
media 159, 161-2, 168, 170-2, 174, 179, 181, 183, 192, 195-6, 202-3, 214, 243, 276, 309, 320-1, 323, 329, 368, 382, 383, 388, 396-7
meeting 17, 31-2, 98, 118, 163, 172, 198, 209, 327, 357, 374, 376, 406
members 32, 83, 102, 153, 155, 163-5, 167, 170-1, 209, 305, 326, 328, 351, 357, 359, 374, 395, 397, 399, 407, 417, 426
MEND (Movement for the Emancipation of the Niger Delta) 441
merger 201, 362, 371, 416-9
MIC (Military Industrial Complex) 22, 279
middle 2-3, 24, 234, 240, 279, 286, 373, 375, 406, 435
militarism 275, 294, 295
military 6-13, 15-6, 19-23, 25-6, 31, 33-4, 37-50, 53-62, 66, 69, 71, 73-5, 77, 79-83, 85, 87-90, 93-6, 99, 101-2, 104-20, 124-58, 174, 186, 201, 203, 221, 225-8, 232, 236, 241, 253-5, 258, 261, 265-6, 270-3, 278-9, 282-9, 290-2, 294, 296-7, 299-300, 307, 313, 332, 349-53, 356-7, 359-60, 365, 370, 372-3, 376, 392, 400-1, 420, 422, 437-8
military administrations 261
military administrators 89
military adventurers 16, 89, 90, 270, 273
military boys 33-4
military coup 225, 372, 420, 437-8
military dictatorship 26, 95, 96, 124, 126-7, 133, 135, 137, 254, 271, 291, 300, 349, 352, 370
military government 43, 136, 226, 258, 352, 439
  present 226, 352
military government prides 226
Military Industrial Complex (MIC) 22, 279
military junta 13, 79-80, 101, 113, 271, 289-90, 359
military misrule 47, 102
military officers 133, 203, 261, 437
military president 201, 203
  former 201
military regime 9-10, 13, 15, 49, 60, 73-4, 80, 82, 85, 95, 108, 114, 128, 130, 133, 226, 228, 266, 270-1, 365
  present 9, 73, 228
  various 228, 246
military rule 16, 26, 33, 43, 45, 50, 69, 73-5, 77, 106, 139, 158, 225-6, 265, 353, 356, 359, 439
  scourge of 353, 356
military rulers 114, 124, 131, 266, 297
  new 114, 131, 297
military tribunals 85
minister 21, 29, 37, 66-8, 80, 84, 87, 89, 96, 99, 101, 103, 109, 144, 163-6, 170, 172-7, 185-6, 251, 266-7, 278, 302, 304-5, 314-5, 320, 327, 332, 334, 366-8, 391, 397-8, 407, 437
  former 407
Minister of Petroleum Resources 163-4, 166, 327, 368, 397-8
ministries 305, 313, 330, 398
mistakes 129, 260, 306
Mobutu 21, 45, 89, 90, 99, 262, 277

Modern Nigeria 24, 150, 210
money 13, 56, 60, 146, 154, 165, 174, 176, 178, 192-3, 197, 205-7, 214, 225, 234, 290, 305, 307, 308, 323-4, 332, 336, 342, 376, 384, 391, 407, 415, 433-4
move the country forward 7, 264, 349-51, 359, 424
Movement for Abacha for President 87
Movement for the Emancipation of the Niger Delta (MEND) 441
mufti-presidents 276-7
murder 12, 56, 77, 83-4, 93, 100, 104, 119, 127, 142, 156, 228, 230, 254-5, 281, 316-7, 337, 356
  of Kudirat Abiola 254
myths 26, 352, 375-6

N

NADECO (National Democratic Coalition) 252, 439, 440
NANS (National Association of Nigerian Students) 395
nation 8, 12, 16, 20, 29, 30-2, 37-41, 48, 54, 59, 61-2, 80-1, 89, 95, 105, 109, 111, 115-9, 121, 123, 129, 131-2, 134, 140, 143-6, 148, 150, 152-4, 162, 164, 169, 175, 177, 187-8, 197, 204-7, 210-1, 214, 216-7, 221-3, 226, 231, 234, 238, 241, 253-4, 257, 260, 264, 268, 272, 276, 281, 289-91, 295, 299-306, 318, 322, 324, 327, 330, 353-5, 358, 361-3, 365-72, 376-83, 386, 389, 392-3, 400, 405, 409, 420, 423-4, 427, 429-31, 434, 436
  most disorderly 214, 384
  prosperous 30, 377-8
National Assembly 130, 144, 154, 171, 173, , 175, 179-80, 185, 187, 211, 310, 342, 375, 384, 392, 395, 414, 430-2, 441
National Association of Nigerian Students (NANS) 395
National Centre Party of Nigeria see NCPN
National Council of Women Societies (NCWS) 395
National Democratic Coalition (NADECO) 252, 439, 440
national dialogue 217, 373, 377
National Electoral Commission of Nigeria in Uyo 101
national ethos 7, 329, 361, 381-2
National Examination Council (NECO) 336
National Film and Video Censors Board (NFVCB) 340
national governments 313
National Institute of Policy and Strategic Studies (NIPSS) 321
National Oil Corporation (NOC) 326
National Orientation Agency (NOA) 309
National Party of Nigeria see NPN
National Population Commission see NPC
National Public Radio (NPR) 215
national question 26, 30, 351, 353, 354-6, 358, 364, 412, 428
National Republican Convention see NRC
National Solidarity People's Alliance (NSPA) 266
national teams 260
national unity 4, 16, 41, 90, 106, 116, 157, 226, 270-2, 353-4, 364, 424
  bastion of 226, 270
National Universities Commission see NUC
National University of Nigeria 338
National Youth Council of Nigeria (NYCN) 395, 441
nationalities 27, 30, 46, 111, 113, 125, 135, 144-5, 149, 227, 253, 355-8, 361-4, 372, 374-7, 382, 394
  oppressed 46
  various 113, 135, 356, 358, 361-2
nationhood 29, 83, 192, 225, 242, 253, 301, 353-4, 362, 375, 400, 429-30
NCDC (Nigeria Centre for Disease Control) 317
NCPN (National Centre Party of Nigeria) 101, 266
NCWS (National Council of Women Societies) 395
NDPVF (Niger Delta People's Volunteer Force) 374
NECO (National Examination Council) 336
neighbours 286, 288-289, 293-4
NEITI (Nigeria Extractive Industries

Transparency Initiative) 169, 328
neo-colonialism 73-5, 273, 296, 354
NERC (Nigerian Electricity Regulatory Commission) 177
Network on Police Reform in Nigeria (NOPRIN) 332
New Nigeria 24, 116, 188, 354, 366, 369, 376, 379, 416
New World Order 59, 229-31, 250, 288-9, 293
newspapers 15, 100, 181, 304-5, 396
NFA (Nigeria Football Association) 260
NFVCB (National Film and Video Censors Board) 340
Niger 174, 193, 267, 375, 406, 422, 436
Niger Delta 71, 104-5, 133-4, 144, 149-52, 207, 282-5, 300, 374, 425-6, 436, 441
Niger Delta People's Volunteer Force (NDPVF) 374, 425
Nigeria
  creation of 105, 383
  democratic 20
  disintegration of 375, 394, 400
  misruled 44, 114
  moving 42, 71, 265, 271
  negotiate 381-2, 423, 425, 427
next civilian president of 80, 109
  primitive regime 50
  reclaiming 371, 435
  ruled 134, 264, 380
  soul of 390, 405
  survival of 373, 390
  territorial integrity of 393-4, 399
Nigeria and Nigerians 42, 79, 88, 90, 92, 111, 165, 380
Nigeria Centre for Disease Control (NCDC) 317
Nigeria constitution 425
Nigeria counter part 273
Nigeria Extractive Industries Transparency Initiative (NEITI) 169, 328
Nigeria Football Association (NFA) 260
Nigeria Labour Congress *see* NLC
Nigeria nationalism 27
Nigeria Obasanjo 125, 142, 210
Nigeria Police 154, 329-33
Nigeria Ports Authority (NPA) 308, 412
Nigeria state 323-4, 326

Nigerian Army 109, 124, 290, 296, 298
Nigerian character 214, 387
Nigerian crisis 42, 58, 120, 135, 156, 209, 255
Nigerian debacle 40, 113, 270
Nigerian economy 38, 61, 226, 437
Nigerian Electricity Regulatory Commission (NERC) 177
Nigerian federation 54, 133, 407-8, 417
Nigerian government 34, 284-5, 316, 437, 440
Nigerian leaders 177
Nigerian masses 371, 373
Nigerian military 43, 47, 126, 141, 285-9, 365
  so-called 365
Nigerian military dictatorship 126
Nigerian military head 285
Nigerian nation 40146, 148, 154, 272, 300, 361-2, 365, 369, 434
Nigerian National Petroleum Corporation *see* NNPC
Nigerian nationhood 429
Nigerian Peoples Party (NPP) 417
Nigerian politics 26, 124, 146-7
Nigerian president 302
Nigerian Presidential Air Fleet 319
Nigerian problem 387
Nigerian project 51, 129, 376
Nigerian psyche 233
Nigerian situation 7, 37, 49, 176, 265, 358, 430433
Nigerian society 118, 125, 213, 240, 391-2
Nigerian soldiers 292
Nigerian state 11, 71-2, 94-5, 102, 112, 116, 126, 130, 135, 136, 138, 145, 156, 204, 207, 210, 226-8, 231-2, 235, 267-9, 317-8, 333, 351, 353, 357, 372, 383, 421, 425, 431, 434
Nigerian Television Authority (NTA) 159, 195
Nigerian Universities 146-7, 259, 385
Nigerian women 213, 243, 319
Nigerian youth 77, 108, 231, 233, 418
Nigerians 5-15, 18-21, 25, 28, 32-4, 38-44, 46, 48-9, 52, 54-5, 57-9, 69-70, 74, 79-82, 87-90, 92-5, 97, 99, 102, 104-9,

111-5, 117-21, 125-6, 128-30, 132, 134-8, 142, 147-9, 151-62, 165, 169-70, 174-5, 181-6, 188, 190, 194-5, 197, 199, 202-5, 207, 211-2, 214, 216, 221-2, 226, 238, 241, 252, 254, 265, 266, 270-1, 273-4, 289-91, 299-303, 306-7, 313, 316-7, 319-24, 328, 337, 340-1, 343-4, 349-50, 353, 359, 365, 368-70, 373, 375, 379-81, 383, 385-8, 392, 395, 398, 400, 402, 405, 408, 413-5, 426, 429, 430-5, 439, 441, 443
- befuddle 15, 20, 44
- cannibalized 119, 365
- few 9, 70, 161, 195, 214
- idle 160, 207
- innocent 94, 302, 316, 380
- million 92, 170
- most 104, 413
- ordinary 38, 221-2, 299, 381, 386
- patriotic 128, 429
- response of 303, 340
- rights of 59, 95
- smart 204, 343

Nigeria's democratic aspirations 86
Nigeria's freest 142, 439
Nigeria's history 28, 55
Nigeria's ignoble military regime 94
Nigeria's independence 53, 357, 362
Nigeria's independence struggle 362
Nigeria's military establishment 73
Nigeria's military junta 101
Nigeria's military ruler 99, 110
Nigeria's military tyrants 38
Nigeria's power base 120
Nigeria's problems 270, 393, 428
Nigeria's ruling elite 149, 333, 399
Nigeria's Senate President 176
Nigeria's tortuous history 19, 54
NIPSS (National Institute of Policy and Strategic Studies) 321
Nkrumah 21, 73-5, 80, 278
NLC (Nigeria Labour Congress) 303, 369, 395, 424
NNPC (Nigerian National Petroleum Corporation) 165, 167, 221-2, 325, 327, 398
NOA (National Orientation Agency) 309
NOC (National Oil Corporation) 327
NOPRIN (Network on Police Reform in Nigeria) 332
North 26, 28-9, 37, 53-4, 103, 120, 124, 125, 130, 137, 144, 146, 157, 339, 357, 364, 372, 374, 390, 406-7, 426, 436, 441-3
Northern Nigeria 137, 300, 436-8
NPA (Nigeria Ports Authority) 412
NPC (National Population Commission) 312-3, 315
NPN (National Party of Nigeria) 103, 290, 417
NPP (Nigerian Peoples Party) 417
NPR (National Public Radio) 215
NRC (National Republican Convention) 25, 84, 202, 204, 439
NSPA (National Solidarity People's Alliance) 266
NTA (Nigerian Television Authority) 159, 195
NUC (National Universities Commission) 200-1, 259, 319, 337, 338, 339-40
NUNS (National Union of Nigerian Students) 123
NYCN (National Youth Council of Nigeria) 395, 441

O

Obasanjo 58-61, 76, 103, 121-6, 132, 134, 138-44, 148-9, 151-2, 187, 202-4, 209-12, 225, 340, 368, 380, 384, 407, 422, 432, 438-440
- emergence of 141, 202

Obasanjo presidency 122, 139
Obasanjo's regime 123, 132
Occupy Nigeria 322, 329, 366, 369, 371, 379, 441
offences 96, 107, 190
office 28, 38, 48, 57, 90, 92, 100, 110, 118, 120, 124-5, 133, 144, 175-, 180, 181, 186-7, 199, 205-6, 209, 225, 260, 263-4, 276, 287, 304-5, 311, 330, 369, 388, 391, 398, 410, 413, 432, 434, 440-1
officers, public 180, 196, 310
Ogoni tragedy 71
Ogonis 71-2, 269, 282
oil 34, 40, 71-2, 92-3, 95, 101, 117, 123, 125, 129, 130, 144, 151, 163, 167, 173, 221-2, 225, 273, 282-6, 306, 318, 321-8,

340, 350, 356, 362, 365, 367, 369, 372-3, 376, 379, 389-91, 396-8, 401, 424, 432, 436
politics of 372-3
oil companies 130, 151, 282-5, 327, 367, 398
oil industry 163, 222, 306, 324, 327, 340, 350, 396
oil sector 163, 168, 321, 324-5, 327
oligarchy 15-6, 19, 44, 50, 130, 143, 150, 152, 271
Olufemi Oyinade Tunde-Oladepo 337
Olusegun Obasanjo 76, 121, 134, 139, 149, 209, 340, 380, 384, 422, 438, 439, 440
omnipotence 49, 227-8, 262, 264
Omolade Adunbi 428
OPEC (Organisation of Petroleum Exporting Countries) 326, 436
opposition 7-8, 11-2, 14, 29, 35, 45, 66, 72, 81, 88, 98, , 106, 118, 123, 142, 148, 182, 187, 201, 226, 262, 276, 296, 303, 359, 397, 399, 415-22, 434, 443
opposition parties 416-7, 419-20
oppression 30, 46, 127, 223, 227, 232, 244, 247, 251, 264, 301, 360, 364
option 11-2, 37, 93, 97, 130, 139, 144, 152, 164, 190-3, 201, 281, 307, 322, 376, 392-3, 419-21
order 29, 43, 45-6, 59-60, 67, 75, 83-5, 89, 102, 106, 118, 135-6, 153-5, 181, 204, 210, 224, 227, 229-31, 233, 237, 249, 250-2, 259, 262-3, 267-9, 276, 279, 288-9, 393, 299, 308, 317, 340, 392, 414, 415, 421
Organisation of Petroleum Exporting Countries (OPEC) 326, 436
Orji Kalu 199-200

P
pain 13, 143, 158, 302, 304, 322, 400, 417
parents 191, 258, 326, 337-8
parties 5, 13, 18, 25, 28, 37, 45, 47, 57, 69-70, 81, 83-4, 89, 92, 96-8, 148, 191, 201-2, 204, 246, 265-6, 296, 416-7, 419-20
new 416, 418-9
PCI (Police College Ikeja) 329-33, 343-4
PDP (People's Democratic Party) 105, 144, 202, 209, 212, 308, 389, 406, 410, 413, 415-22, 440
peace 4-6, 13, 23, 62, 67, 71, 90, 96, 100, 128, 146, 150, 152, 219, 228, 229-31, 242, 247-9, 272, 277, 279, 281, 288, 292, 294, 297-8, 350, 400, 424-6, 433
peace process 297
peasants 25, 27-9, 151, 240
People's Democratic Party see PDP
performance 176, 207, 307, 343, 413
personages 69, 265
petrol 92, 221, 234, 302-3, 305-6, 317, 322-3, 325, 328-9, 368-400, 441
 price of 221, 234, 302-3, 305-6, 322-3, 325, 329, 368-9, 441
petroleum 34, 76, 92, 162-6, 173, 221-2, 282, 302-4, 319, 321, 326-8, 368, 396-9, 408, 436-7
petroleum ministers 397-8
Petroleum Products Pricing Regulatory Agency see PPPRA
Petroleum Resources 163-4, 166, 173, 327, 368, 397, 398
Petroleum Revenue Special Task Force see PRSTF
Pickering 32-4
picture 11, 32, 71, 143, 159, 195, 299, 333-4
planned presidential election 80
Police College 331
Police College Ikeja see PCI
political class 4-6, 8, 11-12, 39, 43-6, 56, 58, 69, 81, 118, 120, 127, 139, 152, 224 253, 357, 359-60, 410, 418
political crisis 12, 17, 24, 43, 83, 86, 120, 137, 156, 254-5, 270, 350
political detainees 31, 79, 93, 114
political office holders 304, 369, 391
political parties 13, 18, 25, 28, 47, 57, 69, 81, 83, 96-8, 201-2, 204, 265-6, 296
political power 15, 29, 30, 45-6, 54-5, 132, 262, 301, 351, 362, 364, 374, 379, 390
political reform 393
political structure 10, 363, 365, 394, 395
politicians 4-5, 17, 25, 38-9, 42, 45-6, 49, 51, 56-7, 60, 69, 77, 80, 89, 99, 100, 103-4, 106, 139-40, 142-4, 153, 193, 201, 203-4, 235, 241, 270, 272, 318, 352, 356, 359-60, 383, 392, 411, 418, 424, 434

politics 9, 16, 25-7, 33, 35, 39, 44, 52, 54, 56, 66, 69, 77, 92, 98, 100, 103, 106, 117, 124, 131, 140, 146, 159, 176, 195, 215, 223-4, 229-30, 235, 237, 252-5, 265, 285, 292, 294, 372-3, 378, 391, 399-400, 408-9, 416-7, 419, 426
  international 117, 285, 292
  playing 9, 159, 399
polity 9-10, 55, 67, 74, 120, 171, 175, 178, 181, 257, 300, 351, 355-8, 397
poll, presidential 51-2
population 7, 37, 243, 248-50, 271-2, 282, 307, 312-6, 372, 377, 395, 405, 424, 430, 432-4
  country's 312-3
position 4-6, 22, 24, 31, 33-5, 58, 69, 80, 114, 122, 144, 160, 170, 173, 185, 236-7, presidency of Nigeria 42, 120, 122, 143
president 10-11, 14-20, 23, 26, 32-3, 35-8, 42, 46-9, 51, 53, 59, 66, 72, 76, 80, 87, 91, 95, 97, 99-103, 106, 109, 113, 115, 120, 122-6, 135, 141-2, 158-60, 162-5, 167, 169-70, 172-6, 178-87, 195-7, 201, 203-12, 216, 229, 237, 243, 263, 277-9, 291, 296-7, 302-15, 318-36, 340-1, 343, 351, 367, 374, 383-4, 388, 390-1, 397-8, 400-2, 405-9, 411-6, 420, 422, 424-8, 431-2, 437, 439-42
  democratically-elected 18, 91
  democratically-selected 18, 91
  first 87, 207, 278, 437
  former 196, 209, 384, 422
  last 405, 409
  next 42, 102, 120, 135, 407
President Abacha 17, 49
President Bill Clinton 91, 115, 278
President Clinton 279
President Goodluck Ebele Jonathan 180
President Goodluck Jonathan 159, 172, 174, 181, 182, 195-6, 210, 333, 383, 405-6, 412, 422, 441-2
President Jonathan 163-5, 169, 173-4, 178-, 181-5, 205, 207-8, 211, 302-3, 305-10, 313, 315, 320-1, 324-5, 327, 329, 331, 341, 343, 388, 390-1, 400-2, 405-9, 412-6, 420, 422, 424-8, 431
President Jonathan fighting corruption 431
President Obasanjo 103, 187
president of Nigeria 18, 42, 80, 91, 96, 99, 109, 120, 203, 405, 409, 426,
President on Niger Delta 425
President on Public Affairs 167, 178, 413
President Yar'Adua 414, 441
presidential ambition 101, 121, 174
presidential election 19, 24-5, 35, 47, 51, 53-54, 66, 80, 84, 85, 91, 94, 96, 98, 99, 109, 121-2, 125, 132, 140-2, 147, 157, 187, 203-4, 211, 237, 264, 271, 296, 302, 405, 412-4, 423, 438-43
presidential jets 123, 143, 411
presidential nomination 150
presidential Villa 196, 312, 335, 441
President's wife 159, 195
presides 408
presiding officers 173, 175,
prison 14, 79, 91, 94, 98, 100, 141, 143, 156, 192, 193, 203, 206, 210-1, 332, 440
pro-democracy 10, 19-20, 33, 35, 49, 76, 78, 79, 85, 91, 93, 95, 98, 108-9, 111, 115, 122, 141-2, 152, 203, 252, 264, 296
pro-democracy forces 33, 35, 115, 152
process 40-1, 48, 51, 57, 60-1, 73, 76, 92, 106, 135, 141, 150, 152, 164-5, 177, 199, 214, 216-7, 255, 257, 271, 297, 301, 308, 321, 331, 341-2, 397, 399, 414, 415, 420, 427-9, 431, 433-5
programmes 42, 57, 69-70, 131, 142, 215, 228, 246, 256, 296, 431
progress 49, 162, 156, 182-3, 186, 223-4, 231, 232, 320, 401, 423
progressives 201, 376, 379, 416, 420, 422,
project 51, 129, 147, 172, 187, 214-6, 221, 317, 342-4, 363, 376, 423, 432
promises 31, 132, 183, 223, 247, 257, 265, 309
property 87, 146, 151, 156, 190, 193, 208, 238-9, 255, 257
PRSTF (Petroleum Revenue Special Task Force) 162-9
PRSTF report 162-9
public schools 334-5, 337
pupils 68, 330, 334-5

R

race 42, 70, 100-, 103, 244, 259, 281, 285,

295, 309, 317, 360, 412, 415
realize 6, 15, 19, 50, 58, 67, 72, 88-9, 120, 131, 133, 175, 192, 212, 221, 232, 241-2, 260, 263, 303, 316, -7, 323, 377-8, 392
Reclaim Nigeria 163, 172, 192, 370, 379, 405, 435
recommendations 167-8, 198-9, 399, 414
refineries 92, 304, 319, 321-2, 324-8, 368-9
regime 7-10, 13-5, 17-22, 28-30, 33-4, 36-7, 42-3, 45-7, 49-50, 55-6, 60, 69, 70, 73-4, 78-3, 85, 87-9, 91, 94-6, 98-9, 106-9, 111-4, 118-9, 123, 126, 128, 130, 132-3, 135, 143, 145, 150-2, 154, 186, 203, 211, 226, 228, 232, 254, 256, 261, 263, 265-6, 270-1, 275-, 284, 296-7, 303, 341, 349, 350, 352-3, 365, 368, 388, 398, 405, 408, 440
  present 9, 29, 37, 43, 70, 106, 113-4, 132, 135, 150, 232, 297
regions 52-3, 212, 263
relationship 190, 230, 247, 251-2, 327, 355-6, 372, 394
release 31-5, 78, 90, 93, 118, 121, 142, 296, 342-3, 423
report 47, 83-4, 115, 162-9, 172, 201, 213, 282, 310, 320, 321, 324, 325, 328, 331, 374, 376, 385, 396-9, 414, 432
representatives 31, 60, 113-6, 128, 152-3, 155, 170, 173, 216, 223, 299, 332, 339, 340, 391, 395, 426, 431-2
Republic 11, 21, 45, 53, 69, 70, 86, 89, 101, 103, 132, 174-5, 177, 180, 186-7, 203-4, 252, 265, 270, 277, 289, 295, 310, 311-2, 340, 375, 400, 408, 436-8, 440
request 33-4, 54, 95, 179-85, 216
resources, natural 20-1, 394, 401, 428
response 5, 35, 130, 138, 148, 165-6, 171-2, 174, 180, 242, 249, 280, 295, 303, 306-7, 309-10, 312, 323, 330, 332, 335, 338, 340-1, 368, 374-5, 378, 380, 396, 398, 409-12, 416, 418-9, 423, 426
  president's 306, 310, 323
Reuters 164, 167, 396-7
revenue 162, 165-6, 170, 260, 282, 326, 328, 391, 394, 396, 407-8
Ribadu 162-3, 165, 166-7, 384, 396-8, 415
Ribadu committee report 397-8

rule Nigeria 11, 99, 102, 121, 125, 144, 186, 202, 271, 659
  post-military 359
rule of law 4, 6, 33, 81, 85, 188, 203, 229, 232, 240, 310, 337, 350, 386, 402, 413, 424
rulers 6, 8, 14, 32, 35, 40, 48, 60, 95, 97, 114, 116, 124, 131, 146, 160, 162, 172, 210, 214, 216, 234, 238, 240-1, 251-2, 263, 266, 268, 275, 295, 297, 300-1, 326, 330-1, 353, 358, 367, 369, 373, 375, 380-2, 386, 402, 407, 424
  traditional 14, 48, 95, 97
rumours 177, 194, 406
Russia 16, 127, 280-1

S
safeguard 12, 245-6, 354
Saharareporters 172, 195, 215
SAIS (School of Advanced International Studies) 317
SAN (Senior Advocate of Nigeria) 167, 367
Sani Abacha 10-1, 13, 17, 20, 31-2, 43, 53, 78, 81-2, 88, 99, 100, 113-4, 146, 151, 157, 204, 273
  late 114, 157
Sani Abacha Foundation for Peace and Justice 100
Sanusi 170-2, 174, 368, 370
SAP (Structural Adjustment Programme) 9, 25, 74, 143, 148, 203, 211, 228, 238, 274, 438
Saro-Wiwa 71-2, 83-4, 93-6, 100, 107, 109, 126-7, 131, 269, 283-4, 356
Saro-Wiwa, Ken 72, 83-4, 93, 100, 109, 126, 269, 283-4, 356
scenarios 420-1
School of Advanced International Studies (SAIS) 317
schools 123, 201, 209-10, 246, 330, 334-7,
SDP (Social Democratic Party) 25, 84, 202, 204, 422, 439
secretary 32-3, 135, 166
security, national 8, 335, 337, 344, 424
selection 9, 412, 414
self-determination 46-7, 61, 94, 125, 131, 227, 292, 295, 356, 362-5

self-government 363, 366
senate 103, 173-8, 186-7, 198-201, 204, 208, 216, 320, 395, 399, 442
Senate President 173-6, 186, 204, 208, 216
Senator Mark 174-6
senators 170-1, 174, 177, 178, 187, 191, 391, 393,
Senior Advocate of Nigeria (SAN) 167, 367
Senior Secondary Certificate Examination (SSCE) 336
shacks 245, 247, 249, 274
shelter, adequate 245-6
Shonekan 29, 53, 80, 86, 140, 144, 439
sick intellectualism 50-1, 53, 55
Sierra Leone 102, 109, 111, 114, 133, 230, 297-8
Sierra Leoneans 40, 298
SNC (Sovereign National Conference) 90, 237, 375-9, 382, 393-5
SNC debate 376-7
Social Democratic Party *see* SDP
socialism 30-1, 280-1
society 8, 16, 22, 26, 61, 67, 75, 76-7, 86, 106-7, 118, 121, 125, 132, 152, 170, 172, 178, 187-9, 207, 213, 223, 224, 227, 229, 234, 238-40, 242, 244, 247, 251, 254, 256, 268, 280-1, 290, 303, 306, 308, 317-9, 329, 331, 353, 364, 369, 386, 391-2, 395, 411
soldiers 11, 78, 81, 101, 109, 118, 123, 130, 210, 270, 272, 282, 284, 291, 297, 438,
Somalia 230, 278, 286-7, 295, 317, 382, 402,
south 20, 22, 26, 28, 35, 42, 44-6, 51, 93, 120, 124, 128, 141, 143, 156, 188, 210, 251-2, 278, 288, 294, 364, 372, 373. 374, 390, 435-6, 442-3
South-south Nigeria 93, 442
Sovereign National Conference *see* SNC
Sovereign National Conference of genuine representatives 113, 116, 128, 152
Sovereign National Conference of genuine representatives of Nigerians 152
Soviet Union 36, 72, 278-80, 286, 292
space, political 212, 371, 379, 420
Speaker 153, 155, 173, 175, 216, 299, 339, 340

SSCE (Senior Secondary Certificate Examination) 336
stability, international 145
stakeholders 163, 168, 259, 298, 302, 303, 369
state, modern 233, 251, 319
State governments 373
steal 111-2, 159, 192, 194, 228, 318, 391
Structural Adjustment Programme *see* SAP
struggle 8, 24-5, 27, 30-1, 43, 45, 59, 72-5, 78, 94-6, 116, 124, 127, 223-4, 236-8, 241, 254, 268-9, 277, 354-5, 357, 359, 362, 369, 405, 419, 434-5
students 26, 44, 79, 90, 123, 147, 186, 209, 259-60, 277, 333-5, 337, 385, 395, 419, 442
submission 55, 162-4, 167-8
subsidy 221, 238, 302-4, 314, 321-5, 327-8, 367-9, 379, 389, 432, 441-2
Sudan 215, 287-8, 292, 295, 424
summit 90, 110, 170, 194, 249, 313-6, 336, 424
superpowers 242-4
sworn 155, 212, 302, 304, 405, 414, 438, 440. 441
system 30, 35, 46, 49, 52, 59, 61, 69, 74, 144, 147, 150, 152, 154, 155, 191-2, 194, 201-2, 204-6, 208224, 233-5, 238-40, 254, 257-8, 260-1, 275, 284, 323-4, 326, 341-2, 344, 353-4, 381, 387, 390, 397, 405, 434
two-party 201-2, 204-5

T
teachers 123, 137, 259-60, 319, 334-6
team 170, 212, 260, 292-3, 321, 327-8, 335
tenants 151, 247
terms 45-, 52, 70, 79, 104, 107, 123, 129, 180, 185, 191, 207, 210, 271, 286-7, 290, 310, 320, 335, 341, 342, 358-9, 362, 369, 380-1, 405, 425
threat 8, 12, 23, 36, 50, 67, 97, 100, 116, 141-2, 144, 158, 189-90, 212, 229, 255, 269, 279, 286, 288-9, 292, 294, 340, 350, 375-6, 381, 390, 417
TIC (Transition Implementation Committee) 80, 266

Time to Reclaim Nigeria 163, 172, 192, 370, 379
totalitarianism 37, 88, 138
tragedy 13, 16, 32, 36-7, 40, 43, 59, 68, 71, 108, 121-2, 128, 134, 139, 176, 208, 210, 256, 258, 265, 269, 275, 281-2, 291, 299, 358-9, 375, 381, 392, 430, 433
   national 32, 291
transition 8-11, 13-20, 23, 25-6, 28-9, 31, 33, 36-44, 46-8, 50, 56-60, 68-70, 72, 77, 80-1, 83, 86, 91, 95, 97-100, 106, 108, 112, 115, 117, 119-120, 122, 124, 128-9
   democratic 60, 98
Transition Implementation Committee *see* TIC
transition programme 8-10, 16-7, 25, 36, 41, 43-4, 47, 56-7, 59, 68-70, 77, 81, 86-7, 91, 95, 97 112, 115, 119, 120, 132-4, 139-41, 143, 154, 203, 235-6, 254, 263, 365-6, 271, 350
treachery 17, 19, 31, 35, 45-6, 67, 98, 112, 131, 140, 223, 259, 275
treatment 160, 162, 197-8, 441
trial 14, 72, 77, 79, 84-5, 88, 94-5, 110, 118, 147, 151, 157-8, 161, 190, 193, 208, 243, 253, 264, 267, 297, 384, 426, 439

U
UAC (United African Company) 18, 140
Uganda 21, 156, 318
Umaru Yar'Adua, late President 197, 310
union 36, 72, 76, 79, 105, 114, 123, 229, 253, 258, 260, 278, 279-80, 286, 292, 303, 369, 371-2, 393, 402, 436
United African Company (UAC) 18, 140
United Nations 114, 137, 243, 249, 288, 292-4, 437, 441
United States 32, 34-5, 40-1, 89, 114, 176, 229, 230-1, 240, 243-4, 278, 343, 385, 443
unity 4-5, 7, 16, 30, 41, 46, 50, 67, 90, 106, 116, 127, 131, 157, 226-7, 254, 269, 270-2, 350-1, 353-4, 356, 358-60, 362, 364-6, 376-8, 380-2, 389, 394, 399, 401-2, 407, 417, 423-4
unity of Nigeria 30, 50, 127, 376-7, 381-2, 389, 424
Unity Party of Nigeria (UPN) 417
universities 79, 146-, 155, 200-1, 211, 258-61, 319, 330, 336-40, 385
   fake 319, 337-40
UPN (Unity Party of Nigeria) 417
US 21-2, 24, 28, 34, 41, 44, 45, 89-90, 115, 140, 213, 215, 237, 243, 278-9, 280, 285-9, 291-5, 297-8, 314, 326, 413
US presidential election 413

V
values 7-8, 187, 206-7, 232, 250, 328, 329, 381
very few Nigerians 9
vice-president 15, 103, 303
   civilian 15
victims 22, 95, 114, 217, 223-4, 226, 228-9, 247, 256, 285, 316-7, 351, 362
violence 4, 12, 79, 89, 94, 104, 111, 134, 153, 177, 230-1, 242-3, 252, 254, 283, 285, 299, 301, 317, 374, 382, 390, 394, 426, 428, 433, 437
votes 84, 89, 135, 215, 425, 432
VP 304-5, 342

W
Wada Nas 87, 96-9
wages 234, 259-60
war 4, 6, 12, 16, 21, 28, 38, 40, 44, 47, 50, 54, 70, 102, 107, 111, 125, 129, 134, 139, 140, 149, 169, 179, 190, 198, 210, 229-30, 243, 248, 250, 254, 258, 262-3, 265, 268-9, 272, 278, 286, 288, 290, 291-2, 294, 300-1, 329, 355, 360, 365, 372-4, 376, 380, 382, 393, 402, 420, 425-6, 431, 433, 437
Washington 20-3, 33, 35-6, 90, 114-5, 150, 215, 243, 309, 329, 442
West 15, 19, 22, 24, 28, 36, 40-1, 52, 59, 61, 81-2, 84, 90-1, 114, 117-8, 124, 142, 150, 156, 189, 211, 230, 238, 239, 242, 251, 263, 280-1, 296-8, 317, 319, 339, 357, 363, 436
WIPO (World International Property Organisation) 87
Wole Soyinka 40, 87, 136, 188, 214-5, 226, 270, 438
women 90, 161, 206-7, 213, 217, 224, 234, 242-4, 255, 261, 284-5, 293, 298, 314-6, 319, 332, 336
   position of 244

work 16, 88, 161, 163-9, 194, 199, 202, 213-4, 240, 264, 270, 297, 299, 318, 329, 331-2, 335, 372, 387, 397, 415, 418, 423-4, 427
workers 22, 25-30, 123, 171-2, 364
world 6, 11, 14, 17-18, 20-21, 23, 32, 41, 47, 52, 55, 59, 67, 71, 73, 83, 85, 89, 93, 98-100, 102, 112-14, 120, 126, 129-30, 139, 149, 150, 155, 159, 161, 172, 183, 188-9, 193, 198, 203, 212-4, 226, 229-31, 234, 237-8, 240, 242, 244, 246, 248-9, 250-2, 261, 266, 278-81, 285-95, 300-1, 313, 326, 337, 344, 371, 384, 390, 401, 436

World International Property Organisation (WIPO) 87
world peace 23, 229-31, 279, 288
world politics 226-7, 248

Y

YEAA (Youth Earnestly Ask for Abacha) 108
year's presidential elections, next 96, 101
Yoruba 53, 104, 125, 143, 299, 357, 429-30
youth 26, 77, 104, 108, 133, 144, 172, 211, 214, 231, 233, 290, 374, 381-2, 418-9, 441
Youth Earnestly Ask for Abacha (YEAA) 108
Yugoslavia 61, 149, 152, 293-5

www.ingramcontent.com/pod-product-compliance
Lightning Source LLC
Chambersburg PA
CBHW071958150426
43194CB00008B/916